# MEAT, POULTRY & GAME

# LAROUSSE
## GASTRONOMIQUE
# RECIPE
## COLLECTION

# MEAT, POULTRY
# & GAME

With the assistance of the Gastronomic Committee
President Joël Robuchon

## hamlyn

First published in Great Britain in 2004 by
Hamlyn, a division of Octopus Publishing Group Ltd
2–4 Heron Quays, London E14 4JP

ISBN 0 600 61162 0
EAN 9780600611622

A CIP catalogue record for this book is available from the British
Library

Printed and bound in Italy

10 9 8 7 6 5 4 3 2 1

# Gastronomic Committee

## President

Joël Robuchon

## Members of the Committee

Michel Creignou, *Journalist*

Jean Delaveyne, *Chef, founder of Restaurant Le Camélia, Bougival*

Éric Frachon, *Honorary president, Evian Water SA*

Michel Guérard, *Chef, Restaurant Les Prés d'Eugénie, Eugénie-les-Bains*

Pierre Hermé, *Confectioner, Paris*

Robert Linxe, *Founder, The House of Chocolate, Paris and New York*

Élisabeth de Meurville, *Journalist*

Georges Pouvel, *Professor of cookery; consultant on cookery techniques*

Jean-François Revel, *Writer*

Pierre Troisgros, *Chef, Restaurant Pierre Troisgros, Roanne*

Alain Weill, *Art expert; member of the National Council of Gastronomy*

# Contributors

Marie-Paule Bernardin
*Archivist*

Geneviève Beullac
*Editor*

Jean Billault
*Member of the College of
Butchery*

Christophe Bligny
*Paris College of Catering*

Thierry Borghèse
*Chief Inspector of Consumer
Affairs*

Francis Boucher
*Confectioner*

Pascal Champagne
*Barman, Hotel Lutetia;
Member, French Association
of Barmen*

Frédéric Chesneau
*Project manager*

Marcel Cottenceau
*Former technical director,
College of Butchery*

Robert Courtine
*President, Marco-Polo Prize*

Philippe Dardonville
*Secretary-general, National
Union of Producers of Fruit
Juice*

Bertrand Debatte
*Officer of the Bakery,
Auchamps*

Jean Dehillerin
*President and managing
director, E. Dehillerin SA
(manufacturers of kitchen
equipment)*

Gilbert Delos
*Writer and journalist*

Christian Flacelière
*Journalist*

Jean-Louis Flandrin
*Professor emeritus,
University of Paris VII;
Director of studies,*

E.H.E.S.S. *(College of Social
Sciences)*

Dr André Fourel
*Economist*

Dominique Franceschi
*Journalist*

Dr Jacques Fricker
*Nutritionist*

Jean-Pierre Gabriel
*Journalist*

Thierry Gaudillère
*Editor,* Bourgogne
Aujourd'hui *(Burgundy
Today)*

Ismène Giachetti
*Director of research, C.N.R.S.
(National Centre for
Scientific Research)*

Sylvie Girard
*Cookery writer*

Catherine Goavec-Bouvard
*Agribusiness consultant*

Jo Goldenberg
*Restaurateur*

Catherine Gomy
*Agribusiness certification
officer,
French Association of
Standardization*

Bruno Goussault
*Scientific director, C.R.E.A.
(Centre of Food and
Nutrition Studies)*

Jacques Guinberteau
*Mycologist; Director of
studies, I.N.R.A. (National
Institute of Agriculture)*

Joseph Hossenlopp
*Director of studies, Cemagref
(Institute of Research for
Agricultural and
Environmental Engineering)*

Françoise Kayler
*Food critic*

Jacques Lacoursière
*Writer*

Josette Le Reun-Gaudicheau
*Teacher (specializing in
seafood)*

Paul Maindiaux
*Development officer,
Ministry of Agriculture*

Laurent Mairet
*Oenologist*

Jukka Mannerkorpi
*Cookery editor*

Pascal Orain
*Manager, Bertie's Restaurant*

Philippe Pilliot
*Secretary-general, Federation
of French Grocers; Editor,*
Le Nouvel Épicier
*(The New Grocer)*

Jean-Claude Ribaut
*Cookery correspondent,*
Le Monde

Isabelle Richard
*Bachelor of Arts*

Michel Rigo
*Deputy head, National
Federation of Fruit Brandies*

Françoise Sabban
*Master of ceremonies,
E.H.E.S.S.
(College of Social Sciences)*

Jacques Sallé
*Journalist*

Jean-Louis Taillebaud
*Chef, Ritz-Escoffier (French
School of Gastronomy); Ritz
Hotel, Place Vendôme, Paris*

Claude Vifian
*Chef and professor, College of
the Hotel Industry, Lausanne*

Leda Vigliardi Paravia
*Writer and journalist*

Jean-Marc Wolff
*College of the Hotel Industry,
Paris*

Rémy Yverneau
*Secretary-general,
National Federation of
Makers of Cream Cheese*

# Contents

# Useful information

## How to use this book

The recipes are divided into five main chapters: Meat, Offal (variety meats), Poultry, Game, and Frogs & snails. Within these chapters, entries are grouped by main ingredient in A–Z order. The last chapter, Basic recipes & classic additions, has recipes for the marinades, sauces, stocks, pastry, garnishes, accompaniments and so on referred to in the first five chapters.

When an entry refers to another recipe, it may be found by first referring to the relevant section and then to the food or dish type. A comprehensive index of entries lists the entire contents.

## Weights & measures

Metric, imperial and American measures are used in this book. As a general rule, it is advisable to follow only one set of measures and not to mix metric, imperial and/or cup quantities in any one recipe.

## Spoon measures

Spoon measures refer to standard measuring utensils. Serving spoons and table cutlery are not suitable for measuring as they are not standard in capacity.

¼ teaspoon = 1.5 ml
½ teaspoon = 2.5 ml
1 teaspoon = 5 ml
1 tablespoon = 15 ml

## Oven temperatures

Below are the standard settings for domestic ovens. However, ovens vary widely and manufacturer's instructions should be consulted. Individual ovens also perform differently and experience of using a particular appliance is invaluable for adjusting temperatures and cooking times to give the best results. Those working with commercial cooking appliances will be accustomed to using the higher temperatures attained. Many chefs' recipes refer to glazing or cooking in a hot oven for a short period: as a rule, the hottest setting for a domestic appliance should be used as the equivalent.

Temperatures and timings in the recipes refer to preheated ovens.

If using a fan-assisted oven, follow the manufacturer's instructions for adjusting timing and temperature.

| Centigrade | Fahrenheit | Gas mark |
|---|---|---|
| 110°C | 225°F | gas ¼ |
| 120°C | 250°F | gas ½ |
| 140°C | 275°F | gas 1 |
| 150°C | 300°F | gas 2 |
| 160°C | 325°F | gas 3 |
| 180°C | 350°F | gas 4 |
| 190°C | 375°F | gas 5 |
| 200°C | 400°F | gas 6 |
| 220°C | 425°F | gas 7 |
| 230°C | 450°F | gas 8 |
| 240°C | 475°F | gas 9 |

# Introduction

*Larousse Gastronomique* is the world's most famous culinary reference book. It was the vision of Prosper Montagné, a French chef who was responsible for the first edition published in Paris in 1938. His aims were to provide an overview of 20th-century gastronomy and its history, as well as a source of reference on the more practical aspects of cookery. Twenty-three years later the first English edition was published and it immediately became the culinary bible of chefs, cooks and food aficionados.

A new English edition of this monumental work was published in 2001. Completely revised and updated, it reflected the social and cultural changes, together with advances in science and technology, that have dramatically influenced our ideas about food, the way we cook and how we eat.

Distilled from the latest edition, in one convenient volume, is this collection of over 800 meat, game and poultry recipes, together with over 180 basic and complementary recipes. Whether your particular interest is in the great traditions of French cuisine or in the wide spectrum of food as the international subject it has become, the recipes reflect the diversity of the world of cooking in the 21st century.

# Meat

# Beef

## Beef Brandenburg

Cut 1 kg (2¼ lb) top ribs of beef (chuck steak) into large dice and season. Heat 40 g (1½ oz, 1½ tablespoons) lard in a heavy based saucepan and brown the meat lightly on all sides. Remove the meat, and fry 800 g (1¾ lb) thinly sliced onions until soft but not brown. Add a bay leaf, 2 crushed cloves, and 600 ml (1 pint, 2½ cups) cold water. Bring to the boil, return the meat to the pan and leave to simmer, covered, for 1½ hours. Drain the meat and keep it warm in a covered serving dish. Blend 2 slices crumbled stale gingerbread, 1 tablespoon drained capers, the juice and zest of 1 lemon, and some ground pepper with the cooking liquor. Simmer, uncovered, for 5 minutes. Pour the sauce over the meat and serve piping hot with a celery purée.

## Beef croquettes

Cut some boiled beef and some lean ham into very small dice. Make a well-reduced béchamel sauce with 50 g (2 oz, ¼ cup) butter, 50 g (2 oz, ½ cup) plain (all-purpose) flour, 500 ml (17 fl oz, 2 cups) milk, grated nutmeg, and salt and pepper; beat in 1 egg yolk. Bind the beef and ham with the béchamel sauce and leave to cool.

Divide the cold mixture into portions of 50–75 g (2–3 oz). Roll these out on a floured flat surface and shape them into corks, balls, eggs or rectangles. Dip them in a mixture of egg and oil beaten together and then cover them completely with fine breadcrumbs.

Place the croquettes in a frying basket, plunge into oil heated to 175–180°C (347–350°F), and deep-fry until they are crisp and golden. Drain on paper towels and arrange on a napkin in a pyramid or turban shape. Garnish with parsley and serve with a well-seasoned tomato sauce.

The béchamel may be replaced by rice, using two-thirds salpicon to one-third rice cooked in meat stock.

## Beef émincés with bordelaise sauce

Make some bordelaise sauce. Poach some slices of beef bone marrow in stock. Arrange thin slices of boiled beef on a lightly buttered ovenproof dish and garnish with the hot slices of bone marrow. Generously coat with bordelaise sauce and heat through gently in the oven.

## Beef émincés with mushrooms

Arrange some thin slices of boiled beef in a long ovenproof dish. Prepare some Madeira sauce. Trim and slice some mushrooms and heat them in butter. Place the mushrooms on the meat and cover generously with hot Madeira sauce; heat through gently in the oven.

## Beef hash à l'italienne

Sauté 3 tablespoons chopped onion in 3 tablespoons olive oil until slightly brown, sprinkle with 1 tablespoon flour and mix well. Then add 200 ml (7 fl oz, ¾ cup) water or stock, 3 tablespoons tomato purée (paste) diluted with 6 tablespoons stock, a bouquet garni and a crushed garlic clove. Cook gently for about 30 minutes. Remove the bouquet garni and allow to cool. Add some of this sauce to some finely chopped braised or boiled beef and reheat gently. Serve with tagliatelle and the remainder of the sauce.

## Beef hash with aubergines au gratin

Prepare and cook the sauce as for beef hash *à l'italienne*, then add the finely chopped beef together with 1 tablespoon chopped parsley. Slice some aubergines (eggplants) into rounds, sauté them in oil and arrange them in a buttered gratin dish. Pour in the beef in its sauce, smooth the surface, sprinkle with a mixture of grated Parmesan cheese and breadcrumbs, pour over a little olive oil and brown in a preheated oven at 230°C (450°F, gas 8).

## Beef miroton

Cook about 10 tablespoons finely sliced onions in 125 g (4½ oz, generous ½ cup) butter in a covered pan. Sprinkle with 1 tablespoon flour. Brown slightly, stirring continuously, then add 2 tablespoons vinegar and an equal amount of stock or white wine. Bring to the boil, then remove from the heat. Pour half the sauce into a long ovenproof dish. Cut 500 g (18 oz) cold boiled beef into thin slices and arrange them in the dish on top of the sauce. Pour the rest of the sauce over the top, sprinkle generously with breadcrumbs and pour on some melted butter (or dripping). Brown in a preheated oven at 220°C (425°F, gas 7) without allowing the sauce to boil. Sprinkle with chopped parsley and serve piping hot.

## Beef on a string

Place 2 kg (4½ lb) veal bones in a roasting tin (pan) with 2 large onions, unpeeled and cut in half, and 1 large glass of water; sprinkle a little caster (superfine) sugar on top. Brown in a hot oven. Then put all the ingredients in a large flameproof casserole with 6 litres (10 pints, 6½ quarts) water. Carefully deglaze the juices in the roasting tin and pour into the casserole with 4 large, peeled carrots, the green tops of 8 leeks, 1 head garlic, peeled and crushed, the stalks of 1 bunch of parsley, 1 thyme sprig, 2 bay leaves, 4 cloves, 10 peppercorns, 2 tarragon sprigs, 1 celery stick and 4 tomatoes (or a small can of tomato purée). Cook, skimming frequently, until only 2 litres (3½ pints, 9 cups) of stock remain. Drain the vegetables and bones thoroughly, then filter the stock.

Put the bouillon back on the heat, skim, degrease, season with salt and add a bunch of 8 small turnips, 8 small carrots with their leaves, the whites of the 8 leeks, 1 small cauliflower and 8 small new potatoes and cook, making sure that the vegetables, except for the potatoes, remain crunchy. Remove the vegetables and set aside in a warm place. Poach 4 marrow bones in the stock for a few minutes over a low heat so that they do not lose their content and put aside. Skim and degrease the stock one final time.

Put an 800 g (1¾ lb) unbarded, loosely tied, seamless piece of beef (in France cut lengthways from rump steak, more conveniently a trimmed beef fillet), in the stock, and cook for 10 minutes. Remove the beef and allow to rest for 10 minutes so that the heat distributes itself evenly inside while the vegetables and marrow bones are reheated. Then slice the rare meat into very thin slices and garnish with the vegetables, surrounding it with marrow bones. Pour some boiling stock over the meat and sprinkle with finely chopped flat-leafed parsley.

## Beef patties à l'andalouse

Soften 50 g (2 oz) chopped onion and a chopped garlic clove in butter. Add salt and pepper. Mix with 400 g (14 oz, 2 cups) minced (ground) beef and form into 4 rounds. Coat these with flour and fry in oil. Sauté 4 large tomato halves in oil and place a cooked patty on each. Arrange them on a plate with a rice pilaf in the centre. Deglaze the cooking juices of the patties with 2–3 tablespoons sherry. Reduce, add some butter, and pour over the patties.

## Beef Stroganov

Cut 800 g (1¾ lb) fillet of beef into fine strips 2.5 cm (1 in) long. Sprinkle with salt and pepper and place in a small ovenproof dish with 4 sliced onions, 3 chopped shallots, 1 large carrot cut into slices, 1 crushed bay leaf and a small sprig of crumbled fresh thyme. Add just enough white wine to cover the meat and leave to marinate in a cool place, covered, for 12 hours. Drain and dry the meat; reduce the marinade by half and set it aside.

Sauté 2 thinly sliced onions in a shallow frying pan in 25 g (1 oz, 2 tablespoons) butter until soft and lightly brown; set aside. Lightly brown 200 g (7 oz, 2⅓ cups) thinly sliced mushrooms in the same pan with 25 g (1 oz, 2 tablespoons) butter, then add them to the onions. Wipe the pan and melt 50 g (2 oz, ¼ cup) butter in it; when hot, add the meat and sauté over a brisk heat, turning it frequently. When the meat is well browned (about 5 minutes), sprinkle it with 3 tablespoons warmed brandy and flame it. Keep warm in a serving dish.

Tip the onions and mushrooms into the frying pan together with the reduced and strained marinade and 150 ml (¼ pint, ⅔ cup) double (heavy) cream; stir over a brisk heat until the sauce thickens. Taste and adjust the seasoning and coat the meat with the sauce. Sprinkle with chopped parsley and serve piping hot.

## Bitoke

A *bitoke* is a French meat cake, moulded into a flat, oval or round shape. To make a single *bitoke*, finely mince (grind) 125 g (4½ oz, ½ cup) lean beef and

17

add 25 g (1 oz, 2 tablespoons) butter, salt, pepper and a little grated nutmeg. Shape the mixture into a flattened ball, coat in flour and sauté in clarified butter. Add 1 tablespoon cream and 1 teaspoon lemon juice to the cooking liquor to make a sauce. Coat the *bitoke* with the sauce and garnish with fried onion. Serve with sauté potatoes. Alternatively, the minced beef may also be coated with egg and breadcrumbs before cooking.

## Boeuf à la mode

Cut about 250 g (9 oz) fat bacon into thick strips and marinate for 5–6 hours in 100 ml (4 fl oz, 7 tablespoons) Cognac. Use the strips to lard a piece of rump weighing about 2 kg (4½ lb). Season with salt and pepper and marinate for 5–6 hours (turning the meat several times) in the Cognac used to marinate the bacon mixed with at least 1 litre (1¾ pints, 4⅓ cups) good red wine, 100 ml (4 fl oz, 7 tablespoons) olive oil, 250 g (9 oz, 2¼ cups) chopped onions, 1 kg (2¼ lb) sliced carrots, 2–3 garlic cloves, a bouquet garni and a few peppercorns.

Blanch a boned calf's foot and some bacon rind from which some of the fat has been removed. Drain the meat and dry it on paper towels, and then drain the other ingredients of the marinade. Brown the meat on all sides in olive oil in a frying pan, then place in a large casserole. Add the drained ingredients from the marinade followed by the bacon rinds and the calf's foot. Moisten with the marinade and about 750 ml (1¼ pints, 3¼ cups) stock and season with salt.

Place the covered casserole in a preheated oven at 200°C (400°F, gas 6) and cook for about 2½ hours, until tender. When the beef is cooked, slice it evenly and serve surrounded with the carrots and the diced meat of the calf's foot. Strain the braising stock over the meat. Small glazed onions may be added to garnish.

## Boeuf à la mode de Beaucaire

This is the traditional dish of the Beaucaire fair. It is delicious but takes a long time to prepare. Take 1.2 kg (2½ lb) thin slices of beef cut from the thigh or shoulder blade allowing about 200 g (7 oz) per person. Bard the meat with fat which has been rolled in salt and pepper and moistened with brandy. Then marinate for 24 hours in 4 tablespoons vinegar, 1 chopped onion, a bouquet garni, 4 tablespoons brandy and 4–5 teaspoons olive oil.

Cover the bottom of an earthenware cooking pot with 225 g (8 oz) bacon, cut in thick rashers (slices). Chop 4 onions and 2 garlic cloves and place on top of the bacon. Add the slices of beef, season with salt and pepper, then pour the marinade over the meat. Cover and cook in a preheated oven at 120°C (250°F, gas ½) for 2 hours. Then slowly (so as not to overcool the contents) add 1 litre (1¾ pints, 4⅓ cups) red wine, a bouquet garni, 1 tablespoon capers and an onion stuck with 3 cloves. Cover and cook gently for a further 2 hours.

Just before serving, thicken the sauce with a generous 1 tablespoon flour and add 3 pounded anchovy fillets. When the dish is ready, pour 3 tablespoons olive oil over and serve.

## Boeuf bourguignon

Cut 1 kg (2¼ lb) braising steak (rump) into cubes and coat with flour. Cut 150 g (5 oz) belly pork into thin strips and fry in a flameproof casserole or heavy based saucepan. Add the steak, a chopped shallot and 2 sliced onions and continue to fry. If desired, add a small glass of brandy and set alight. Add 500 ml (17 fl oz, 2 cups) red wine and a generous glass of stock. Season with salt and pepper and add a bouquet garni and a crushed clove of garlic. Cover and simmer gently for at least 2 hours. A dozen small onions lightly fried in butter may be added 20 minutes before cooking ends. Just before serving, bind the sauce with 1 tablespoon beurre manié.

## Boiled beef

For 6 servings, place about 800 g (1¾ lb) beef or veal bones in a large saucepan with 2.5 litres (4¼ pints, 11 cups) water, and bring to the boil. Skim the surface of the liquid and remove the foam deposited on the sides of the pan. Boil for about 1 hour, then remove the bones. Add 1.25–2 kg (2¾–4½ lb) beef, depending on the cut and the proportion of bone to meat: silverside (bottom round), cheek, shoulder, chuck, flank or oxtail may be used. Bring back to the boil and skim. Then add the following vegetables: 6 carrots, 3 medium turnips, 6 small leeks (tied together), 2 celery sticks (cut into short lengths and tied together), a piece of parsnip, 2 onions (one stuck with 2 cloves), a bouquet garni and, if desired, 1–2 garlic cloves. Season with salt and pepper, cover to bring back to the boil, and simmer for about 3 hours. Drain the meat, cut into even-sized pieces, and serve with the drained vegetables. Serve with coarse salt, pickled onions, gherkins and mustard.

If a marrow bone is available, wrap this in muslin (cheesecloth) and add it to the pan not more than 15 minutes before serving. The bone may be served with the dish or the marrow can be removed and spread on toasted croûtons. To make the dish look more attractive, select vegetables of a similar size, cut the leeks and celery to the same length and form into neat bunches, and serve the onions slightly browned.

## Boiled beef hash

Chop very finely (by hand or in a food processor) 500 g (18 oz) boiled beef. Cook 2 large finely chopped onions in 15 g (½ oz, 1 tablespoon) butter until tender. Sprinkle with 1 tablespoon flour and cook until golden brown. Add 200 ml (7 fl oz, ¾ cup) stock, season with salt and pepper, and bring to the boil, stirring constantly. Simmer for 15 minutes. Cool, add the boiled beef, and cook, covered, in a preheated oven at 200°C (400°F, gas 6) for 25 minutes.

## Bollito misto

Put 500 g (18 oz) flank of beef, 500 g (18 oz) oxtail and 500 g (18 oz) blade-bone of beef (or silverside) into a braising pan and fill with water. Bring to the boil, skimming often and removing the foam deposited on the sides of the pan. Add 2 onions, 3 celery sticks, 3 peeled garlic cloves, 5 sprigs flat-leaf parsley, 1 rosemary sprig, 10 peppercorns and a little sea salt. Cover and cook for 1½ hours. Remove the pieces of meat gradually as and when they become tender. Meanwhile, cook 1 split calf's head and 1 split calf's foot in water flavoured with 1 onion and 1 celery stick. In another braising pan, cook 1 calf's tongue then skin it very carefully and set aside. Prick a *cotechino* (Italian sausage) and cook it in a little stock. Arrange the meats on a serving dish and serve very hot. Traditional accompaniments to this celebrated Italian stew from Piedmont include a green herb sauce or tomato sauce, spring onions (scallions), gherkins, capers, Verona mustard (a type of mustard with apple purée) and Cremona mustard (made from several kinds of fruit, cooked in a very hot mustard syrup).

## Braised beef

Brown a joint of beef in a large saucepan. Remove the joint and set aside and then brown a large mirepoix of carrots and onions in the fat from the meat. Brown some small pieces of bone from a loin of veal and some chicken bones in butter. Put them into a braising pan with the skimmed mirepoix, the joint of beef, a blanched pig's foot and some crushed tomatoes. Season with salt and pepper, add 250 ml (8 fl oz, 1 cup) white wine and simmer steadily on the hob (stove top) until all the liquid has evaporated. Then add a bouquet garni and sufficient red wine and stock (1 part wine to 2 parts stock) to cover three-quarters of the beef. Cover the pan and cook gently for 3 hours, turning the meat occasionally.

## Braised beef à l'ancienne

Trim and tie a piece of rump and braise until almost cooked, but still slightly firm. Drain and untie the meat and place it either under a press or on a plate under a weight until cool. Trim the sides of the cooled meat. Cut away the central portion, leaving a thickness of about 2 cm (¾ in) of meat on the sides and bottom. Brush with beaten egg and cover with a mixture of soft breadcrumbs and grated Parmesan cheese (3 parts breadcrumbs to 1 part cheese). Ensure that the breadcrumb mixture covers the meat completely. Place the hollow meat case on a plate, sprinkle with melted butter and brown in the oven.

Meanwhile, slice the remaining portion of meat very thinly. Place the slices in a sauté dish, add some thin slices of tongue and some sliced mushrooms, which have been gently fried in butter, and moisten with a few tablespoons of the reduced, strained, braising stock (from which the fat has been removed). Add 2½ tablespoons Madeira and simmer without boiling. To serve, place the hollow piece of beef on a large serving dish and arrange the sautéed meat slices inside it. Serve any extra sauce in a sauceboat.

## Braised beef à la bourgeoise

Marinate a rump cut of beef in white wine and then braise it in the wine, in a saucepan with a calf's foot. When the meat is half cooked, transfer it to a casserole with the calf's foot and cooking liquor. Add some sliced carrots and small glazed onions. Complete the cooking in the casserole, in a preheated oven at 180°C (350°F, gas 4).

## Braised beef à la créole

Cut 1 kg (2¼ lb) braising steak (top round or rump) into cubes and thread a large piece of larding bacon into each cube. Marinate in a mixture of spices (especially cayenne) and Cognac for 5–6 hours. Heat some lard and oil in a heavy frying pan, then add 3 large sliced onions and the drained pieces of beef. Sauté together for several minutes, then turn into a casserole. Add 2 tablespoons tomato purée (paste), 1 crushed garlic clove, a sprig of thyme, a small bunch of parsley and a pinch of saffron powder. Season with salt and pepper, cover and cook very gently in a low oven for 3 hours. During the cooking period, add a few tablespoons of either boiling water or, even better, stock. Adjust the seasoning.

## Braised beef à la gardiane

Ask the butcher to lard and tie a piece of topside (beef round) weighing about 1.25 kg (2¾ lb). Peel and slice 800g (1¾ lb) onions. Heat some olive oil in a flameproof casserole and brown the meat in the oil. Add the sliced onions, 5–6 peeled garlic cloves, 2 cloves, a pinch of nutmeg and the same amount of basil, bay, rosemary, savory and thyme. Cover and cook very gently for at least 2½ hours. Serve the meat sliced and coated with the cooking liquor.

## Braised beef à la mode

This is prepared as for beef à la bourgeoise, using red instead of white wine (opposite).

## Braised beef porte-maillot

Cut 100 g (4 oz) fat (slab) bacon into thin strips and marinate for 12 hours in a mixture of oil and brandy (one-third brandy, two-thirds oil), mixed herbs, chopped garlic, and salt and pepper. Interlard 1.5 kg (3¼ lb) trimmed beef aiguillettes (thin strips of meat) with the bacon strips. Braise the meat in a flameproof casserole with 200 ml (7 fl oz, ¾ cup) white wine, the same amount of stock and the ingredients of the marinade.

Glaze 250 g (9 oz) small (pearl) onions, 250 g (9 oz) small turnips and 500 g (18 oz) new carrots. Cook the beef for at least 2¾ hours; 10 minutes before the end of the cooking time add the onions, carrots and turnips and finish cooking. Steam some green beans until just tender and drain. Arrange the meat on a long serving dish (platter) and surround with the vegetables in separate piles. Keep warm.

Skim the fat off the cooking juices, then strain and boil rapidly until reduced. Sprinkle the meat with chopped flat-leaf parsley and serve the sauce separately in a sauceboat.

## Braised paupiettes of beef

Flatten some thin slices of beef fillet, sirloin or chuck steak, season with salt and pepper, and spread with a layer of well-seasoned sausagemeat. Roll them up, wrap in thin rashers (slices) of fat bacon and tie with string. Braise the paupiettes in white wine or Madeira, drain them, untie the string, remove the bacon and arrange them on a heated dish. Coat with the cooking juices (reduced and strained).

All the accompaniments for small cuts of braised meat are suitable for these paupiettes: noisette potatoes, braised vegetables, vegetable purée, stuffed artichoke hearts, risotto, rice pilaf. Some garnishes (bourgeoise or chipolata) can be added to the casserole halfway through the braising time.

Paupiettes of beef can also be braised in red wine. In this case, the accompaniments (baby onions, bacon and mushrooms) can also be added while the paupiettes are cooking.

## Braised rib of beef

The cooking method is the same as for braised rump of beef. Ask the butcher to cut a large rib weighing 2–3 kg (4½–6½ lb).

# Braised rump of beef

Cut 200 g (7 oz) fat pork or bacon into larding strips. Season with spices, soak in Cognac and use them to lard a piece of beef (cut from the rump) weighing 3 kg (6½ lb). Season the meat with salt, pepper and spices, and tie into a neat shape with string. Marinate for 5 hours in either red or white wine with thyme, bay, parsley and 2 crushed garlic cloves. Blanch, cool and tie 2 boned calf's feet. Peel and slice 2 large onions and 2 carrots and heat gently in butter. Crush into small pieces a mixture of 1.5 kg (3¼ lb) beef bones and veal knuckle bones together with the bones from the calf's feet. Brown in the oven. Place the browned bones and the vegetables in a flameproof casserole or a braising pan. Add the beef, a bouquet garni and the marinade. Cover and simmer gently until the liquid has almost completely reduced. Add 3 tablespoons tomato purée (paste) and enough veal stock to cover the meat. Place the covered casserole in a preheated oven at 180°C (350°F, gas 4) and cook for about 4 hours until tender. To serve, drain the meat, untie it and glaze in the oven, basting it with the strained cooking liquor. Arrange the meat on a large serving dish and surround with the chosen garnish. Keep warm. Remove the fat from the braising pan, reduce the cooking liquid and pour over the meat.

# Braised sirloin

Ask the butcher to prepare a piece of sirloin weighing about 2–3 kg (4½–6½ lb), cut along the grain of the meat. Lard the joint with lardons of bacon that have been marinated for at least 1 hour with a little brandy, pepper, spices, chopped parsley, sliced carrot and sliced onion. Tie up the sirloin, brown it on all sides in hot fat, then place it in a large braising pan on a mirepoix of vegetables. Add a bouquet garni and pour over about 600 ml (1 pint, 2½ cups) stock. Cover the pan and braise the joint in a preheated oven at 150°C (300°F, gas 2) for about 4 hours, or until the meat is very tender. After braising, the meat may be sliced and served with the cooking liquid, deglazed, reduced and strained.

## Brochettes of marinated fillet of beef

Prepare a marinade using 150 ml (¼ pint, ⅔ cup) olive oil, salt, pepper and chopped herbs. Cut up 500 g (18 oz) fillet of beef into 2.5 cm (1 in) cubes and cut 150–200 g (5–7 oz) smoked belly pork or bacon into strips; marinate these for 30 minutes. Remove the seeds from a green (bell) pepper and cut the flesh into 2.5 cm (1 in) squares. Cut off the stalks from 8 large button mushrooms, sprinkle with lemon juice and sauté briskly in oil with the pieces of pepper; drain as soon as the pepper is slightly softened. Thread the ingredients on to skewers, adding 2 whole baby onions to each skewer, one at each end. Grill (broil) under a very high heat for 7–8 minutes.

## Broufado

Cut 900 g (2 lb) stewing beef into 5 cm (2 in) cubes. Marinate in a cool place for 24 hours in a mixture of 5 tablespoons red wine vinegar, 3 tablespoons olive oil, a large bouquet garni, a large sliced onion and some pepper. Desalt 6 anchovies by soaking in milk. Drain the meat and heat in a flameproof casserole with 2 tablespoons olive oil. Add a large chopped onion, then the marinade and 175 ml (6 fl oz, ¾ cup) red or white wine. Bring to the boil, then cover and cook in a preheated oven at 200°C (400°F, gas 6) for 2 hours. Add a few small pickled onions and 3–4 sliced gherkins (sweet dill pickles). Cook for a further 15 minutes. Wash the desalted anchovies, remove the fillets and cut them into small pieces, mix with 2 teaspoons beurre manié and add to the casserole. Stir the broufado well for 2 minutes and serve piping hot with jacket potatoes.

## Carbonade à la flamande

Slice 250 g (9 oz, 1½ cups) onions. Cut 800 g (1¾ lb) beef flank or chuck steak into pieces or thin slices, and brown over a high heat in a frying pan in 40 g (1½ oz, 3 tablespoons) lard (shortening). Remove the meat and set aside. Fry the onions until golden in the same fat. Arrange the meat and onions in a flameproof casserole in alternate layers, seasoning each layer with salt and a grinding of pepper. Add a bouquet garni. Deglaze the frying pan with 600 ml (1 pint, 2½ cups) beer and 3 tablespoons beef stock (fresh or made with concentrate). Make a brown roux with 25 g (1 oz, 2 tablespoons) butter and 25 g (1 oz, ¼ cup) plain (all-purpose) flour, and add the beer mixture, then ½ teaspoon brown sugar. Adjust the seasoning. Pour the mixture into the casserole, cover and leave to cook very gently for 2½ hours. Serve the carbonade in the casserole.

## Carpaccio

Remove the fat, nerves and gristle from a piece of very tender sirloin weighing 1.25 kg (2¾ lb) so as to obtain a neat cylinder. Put in the freezer. When it has hardened sufficiently, cut into very thin slices using a very sharp knife. Arrange these slices on plates, season lightly with salt and put back in the refrigerator for at least 15 minutes. Mix 200 ml (7 fl oz, ¾ cup) mayonnaise with 1 or 2 teaspoons Worcestershire sauce and 1 teaspoon lemon juice. Season with salt and white pepper. Pour a little of this sauce over the slices of meat, making a few decorative motifs with it.

## Cold fillet of beef à la niçoise

Garnish the cold roasted fillet with small tomatoes that have been marinated in olive oil and stuffed with a salpicon of truffles, small artichoke hearts filled with a salad of asparagus tips, large olives, anchovies and pieces of aspic jelly.

## Cold fillet of beef à la russe

Surround the cold roasted fillet with halves of shelled hard-boiled (hard-cooked) eggs and artichoke hearts stuffed *à la russe*, with a macédoine of vegetables bound with mayonnaise, and covered with aspic jelly, and chopped aspic.

## Cold fillet of beef in aspic

Cold roasted fillet either whole, or cut into thin slices, may be covered with aspic jelly. If the piece is big enough to be served whole, place it on a rack and coat with several layers of aspic jelly, which may be flavoured with Madeira, port or sherry. (It must be placed in the refrigerator between each coating.) Then arrange it on a serving dish and garnish with chopped aspic or with croûtons and watercress. Slices of fillet are either coated separately or placed in a row on the serving dish and coated with aspic. They are garnished in the same way.

Serve with a cold sauce, such as mayonnaise or tartare sauce, and cold vegetable barquettes or a salad.

## Consommé croûte au pot

Use beef consommé. Dry some hollowed-out bread crusts in the oven. Sprinkle each one with a little stockpot fat and brown lightly or garnish with chopped stockpot vegetables. Serve with the consommé.

## Consommé Florette

Use beef consommé. Cook 150 g (5 oz, ¾ cup) shredded leek lightly in butter, moisten with consommé and reduce. Cook 1½ tablespoons rice in consommé and add the leek. Serve with double (heavy) cream and grated Parmesan cheese.

## Consommé Léopold

Use beef consommé. Cook 2 tablespoons shredded sorrel in butter. Cook 4 teaspoons semolina in the consommé, then add the sorrel and some chervil.

## Consommé Monte-Carlo

Use beef consommé. Cut some very thin slices of bread into circles; butter, sprinkle with Parmesan and toast lightly. Serve with the consommé.

## Consommé Princess Alice

Use beef consommé. Separately cook shredded artichoke hearts (enough for 2 tablespoons) and finely shredded lettuce (enough for 1 heaped tablespoon) in butter. Cook 2 tablespoons fine vermicelli in the consommé, add the artichoke and lettuce garnishes, and finally some chervil leaves.

## Consommé with profiteroles

Use beef, chicken or game consommé. Prepare 20 small profiteroles filled with a purée of meat, game, vegetables or chicken. Thicken the consommé with tapioca and sprinkle with chervil leaves. Place the profiteroles in an hors d'oeuvre dish and serve with the consommé.

## Consommé with rice

Use beef, fish or game consommé. Cook 65–75 g (2½–3 oz, ½ cup) rice in simple beef consommé. Add it to the consommé chosen for a base and cook for about 20 minutes. Serve with grated cheese.

## Consommé with wine

Use beef consommé. Strain the consommé and when nearly cold add 150 ml (¼ pint, ⅔ cup) Madeira, Marsala, port or sherry.

## Daube of beef à la béarnaise

Cut 2 kg (4½ lb) top rump or chuck beef into 5 cm (2 in) cubes. Lard each cube crossways with a small piece of pork streaky (slab) bacon rolled in chopped parsley and garlic seasoned with some crushed thyme and bay leaf. Marinate these beef cubes for at least 2 hours in a bowl with 1 bottle red wine and 4 tablespoons brandy with 1 large sliced onion, 2 sliced carrots and a bouquet garni of parsley, thyme and bay leaves. Drain the beef, reserving the marinade, then pat the meat dry and roll it in flour. Brown the meat and vegetables separately.

Line the bottom of a flameproof casserole with slices of Bayonne ham, then add alternate layers of the meat cubes and vegetables. Add the bouquet garni, 2–3 crushed garlic cloves to the reserved marinade and a few spoonfuls of stock; then boil for 30 minutes. Strain and pour over the meat. Cover the casserole and seal on the lid with a flour-and-water paste. Bring to the boil on the hob (stove top), then cook in a preheated oven at 120°C (250°F, gas ½) for 4–5 hours.

Serve the daube from the casserole after skimming off some of the fat. In Béarn this daube is served with a cornmeal (maize) porridge, which is eaten cold and sliced as an alternative to bread.

## Daube of beef à la provençale

Cut 1.5 kg (3¼ lb) lean chuck or silverside (bottom round) into 6 cm (2½ in) cubes. Lard each cube crossways with a piece of fat bacon rolled in chopped parsley and garlic. Put the meat into an earthenware dish or casserole with a calf's foot, if available, and cover with 600 ml (1 pint, 2½ cups) white wine mixed with 2 tablespoons olive oil, 1 tablespoon brandy, salt and pepper. Marinate for 24 hours; reserve the marinade. Mix together 150 g (5 oz, 1⅔ cups) mushrooms, 75 g (3 oz, ⅔ cup) chopped raw onion, 2 crushed tomatoes, 150 g (5 oz, 1 cup) diced and blanched thick streaky (slab) bacon and 100 g (4 oz, 1 cup) black olives.

Remove the fat from some bacon rinds, blanch, wipe and use the rinds to line the bottom of an earthenware casserole just large enough to contain the meat and its garnishes. Add 2 sliced carrots, then add alternating layers of meat cubes and the vegetable and bacon mixture. In the centre of the meat place a large bouquet garni consisting of parsley stalks, thyme, a bay leaf and a small piece of dried orange peel. Add the white wine mixture from the marinade plus an equal volume of beef stock so that it just covers the meat.

Cover the casserole, seal the lid with a flour-and-water paste, and cook in a preheated oven at 120°C (250°F, gas ½) for 6 hours. Remove the bouquet garni, allow to cool, then skim off the fat. Serve the daube cold in slices, like a terrine, or hot (reheated in the oven).

## Devilled beef

Cut some cold boiled beef into fairly thick slices. Coat each slice with mustard, sprinkle with oil or melted butter, coat with fresh breadcrumbs and grill (broil) under a low heat until each side is golden brown. Serve with devilled sauce.

## Empanada

Cut 500 g (18 oz) lean beef into small cubes and cook gently in a little oil with 100 g (4 oz, ⅔ cup) chopped onion, ½ seeded and diced sweet (bell) green pepper and leaf pimento (*ignara*), 1 teaspoon ground cumin and 1 crushed garlic clove. When the meat is cooked, add 2 tablespoons raisins, previously soaked, and 1 chopped hard-boiled (hard-cooked) egg. Put a layer of this mixture on pieces of pastry and make little pasties. Bake in a preheated oven at 180°C (350°F, gas 4) for 30 minutes and serve very hot.

## Entrecôte à la ménagère

Gently cook 250 g (9 oz) small carrots, 150 g (5 oz) small onions and 150 g (5 oz, 1½ cups) mushrooms in butter. Season the steak with salt and pepper and brown it in butter in a frying pan over a brisk heat. Add the vegetables and fry for a further 3–4 minutes. Arrange the entrecôte and the vegetables on a serving dish and keep hot. Make a sauce in the frying pan by adding 5 tablespoons white wine and 3 tablespoons stock. Boil down to reduce and pour it over the entrecôte.

## Entrecôte Bercy

Grill (broil) a steak and garnish with Bercy butter.

## Entrecôte grand-mère

Prepare 12 small glazed onions, 12 blanched mushroom caps and 50 g (2 oz, ⅓ cup) diced blanched salt pork or bacon. Sauté the steak in butter, browning both sides, then add the vegetables and bacon to the pan and cook all together. Meanwhile, prepare and fry some small new potatoes until browned. Arrange the steak on the serving dish surrounded by the garnishes and keep hot. Dilute the pan juices with a little stock, bring to the boil and pour over the steak. Sprinkle with parsley and serve with the potatoes.

## Entrecôte marchand de vin

Grill (broil) an entrecôte steak under a high heat. Season with salt and pepper and garnish with rounds of marchand de vin butter.

## Entrecôtes mirabeau

Stone (pit) about 15 green olives and blanch them in boiling water. Prepare 2 tablespoons anchovy butter. Blanch a few tarragon leaves. Grill (broil)

2 thin sirloin steaks. Garnish with strips of anchovy fillets arranged in a criss-cross pattern, the tarragon leaves and olives, and anchovy butter, which may be piped into shell shapes.

## Estouffade of beef

Dice and blanch 300 g (11 oz, 15 slices) lean bacon. Brown the bacon in butter in a flameproof casserole, drain and set aside. Cut 1.5 kg (3¼ lb) beef – half chuck steak, half rib – into cubes of about 100 g (4 oz) and brown in the same pan. Cut 3 onions into quarters, add them to the beef and brown. Season with salt, pepper, thyme, a bay leaf and a crushed garlic clove. Then stir in 2 tablespoons flour and add 1 litre (1¾ pints, 4⅓ cups) red wine with an equal quantity of stock. Add a bouquet garni and bring to the boil. Cover and cook in a preheated oven at 160°C (325°F, gas 3) for 2½–3 hours.

Drain the ragoût in a sieve placed over an earthenware dish. Place the pieces of beef and the strips of bacon in a pan and add 300 g (11 oz, 3½ cups) sautéed sliced mushrooms. Skim the fat from the cooking liquid, strain and reduce. Pour it over the meat and mushrooms and simmer gently, covered, for about 25 minutes. Serve in a deep dish.

## Faux-filet braised à la bourgeoise

The faux-filet is also known as *contre-filet*. Part of the beef sirloin located on either side of the backbone above the loins. It is fattier and less tender than the fillet but has more flavour; when boned and trimmed, it can be roasted or braised. Unlike fillet, it is not essential to bard the meat, unless it is to be braised. Slices of faux-filet can be grilled (broiled) or fried.

Marinate some lardons of bacon in brandy for about 30 minutes. Season with salt, pepper and ground allspice. Insert the lardons into the faux-filet (tenderloin). Season and marinate the meat for 12 hours in red or white wine flavoured with thyme, bay leaf, chopped parsley and 1 crushed garlic clove. Drain the meat and brown it in either butter or oil. Fry 2 large sliced onions and 2 large diced carrots in butter, and brown a few crushed veal bones in the oven. Place the vegetables in the bottom of a braising pan and lay the faux-filet on top. Add the browned bones, 1 or 2 blanched boned calves' feet, the marinade, 2–3 tablespoons tomato purée (paste) and enough stock just to cover the meat. Then add a bouquet garni and season with salt and pepper. Cover, bring to the boil on the hob (stove top) and then transfer to a preheated oven at 150°C (300°F, gas 2) for about 2½ hours. Add some wedges of carrot and continue cooking for another hour. Prepare some small glazed onions. When the meat is cooked, drain it, and keep it warm in a deep dish. Skim the fat off the cooking liquid, boil to reduce and add a knob of softened butter. Dice the meat from the calves' feet and arrange it around the meat together with the carrots and small onions. Coat with the cooking liquid.

## Filets mignons of beef en chevreuil

Prepare an *en chevreuil* marinade. Cut the filets mignons into triangles, flatten them slightly and lard with fat bacon. Marinate them for between 36 hours (in summer) and 3 days (in winter), turning them frequently in the marinade. Drain, wipe and sauté briskly in oil or clarified butter. They may be served with a purée (of celeriac, lentils, chestnuts or onions) and a sauce (for example chasseur, hongroise, poivrade or romaine).

## Fillet of beef à la Frascati

Prepare a demi-glace sauce flavoured with port. Sauté some very large mushrooms in butter or bake them in the oven. Cook some very short green asparagus tips in butter and quickly sauté some small slices of foie gras (preferably duck) in butter. Keep all these ingredients hot. Roast a fillet of beef and place it on a serving dish. Fill two-thirds of the mushroom caps with the asparagus tips and the remainder with a salpicon of truffles braised in Madeira. Arrange the mushrooms and the slices of foie gras around the meat. Pour the demi-glace over the top.

## Fillet of beef à la matignon

Stud a fillet of beef with strips of pickled ox (beef) tongue and truffle (optional). Cover with a matignon mixture and wrap in very thin slices of bacon. Secure with string. Put into a braising pan and add enough Maderia to cover one-third of it. Cover and braise in a preheated oven at 160°C (325°F, gas 3) until the meat is tender. Drain the fillet and remove the bacon and matignon. Skim the fat from the cooking liquid, strain it, pour a few tablespoons over the fillet, and put it into the oven to glaze. Serve surrounded with a matignon garnish and a little of the sauce. Serve the remainder of the sauce separately.

## Fillet of beef à la périgourdine

Trim the fillet of beef, stud it with truffles, cover it with bacon rashers (slices), tie it with string and braise in Madeira-flavoured stock. Drain, remove the bacon, glaze in the oven and arrange it on the serving dish. Surround it with small slices of foie gras that have been studded with truffles and sautéed in clarified butter. Reduce the stock by half, strain it and pour it over the fillet.

## Fillet of beef en brioche

Prepare some brioche dough without sugar, using 500 g (1 lb 2 oz, 4½ cups) plain (all-purpose) flour, 20 g (¾ oz) fresh yeast (1½ cakes compressed yeast), 100 ml (4 fl oz, 7 tablespoons) water, 2 teaspoons salt, 6 medium-sized eggs, and 250 g (9 oz, 1 cup) butter. Melt 25 g (1 oz, 2 tablespoons) butter and

3 tablespoons oil in a pan and lightly brown a piece of fillet of beef weighing about 1.5 kg (3¼ lb), tied with string to maintain its shape. Then place the pan, uncovered, in a preheated oven at 240°C (475°F, gas 9) and cook for 10 minutes, basting the meat 2 or 3 times. Drain it, season with salt and pepper and leave to cool completely.

Lower the temperature of the oven to about 220°C (425°F, gas 7). Roll out the brioche dough into a fairly large rectangle. Remove the string from the beef and place it in the centre of the dough lengthways. Brush the meat with beaten egg and fold one of the sides of the dough over it. Brush the other side of the rectangle with beaten egg and wrap the fillet completely in the dough, tucking in the edges. Trim and cut both ends of the dough just beyond the meat and seal the edges with beaten egg. Brush the top with beaten egg. Garnish the top with the remaining pieces of dough. Brush with beaten egg. Place on a floured baking sheet and bake in a preheated oven at 220°C (425°F, gas 7) for about 30 minutes. Fillet of beef *en brioche* is traditionally served with a Périgueux sauce.

## Fillet of beef Prince Albert

Marinate a raw goose foie gras studded with truffle in a little Cognac with salt and pepper for 24 hours in a cool place. Lard a piece of beef cut from the middle of the fillet with fine strips of bacon. Slice the meat along its length without separating the 2 halves completely. Drain the foie gras, place it in the meat and tie together firmly to keep the liver in place. Fry the meat in butter in a braising pan over a brisk heat until it is well browned on all sides, then cover it with a layer of matignon mixture, wrap in very thin rashers (slices) of bacon and secure with string.

Prepare a braising stock with a calf's foot and aromatic herbs, adding the liver marinade; pour into the braising pan and add the beef. Pour on a little port, cover, bring to the boil, then transfer to a preheated oven at 200°C (400°F, gas 6) and cook for 1 hour. Untie the fillet, remove the bacon and the matignon mixture, but leave the string holding the foie gras in place. Strain the braising stock, pour some over the meat and glaze quickly in a very hot oven. Untie the meat, place it on a serving dish and garnish with whole truffles, stewed in butter or poached in Madeira. Serve the braising stock, skimmed of fat and strained, in a sauceboat.

## Flank with shallots

Flank steaks come from the abdominal muscles of beef, which form a second-category joint. Thick flank steaks cut on the perpendicular from the internal muscles are lean, tasty, coarse-grained and slightly tough (they must therefore be hung); they are eaten grilled (broiled) or sautéed. Thin flank is similar but slightly tougher. Cuts taken from the two external muscles give fibrous, rather tough meat, suitable for broths and stews.

Chop some shallots, allowing 1 level tablespoon chopped shallots for each steak. Fry the flank steaks quickly in butter, add the chopped shallots to the frying pan (skillet) and brown. Season with salt and pepper. Remove the steaks and deglaze the meat juices with vinegar (1 tablespoon per steak) and a little stock, then reduce. Pour the shallots and juice over the steaks.

## Fried entrecôte

Season the steak with salt and pepper. Melt some butter in a frying pan. When it bubbles, add the steak and brown both sides over a high heat. Then drain, arrange on the serving dish, and garnish with a knob of butter (plain butter, maître d'hôtel butter or *marchand de vin* butter). Alternatively, serve with a red wine sauce or sprinkle with the cooking butter plus a few drops of lemon juice and some chopped parsley.

## Fried entrecôte à la bourguignonne

Fry a 400–500 g (14–18 oz) steak in butter, drain and keep hot on the serving dish. Pour 100 ml (4 fl oz, 7 tablespoons) each of red wine and demi-glace into the frying pan and heat until reduced, then coat the steak with this sauce.

The demi-glace can be replaced by the same amount of well-reduced consommé bound with 1 teaspoon beurre manié.

## Fried entrecôte à la fermière

Prepare about 450 g (1 lb) vegetable fondue. Fry a 450 g (1 lb) steak in butter, place in a serving dish and keep hot. Surround with the vegetable fondue. Deglaze the pan with 100 ml (4 fl oz, 7 tablespoons) white wine and the same amount of beef consommé, reduce and bind with 1 teaspoon beurre manié. Pour this sauce over the steak.

## Fried entrecôte à la hongroise

Season a 450 g (1 lb) steak, then fry it in butter. When it is three-quarters cooked, add 1 tablespoon chopped onion. Drain the steak, place it on a serving dish and keep hot. Finish cooking the onions, add a little paprika and adjust the seasoning. Deglaze the frying pan with 100 ml (4 fl oz, 7 tablespoons) white wine and the same amount of velouté. Reheat and pour over the steak. Serve with boiled potatoes.

## Fried entrecôte à la lyonnaise

Thinly slice 2 large onions and fry them gently in butter. Fry a 450 g (1 lb) steak in butter; when it is three-quarters cooked, add the fried onions to the pan. When cooked, drain the steak and onion, place in a serving dish and keep hot. Deglaze the frying pan with 2 tablespoons vinegar and 100 ml (4 fl oz, 7 tablespoons) demi-glace. Reduce, stir in 1 tablespoon chopped parsley and pour over the steak. (If you wish, the demi-glace can be replaced with reduced consommé bound with 1 teaspoon beurre manié.)

## Fried entrecôte with mushrooms

Fry a 450 g (1 lb) steak in butter. When three-quarters cooked, add 8–10 mushroom caps to the frying pan. Place the steak in a serving dish and keep hot. Finish cooking the mushrooms, then arrange them around the steak. Deglaze the frying pan with 100 ml (4 fl oz, 7 tablespoons) each of white wine and demi-glace, and reduce. Sieve, add 1 tablespoon fresh butter, stir and pour the sauce over the steak.

Instead of demi-glace, the same quantity of well-reduced consommé bound with 1 teaspoon beurre manié can be used.

## Fried fillet steaks

Cut the fillet into thick 125–150 g (4–5 oz) steaks. Slightly flatten the steaks, then seal in very hot butter. Season with salt and pepper. Remove the steaks and keep them hot. Make a sauce with the pan juices mixed with a little Madeira; reduce and coat the steaks.

## Fried onglet with shallots

The onglet is a French cut of beef consisting of two small muscles joined by an elastic membrane (the supporting muscles of the diaphragm). The butcher splits it open, trims it and removes all the skin and membrane. Onglet must be well hung; the meat is then tender and juicy. In the past it was not a popular cut, but it is now generally accepted that it makes a prime steak. Whether fried or grilled (broiled), it should be eaten rare, otherwise it becomes tough.

Make shallow criss-cross incisions on both sides of the meat. Peel and chop 3–4 shallots. Heat about 25 g (1 oz, 2 tablespoons) butter in a frying pan; when it is very hot, put in the meat and brown it quickly on both sides. Season with salt and pepper, drain it and keep it hot. Cook the shallots in the frying pan until golden. Add 2–3 tablespoons vinegar to the pan and reduce the liquid by half. Pour this gravy over the meat.

## Grilled beef fillet steaks

Cut the trimmed fillet into thick steaks, each weighing 125–150 g (4–5 oz). Slightly flatten each steak with a meat mallet, sprinkle with pepper, brush with oil and season with herbes de Provence (or mixed dried herbs). Cook the steak under a hot grill (broiler) or over glowing embers, so that the outside is sealed while the inside remains pink or rare. Top each steak with a pat of maître d'hôtel butter.

## Grilled Chateaubriand

Brush the chateaubriand with oil, sprinkle with pepper and cook under a grill (broiler) under a brisk heat. Sprinkle with salt and serve very hot. A very hot grill is perfect for cooking chateaubriand to a turn, so that it is sealed on the outside and underdone inside.

## Grilled entrecôte

Lightly brush the steak with oil or melted butter, season with salt and pepper and cook over very hot wood charcoal or grill (broil) in a vertical grill, under the grill (broiler) of the cooker (stove), or over an iron grill. The surface of the steak must be sealed so that the juices will not escape. (Some cooks advise against seasoning with salt before cooking because this draws out the blood.) Serve with château potatoes, bunches of cress and béarnaise sauce (separately), if liked.

# Grilled entrecôte à la bordelaise

In the authentic recipe, the steak is simply grilled (broiled) over vine-shoot embers, seasoned, then served with a knob of butter. However, in certain gastronomic circles, the steak is grilled, garnished with slices of beef bone marrow poached for a few minutes in stock and sprinkled with chopped parsley. It is served with bordelaise sauce.

# Grilled filets mignons

Slightly flatten some filets mignons of beef, each weighing about 125–150 g (4–5 oz). Season with salt and pepper, dip in melted butter and coat with fresh breadcrumbs. Moisten them with clarified butter and cook under a low grill (broiler). Serve with maître d'hôtel butter, Choron sauce, lemon butter or tarragon-flavoured tomato sauce mixed with white wine.

# Grilled flank

Brush some flank steaks with oil, sprinkle with chopped thyme and parsley and grill (broil) quickly for 7–8 minutes then season with salt and pepper.

# Grilled onglet

Onglet is a French cut of beef made up of two small muscles connected by an elastic membrane (the supporting muscles of the diaphragm). It is split open by the butcher who removes all the skin and membrane. This is a cut which must be well hung; the meat is then tender and juicy. In the past, it was not popular, but it is now regarded as a prime steak. Whether fried or grilled (broiled), onglet should be eaten rare, otherwise it becomes tough.

Make shallow criss-cross incisions on both sides of the meat and rub it with a little oil and pepper. Cook under a very hot grill (broiler), seasoning with salt halfway through cooking, and serve rare.

## Hachis Parmentier

Dice or coarsely chop 500 g (18 oz, 4½ cups) boiled or braised beef. Melt 25 g (1 oz, 2 tablespoons) butter in a shallow frying pan and cook 3 chopped onions in it until they are golden. Sprinkle with 1 tablespoon flour, cook until lightly brown, and then moisten with 200 ml (7 fl oz, ¾ cup) beef stock (or braising stock with water added to it). Cook for about 15 minutes, leave to cool, then add the beef and mix well. Place the beef and onions in a buttered gratin dish, cover with a layer of potato purée, sprinkle with breadcrumbs and moisten with melted butter. Brown in a preheated oven at 230°C (450°C, gas 8) for about 15 minutes.

Although it is not traditional, a small cup of very reduced tomato sauce can be added to the chopped meat and a little grated cheese may be mixed with the breadcrumbs.

## Hamburgers

Mix 400 g (14 oz) best-quality minced (ground) beef with 50 g (2 oz, ⅓ cup) chopped onion, 2 beaten eggs, salt, pepper and 1 tablespoon chopped parsley if liked. Shape the mixture into 4 thick flat round patties, and fry in very hot clarified butter or grill (broil). They are cooked when droplets of blood appear on the surface. Fry 100 g (4 oz, ⅔ cup) chopped onion in the same butter to garnish the hamburgers. Serve very hot in a round bun.

## Hungarian goulash

Peel 250 g (9 oz) onions and slice them into rings. Cut 1.5 kg (3¼ lb) braising steak (chuck beef) into pieces of about 75 g (3 oz). Melt 100 g (4 oz, ½ cup) lard in a casserole. When it is hot, put in the meat and onions and brown them. Add 500 g (18 oz) tomatoes, peeled, seeded and cut into quarters, then 1 crushed garlic clove, a bouquet garni, salt, pepper and finally 1 tablespoon mild Hungarian paprika. Add enough stock to cover the meat, bring to the boil, then reduce the heat, cover and cook very gently for 2 hours. Add 600 ml (1 pint, 2½ cups) boiling water and 800 g (1¾ lb) potatoes, peeled and cut into quarters. Again bring to the boil and continue boiling until the potatoes are cooked. Adjust the seasoning. Serve very hot.

## Jellied beef aiguillettes

Aiguillette is the French name for a long narrow fillet, taken from either side of the breastbone of poultry (mainly duck) and game birds. This separates easily from the underside of the breast meat and is a popular chef's item for small dishes. An aiguillette can also be a thin strip of any meat. In France the tip of a rump of beef is called *aiguillette baronne*.

Put 1 calf's foot and some veal bones into a saucepan, cover with cold water and bring slowly to the boil. Drain, then cool and wipe dry. Slice 575 g (1¼ lb) new carrots and 1 large onion, quarter 2 tomatoes and peel 2 small garlic cloves.

Heat 2 tablespoons oil in a flameproof casserole and brown 1.25 kg (2¾ lb) slivers of beef aiguillettes which, if possible, have been larded by the butcher. Add the sliced carrot and onion, the calf's foot and the veal bones; continue to cook until the onions are coloured. Remove any excess oil with a small ladle, then add the tomato quarters, a bouquet garni, a small piece of orange zest, a pinch of salt, pepper (a few turns of the pepper mill), a dash of cayenne pepper, 250 ml (8 fl oz, 1 cup) dry white wine and 500 ml (17 fl oz, 2 cups) water. Cover and slowly bring to the boil, then place the casserole in a preheated oven at 180°C (350°F, gas 4). Cook for about 2½ hours or until the meat is tender, stirring the meat from time to time.

In a large uncovered pan, simmer 30 small peeled button onions with 25 g (1 oz, 2 tablespoons) butter, 2 teaspoons caster (superfine) sugar, a pinch of salt and just enough water to cover them. Cook until the onions are tender and the liquid has evaporated. Toss the onions in the caramel which has formed. Drain the aiguillettes (reserving the cooking liquid) and arrange them in a deep dish or terrine with the sliced carrots and the small onions. Set aside until cold, then refrigerate.

Remove the bones from the calf's foot and cut the flesh into cubes. Strain the cooking liquid back into a saucepan, add the calf's foot cubes and boil for about 10 minutes, then strain. Dissolve 15 g (½ oz, 2 envelopes) powdered gelatine in the minimum of water, then add the strained cooking liquid and 100 ml (4 fl oz, ½ cup) Madeira; check seasoning, then leave to cool until syrupy. Coat the aiguillettes with the setting liquid, then refrigerate until set and ready to serve.

## Kromeskies à la bonne femme

A kromesky is a type of rissole or fritter, often served as a hot hors d'oeuvre and originating in Poland, but also traditional in Russia. It is made by binding the ingredients in a thick sauce and using as a filling for thin pancakes. The filled pancakes are coated in breadcrumbs and fried. Alternatively the mixture may be coated in batter or breadcrumbs.

Boil 500 g (18 oz) beef and retain the cooking stock. Soften 2 tablespoons chopped onion in 15 g (½ oz, 1 tablespoon) butter or lard and add 1 tablespoon flour. Brown lightly and then add 200 ml (7 fl oz, ¾ cup) very reduced beef stock. Stir well, then cook over a very gentle heat for about 15 minutes. Dice the beef very finely and mix it with the sauce. Reheat and then cool completely. Divide the mixture into portions weighing about 65 g (2½ oz), shaping them into cork shapes. Roll them in flour, dip them in batter and fry in very hot fat.

The beef may be replaced by pieces of cooked chicken or game.

## Oven-roast rib of beef

Place the rib in a roasting tin (pan), brush with butter or dripping, and roast uncovered in a preheated oven at 240°C (450°F, gas 9) for 15–18 minutes per 450 g (1 lb) plus 15 minutes. To ensure that it is cooked through completely, treat as for spit-roast rib of beef.

To ensure the meat is cooked through, remove from the spit just before completely cooked, wrap in foil and leave in a hot oven that has been turned off or in a very low oven for 30 minutes.

## Paleron ménagère

Cut 1 kg (2¼ lb) chuck steak into large dice and season with salt and pepper. Brown in hot oil in a saucepan for 5 minutes. Then pour off the oil, add a large, finely diced onion and cook until brown. Sprinkle with 1 tablespoon flour, stirring well to coat the meat and the onion, then moisten with 500 ml (17 fl oz, 2 cups) dry white wine. Add 2 whole tomatoes, 2 chopped garlic cloves and a bouquet garni. Cover with a mixture of half water and half stock, add 1 tablespoon coarse salt and cook gently with the lid on for 1 hour, stirring from time to time. Add 400 g (14 oz, 3 cups) carrots and 200 g (7 oz, 1½ cups) turnips cut into small sticks. Leave to simmer for 10 minutes. Finally add 20 button (pearl) onions, which have been cooked in salted water, and adjust the seasoning. Sprinkle with roughly chopped parsley and serve.

## Pâté en croûte 'pavé du roy'

Cut 300 g (11 oz) lean fillet of veal and 300 g (11 oz) lean fillet of pork into small cubes and marinate for 12 hours in 175 ml (6 fl oz, ¾ cup) white wine and 175 ml (6 fl oz, ¾ cup) Cognac, salt, pepper and a pinch of allspice. Mince (grind) 500 g (18 oz) lean boneless pork and season. Add 100 g (4 oz, ¾ cup) foie gras to the marinated meat.

Make an extra-rich butter pastry with 500 g (18 oz, 4½ cups) plain (all-purpose) flour, 300 g (11 oz, 1⅓ cups) butter and 2 eggs and use to line a pâté mould, reserving enough for the lid. Cover the bottom with bacon and add half the meat mixture. Cover with a thin layer of bacon and use the remaining pastry for the lid. Make two holes in the lid and brush with beaten egg.

Cook in a preheated oven at 220°C (425°F, gas 7) for 15 minutes, then reduce the temperature to 180°C (350°F, gas 4) and continue to bake for 1¼ hours. If necessary, cover the top of the pâté en croûte loosely with foil to prevent the crust from becoming too brown. Leave to cool and pour some cold aspic jelly through the holes in the lid to top up the filling. Place in the refrigerator for 12 hours.

## Paupiettes of beef à la hongroise

Flatten some thin slices of beef fillet, sirloin or chuck steak, season with salt and pepper, and spread with veal forcemeat mixed with chopped onion fried in butter, then wrap in thin slices of bacon, place in a pan on a bed of more fried onion and season with salt and paprika. Cover the pan and simmer for 10 minutes. Moisten with dry white wine, allowing 200 ml (7 fl oz, ¾ cup) for 10 paupiettes. Boil down, then add about 400 ml (14 fl oz, 1¾ cups) light velouté sauce. Put a bouquet garni in the middle of the dish. Bring to the boil, cover the pan and cook in a preheated oven at 220°C (425°F, gas 7) for 25 minutes, basting frequently.

When the paupiettes are nearly ready, drain them, remove the barding, put back into the pan and add 20 small mushrooms lightly tossed in butter. Add some double (heavy) cream to the sauce, boil down a little, strain and pour over the paupiettes. Cook until they are done.

Serve on croûtes fried in butter, covering them with the sauce and mushrooms.

## Paupiettes of beef Sainte-Menehould

Flatten some thin slices of beef fillet, sirloin or chuck steak, season with salt and pepper, and spread with a layer of well-seasoned sausagemeat. Roll them up, wrap in thin rashers (slices) of fat bacon and tie with string. Braise the paupiettes in white wine or Madeira, drain them, untie the string, remove the bacon and arrange them on a heated dish. Coat with the cooking juices (reduced and strained).

All the accompaniments for small cuts of braised meat are suitable for these paupiettes: noisette potatoes, braised vegetables, vegetable purée, stuffed artichoke hearts, risotto, rice pilaf. Some garnishes (bourgeoise or chipolata) can be added to the casserole halfway through the braising time.

When three-quarters cooked, remove from the heat and leave to cool in their strained cooking juices, then drain, pat dry and spread with French mustard mixed with a little cayenne. Moisten with melted butter, roll in fresh breadcrumbs and gently grill (broil) them. Arrange the paupiettes on a serving dish garnished with watercress. Reheat the cooking juices and serve, strained, in a sauceboat.

## Petite marmite à la parisienne

Pour 2.5 litres (4½ pints, 11 cups) cold consommé into a pan. Add 500 g (18 oz) rump roast (standing rump) and 250 g (9 oz) short rib of beef. Bring to the boil and skim. Then add 100 g (4 oz, ¾ cup) chopped carrots, 75 g (3 oz, ⅔ cup) chopped turnips, 75 g (3 oz) leeks (white part only, cut into chunks), 2 baby (pearl) onions browned in a dry frying pan, 50 g (2 oz) celery hearts (cut into small pieces and blanched) and 100 g (4 oz) cabbage (blanched in salted water, cooled and rolled into tight balls). Simmer these ingredients for 3 hours, occasionally adding a little consommé to compensate for the evaporation.

Lightly brown 2 sets of chicken giblets in a preheated oven at 200°C (400°F, gas 6), add them to the pan and cook for a further 50 minutes. Finally, add a large marrow bone wrapped in muslin (cheesecloth) and simmer for another 10 minutes. Skim off the surplus fat, unwrap the marrow bone and replace it in the pan. Serve the soup hot with small slices from a long thin French loaf that have been crisped in the oven and sprinkled with a little fat from the stew. Spread some of the bread with bone marrow and season with freshly ground pepper.

## Poached rump of beef

Lard the meat or not, as preferred. Tie the meat into a neat shape with string and cook in a large pan using the same method as for a pot-au-feu and the same vegetables. Bring to the boil, skim and season. Simmer gently for 4–5 hours, but do not cover the pan completely. To serve, drain and untie the meat and place it on a large serving dish with the garnish. Serve with the strained cooking liquor, grated horseradish and coarse salt. Cooked in this way, rump provides both a soup and a main course. To provide additional flavour to the soup, add small pieces of fleshy beef bones to the liquid.

## Pot-au-feu

Place 800 g (1¾ lb) flank (flank or short plate) in a large stockpot and pour in 3 litres (5 pints, 13 cups) cold water. Heat until just simmering, then skim the water, cover and continue to simmer for 1 hour. Stud 1 onion with 4 cloves and add it to the pan with 4 coarsely crushed or chopped garlic cloves, a bouquet garni, 1 teaspoon salt and pepper. Add 800 g (1¾ lb) each of sirloin and chuck steak. Bring back to simmering point, skim the soup, then cover and simmer gently for 2 hours.

Cut 6 carrots, 6 turnips and 3 parsnips into large even-sized pieces, turning them into neat ovals if liked. Cut the white parts of 3 leeks and 3 celery sticks into similar lengths. When the pot-au-feu has cooked for 3 hours, add the celery and leeks, then simmer for 10 minutes before adding the carrots, turnips and parsnips. Continue to cook for a further 1 hour.

Towards the end of the cooking time, poach 4 sections of marrow bone in lightly salted water for 20 minutes. Drain the meats and vegetables, and place on a large serving platter. Drain the marrow bone and add to the platter. Skim the fat off the broth and spoon a little over the meat and vegetables. Serve at once, with coarse salt, gherkins, mustard and toasted French bread on which to spread the marrow.

## Pressed beef

Take 3 kg (6½ lb) lightly larded brisket. Prick with a large larding needle and soak the meat in brine for 8–10 days (brine penetrates the meat more quickly in summer). The meat must be completely submerged and it is advisable to use a weighted board to achieve this. Just before cooking, wash the meat in cold water. If more than one mould is used, then cut the meat into pieces to fit them. Cook in water until tender with some carrots, cut into pieces. Place the meat in square moulds, each covered with a weighted board. When the meat is quite cold, turn it out of the moulds and coat with several layers of meat aspic, coloured reddish brown by adding caramel and red food colouring. This provides the meat with a strong protective coating that retards deterioration. To serve, cut into very thin slices and garnish with fresh parsley.

## Roast faux-filet

Also known as *contre-filet*, this cut is part of the beef sirloin located on either side of the backbone above the loins. It is fattier and less tender than the fillet but has more flavour; when boned and trimmed, it can be roasted or braised.

Bone and trim the meat. Bard it on top and underneath, shape into a square and tie. Cook in a preheated oven at 240°C (475°F, gas 9) so that the outside is sealed but the inside remains pink or rare, allowing 10 minutes per 450 g (1 lb). The meat can be untied and debarded to brown the outside thoroughly 5 minutes before the end of the cooking time. Season with salt and pepper.

## Roast fillet of beef

Trim the fillet, bard it top and bottom (or brush with melted butter) and tie with string. Cook it in a preheated oven at 240°C (475°F, gas 9), allowing 10–12 minutes per 450 g (1 lb) and basting it several times with the meat juices, to which a very small amount of water has been added. Drain the meat, remove the barding strips and keep it hot on a serving dish. Make a sauce with the pan juices mixed with stock or reduced veal gravy. Reduce and serve.

## Roast rib of beef à la bouquetière

A *bouquetière* is a French garnish composed of vegetables that are arranged in bouquets of different colours around large meat roasts, fried chicken or tournedos (filet mignon) steaks.

Season a thick (two-bone) slice of rib of beef with salt and pepper, brush with melted butter. Roast in a preheated oven at 240°C (475°F, gas 9) for about 16–18 minutes per 1 kg (2½ lb) or until cooked as required.

To prepare the garnish, cook some small carrots, pod-shaped pieces of turnip, small green (French) beans, artichoke hearts and small cauliflower florets in salted water. Drain the vegetables and warm them in clarified butter. Cook some peas and use them to stuff the artichoke hearts. Fry some small new potatoes in butter.

Drain the fat from the meat juices and place the meat on a serving dish surrounded by the vegetables arranged in bouquets. Deglaze the dish in which the meat was cooked with a mixture of Madeira and stock. Reduce and pour the meat juices over the rib of beef.

## Roast sirloin

This very large joint is not normally cooked in one piece except by professional chefs. They trim off the top a little to give the joint a more regular shape, then cut the ligament that runs along the chine into regular sections and remove part of the fat that surrounds the fillet. The joint is then seasoned with salt and pepper and generally roasted in the oven or on a spit – allowing 10–12 minutes per 1 kg (5–6 minutes per 1 lb); it should be pink on the inside. It is served surrounded with sprigs of watercress or with a bouquetière or printanière garnish.

## Salt (corned) beef

This method is mostly used for preparing brisket, but may also be used for flank and chuck. The meat is soaked in brine for 6–8 days in summer and 8–10 days in winter. It is then rinsed to desalt, and cooked in water for 30 minutes per 1 kg (2¼ lb). Salt beef is served hot with vegetables that are traditionally associated with it, such as braised red or green cabbage and sauerkraut. It is also used for pot roasting.

## Sautéed Chateaubriand

Sauté the chateaubriand briskly in butter: the outside must be sealed, the inside underdone. Use the butter in which the steak was cooked to make a chasseur sauce and coat the steaks, or keep the meat hot and surround it with boiled vegetables mixed with the butter. Alternatively, remove the cooking butter and serve with a pat of maître d'hôtel or marchand de vin butter.

## Sautéed filet mignons

Slightly flatten some filets mignons of beef, season with salt and pepper and sauté them quickly in very hot clarified butter. Garnish as for tournedos.

## Sautéed or grilled tournedos

Sauté the tournedos very rapidly in butter, oil or a mixture of both, so that the interior remains pink. They can also be grilled (broiled). Depending on the choice of garnish, or to prevent the garnish from masking the tournedos, the steaks are sometimes arranged on fried or grilled croûtons, potato cakes, artichoke hearts or rice. The following are a few suggestions for garnishes and sauces.

- *à la béarnaise* Grill and garnish with château potatoes; serve béarnaise sauce separately.

- *à la d'abrantès* Season with paprika, sauté in oil, then arrange on a grilled slice of aubergine (eggplant); add to the cooking juices some lightly fried onion, a salpicon of sweet (bell) pepper and tomato sauce.

- *à la périgourdine* Sauté in butter; place on a fried croûton; garnish with slices of truffle tossed in butter; pour over a sauce made from the pan juices mixed with Madeira.

- *archiduc* Sauté in butter and arrange on a potato cake; garnish with croquettes of calves' brains and slivers of truffle; cover with the pan juices deglazed with a little sherry, diluted with crème fraîche and veal stock, and flavoured with paprika.

- *Clamart* Sauté in butter and garnish with artichoke hearts filled with peas or fresh pea purée; pour over a sauce made from the pan juices mixed with white wine and veal stock.

- *Saint-Germain* Sauté in butter, place on a fried croûton and garnish with thick pea purée.

- *with anchovies* Sauté in butter and arrange on a slice of fried bread; pour over a sauce made from the pan juices mixed with thickened veal stock, white wine and a little anchovy butter; garnish with half fillets of anchovies in oil, placed in a crisscross pattern on the tournedos.
- *with mushrooms* Sauté in butter; pour over a sauce made from the pan juices mixed with thickened veal stock and Madeira; garnish with mushrooms sautéed in butter.

## Sirloin à la d'Albufera

*Aloyau à la d'Albufera* (from Carême's recipe) Braise a sirloin joint. Make some tortue sauce, add a little butter and some of the beef juice, then stir in a plateful of sliced and sautéed calves' sweetbreads, a plateful of sliced pickled ox (beef) tongue and some mushrooms. Spoon some of this ragoût round the beef and then cook to reheat. Garnish the dish with slices of young rabbit fillet *à la d'Orly* (egged, crumbed and deep-fried) and 10 skewers laid on the beef, each assembled as follows: first a fine double cockscomb, a slice of young rabbit *à la d'Orly*, a cockscomb, a large glazed truffle, a cockscomb, and finally a glazed black truffle. Serve more ragoût in two sauceboats.

## Sliced meat à l'italienne

Prepare some Italian sauce and keep it very hot. Cut thin slices of boiled or braised beef, mutton or veal. Pour some of the sauce into a flameproof dish and put the meat on top. Cover with the remaining sauce and sprinkle with grated Parmesan cheese. Reheat on the stove without letting the sauce boil.

## Soupe albigeoise

Fill a large flameproof casserole with salted water and boil some beef flank (flank steak), calf's foot, salt pork and cooking sausage, together with vegetables such as cabbage, carrots, turnips, leeks and potatoes. Add 1 whole head of garlic per 6 servings. Brown some thin slices of goose confit in butter and garnish the soup with them.

## Spit-roasted fillet of beef

Trim the fillet, put it on the spit, season with salt and pepper and coat with melted butter. Roast, allowing about 10–12 minutes per 450 g (1 lb). Remove from the spit and leave the meat to rest for a few minutes. Cut it into even slices and serve with the reserved meat juices.

## Spit-roast rib of beef

Trim the boned rib and tie firmly to hold in shape, covering the exposed meat with thin rashers (slices) of fat bacon. Pierce evenly on to a spit and brush with butter or oil. Cook rapidly at first and then at a moderate heat, allowing 15–18 minutes per 1 kg (2¼ lb). Remove from the spit, untie, trim, season with salt and serve with the desired garnish. To ensure the meat is cooked through, remove from the spit just before it is completely cooked, wrap in foil and leave in a hot oven that has been turned off or in a very low oven for about 30 minutes.

## Steak and kidney pie

Make some puff pastry, using 225 g (8 oz, 2 cups) plain (all-purpose) flour and 225 g (8 oz, 1 cup) butter. (Traditionally, steak and kidney pie can also be made with flaky or shortcrust pastry.)

Cut 675 g (1½ lb) stewing steak into cubes. Clean an ox (beef) kidney and cut it into small pieces. Season 25 g (1 oz, ¼ cup) plain flour with salt and pepper to taste and coat the steak and kidney with the mixture. Finely chop 1 onion. Melt 50 g (2 oz, ¼ cup) butter in a saucepan, add the meats and onion and fry until golden. Stir in 600 ml (1 pint, 2½ cups) beef stock. Continue to stir until the mixture boils and thickens, then cover the pan, reduce the heat and simmer for 1½ hours, until the meat is almost tender.

Spoon the mixture into a 1.15 litre (2 pint, 5 cup) pie dish, reserving excess liquid for gravy. Wet the rim of the pie dish and put a strip of pastry around it; brush with water, then cover the dish with pastry. Trim, knock up and flute the edges with the back of a knife and brush with beaten egg. Make a small hole in the centre of the pie crust to allow steam to escape, and bake in a preheated oven at 190°C (375°F, gas 5) for about 45 minutes. Cover the pastry with foil if overbrowning. Serve piping hot in the pie dish.

## Steak à cheval

Season a steak with salt and pepper and sauté in butter. Arrange it on a plate, place a fried egg on top and sprinkle with the cooking butter.

## Steak au poivre

Generously sprinkle a thick steak (preferably rump steak) with coarsely ground black pepper. Seal the steak in hot clarified butter or oil in a sauté pan; when half-cooked, season with salt. When it has finished cooking, remove from the pan and keep hot. Skim the fat from the sauté pan and dilute the cooking juices with white wine and brandy. Boil down a little, then add 2 tablespoons demi-glace sauce or thick veal stock. Reduce further until the sauce becomes thick and glossy. Finish off with fresh butter and adjust the seasoning with salt.

Serve the steak coated with the sauce. Some cooks flame the steak with Cognac, Armagnac, whisky or liqueur brandy, and it is standard practice to finish the sauce with cream. It has also become common practice to prepare this dish using whole green peppercorns.

## Steak Dumas

Poach 12 rounds of beef marrow in some court-bouillon. Sauté 4 sirloin steaks in butter in a frying pan, season with salt and pepper and garnish with the marrow slices; remove from the frying pan and keep warm. Add 100 ml (4 fl oz, 7 tablespoons) dry white wine and 2 tablespoons chopped shallots to the frying pan and reduce by three-quarters. Add 100 ml (4 fl oz, 7 table-spoons) stock and bring to the boil. Stir in 100 g (4 oz, ½ cup) butter and season with salt and pepper. Coat the steaks with the sauce and sprinkle with chopped parsley.

## Steak tartare

Mince (grind) 150–200 g (5–7 oz) lean beef (rump steak, sirloin or top rump). Season with salt and pepper, a little cayenne and a few drops of Worcestershire sauce or Tabasco. Shape the meat into a ball, place it on a plate, hollow out the centre and put a raw egg yolk in the hollow. Around the meat arrange 1 tablespoon each of chopped onion, chopped parsley and chopped shallots and 1 teaspoon drained capers. Serve with tomato ketchup, olive oil and Worcestershire sauce.

## Steak with oysters

Open 8 oysters. Slice through a piece of beef fillet (sirloin) weighing about 300 g (11 oz), without separating the 2 halves. Flatten it slightly, season with salt and pepper, brush the inside surfaces with a mild mustard and then sear it rapidly in a mixture of equal quantities of oil and butter. Flame it with brandy and keep hot. In another pan put the strained water from 4 oysters, 1 chopped garlic clove, 1 finely chopped shallot, a knob of butter, 3 table-spoons double (heavy) cream and 1 teaspoon brandy. Add pepper and reduce. Slip the oysters into the steak, press it closed and secure it with 1 or

2 cocktail sticks (toothpicks). In a small saucepan put the juices which have run from the meat, the reduced sauce, a few drops of Worcestershire sauce, pepper and 1 tablespoon brandy; reduce once more. To serve, cover the steak with this sauce, arrange the last 4 oysters on top of the meat and sprinkle with chopped parsley.

## Sukiyaki

Before proceeding with the cooking, which is done in the course of the meal, prepare the ingredients: 450 g (1 lb) lean beef (fillet or sirloin), cut into very fine strips; 250 g (9 oz) shirataki (vermicelli made with starch), dipped in boiling water and drained (this may be replaced by fresh small noodles); 100 g (4 oz, 1⅓ cups) thinly sliced mushrooms; 150 g (5 oz, 1 cup) canned bamboo shoots, drained and finely sliced; 4 large leeks, thinly sliced; 150 g (5 oz, ¾ cup) bean curd cut into small dice; 100 g (4 oz, 1½ cups) blanched shredded Chinese cabbage; and a few coarsely shredded spinach leaves.

Heat a large heavy-based pan on a table hotplate, over a brisk flame, and grease it lightly with a piece of beef fat, which should be removed before cooking begins. Place one-third of the strips of meat in the pan, heat them through, then add 60 ml (2 fl oz, ¼ cup) soy sauce and 2 tablespoons sugar; turn over the meat, cook for 1–2 minutes, then push towards the edge of the pan. Next, add one-third of the vegetables, together with some shirataki and bean curd, and sprinkle with 60 ml (2 fl oz, ¼ cup) sake; leave to cook for 4–5 minutes. Distribute the vegetables and meat between the plates (the proportions given here are for four), and repeat the operation until all the ingredients have been used up.

Sukiyaki is eaten with chopsticks: each mouthful is dipped in raw beaten egg before being eaten; each guest breaks an egg into a small bowl for this purpose. Sukiyaki is served with plain boiled rice.

## Tajine of beef with cardoons

Pour 60 ml (2 fl oz, ¼ cup) olive oil into a tajine and brown 1 kg (2¼ lb) cubed beef, 2 sliced onions, 2 chopped garlic cloves, ½ teaspoon cumin, ½ teaspoon ginger, 2 pinches saffron strands, ½ teaspoon grey pepper (mixed ground black and white peppers) and 1 teaspoon salt. Cover with water and simmer gently for 1 hour. Peel 1.5 kg (3¼ lb) cardoons, cut into strips, placing them in water and lemon juice to prevent discoloration. Add to the tajine and cook for 30 minutes, then add the juice of 1 lemon and cook for 10 minutes.

## Tournedos (filet mignons) à la bordelaise

Poach some slices of bone marrow in salt water, drain and keep warm. Grill the steaks over very hot charcoal. Place a slice of bone marrow on each steak and sprinkle with chopped parsley. Serve with bordelaise sauce.

## Tournedos à la portugaise

The term *à la portugaise* describes various dishes (eggs, fish, kidneys, small pieces of meat and poultry) in which tomatoes predominate.

Prepare very small stuffed tomatoes, for example filling them with a cooked forcemeat bound with breadcrumbs, and browning them with some château potatoes. Fry the steaks in a mixture of butter and oil, drain and keep warm. Deglaze the cooking juices with white wine and thick tomato sauce and thicken with a little beurre manié. Arrange the tournedos on the serving dish with the tomatoes and the potatoes. Serve the sauce separately.

## Tournedos au lissé fermier

Cut off the base of the stalks of 800 g (1¾ lb) button mushrooms. Wash, sprinkle with lemon juice, slice thinly and brown gently in a frying pan with 50 g (2 oz, ¼ cup) butter. Set aside.

In another frying pan, melt 40 g (1½ oz, 3 tablespoons) butter with 2 tablespoons oil. As soon as it starts to boil, put in six 175 g (6 oz) tournedos and seal on both sides. Season with salt and pepper and cook for 5–8 minutes, according to the thickness of the meat. Drain, place in a hot serving dish, surround with the mushrooms and keep warm.

Stir into the second pan 250 g (9 oz) smooth cream cheese and reduce for 1 minute. Heat 100 ml (4 fl oz, 7 tablespoons) Calvados in a frying pan, reduce and add to the cheese. Add 1 tablespoon crème fraîche and reduce by half. Adjust the seasoning and pour over the tournedos. Sprinkle with chopped chives and serve immediately.

## Tournedos Brillat-Savarin

Wash 250 g (9 oz) fresh morels, cut off the stems and make small cuts in the caps. Simmer them in a little water for 15 minutes, then drain thoroughly. Brown a chopped shallot in butter in a frying pan. Add the morels to the pan with a little mustard and a few tablespoons of double (heavy) cream then finish cooking over a low heat. Taste and adjust the seasoning then set the morels aside and keep warm.

Gently fry the tournedos in butter. Remove and keep warm on a serving dish. Stir into the pan 175 ml (6 fl oz, ¾ cup) port and 5 tablespoons gravy and heat. Remove from the heat and thicken the sauce with butter. Adjust the seasoning. Arrange the morels around the tournedos and pour over the strained sauce.

## Tournedos chasseur

Sauté some tournedos steaks (filets mignons) in butter and then drain them. Use the butter in which they were cooked to prepare a chasseur sauce, and coat the steaks with it.

## Tournedos Helder

Prepare a béarnaise sauce and a very thick tomato fondue. Also prepare noisette potatoes. Brown the steaks in butter, drain them and keep warm. Deglaze the pan with white wine and consommé, and boil down to reduce to a thick syrupy consistency. Put a ribbon of béarnaise sauce on each steak with a little tomato fondue in the centre. Garnish with the noisette potatoes. Pour the reduced pan juices over the steaks.

## Tournedos marigny

Gently cook some artichoke hearts in butter. Prepare some buttered sweetcorn and some noisette potatoes. Sauté the steaks in butter and keep them warm. Deglaze the pan with a little white wine and reduce; complete the sauce by adding thickened veal stock. Surround the steaks with artichoke hearts stuffed with sweetcorn and noisette potatoes. Serve with the sauce.

## Tournedos masséna

Gently cook some artichoke hearts in butter and poach some slices of bone marrow (2–3 per steak) in a court-bouillon. Prepare a thin Périgueux sauce. Sauté the steaks in butter and arrange them on a dish with the artichoke hearts. Garnish each steak with 2–3 slices of bone marrow and pour a little of the Périgueux sauce over the artichokes. Serve the remaining sauce separately.

## Tournedos Rossini

Sauté 1 slice of foie gras and 2 slices of truffle per steak in butter. Fry some slices of bread trimmed to the shape of the steaks. Fry the fillet steaks (filets mignons) in butter and place each steak on a croûton. Arrange the foie gras and truffle slices on top. Deglaze the pan in which the steak was cooked with Madeira and pour the sauce over the meat.

## West Indian ragoût

Cut 800 g (1¾ lb) shoulder of beef or neck of mutton into small pieces. Chop 3 onions and slice 3 carrots, 6 potatoes and 3 ripe tomatoes. Brown the meat in oil or butter in a flameproof casserole, add the vegetables and mix together. Then pour in 175 ml (6 fl oz, ¾ cup) water and simmer over a low heat, stirring occasionally. When the ragoût has been cooking for 45 minutes, take out the vegetables, drain them and keep warm.

Add 1 small chopped chilli, salt and pepper, 3 tablespoons vinegar and 1 tablespoon peanut butter to the casserole.

Bone a herring and grill (broil) it gently, turning once, until cooked through. Mash the flesh and mix it into the sauce, adding a little hot water if necessary. Cover the casserole and simmer for a further 1 hour. Transfer the vegetables and the meat to a deep dish, pour the sauce over and serve very hot with rice *à la créole*.

# Veal

## Ballotine of veal

Prepare using boned shoulder or breast of veal, in the same way as for ballotine of lamb.

## Blanquette of veal

This is prepared with shoulder, breast and flank, either on or off the bone. Cut the meat into about 5 cm (2 in) cubes. Seal by frying the cubes in butter without browning. Cover with bouillon, season, quickly bring to the boil and skim. Add 2 onions (one stuck with a clove), 2 medium-sized carrots cut into quarters and a bouquet garni. Simmer gently for 1¼ hours. Drain the pieces of meat and place in a sauté pan with 200 g (7 oz) baby onions and 200 g (7 oz) mushrooms (preferably wild) that have been cooked *au blanc*, in a thin white sauce. Heat gently and, just before serving, bind the sauce with 50 g (2 oz, 1 cup) butter and 50 g (2 oz, ¼ cup) plain (all-purpose) flour for the roux, then 3 egg yolks, 150 ml (¼ pint, ⅔ cup) double (heavy) cream, the juice of ½ lemon, and a pinch of grated nutmeg. Place in a deep serving dish, sprinkle with parsley and garnish with heart-shaped croûtons fried in butter.

## Braised breast of veal à l'alsacienne

Open a breast of veal and remove the bones without piercing the flesh. Make a forcemeat by mixing 500 g (18 oz, 2¼ cups) fine sausagemeat, 250 g (9 oz, 2¼ cups) dry breadcrumbs (soaked in milk and well drained), a bunch of chopped parsley, 1 crushed garlic clove, 125 g (4½ oz, ⅔ cup) chopped onions and 125 g (4½ oz, 1½ cups) sliced mushrooms fried gently in butter, salt, pepper and a little grated nutmeg or mixed spice. Stir the mixture well until it is smooth. Stuff the veal with this forcemeat and sew up. Line the bottom and halfway up the sides of a lightly buttered casserole with pork rind from which most of the fat has been remove

Prepare some sauerkraut *à l'alsacienne*. Add the stuffed partly cooked breast of veal 1 hour before the sauerkraut has finished cooking. Remove the string from the veal and serve piping hot with the meat cut in slices.

## Braised stuffed breast of veal

Open a breast of veal and remove the bones without piercing the flesh. Season inside and out with salt and pepper. Prepare the forcemeat as follows: soak

400 g (14 oz, 3½ cups) dry breadcrumbs in milk and squeeze, then mix with 2 chopped garlic cloves, a chopped bunch of parsley, 250 g (9 oz) mushroom duxelles, 2 egg yolks, 100 g (4 oz, 1 cup) chopped onions and 2 chopped shallots fried gently in butter, salt, pepper and a little cayenne pepper. Stuff the breast and sew up the opening.

Line the bottom and halfway up the sides of a lightly buttered casserole with pork rind from which most of the fat has been removed. Finely dice a carrot, the white part of 1 leek, 3 celery sticks and 1 onion. Sweat them together in 25 g (1 oz, 2 tablespoons) butter in a covered pan for about 10 minutes and then spread them over the rind in the casserole. Brown the stuffed breast on both sides in 25 g (1 oz, 2 tablespoons) butter and place it in the casserole. Add half a boned calf's foot and 2 tablespoons tomato purée (paste) diluted with 200 ml (7 fl oz, ¾ cup) dry white wine and an equal quantity of stock.

Cover the casserole and bring to the boil. Then cook in a preheated oven at 200°C (400°F, gas 6) for 1¾ hours. Drain the meat. Skim the fat from the cooking stock, strain it, then reduce by one-third. Pour it over the meat. Spinach in butter or braised artichoke hearts may be served as a garnish.

## Braised tendrons of veal à la bourgeoise

A tendron is a piece of beef or veal cut from the extremities of the ribs, from the point at which the chops are generally cut, to the sternum.

Braise 4 tendrons of veal; when half-cooked, add 12 small glazed onions, 12 shaped and glazed carrots, and 50 g (2 oz, ¼ cup) diced streaky (slab) bacon (blanched and fried). Finish the cooking, drain the tendrons and arrange them on an ovenproof serving dish. Sprinkle them with a little of the cooking juices and glaze in a preheated oven at 230°C (450°F, gas 8). Serve piping hot, garnished with the vegetables and the diced bacon.

## Braised veal chops à la custine

(from Carême's recipe) Braise some veal chops; coat them first with 1 generous tablespoon duxelles, then with breadcrumbs, then dip in beaten egg and finish with another coating of breadcrumbs. Fry in well-browned butter and serve with a light tomato sauce.

## Braised veal grenadins

A grenadin is a small slice of fillet of veal, about 2 cm (¾ in) thick and 6–7 cm (2½–3 in) long, cut from the loin, the fillet or the chump end of the loin.

Trim four 100 g (4 oz) grenadins and interlard with bacon fat. Butter a casserole and line it with unsmoked bacon rinds or pork skin with the fat removed. Peel and finely slice a large carrot and a medium-sized onion and brown them in butter, with any trimmings of meat from the grenadins. Put the vegetables on top of the bacon rinds, arrange the grenadins on top, cover and cook gently for 15 minutes. Add 200 ml (7 fl oz, ¾ cup) white wine and boil down almost completely. Then add a little stock, bring to the boil, cover the casserole and cook in a preheated oven at 220°C (425°F, gas 7) for about 40 minutes, basting the meat several times. Arrange the grenadins on an ovenproof dish, coat with a little of the strained cooking liquid and glaze in the oven. Dilute the cooking juices in the casserole with consommé, strain and remove the fat. Pour the sauce over the grenadins and serve with spinach.

## Breaded veal chops à la milanaise

Flatten the chops and season with salt and pepper. Dip in beaten egg and coat in a mixture of half breadcrumbs and half grated Parmesan cheese. Cook gently in clarified butter in a sauté pan, then arrange on a serving dish garnished with cannelled lemon slices and sprinkled with noisette butter. Serve macaroni *à la milanaise* separately.

## Casserole of veal chops à la Parmentier

Season 2 fairly thick veal chops with salt and pepper and brown them on both sides in 25–40 g (1–1½ oz, 2–3 tablespoons) butter in a flameproof casserole. Place the casserole in a preheated oven at 200°C (400°F, gas 6) and cook for about 1 hour. Drain the meat and the potatoes and keep them hot in the serving dish. Deglaze the casserole with 4 tablespoons white wine and the same amount of stock (traditionally veal stock); reduce. Pour this sauce over the chops and sprinkle with chopped parsley.

## Casserole of veal chops à la paysanne

Prepare a vegetable fondue with 4 carrots, 2 onions, 2 leeks (white part), a turnip and 4 celery sticks, all diced and softened in 25 g (1 oz, 2 tablespoons) butter. Add 1 tablespoon chopped parsley and season with salt and pepper. Fry 2 firm diced potatoes in a mixture of 20 g (¾ oz, 1½ tablespoons) butter and 2 tablespoons oil. Brown 200 g (7 oz) diced smoked streaky (slab) bacon in butter. Mix all these ingredients together. Fry 4 veal chops in butter, place them with the other ingredients in a casserole, season with salt and pepper, reheat thoroughly and serve.

## Casseroled veal chops

Season some veal chops with salt and pepper and cook gently in 20 g (¾ oz, 1½ tablespoons) butter or 2 tablespoons oil per chop, at first uncovered, then covered, until they are browned. Deglaze the pan with 2 tablespoons each of veal stock and white wine per chop, reduce by half and pour over the chops.

Alternatively, half-cook the chops, remove them from the pan, put in the chosen accompanying vegetable (also half-cooked), replace the chops in the pan and complete the cooking. The accompanying vegetables could include: diced aubergine (eggplant) sautéed in butter or oil; glazed carrots, turnips or small (pearl) onions; mushrooms sautéed in butter; celeriac, cucumber or artichoke hearts cut into quarters and cooked in butter; or green beans.

Alternatively, the chops may be completely cooked and garnished with vegetables cooked separately, either by braising, sautéeing or steaming.

Other vegetables that may be used are chicory, Brussels sprouts, cauliflower, endive, spinach, hop shoots, beans, lettuce, chestnuts, sorrel, peas or tomatoes. Buttered noodles or rice can also be served.

## Casseroled veal chops à la bonne femme    -

Sauté the chops in butter or oil in a flameproof casserole until they are half cooked. Add the *bonne femme* garnish, consisting, for each chop, of 4 small pieces of bacon, 5 small onions and 6 small new potatoes, all well browned. Cover the casserole and complete the cooking in a preheated oven at 220°C (425°F, gas 7).

## Casseroled veal chops à la dreux

Choose thick veal chops and stud them with strips of pickled tongue and truffle, so that the studding shows. Fry gently in butter on both sides until completely cooked. Arrange on a serving plate and surround with a financière garnish; keep warm. Deglaze the pan with Madeira and veal stock and reduce; use this sauce to coat the chops.

## Cold best end of neck of veal

Trim a shortened best end of neck (rib) of veal and season it with salt and pepper. Cook in a preheated oven at 220°C (425°F, gas 7), allowing 30–40 minutes cooking time per 1 kg (2¼ lb). Allow to cool completely, then glaze with aspic jelly. Chill until ready to serve. Garnish with watercress and artichoke hearts stuffed with asparagus tips, glazed with aspic if desired.

# Cold veal à l'italienne

Cook some small white (pearl) onions in olive oil in a flameproof casserole and set aside. Using the same pan, brown a noix of veal; then add to the casserole 300 g (11 oz) canned tuna in oil, 100 g (4 oz) desalted anchovy fillets, 2 peeled and diced lemons, salt, pepper and a bouquet garni. Replace the onions in the casserole. Moisten with an equal mixture of white wine and veal stock, cook for 1½ hours, then allow to cool in the casserole. Remove the veal and purée the rest of the contents of the casserole in a blender. Prepare a mayonnaise, add the strained sauce to it and serve with the veal.

# Dagh kebab

Cut boneless veal into even-sized cubes. Also cut very firm small tomatoes into quarters and seed them. Cut some onions into quarters. Marinate these ingredients in a little oil flavoured with aromatic herbs. Thread the meat on to skewers alternating with the tomatoes and onion. Season, sprinkle with crumbled thyme and grill (broil) under a medium to high heat.

# Escalopes à l'anversoise

Cut some round slices of bread, 1 cm (½ in) thick, and fry them in butter. Lightly fry some very small new potatoes in butter. Prepare some hop shoots in cream: drop them into salted boiling water and remove them while they are still firm. Drain, braise in butter in a covered pan, then add 200 ml (7 fl oz, ¾ cup) double (heavy) cream per 350 g (12 oz) hop shoots. Flatten some round veal escalopes (scallops), sprinkle with salt and pepper, and sauté in a frying pan with clarified butter. Drain and arrange on the fried bread slices. Add to the frying pan a little white wine or beer and some very concentrated consommé. Reduce to a sauce and pour over the escalopes. Serve hot with the potatoes and the hop shoots.

## Escalopes à la mandelieu

Flatten some veal escalopes (scallops), sprinkle them with salt and pepper, and sauté in clarified butter until golden. Then flame in Cognac, using 1 tablespoon Cognac for 4 escalopes. Cover each with a thin slice of Gruyère or Comté cheese and sprinkle with a few dried breadcrumbs. Moisten with melted butter and brown in a preheated oven at 240°C (475°F, gas 9). Prepare 250 g (9 oz, 3 cups) mushrooms and sauté them in the butter in which the escalopes were cooked. Add 2 tablespoons tomato purée (paste) and 250 ml (8 fl oz, 1 cup) reduced consommé; cook for about 5 minutes. Adjust the seasoning and serve this sauce with the escalopes.

## Escalopes à la viennoise

Flatten 4 veal escalopes (scallops) well and sprinkle with salt on both sides. Put 4 tablespoons flour with a little salt on one plate, 175 g (6 oz, 2 cups) dried breadcrumbs on another and 2 beaten eggs on a third. Melt 100 g (4 oz, ½ cup) lard (shortening) in a large frying pan. Dip the escalopes into the flour so that they are completely covered with a very fine coating, then in the beaten egg and finally in the breadcrumbs, coating them evenly on both sides. Place in the lard when it is on the point of smoking and cook gently for 8 minutes on each side. Serve well browned.

## Escalopes casimir

Slowly cook in butter as many artichoke hearts as there are veal escalopes (scallops). Stew 4 tablespoons julienne of carrots in butter and, separately, a little julienne of truffles. Cut some escalopes from the fillet, flatten them, season with salt, pepper and paprika, then sauté in clarified butter; halfway through cooking, add 1 tablespoon chopped onion. Arrange the artichoke hearts in the serving dish, place an escalope on each one and garnish with the julienne of carrots. Add some cream to the pan juices from the escalopes and reduce. Coat the escalopes with this sauce and garnish with the truffles.

## Escalopes with aubergines and courgettes

Slice, without peeling, 2 medium-sized courgettes (zucchini) and a choice aubergine (eggplant). Sauté them in seasoned olive oil in a frying pan. Cut veal escalopes (scallops), flatten them, sprinkle with salt and pepper, and sauté in clarified butter. Arrange them in a serving dish, garnish with the aubergine and courgettes, and keep hot. Add to the pan juices 5 tablespoons white wine and 2–3 tablespoons meat juices; reduce by half. Add a small chopped garlic clove and reduce further. Pour the sauce over the escalopes and sprinkle with chopped parsley.

## Feuilleton of veal à l'ancienne

A feuilleton consists of thin slices of veal or pork beaten flat, spread with layers of forcemeat, and laid one on top of the other. The layers are then wrapped in strips of bacon or caul and tied with string. A feuilleton may also be made with a single piece of meat that is cut into parallel slices but not completely through, leaving them attached at one end.

For a feuilleton weighing 2 kg (4½ lb), cut 10 thin slices from a noix or sous-noix (loin) of veal and flatten them into rectangles with a mallet. Season with salt, pepper and a pinch of mixed spice. Prepare a fine pork forcemeat and add one-third of its weight of *à gratin* forcemeat and an equal amount of dry duxelles. Bind the forcemeat with egg. Cut a thin slice of pork fat slightly larger than the slices of veal and spread it with a layer of forcemeat. Top with a piece of veal and spread it with some forcemeat. Continue to build up the feuilleton in this way, ending with a layer of forcemeat. Coat the sides of the feuilleton with the remaining forcemeat and cover with a second strip of pork fat that is also larger than the slices of veal. Fold the edges of the bottom slice of pork fat upwards and the edges of the top piece of pork fat downwards so that the feuilleton is covered.

Tie the feuilleton into a neat shape. Put it in a buttered casserole lined with bacon rinds, sliced onions and carrots. Add a bouquet garni. Cover and simmer for 20 minutes. Moisten with 250 ml (8 fl oz, 1 cup) white wine and boil to reduce by half. Add 250 ml (8 fl oz, 1 cup) veal stock and boil to reduce to a concentrated glaze. Moisten with 500 ml (17 fl oz, 2 cups) good stock. Cover and cook in a preheated oven at 190°C (375°F, gas 5) for 1¾ hours, basting frequently. Drain the feuilleton, untie and arrange it on an ovenproof serving dish. Pour over a few tablespoons of braising stock and glaze in the oven, basting frequently.

## Feuilleton of veal l'Echelle

Season a boned fillet of veal and brown it quickly in very hot butter to seal. Leave it to cool. Cut it into slices lengthways, but do not cut completely through the joint. Prepare a forcemeat with a mixture of dry mushroom duxelles, chopped lean ham, diced truffles, and a vegetable mirepoix, bound with a beaten egg. Spread each of the slices with some of the forcemeat and reshape the fillet.

Cover the feuilleton with mirepoix and wrap it in a pig's caul (caul fat). Braise the feuilleton for 2–3 hours in butter, very slowly, then place it in an ovenproof dish. Garnish it with lettuce and potatoes that have been braised in butter. Pour over a little of the pan juices and return it to the oven to glaze. Make a sauce with the remainder of the juices in the pan by adding some Madeira and some veal stock.

This feuilleton may be served cold in aspic. In this case, a boned calf's foot is cooked in the stock.

## Filets mignons of veal with lemon

Pare the zest of ½ lemon and cut into fine strips. Put into a saucepan with 6 tablespoons cold water and bring to the boil, then drain and rinse in cold water. Put the lemon strips back into a saucepan with 1 tablespoon water and 1½ teaspoons sugar; cook until the water has evaporated, then set aside.

Heat 20 g (¾ oz, 1½ tablespoons) butter in a frying pan. When it starts to sizzle, add 4 veal filets mignons, each weighing 75 g (3 oz), sprinkled with salt and pepper on both sides. Brown them for 5 minutes on each side, then set aside and keep hot on a plate.

Pour off the butter from the pan and deglaze with 4 tablespoons dry white wine, reducing to 1 tablespoon liquid. Mix in 40 g (1½ oz, 3 tablespoons) butter, then 1 tablespoon chopped parsley.

Transfer the filets mignons to hot serving plates. Pour any meat juices into the sauce and coat the fillets with the sauce. Garnish each fillet with a peeled slice of lemon and a little of the shredded zest cooked in sugar.

## Fried grenadins in cream

A grenadin is a small slice of fillet of veal, about 2 cm (¾ in) thick and 6–7 cm (2½–3 in) long, cut from the loin, the fillet or the chump end of the loin.

Season four 100 g (4 oz) grenadins with salt and pepper and sauté them in oil until brown on both sides. Reduce the heat, cover and cook gently for about 15 minutes until tender. Drain the grenadins and keep them hot in a serving dish. Remove the cooking oil from the pan and add 200 ml (7 fl oz, ¾ cup) white wine or cider. Scrape the pan with a spatula, add a small sprig of tarragon and boil down to reduce the liquid by half. Remove the tarragon, add 200 ml (7 fl oz, ¾ cup) single (light) cream, and boil down, stirring continuously. Taste and adjust the seasoning then pour the sauce over the grenadins and serve.

## Grilled veal chops

Flatten the chops and season with salt and pepper; coat with tarragon-flavoured oil and leave to marinate for 30 minutes. Grill (broil) gently until the meat is cooked through (about 15 minutes), turning over once. Serve the chops with a green salad, a mixed salad or green beans, steamed and served with green butter.

## Grilled veal chops en portefeuille

Soak a pig's caul (caul fat) in cold water for 2 hours. Take thick veal chops from the loin, cut open the lean meat and season the pocket with salt and pepper; fill with mushroom duxelles or with a salpicon of pressed tongue and mushrooms cooked slowly in butter, bound with a thick béchamel sauce. Wrap each chop in a piece of caul and grill (broil) gently.

## Knuckle of veal à la provençale

Cut about 800 g (1¾ lb) veal knuckle (shank) into slices 4 cm (1½ in) thick and season with salt and pepper. Brown in a sauté pan in 3 tablespoons very hot olive oil. Chop150 g (5 oz) onions finely and fry until golden in the sauté pan; add 575 g (1¼ lb) peeled, seeded and coarsely chopped tomatoes – or 500 g (18 oz) tomatoes and 1 tablespoon tomato purée (paste) – together with 150 ml (¼ pint, ⅔ cup) dry white wine and a bouquet garni. Stir well, then add 100 ml (4 fl oz, 7 tablespoons) stock or consommé and 2 crushed garlic cloves. Cover the pan and cook gently for about 1¼ hours, then remove the lid and reduce the liquid for 10 minutes. Adjust the seasoning.

## Knuckle of veal braised in cider

Melt 25 g (1 oz, 2 tablespoons) butter in a large saucepan and in it lightly brown a knuckle of veal weighing about 1.7 kg (3¾ lb), having cut 3 cm

(1¼ in) off the end. Peel and chop 6 shallots, add three-quarters of them to the pan, leave to colour and flame with Calvados. Then pour in ½ bottle of dry sparkling cider, add salt and pepper, cover and cook for 2½ hours over a gentle heat. Turn the knuckle over once or twice during cooking.

Meanwhile, peel about 30 small white (pearl) onions and cook them gently in a covered saucepan with 50 g (2 oz, ¼ cup) butter until they are soft. Add salt and pepper. Peel and core 3 dessert (eating) apples and cut them into slices, about 3 mm (⅛ in) thick. Brown lightly in a frying pan with 25 g (1 oz, 2 tablespoons) butter. Keep them hot.

When the knuckle is nearly ready, sauté 200 g (7 oz) fresh chanterelle mushrooms in butter, along with the remaining chopped shallots; cover. The knuckle is cooked when the flesh comes away from the bone by itself. Remove the pieces of skin and the gelatine that surround the meat, cut the meat into pieces and arrange in a warmed serving dish.

Lightly brown the apple slices under the grill (broiler). Mix 1 egg yolk with 1 tablespoon double (heavy) cream, add it to the veal cooking liquor, then strain everything. Beat this sauce with a whisk and adjust the seasoning. Arrange the onions and mushrooms around the knuckle. Coat the knuckle with the sauce, putting a little on the garnish too. Sprinkle with chopped parsley and serve the apple slices separately.

## Medallions of veal Alexandre

Sauté the medallions of veal in butter in a sauté pan. Arrange them on a hot dish, place a sliver of truffle on each if wished, and keep warm. Cook some fresh artichoke hearts in white stock, brown them in butter, garnish with morels in cream, and arrange them in a circle around the medallions. Deglaze the sauté pan with 1 tablespoon brandy and 1 tablespoon Marsala, boil to reduce and pour the sauce over the medallions.

## Minute sauté of veal

Cut 800 g (1¾ lb) shoulder of veal into small pieces and sauté in butter or oil over a brisk heat for 15 minutes. Season with salt and pepper. When serving, keep the meat hot in a serving dish and deglaze the pan with 175 ml (6 fl oz, ¾ cup) white wine. Reduce, add the juice of ½ lemon and whisk in 25 g (1 oz, 2 tablespoons) butter. Pour the sauce over the meat and sprinkle with chopped parsley.

## Mousseline forcemeat

Pound 1 kg (2¼ lb) boned veal, poultry or game in a mortar (or reduce to a purée in a food processor). Then press through a fine sieve. Whisk 4 egg whites lightly with a fork and add them to the meat purée a little at a time. Season with 4 teaspoons salt and a generous pinch of ground white pepper. Press through the sieve a second time, place in a terrine, and then chill for 2 hours. Remove the terrine from the refrigerator and place in a bowl of crushed ice. Then work in 1.5 litres (2¾ pints, 6½ cups) double (heavy) cream using a wooden spoon. (It is essential to keep the cream and the pâté as cold as possible to prevent them from curdling.) This forcemeat is used for fine quenelles, mousses and mousselines.

## Noix of veal Brillat-Savarin

Bone a whole noix of veal. Flatten it, then sew the cut parts together to reform the noix. Chop 3 shallots. Cook 100 g (4 oz) black morels in cream. Spread a 1 cm (½ in) layer of *à gratin* forcemeat mixed with the shallots over the veal. Sprinkle on some of the cooked morels, then place a piece of duck foie gras weighing about 200 g (7 oz) in the centre. Roll up the noix and tie it securely. Bard with strips of fat pork, brown the veal in butter, then place in a flameproof casserole on a bed of mirepoix. Moisten with equal quantities of dry white wine and beef stock. Add some peeled, seeded, roughly chopped tomatoes and a bouquet garni. Cover the pan and cook slowly for 2 hours.

Take out the meat, then reduce and strain the cooking liquid. Serve the veal sliced, with a little of the sauce poured over, accompanied by leaf spinach and the remaining morels. Serve the rest of the sauce separately.

## Osso bucco à la milanaise

An Italian dish, originally from Milan, whose name means literally 'bone with a hole'. It consists of a stew of pieces of veal shin braised in white wine with onion and tomato. It is generally served with pasta or rice. The variation called *alla gremolata* is prepared with the addition of a mixture of chopped garlic, orange and lemon peel, and grated nutmeg.

Season 8 veal shins, weighing about 1.6 kg (3½ lb), with salt and pepper, sprinkle with flour, then brown them in olive oil in a large flameproof casserole. Chop enough onions to give 5 level tablespoons; add these to the casserole and cook until golden. Moisten with 200 ml (7 fl oz, ¾ cup) white wine, reduce this, then add 4 large tomatoes, skinned, seeded and coarsely chopped. Pour in 250 ml (8 fl oz, 1 cup) stock. Finally add 1 large crushed garlic clove and a bouquet garni. Cover the casserole and cook in a preheated oven at 200°C (400°F, gas 6) for 1½ hours. Arrange the pieces of knuckle in a deep dish and cover them with the reduced cooking liquid. Squeeze on a little lemon juice and sprinkle with chopped parsley.

## Paupiettes of veal braised à brun

Coat some flattened veal escalopes (scallops) with a pork forcemeat mixed with dry mushroom duxelles and chopped parsley and bound with egg. Roll them up, bard them with thin rashers (slices) of fat bacon and tie with string. Arrange them in a buttered flameproof casserole lined with pieces of pork skin or bacon rinds and sliced onions and carrots browned in butter. Place a bouquet garni in the middle and season with salt and pepper. Cover and cook over a gentle heat for 10 minutes.

Add some dry white wine or (depending on the accompaniments) Madeira – 200 ml (7 fl oz, ¾ cup) per 10 paupiettes. Reduce almost completely, then pour in some thickened veal stock to cover the paupiettes by two-thirds. Cover and braise in a preheated oven at 200°C (400°F, gas 6), basting frequently, for 45–60 minutes. Drain the paupiettes and remove the barding, then glaze in the oven. Arrange in a serving dish and coat with the braising liquor, reduced and strained. Serve with braised buttered vegetables.

## Roast noix of veal

The fleshy upper part of the fillet end of a leg of veal, cut lengthways. The meat is lean and tender, but tends to be rather dry. It can be sliced into escalopes (scallops) or grenadins, or it can be roasted. Various garnishes may be used to accompany it; for example, bouquetière, bourgeoise, Clamart, milanaise, or piémontaise. It can also be served with mushrooms, braised chicory (endive), buttered spinach, mixed vegetables or a risotto. The noix can also be braised, which enhances its tenderness.

The lean plump 'eye' of a veal cutlet (chop) is also known as the noix.

Heat some butter in a flameproof casserole. Lard a noix of veal with thin pieces of bacon and brown it on all sides in the butter. Sprinkle with salt and pepper, then cook in a preheated oven at 200°C (400°F, gas 6), allowing 16 minutes per 450 g (1 lb).

## Sausage rolls

Mince (grind) together 2 peeled shallots, 100 g (4 oz) mushrooms, 200 g (7 oz) veal, 200 g (7 oz) smoked pork and a bunch of parsley (a food processor may be used). Add 1 tablespoon cream and season with salt and pepper. Mix together well. Dust the work surface with flour and roll out 500 g (1 lb 2 oz) puff pastry to a thickness of about 3 mm (⅛ in); cut into 6 rectangles of equal size. Divide the filling into 6 portions and roll into sausage shapes the same length as the width of the pastry rectangles. Put a 'sausage' at one end of each rectangle and roll it up. Score the top with the point of a knife and glaze with beaten egg. Bake in a preheated oven at 220°C (425°F, gas 7) for about 30 minutes.

The filling can also be made with fine sausagemeat mixed with chopped onion, parsley, salt and pepper.

## Sauté of veal clamart

Cut 1 kg (2¼ lb) shoulder of veal into uniform pieces. Season with salt and pepper and brown in a heavy-based saucepan with 25 g (1 oz, 2 tablespoons) butter or 3 tablespoons oil. Drain the meat, pour the fat out of the pan, deglaze the pan with 175 ml (6 fl oz, ¾ cup) white wine, then replace the meat and add 300 ml (½ pint, 1¼ cups) stock. Bring to the boil over a brisk heat, then reduce, cover and leave to cook for about 1 hour. Add 1 kg (2¼ lb, 7 cups) shelled peas and 12 baby (pearl) onions. Bring back to the boil and continue cooking for another 30 minutes. Adjust the seasoning, pour into a hot dish and sprinkle with chopped parsley.

## Sauté of veal with red wine

Cut 1 kg (2¼ lb) shoulder of veal into 50 g (2 oz) pieces and brown in 25 g (1 oz, 2 tablespoons) butter. Add 1 large sliced onion and season with salt and pepper. Then add 300 ml (½ pint, 1¼ cups) red wine, 150 ml (¼ pint, ⅔ cup) stock, 1 bouquet garni and 1 crushed garlic clove. Cover and leave to cook gently for 1¼–1½ hours. In the meantime, glaze 20 baby (pearl) onions until brown and fry 150 g (5 oz, 1¾ cups) sliced mushrooms in butter. Drain the pieces of meat, strain the sauce and thicken it with 1 tablespoon beurre manié. Return the meat to the sauté pan and add the onions, mushrooms and sauce. Reheat gently for 10–15 minutes.

## Sautéed veal à la lyonnaise

Take 4 loin chops or 4 escalopes (scallops) of veal and sauté in butter. When they are almost done, add 4 tablespoons sliced onions gently cooked in butter. Complete the cooking. Keep the meat warm on a serving dish. Add to the sauté pan 60 ml (2 fl oz, ¼ cup) wine vinegar, 1 tablespoon chopped parsley and 2 tablespoons meat stock. Reduce and pour over the meat.

## Sautéed veal chops à la crème

Brown some veal chops, seasoned with salt and pepper, in a frying pan using 1 tablespoon oil per chop; cover and finish cooking over a low heat (about 15 minutes). Strain off the oil from the pan and add 1 chopped shallot per chop; cook, uncovered, until browned. Remove the chops and shallots and keep hot. Add to the pan 2–3 tablespoons cider or white wine and 1 tablespoon double (heavy) cream per chop; boil over a brisk heat until the sauce is reduced and smooth. Adjust the seasoning and coat the chops with the sauce.

## Sautéed veal chops à la duxelles

Prepare 4 tablespoons mushroom duxelles. Sauté 4 veal chops in butter. When the chops are almost cooked, add the duxelles to the pan and complete the cooking over a low heat. Drain the chops and arrange on a serving dish; keep hot. Add 100 ml (4 fl oz, 7 tablespoons) double (heavy) cream and ½ glass of white wine or 2 tablespoons Madeira to the duxelles in the pan and reduce until the mixture thickens. Coat the chops with this sauce.

## Sautéed veal chops en portefeuille

Soak a pig's caul (caul fat) in cold water for 2 hours. Take thick veal chops from the loin, cut open the lean meat and season the pocket with salt and pepper; fill with mushroom duxelles or with a salpicon of pressed tongue and mushrooms cooked slowly in butter, bound with a thick béchamel sauce. Wrap each chop in a piece of caul, then cook in butter in a frying pan. Arrange the chops on a round dish with small braised carrots. Keep warm. Deglaze the cooking juices with white wine and stock, bind with beurre manié and pour over the chops.

## Sautéed veal chops à la provençale

First prepare a garlic-flavoured tomato sauce and then some small round tomatoes stuffed with mushroom duxelles and browned in the oven. Quickly brown some veal chops in olive oil in a frying pan. Season with salt and pepper, cover, reduce the heat and leave to complete cooking for about 15 minutes. Drain the chops and arrange them in the serving dish surrounded by the stuffed tomatoes. Keep hot in the oven with the door ajar.

Pour the oil out of the frying pan, add the tomato sauce and 3–4 tablespoons white wine, stir well and reduce by half over a brisk heat. Pour the sauce over the chops, sprinkle with chopped parsley or basil and serve.

## Sautéed veal Marengo

Cut 1 kg (2¼ lb) shoulder of veal into large even-sized cubes and sauté in 25 g (1 oz, 2 tablespoons) butter and 2 tablespoons oil in a flameproof casserole until lightly browned. Add 2 chopped onions and brown them, sprinkle with 1 tablespoon flour and cook until golden brown. Add 1 glass of white wine, scraping the bottom of the casserole to incorporate all the residue, then 500 g (18 oz) seeded chopped tomatoes, a bouquet garni, a crushed garlic clove, and salt and pepper. Add enough hot water just to cover the ingredients, bring to the boil, cover and simmer for 1 hour.

Meanwhile, glaze 24 small (pearl) onions in 1 tablespoon granulated sugar, 25 g (1 oz, 2 tablespoons) butter, salt and pepper. Keep hot. Sauté 150 g (5 oz, 1½ cups) finely sliced mushrooms in 20 g (¾ oz, 3 tablespoons) butter. Cut 2 slices of bread into croûtons and fry in 3 tablespoons oil until golden brown. Five minutes before the meat is cooked, add the mushrooms and complete the cooking.

Pour the sautéed veal into a deep warmed dish, sprinkle with chopped parsley and garnish with the glazed onions and the croûtons.

## Stuffed shoulder of veal

Bone a shoulder of veal weighing about 1.5 kg (3¼ lb), flatten it out carefully, then season it with salt and pepper. Mix 450 g (1 lb) fine sausagemeat with 200 g (7 oz) mushrooms, 1 garlic clove and some chopped herbs and season with salt and pepper. Cover the meat with this stuffing, roll it up and tie with string. Crush the bones and brown them in butter with the trimmings. Trim the fat off some pork rind and line a braising pan with the rind. Peel and finely slice 2 carrots and 1 onion, cook in butter for 10 minutes, then add to the braising pan. Put the shoulder in the braising pan and season with salt and pepper. Add 150 ml (¼ pint, ⅔ cup) white wine and reduce. Add 250 ml (8 fl oz, 1 cup) unthickened gravy, 100 ml (4 fl oz, 7 tablespoons) tomato purée, 1 bouquet garni and the bones and trimmings. Cover and cook in a preheated oven at 220°C (425°F, gas 7) for about 1–1½ hours, depending on the size of the joint. The juices should run clear when the meat is pricked. Remove and drain the meat and untie.

Reduce the cooking juices, strain and pour over the joint. Glaze the joint in a very hot oven, then arrange on a serving dish and pour more juice over it.

Serve the rest of the cooking juices in a sauceboat. Aubergines (eggplants) fried in oil or glazed carrots, turnips or onions make an ideal garnish.

## Stuffed shoulder of veal à l'anglaise

Bone a shoulder of veal weighing about 1.5 kg (3¼ lb). Prepare a stuffing consisting of one-third chopped calf's or ox kidney, one-third chopped breast of veal or veal fat and one-third breadcrumbs soaked in milk, then squeezed. Season well and bind using 1 egg per 450 g (1 lb) stuffing. Season the veal with salt and pepper and cover it evenly with the stuffing; roll it up and tie with string. Braise or roast, as preferred. Serve with the reduced cooking juices and garnish with slices of boiled bacon, cabbage and boiled potatoes.

## Tendrons of veal chasseur

Tendron is a piece of beef or veal cut from the extremities of the ribs, from the point at which the chops are generally cut, to the sternum. Tendrons of veal, which contain a few small cartilages, are streaked with fat and very smooth. They are used for blanquette, braised or sautéed veal, or veal Marengo.

Cook 4 tendrons in a frying pan with 25 g (1 oz, 2 tablespoons) butter for10 minutes on each side. Drain them and keep them hot on a serving dish. Add 200 g (7 oz, 2⅓ cups) finely sliced mushrooms to the pan, brown them, and then add 3 tablespoons each of stock, white wine and tomato sauce. Add 2 chopped shallots, then boil down by at least half. Pour the mushrooms and sauce over the tendrons, sprinkle with chopped herbs and serve hot.

## Tendrons of veal with spinach or sorrel

Braise some tendrons of veal and some spinach (or sorrel) in butter in separate pans. Drain the tendrons, arrange them on a hot dish and sprinkle with the cooking juices. Garnish with the drained and buttered vegetables.

## Terrine de Body

Cut 575 g (1¼ lb) veal escalopes and 400 g (14 oz) smoked belly of pork into fine strips. Finely chop 16 shallots and a bunch of parsley and season with 2 teaspoons ground black pepper. Arrange the ingredients in a terrine as follows: first a layer of pork belly, then a layer of veal, then a layer of shallots and parsley, continuing this way until the ingredients are used up, finishing with a layer of pork. Moisten each layer with a little dry white wine and press down hard.

Cover the terrine and place it in a bain marie. Bring to the boil on the hob (stove top), then cook in a preheated oven at 180°C (350°F, gas 4) for 1 hour. Place a small board with a weight on the terrine before allowing it to cool. Chill for at least 24 hours before serving.

## Terrine of veal with spring vegetables

Poach 500 g (18 oz) lean, boneless loin, fillet or leg of veal in a well-seasoned court-bouillon until very tender. Allow to cool in the stock. Cut half of the meat into neat, even, rather thick strips or cubes. Prepare a jelly with the clarified cooking stock.

Shell 40 g (1½ oz) petits pois and cook in salted boiling water until tender. Drain and refresh in cold water; drain well. Thinly slice 250 g (9 oz) baby carrots and cook in boiling salted water until just tender. Drain, refresh and drain well. Blanch and drain 4 sliced courgettes (zucchini).

Line the bottom of a terrine or mould with plenty of dill. Add layers of the vegetables, alternating them with the meat until the terrine or mould is almost full, seasoning each layer with pepper and sprinkling it with a few dill leaves. Press to settle the contents. Pour in the cooled, but not set, jelly. Allow to set in the refrigerator for a few hours, or preferably overnight, then unmould and serve chilled.

## Tourte of veal with Parmesan cheese

Make 400 g (14 oz) shortcrust pastry (basic pie dough). Soak a pig's caul (fat) in cold water. Cut into strips 250 g (9 oz) noix of veal, a large slice of smoked ham and 200 g (7 oz) bacon fat; marinate in a bowl with 100 ml (4 fl oz, 7 tablespoons) white wine, 2 tablespoons Cognac, thyme, salt and pepper.

Meanwhile, chop 200 g (7 oz) breast of veal, a large slice of smoked ham, 200 g (7 oz) bacon fat, 300 g (11 oz) calf's liver and 3–4 shallots. Add 100 g (4 oz, 1 cup) grated Parmesan cheese and mix with 2 beaten eggs, salt and pepper.

Roll out two-thirds of the pastry and line a buttered *tourtière* or deep flan dish with it. Lay the caul inside, letting the edges overhang. Spread half of the forcemeat on top; add the strips of meat, then the remaining forcemeat. Fold over the edges of the caul. Roll out the remaining pastry and place it on top of the dish, sealing the edges by moistening and pinching them. Make a small hole in the middle and slide a funnel made of foil inside to let the steam escape. Brush the top of the tourte with beaten egg and bake in a preheated oven at 220°C (425°F, gas 7) for 1½ hours. Cover loosely with foil during cooking once the pastry is brown to prevent it from becoming too dark.

## Veal and ham pâté

Remove the sinews from 300 g (11 oz) noix of veal and cut into matchsticks about 10 cm (4 in) long. Prepare 300 g (11 oz) lean pork and 200 g (7 oz) ham in the same way. Put all these meats into a terrine, sprinkle with 1 tablespoon spiced salt, add 100 ml (4 fl oz, 7 tablespoons) Madeira and leave to marinate for 6–12 hours (some herbs and chopped shallots can also be added to the marinade).

Line a round or oval pâté mould with pastry for pâté en croûte made with butter. Coat the bottom and sides with very thin strips of fatty bacon (200 g,

7 oz) and cover this with a layer of about 250 g (9 oz, 1 cup) fine forcemeat. Fill up with layers of the veal, pork and ham matchsticks, separating them with thin layers of forcemeat. If desired, add 1 or 2 truffles cut into quarters or a few pistachio nuts. Finish with a layer of 200 g (7 oz, ¾ cup) forcemeat. Place a sheet of pastry over the top and pinch all round to seal.

Glaze the top with egg and garnish with shapes cut out from leftover pastry (rolled out thinly). Make a hole in the centre and insert a small smooth metal piping nozzle. Glaze the top again.

Bake the pâté in a preheated oven at 190°C (375°F, gas 5) for about 1¼ hours. Pour a few tablespoons of melted butter, lard (shortening) or aspic in through the 'chimney'. Turn the pâté out of the mould when it has cooled and set completely.

## Veal chop cussy en portefeuille

Cut a pocket in a thick veal chop taken from the middle of the loin. Stuff with a salpicon of mushrooms, carrot and lean ham bound with a thick, seasoned béchamel sauce. Secure with a wooden cocktail stick (toothpick). Coat the chop with beaten egg and breadcrumbs and cook in clarified butter until golden on both sides. Prepare a risotto and add cream, grated cheese and a salpicon of truffles. Arrange the chop on a round dish garnished with the truffle risotto. Pour a ring of brown veal gravy, flavoured with tomato, around the dish; sprinkle the chop with noisette butter.

## Veal chop Foyot

Make a thick cheese paste with dried breadcrumbs, 25 g (1 oz, ¼ cup) grated Gruyère cheese, and 20 g (¾ oz, 1½ tablespoons) butter. Season and flour a large veal chop, weighing about 250 g (9 oz) and roast it in a preheated oven at 150°C (300°F, gas 2) with 20 g (¾ oz, 1½ tablespoons) butter for 20–30 minutes. When half-cooked, turn it over and cover with the cheese paste. Stuff a small tomato with a mixture of breadcrumbs, parsley and butter and place it in the roasting pan. Finish cooking the chop and baste regularly with the butter. Drain the meat and the tomato and arrange them on a serving dish. Add a peeled and chopped shallot to the cooking juices and deglaze the pan with 4 tablespoons dry white wine and an equal quantity of veal stock. Boil and reduce by half. Add 10 g (1½ teaspoons, ¼ oz) butter and pour the sauce over the veal.

## Veal chop Pojarski

Bone a veal chop and keep the bone. Weigh the flesh and chop finely. Add an equal weight of stale breadcrumbs soaked in milk and strained, a quarter of its weight of butter and a little chopped parsley. Season with salt and pepper and add a pinch of grated nutmeg. Stir the mixture thoroughly until smooth. Scrape the chop bone thoroughly and blanch in boiling water for 5 minutes. Cool and wipe dry. Press the meat mixture along the bone and reshape the chop. Leave to dry for 30 minutes, then cover with flour and cook in clarified butter for about 15 minutes until brown on both sides and cooked through. Arrange the chop on a serving dish, garnish with a canelled slice of lemon, sprinkle with a little noisette butter and serve with a selection of vegetables cooked in butter.

## Veal chops à la piémontaise

Season 4 veal chops with salt and pepper; dip them in flour, beaten egg and fresh breadcrumbs mixed with grated Parmesan cheese – 40 g (1½ oz, ⅓ cup) Parmesan to 50 g (2 oz, 1 cup) breadcrumbs. Cook gently in 40 g (1½ oz, 3 tablespoons) clarified butter. Serve with risotto *à la piémontaise*, prepared with 200 g (7 oz, 1 cup) rice, and a well-reduced tomato sauce.

## Veal chops en papillotes

Sauté some veal chops in butter until they are cooked through and golden. Cut out some squares of greaseproof (wax) paper, big enough to wrap up each chop, and oil them. Place on half of each square of paper 1 slice of ham cut to the dimensions of the chop, 1 veal chop, 1 tablespoon mushroom duxelles and another slice of ham the same size as the first. Fold over the paper and press the edges together. Place the papillotes in a preheated oven at 240°C (475°F, gas 9) until the paper turns golden.

## Veal chops with fines herbes

Sauté some veal chops in butter in a frying pan (skillet), drain them and arrange on a hot serving dish. Add some chopped shallots and white wine to the butter and cook for a few minutes to reduce. Then add some chopped parsley, chervil and tarragon, adjust the seasoning, stir and pour the sauce over the chops. Formerly, demi-glace sauce was added to the white wine to make a richer, smoother and creamier sauce.

## Veal émincés à blanc

Lightly butter an ovenproof dish. Cut some poached or boiled veal into thin slices and arrange them in the dish. Prepare some Madeira sauce. Trim and slice some mushrooms and heat them in butter. Place the mushrooms on the meat and cover generously with hot Madeira sauce; heat through gently in the oven. Alternatively, the meat can be coated with tomato, Breton, royal or suprême sauce.

## Veal fricandeau with sorrel

Lard a slice of noix of veal, about 3–4 cm (1¼–1½ in) thick, with some thin strips of fat bacon that have been marinated for 30 minutes in a mixture of oil, chopped parsley, salt and pepper. Then brush the veal with melted butter or with oil containing crushed veal bones. Sauté 2 diced carrots and 2 sliced onions in butter until golden brown and put them in a braising pan. Place the veal on top of the vegetables with the crushed bones, a bouquet garni and half a calf's foot that has been boned and blanched. Add enough white or red wine to half-cover the meat; season with salt and pepper. Cover the pan and bring to the boil. Place the pan in a preheated oven at 220°C (425°F, gas 7) and cook, uncovered, for 1 hour. Remove the pan and replace on the top of the cooker.

Mix 1 tablespoon tomato purée (paste) with 500 ml (17 fl oz, 2 cups) stock and add it to the pan so that the veal is now covered. Bring back to the boil, return to the oven and cook for a further 1½ hours. Drain the meat and arrange it on an ovenproof dish. Strain the liquid in the pan, pour some of it over the meat and glaze it in the oven. Serve the fricandeau with a sorrel fondue and the remainder of the sauce in a sauceboat (gravy boat).

## Veal grenadins with salsify

Grenadin is the term used for a small slice of veal fillet, about 2 cm (¾ in) thick and 6–7 cm (2½–3 in) long, cut from the loin, the fillet or the chump end of the loin.

Interlard 8–12 grenadins with strips of bacon fat. Cover the base of a flameproof casserole with pork or bacon rind. Finely slice 1 onion and 1 carrot, then brown them together in butter and place in the casserole. Add the veal grenadins, cover the casserole and cook gently for 15 minutes. Pour in 200 ml (7 fl oz, ¾ cup) dry white wine and bring to the boil, then continue cooking until the wine has almost dried up. Pour in enough stock to come a short way up the meat, add seasoning to taste, bring to the boil and cover. Cook in a preheated oven at 220°C (425°F, gas 7) for about 40 minutes, basting the grenadins occasionally.

Meanwhile, cook 675 g (1½ lb) salsify in boiling water for 10 minutes. Allow to cool, then drain, peel and trim. Cut the salsify into fine strips and toss in lemon juice, seasoning and a little melted butter. Cover and set aside.

When the grenadins are cooked, transfer them to a serving dish. Spoon a little of the cooking juices over the meat. Then arrange the strips of buttered salsify around the edge and keep the dish warm in the oven until the meat and salsify are lightly glazed. Sprinkle with chives and serve.

## Veal hash à l'italienne

Prepare an allemande sauce and allow to cool. Mix it with finely diced leftover roast or sautéed veal. Pour the mixture into a sauté pan and heat gently but thoroughly. The hash may be served in a flaky pastry case or with fresh pasta.

## Veal hash à la Mornay

Finely dice leftover roast or sautéed veal. Prepare a well-seasoned béchamel sauce and add a little crème fraîche. Divide the sauce into 2 equal portions. Add some chopped *fines herbes* to one portion and some grated Gruyère cheese to the other. Mix the sauce containing the herbs with the diced veal and pour into a buttered gratin dish. Smooth the surface and cover with the cheese sauce. Sprinkle with more grated Gruyère, pour melted butter over the top, and brown in a preheated oven at 240°C (475°F, gas 9). Sliced mushrooms, braised in butter with a little lemon juice, can be added.

## Veal Orloff

Thinly slice 500 g (18 oz) onions, 1 large carrot and 800 g (1¾ lb) button mushrooms. Melt 50 g (2 oz, ¼ cup) butter in a casserole and brown 150 g (5 oz) bacon rinds, then a boned loin of veal weighing about 1.8 kg (4 lb). Add the carrot, 1 tablespoon sliced onions, a bouquet garni, salt and pepper.

Add enough water to cover the meat, cover and cook gently for 1¼ hours.

Meanwhile, melt 25 g (1 oz, 2 tablespoons) butter in a sauté pan and quickly brown the sliced mushrooms. Chop them, replace in the pan with salt, pepper, 1 tablespoon flour and a pinch of grated nutmeg, and cook for about 10 minutes. Put the rest of the sliced onions through a food processor or vegetable mill and cook in 40 g (1½ oz, 3 tablespoons) butter until golden. Then moisten them with water, cover the pan and cook for 20–25 minutes until puréed. Add the mushrooms and 200 ml (7 fl oz, ¾ cup) double (heavy) cream, then boil the cream down.

Cut the veal into thin even slices, cutting transversely from one long side to the other; spread each slice with a little of the onion and mushroom purée. Put the slices together again and reshape the loin. Tie it, place in a gratin dish and spread it with the rest of the purée. Mask it with Maintenon sauce, sprinkle with grated Parmesan cheese, dot with butter and brown in a hot oven for 10 minutes. Skim the fat from the liquid, strain it and serve separately.

## Veal piccata with aubergines and tomatoes

Cut a fillet of veal weighing about 1.4 kg (3 lb) into 12 round slices (*piccatas*). Cut an aubergine (eggplant) into round slices and dust them with flour. Fry the piccatas in a frying pan in 50 g (2 oz, ¼ cup) clarified butter and drain them. Fry the aubergine slices in the same butter. Sauté 2 sliced white onions gently in a covered pan. Cut a sweet red (bell) pepper into strips and fry them in butter for about 15 minutes. Crush 450 g (1 lb) ripe tomatoes.

Arrange the piccatas on an ovenproof serving dish, alternating them with small strips of cooked ham and the aubergine slices. Garnish with the onions, the strips of red pepper and the tomatoes. Cook in a preheated oven at 200–220°C (400–425°F, gas 6–7) for 5 minutes. Sprinkle with noisette butter and garnish with parsley just before serving.

## Veal quenelles

Prepare a forcemeat for the quenelles: godiveau with cream. With floured hands, roll the mixture into balls. Press these into large olive shapes, poach them and drain thoroughly and leave to cool. The quenelles can be served in many ways or used in recipes. For example, coat them in a béchamel sauce enriched with crème fraîche. Finish in the oven, with a topping of grated cheese and butter.

For *quenelles à la florentine*, arrange the quenelles on a bed of spinach in cream before coating with the sauce.

Chicken meat can be used to make quenelles in the same way.

## Veal sauté à la portugaise

Cut 1 kg (2¼ lb) shoulder of veal into 50 g (2 oz) pieces. Season them with salt and pepper and brown them in 3–4 tablespoons olive oil. Add 1 very large chopped onion and 1 crushed garlic clove. Deglaze the frying pan with 175 ml (6 fl oz, ¾ cup) white wine, then add 300 ml (½ pint, 1¼ cups) veal or chicken stock and 200 ml (7 fl oz, ¾ cup) tomato sauce. Add 1 bouquet garni and leave to simmer for about 1¼ hours. Drain the meat. Strain the sauce and reduce it by half. Return the meat to the sauté pan and add 8 tomatoes, which have been peeled, seeded and fried in oil, 1 tablespoon chopped parsley and the reduced sauce. Cover and simmer for 20 minutes. Arrange in a hot dish.

## Veal soup with quenelles

Prepare small veal quenelles. Make a roux with 40 g (1½ oz, 3 tablespoons) butter and 40 g (1½ oz, 6 tablespoons) plain (all-purpose) flour. Pour on to it 1.5 litres (2¾ pints, 6½ cups) well-seasoned veal stock, whisk well and reheat. Pour the soup into a tureen, add the quenelles, garnish with chopped herbs and serve piping hot.

# Veal steamed with vegetables

Cut a shoulder of veal into 24 pieces and place in a heavy-based casserole, together with 18 small trimmed carrots, 18 olive-sized turnip pieces, the white part of 18 leeks cut into 2 cm (¾ in) pieces and 18 small young onions. Cover and cook over a very low heat without fat or liquid, shaking the pan occasionally to prevent sticking. After 20 minutes, remove the turnips, season them with salt and keep hot. Ten minutes later, remove and season the leeks; after a further 10 minutes, do the same with the carrots and onions. Continue to cook the veal over a very low heat, so that it does not burn, for a further 20 minutes. Moisten with 120 ml (4½ fl oz, ½ cup) white wine and reduce until almost dry. Then add 500 ml (17 fl oz, 2 cups) whipping cream and leave to cook for 10 minutes. Replace the vegetables in the casserole and bring to a final boil. Serve the veal with its vegetables piled into a dish.

# Vitello tonnato

Bone a 2 kg (4¼ lb) loin of veal and tie it neatly with string. Chop the bones into short lengths and set aside. Season the meat with salt and pepper. Brown it on all sides in a sauté pan in 2 tablespoons olive oil, then remove the roast from the pan. Put the bones in the bottom of a large roasting tin (pan), then place the meat on top and dot with 50 g (2 oz, ¼ cup) butter. Cook in a preheated oven at 220–230°C (425–450°F, gas 7–8) for 20 minutes. Add 1 diced carrot, 1 chopped onion and 2 garlic cloves in their skin, then continue cooking for a further 10 minutes. Season the meat and allow to cool. Discard the bones, then degrease the cooking juices in the pan and reduce them by half. Deglaze the pan with 100 ml (4 fl oz, 7 tablespoons) white wine and 200 ml (7 fl oz, ¾ cup) water. Reduce, then strain the juice and set aside.

Purée 150 g (5 oz) cooked or drained canned tuna, with 3 preserved anchovies (desalted and boned), 40 g (1½ oz) drained capers and 2 tablespoons of the meat cooking juices. Mix with 450 ml (¾ pint, 2 cups) mayonnaise. Add seasoning to taste and, if necessary, thin the sauce with up to 4 tablespoons chicken stock.

Cut the meat into 2–3 cm (¾–1¼ in) thick slices. Arrange on a platter and pour the tuna sauce over. Sprinkle with sprigs of flat-leafed parsley and 25 g (1 oz) capers. Serve with quartered radicchio hearts, dressed with olive oil and lemon juice.

# Pork & ham

## Aspic of ham and veal (or chicken)

Prepare an aspic jelly flavoured with herbs, and coat the mould with it. Garnish the mould with some diced cooked ham and some casseroled veal (or chicken) cut into even-sized slices. Fill the centre with a layer of ham mousse, then a layer of Russian salad, finishing with a layer of aspic jelly. Place in the refrigerator to set. Unmould before serving.

## Boiled salt pork with pease pudding

Boil a piece of salted belly pork with some carrots, turnips, celery, leeks, onions and parsnips. Meanwhile, prepare a very smooth purée of split peas (preferably yellow) using 500 g (18 oz, 2¼ cups) cooked split peas, 100 g (4 oz, ½ cup) butter, 3 eggs, grated nutmeg, salt and pepper. Butter a pudding basin (mould) and pour the mixture into it. Place the basin in a roasting tin (pan) containing 2.5 cm (1 in) boiling water and cook in a preheated oven at

190°C (375°F, gas 5) for 40 minutes. Drain the cooked pork, place in a serving dish and surround with the well-drained vegetables. Turn out the pease pudding and serve separately.

## Braised ham

A few hours before cooking a fresh ham (or a corner or middle gammon), rub it with salt mixed with powdered thyme and bay leaf. When ready to cook, wipe the ham dry, then brown it lightly in 50 g (2 oz, ¼ cup) butter. Prepare a meatless matignon with 250 g (9 oz, 1½ cups) peeled, finely diced and cored carrots, 100 g (4 oz) celery sticks with the strings removed, and 50 g (2 oz, ⅓ cup) coarsely chopped onions. Cook these vegetables gently in 50 g (2 oz, ¼ cup) butter, in a covered pan, with a bay leaf, a sprig of thyme, salt, pepper and a pinch of sugar, for about 30 minutes. Then add 200 ml (7 fl oz, ¾ cup) Madeira or 200 ml (7 fl oz, ¾ cup) Meursault or Riesling and let it reduce with the lid off until the vegetables are soft and all the liquid has been used up.

Put the ham in a roasting tin (pan), coat it with the matignon and sprinkle it with melted butter, then cover with buttered greaseproof (wax) paper. Cook in a preheated oven at 200°C (400°F, gas 6), allowing 20–25 minutes per 450 g (1 lb), basting frequently with the cooking butter (if this seems to be getting too brown, add a few tablespoons of stock). When the ham is cooked, remove the greaseproof paper and the matignon and place the ham on a hot serving dish. Deglaze the roasting tin with a mixture of one-third Madeira and two-thirds stock, and reduce by half. Put the matignon and the cooking juices through a blender and pour this sauce over the ham.

## Braised ham à la bayonnaise

Soak a Bayonne ham in cold water for at least 6 hours to remove the salt, then poach it in salted water until it is three-quarters cooked (the meat should still resist a trussing needle stuck into it). Drain and skin it by removing the rind and excess fat, leaving about 1 cm (½ in) of fat on the ham. Complete the cooking as for braised ham. When it is cooked, put it on an ovenproof dish, with a little of the strained cooking juices poured over, and glaze in the oven.

Meanwhile, prepare a well-seasoned rice pilaf, adding chopped tomatoes (use slightly less water to cook the rice, as tomatoes are very watery). Sprinkle some cleaned button mushrooms with lemon juice and cook them gently in butter. Fry some very thin chipolata sausages in butter. Mix the rice and the mushrooms, and arrange this garnish around the ham, with the chipolatas around the edge of the dish. Serve the rest of the cooking juices separately in a sauceboat.

## Braised ham à la crème

Cover a fresh ham with water and cook until three-quarters done (the meat should still resist a trussing needle stuck into it). Remove the rind and surplus fat, leaving about 1 cm (½ in) of fat on the ham. Prepare a mirepoix with 200 g (8 oz) peeled and cored carrots, 125 g (4½ oz) onions, 75 g (3 oz) celery sticks and 125 g (4 oz) raw ham or blanched belly pork. Melt 50 g (2 oz, ¼ cup) butter in a saucepan and add the mirepoix with a sprig of thyme and a few sprigs of chopped parsley; cook very gently with the lid on until the vegetables are quite soft.

Spread the mirepoix in a roasting tin (pan) and place the skinned ham on top; pour over 6 tablespoons stock, 50 g (2 oz, ¼ cup) melted butter and 200 ml (7 fl oz, ¾ cup) Madeira. Cover the ham with buttered greaseproof (wax) paper and cook in a preheated oven at 200°C (400°F, gas 6) for about 1½ hours, basting frequently with the cooking juices and adding a little stock if necessary to keep it moist. When cooked, drain the ham and place it on a hot serving dish.

Reduce the cooking liquid a little, then add 500 ml (17 fl oz, 2 cups) crème fraîche and reduce by one third. Put this sauce through a blender and serve it with the ham.

## Braised ham porte-maillot

Braise, drain and dress the ham. Place it in a small braising pan, pour over 500 ml (17 fl oz, 2 cups) Madeira, cover and simmer gently for 30 minutes. Prepare a garnish of glazed carrots and onions, green (French) beans cooked in salted water and braised lettuce. When the ham is cooked, glaze it in the oven. Arrange on a long serving dish (platter), surrounded by the vegetables in separate piles and keep warm. Skim the fat off the cooking juices, strain and serve separately.

## Braised ham with Madeira

Braise the ham and cut it into slices. Remove the fat from the meat juices, reduce them and add Madeira. Strain and then thicken with arrowroot or cornflour (cornstarch). Arrange the slices of ham in an ovenproof dish and cover with the Madeira-flavoured stock. Cover and heat through in the oven without boiling.

## Braised ham with pineapple

Put a fresh ham weighing about 5 kg (11 lb) into cold water, bring to the boil, and simmer very gently for 2 hours. Drain the ham and leave until cold, then remove the rind, leaving a 1 cm (½ in) layer of fat on the ham. Stud the ham with cloves and sprinkle with 125 g (4½ oz, ½ cup) caster (superfine) sugar. Place in a roasting tin (pan) and bake in a preheated oven at 220°C (425°F, gas 7) for 1½ hours.

Heat about 12 canned pineapple slices in their syrup. Put 250 ml (8 fl oz,

1 cup) wine vinegar and 20 peppercorns into a saucepan, bring to the boil, and then add 500 ml (17 fl oz, 2 cups) stock. Prepare a pale caramel with 125 g (4½ oz, ½ cup) caster (superfine) sugar and strain the flavoured stock on to the caramel. Add 2 glasses of sherry and reduce until syrupy; pour into a sauceboat. Put the ham on a hot dish and surround it with the drained slices of pineapple; serve the sauce separately.

## Cassoulet (1)

(from a recipe given by a gourmet from Castelnaudary) Use a glazed earthenware pot, known as a *toupin*, to cook white haricot (navy) beans – those from Pamiers and Cazères are best – with seasoning, plus the usual meat – pork (loin, ham, leg, sausages and fresh rinds) with perhaps a piece of preserved goose – vegetables, garlic and herbs. When the beans are well cooked but still whole, put them in a special cooking pot (of Issel earthenware), the sides of which have been lined with fresh bacon rinds (these are cooked with the beans). Add the pork hock, fat, sausage and a leg of preserved goose. Sprinkle the top with coarse breadcrumbs and then with goose fat. Place in a baker's oven (ideally fuelled by mountain gorse) and cook gently for several hours. When a beautiful golden crust has formed, break it with a wooden spoon; repeat this essential operation two or three times. Then you will have a fine cassoulet that can be served with either a fine red Aquitaine wine or an old Minervois wine.

## Cassoulet (2)

(from a recipe by Prosper Montagné) For 8 people, soak 1 litre (1¾ pints, 4⅓ cups) white haricot (navy) beans in cold water for a few hours (but do not allow them to ferment). Drain, then add to them 300 g (11 oz) pork fat, 200 g (7 oz) fresh pork rind tied in a bundle, a carrot, an onion studded with cloves and a bouquet garni containing 3 garlic cloves. Season carefully, using very little salt as the fat contains salt. Add enough water to allow the beans to 'swim' well. Simmer gently so that the beans are cooked but intact.

Place some dripping or goose fat in a separate pan and brown 800 g (1¾ lb) pork sparerib or bladebone and 500 g (18 oz) boned shoulder of mutton, well seasoned with salt and pepper. When the meats are well browned, put them in a large frying pan containing 200 g (7 oz, 1¾ cups) cooked chopped onion, a bouquet garni and 2 crushed garlic cloves. Cover and cook. Moisten from time to time with good meat juice or stock from the stockpot. If desired, add some spoonfuls of tomato purée or 3 peeled, seeded and crushed tomatoes.

When the beans are almost cooked, remove the vegetables and bouquet garni and add the pork, mutton and onions, together with some garlic sausage, a leg of preserved goose or duck, and, if desired, a piece of home-made sausage. Simmer gently for a further hour. Remove all the meat from the beans and drain. Cut the mutton, pork and goose (or duck) into equal pieces and cut the rind into rectangles, the sausage into slices (removing the skin) and the fresh sausage into small rings.

Line a large earthenware dish or individual dishes with the rind, then add a layer of beans, a layer of the various meats (moistened with their sauce) and another layer of beans, seasoning each layer with pepper. Top the final layer with the pieces of fat, the remaining rind and some sliced sausage. Sprinkle with white breadcrumbs and melted goose fat. Cook gently in the oven (preferably a baker's oven) for about 1½ hours. Serve in the cooking dish.

## Cold ham mousse

Mince (grind) 500 g (18 oz) cooked lean ham, adding 200 ml (7 fl oz, ¾ cup) cold thick velouté sauce. Purée in a blender, then put it into a bowl and stand it on ice; season and stir with a spatula for a few minutes, adding 150 ml (¼ pint, ⅔ cup) liquid aspic, a little at a time. Finally, gently fold in 400 ml (14 fl oz, 1¾ cups) double (heavy) cream whipped until fairly stiff. Pour into a mould lined with aspic, and chill until set. Turn out on to the serving dish and garnish with chopped aspic.

## Croûtes à la diable

Fill some croûtes with a salpicon of York ham and mushrooms which have been cooked slowly in butter, bound with well-reduced demi-glace and seasoned with a pinch of cayenne. Sprinkle the croûtes with breadcrumbs fried in butter, and brown in a preheated oven at 220°C (425°F, gas 7).

## Enchaud

This speciality from Périgord consists of a piece of boned pork fillet (tenderloin) rolled up, tied with string and cooked in the oven in a casserole. Bone a piece of pork fillet (tenderloin) weighing about 1.5 kg (3¼ lb), and keep the bone. Spread out the fillet on the work surface. Season with salt and pepper, sprinkle lightly with crushed thyme and insert small pieces of garlic. Roll up the meat tightly, tie it up with string and keep it cool.

The next day, heat 2 tablespoons lard (shortening) in a flameproof casserole and brown the enchaud on all sides. Add a small glass of warm water, a sprig of thyme and the pork bone. Season with salt and pepper. Cover and seal the lid with a flour and water paste. Cook in a preheated oven at 180°C (350°F, gas 4) for about 2 hours. When the enchaud is cooked, drain it and keep it hot on the serving dish. Remove the bone and the thyme from the casserole and skim as much fat as possible from the cooking juices; add 4 tablespoons stock and reduce. Serve the enchaud with this sauce, accompanied by potatoes sautéed with garlic.

The garlic can be replaced by small sticks of truffle. In this case, the pork is stuffed with about 400 g (14 oz, 1¾ cups) well-seasoned fine forcemeat, to which 1 teaspoon brandy and some truffle peel have been added. Roll up and cook the enchaud as in the previous method and serve cold, with a salad dressed with walnut oil.

## Farci

This speciality of Périgord consists of forcemeat wrapped in cabbage leaves. It is traditionally cooked inside a boiling fowl in meat or vegetable stock; however, it is now more usually made by wrapping the stuffed cabbage leaves in muslin (cheesecloth).

Crumble 350 g (12 oz, 12 slices) stale crustless bread and soak it in fatty stock or in milk. In a bowl, mix together 350 g (12 oz, 2 cups) chopped gammon (ham or bacon, 2 chopped garlic cloves, 2 chopped shallots (or 1 chopped onion), a bunch of chopped parsley, tarragon or other herbs. If liked, add some chopped chicken liver. Squeeze out the bread and mix it with the chopped ingredients. Season with salt, pepper and a generous pinch of mixed spice and bind with 2 or 3 egg yolks. Mix well until smooth, and keep in a cool place.

Blanch some large cabbage leaves in a saucepan of boiling water for 5 minutes. Cool quickly under cold running water then pat them dry on paper towels and arrange them like flower petals on a flat surface. Shape the forcemeat into a ball, place it on the cabbage leaves and fold them over. Secure the cabbage leaves with string to keep the shape, or wrap the package in muslin (cheesecloth), and cook in vegetable or meat stock for about 1¾ hours. Remove the muslin or string. Cut the farci into slices and serve very hot with the stock or with a chicken, depending on the recipe. (Farci can also be served cold.)

## Fresh figs with Parma ham

Choose some very fresh green or purple figs that are ripe but still slightly firm. Split them into four without completely separating the quarters (these should be held together by the stalk). Gently loosen the skin near the stalk. Roll some very thin slices of Parma or Bayonne ham into cornets. Arrange the figs and ham in a dish and serve cold.

## Glazed ham

Soak a medium-sized ham in cold water for at least 6 hours, then scrub it and bone it at the loin end. Put it in a large saucepan with plenty of cold water but no seasoning. As soon as the water boils, reduce the heat and let it simmer very gently, allowing no more than 20 minutes per 450 g (1 lb). After draining and skinning the ham, put it in a roasting tin (pan), sprinkle with icing (confectioner's) sugar and glaze in a preheated oven at 180°C (350°F, gas 4) for about 30 minutes. As it caramelizes, the sugar turns into a sort of golden lacquer, enhancing the appearance and flavour of the ham.

## Glazed ham reine pédauque

Poach a middle or corner gammon in Meursault for 20 minutes per 450 g (1 lb). Cut it into thin slices and leave until cold. Spread each slice with a layer of foie gras mixed with diced truffle, and put the slices together to re-form the original shape. Coat with a port-flavoured chaud-froid sauce. Garnish with slices of truffle and glaze with port-flavoured aspic. Place the glazed ham on a long serving dish and surround it with little squares of aspic.

## Glazed spare ribs

Prepare a marinade with 1 tablespoon sugar, 1 teaspoon salt, a pinch of ground ginger, 60 ml (2 fl oz, ¼ cup) soy sauce and the same quantity of ketchup, 1 chopped garlic clove and some black pepper. Marinate the spare ribs for at least 30 minutes, then drain and grill (broil) briskly on one side. Baste with a little marinade and grill the other side. Baste once more and grill the ribs until they are stickily glazed on both sides. The ribs may also be baked in a preheated oven, and require basting occasionally.

## Grilled andouillette

This sausage made from pork intestines (*chaudins*), often with the addition of pork stomach and calf's mesentery, precooked in stock or milk and packed into a skin may be cooked simply by grilling. Prick the andouillette and grill (broil) it slowly, preferably over charcoal, so that it warms right through.

## Grilled pork chops

Season the chops with salt and pepper, brush with melted butter or oil and grill (broil) under a moderate heat, turning once. Arrange on a serving dish and garnish with watercress. Serve with lemon wedges.

## Ham à la chablisienne

Remove the stalks from 1.5 kg (3¼ lb) spinach, wash the leaves and cook them briskly in salted boiling water until wilted. Cool them down in iced water, then squeeze out all the water. Finely chop 1 small shallot and sweat in a saucepan in 10 g (¼ oz, 1½ teaspoons) butter, without letting it brown. Add 200 ml (7 fl oz, ¾ cup) Chablis and reduce to 4 teaspoons. Add 200 ml (7 fl oz, ¾ cup) chicken stock and reduce by half. Pour in 200 ml (7 fl oz, ¾ cup) double (heavy) cream and cook until it thickens slightly. Season with salt and pepper. In another saucepan, heat 50 g (2 oz, ¼ cup) butter until it turns brown. Add the spinach and stir with a fork spiked with a peeled garlic clove. Adjust the seasoning. Place the spinach in an ovenproof dish. On top arrange

4 thick slices of ham previously warmed in stock and then drained. Pour the sauce on top and put in a preheated oven at 180°C (350°F, gas 4) to heat through for a few minutes.

## Ham cornets with foie gras mousse

Roll up some small but fairly thick slices of ham into cornets. Fill them with a duck or goose foie gras mousse (using a piping bag). Arrange on a bed of lettuce or on a dish garnished with cubes of port-flavoured aspic jelly.

## Ham crêpes

Prepare 12 savoury crêpes. Prepare separately a béchamel sauce with 40 g (1½ oz, 3 tablespoons) butter, 40 g (1½ oz, 6 tablespoons) plain (all-purpose) flour, 500 ml (17 fl oz, 2 cups) milk, nutmeg, salt and pepper. Add 150 g (5 oz, ⅔ cup) diced Paris or York ham and 50 g (2 oz, ½ cup) grated cheese to the sauce. Cool and fill each crêpe with one-twelfth of this mixture. Roll up the crêpes and arrange them in a buttered ovenproof dish. Sprinkle with 50 g (2 oz, ½ cup) grated cheese and 25 g (1 oz, 2 tablespoons) melted butter and brown in a preheated oven at 230°C (450°F, gas 8).

## Ham saupiquet

Cut 8 thick slices of boned ham, which has been thoroughly desalted, and fry them in lard over a brisk heat. Make a roux with 25 g (1 oz, ¼ cup) plain (all-purpose) flour and 25 g (1 oz, 2 tablespoons) butter, then add 200 ml (7 fl oz, ¾ cup) white wine and 200 ml (7 fl oz, ¾ cup) ham, chicken or veal stock. Add the ham trimmings, 7 or 8 juniper berries and some chopped tarragon and reduce for 15 minutes. Reduce some wine vinegar seasoned with 10 crushed peppercorns. Pour the sauce over this and simmer for another 15 minutes. Thicken with 200 ml (7 fl oz, ¾ cup) crème fraîche, then rub through a very fine sieve. Drain the slices of ham, arrange them on a hot serving dish and pour the sauce over them.

## Ham soufflé

Make a béchamel sauce using 40 g (1½ oz, 3 tablespoons) butter, 40 g (1½ oz, 6 tablespoons) plain (all-purpose) flour and 200 ml (7 fl oz, ¾ cup) cold milk. Season with salt, pepper, nutmeg, 75–90 g (3–3½ oz, ¾ cup) grated Gruyère cheese or 50 g (2 oz, ½ cup) grated Parmesan cheese and 150 g (5 oz, 1 cup) ham that has been chopped and processed or finely minced twice. Then add 4–5 egg yolks (use fairly large eggs) and fold in 4–5 egg whites which have been whisked to stiff peaks. Preheat the oven for 15 minutes at 220°C (425°F, gas 7). Butter a 20 cm (8 in) soufflé mould and coat with flour. Pour in the mixture and bake in the preheated oven at 200°C (400°F, gas 6) for 30 minutes, without opening the door during cooking, until well risen and a deep golden-brown on top.

## Home-salted pork

Choose fairly even-sized pieces of belly pork, knuckles of ham, spare rib or shoulder chops, and trimmed rind. Rub them with fine salt and place in a salting tub, putting the largest pieces at the bottom: start with the pieces of belly pork, pressing them down well. Cover with cooking salt, making sure that there are as few air pockets as possible. A few garlic cloves, peppercorns and a bay leaf may be added, but not to excess. Then pile on the knuckles of ham, filling up the holes with the spare rib or shoulder chops. Cover each layer with salt, pressing down well, and finish with the pork rinds. Preservation time is 2–3 weeks for spare rib chops, 1 month for knuckles of ham, and much longer for belly of pork. Knuckle, brushed and wiped, can be stored hung up in a cool, airy place.

## Home-salted pork: rolled belly

Choose a piece of streaky belly pork that is not too fatty. Trim it, cut into a rectangle and slash the inside. Rub with salt mixed with chopped garlic, then sprinkle with chopped thyme. Roll up the belly and tie tightly. Rub the outside – the rind side – with fine salt for some time, so that it penetrates thoroughly. Cut the belly into 2 or 3 pieces, according to the size of the salting tub. Layer in the tub as above.

## Landes ham with honey

Cook 450 g (1 lb, 2 cups) rice in salted water and drain. Coat 4 slices of slightly salted raw ham on both sides with a little clear chestnut honey. Butter an ovenproof dish, line it with the rice, add the slices of ham and sprinkle with cinnamon. Grill (broil) for 10 minutes. Season with pepper and serve hot.

## Loin of pork à l'alsacienne

Salt and pepper a loin of pork and cook in a preheated oven at 200°C (400°F, gas 6), allowing 50 minutes per 1 kg (22 minutes per 1 lb) and turning it over halfway through the cooking time. Prepare a braised sauerkraut with a garnish of bacon and sausages. Drain the loin, place in the centre of the sauerkraut and continue cooking for a further 15 minutes. To serve, cut the bacon into slices and separate the loin chops. Arrange on the sauerkraut with the sausages and boiled potatoes.

## Loin of pork à la languedocienne

Stick the loin with garlic cloves cut into sticks, sprinkle with salt and pepper, brush with oil and leave to stand for 12 hours. Roast it in a preheated oven at 220°C (425°F, gas 7) for 1 hour per 1 kg (25–30 minutes per 1 lb), or on a spit, and serve with its cooking juices accompanied by sautéed potatoes.

## Loin of pork bonne femme

Salt and pepper a loin of pork. Heat 15 g (½ oz, 1 tablespoon) butter or lard per 1 kg (2¼ lb) meat in a flameproof casserole. Brown the meat on all sides, then place it in the casserole in a preheated oven at 200°C (400°F, gas 6) and cook according to the weight of the meat, allowing 50 minutes per 1 kg (22 minutes per lb). About 25 minutes before the end of the cooking time, add 500 g (18 oz) peeled potatoes per 1 kg (2¼ lb) meat and 20 small (pearl) onions fried in butter to the casserole. Season with salt and pepper, cover and finish cooking. Separate the loin chops and serve very hot, sprinkled with chopped parsley.

## Loin of pork with pineapple

Brown a loin of pork in a flameproof casserole with a little butter and oil. Season with salt and pepper, cover the casserole and cook gently for about 1½ hours, either on the top of the stove or in a preheated oven at 200°C (400°F, gas 6). Brown some pineapple slices and apple quarters in butter and add them to the casserole 5 minutes before the end of the cooking time. Arrange the pork on a warm serving plate with the apples and pineapple and keep hot. Deglaze the casserole with a little hot water or rum and serve this separately as a sauce.

## Loin of pork with pistachios

Marinate a loin of pork – or unsmoked (fresh) ham – for 24 hours in white Bordeaux wine. Soak 800 g (1¾ lb) prunes in warm white Bordeaux. Stud the pork joint with garlic and pistachios. Place it in a flameproof casserole, add 500 ml (17 fl oz, 2 cups) of the marinade, cover and cook for 3 hours over a moderate heat. Then add the strained prunes, cook for a further 45 minutes and serve very hot.

## Loin of pork with red cabbage

Prepare a braised red cabbage while roasting a loin of pork. Arrange the pork on a hot serving dish; surround with red cabbage and boiled potatoes or braised chestnuts. Serve very hot.

## Melon with Parma ham

Arrange seeded and peeled, fine slices of melon on individual plates, allowing 3–4 per portion. Add 3–4 fine slices Parma ham, loosely folded to one side of the melon. The ham and melon are eaten together as a simple starter.

## Mother's cretons

In a heavy-based saucepan place 500 g (18 oz, 2¼ cups) minced (ground) shoulder of pork, 1 chopped onion, 2 crushed garlic cloves, 1 cup breadcrumbs, 1 cup milk, 1 cup chopped parsley, salt, pepper and cinnamon. Mix thoroughly, cover and cook for 2 hours over a gentle heat, stirring frequently. Leave to cool, then process in a food processor or blender for 2 minutes. Pour into a buttered terrine and refrigerate until firm.

## Neck of pork with broad beans

Soak 1 kg (2¼ lb) smoked neck of pork for 12 hours in fresh water, changing the water two or three times if the meat seems too salty. Place the pork in a braising pan and cover with cold water. Bring to the boil and skim. Add 1 leek, 1 carrot, 1 onion, 1 celery stick, 1 bay leaf, 6 peppercorns, 3 cloves and 200 ml (7 fl oz, ¾ cup) Rivaner or Riesling. Cover and cook for 2–3 hours. Prepare a roux with 50 g (2 oz, ¼ cup) butter and 2 tablespoons plain (all-purpose) flour. Dilute with stock from the braising pan to make a sauce. Cook 1 kg (2¼ lb) broad (fava) beans with a few sprigs of summer savory. Serve the meat, sliced, with the beans and boiled potatoes.

## Palette of pork with haricot beans

Soak a salted blade or butt of pork in cold water to remove the salt, changing the water once. Stud the meat with pieces of garlic and place it in a saucepan. Cover it generously with cold water, add a bouquet garni and leave to simmer for about 2 hours. Cook separately some dried or fresh white haricot (navy) beans or lentils. When the beans are half-cooked, add the meat (drained), adjust the seasoning and complete the cooking gently with the lid on. Alternatively, the cooked shoulder may be lightly fried in lard (shortening) before being added to the beans.

## Palette of pork with sauerkraut

Soak a salted blade or butt of pork in cold water to remove the salt, changing the water once. Prepare some sauerkraut, place the drained shoulder in it and cook for about 2 hours over a very low heat or in a preheated oven at 180°C (350°F, gas 4). The sauerkraut may be garnished with a few vegetables (potatoes, carrots, turnips and small onions) added 45 minutes before the end of the cooking time.

## Pigs' trotter sausages

Soak a large pig's caul (caul fat) in cold water. Cook the trotters (feet) in stock until really tender and bone them completely. Dice the flesh and mix it with an equal quantity of fine pork forcemeat (diced truffle may be added if wished). Add salt, pepper, a pinch of mixed spice and a dash of Cognac. Divide the mixture into 4 portions of about 100 g (4 oz). Shape into little flat sausages (*crépinettes*) and top with a slice of truffle if wished. Wipe the caul, spread it out on the work surface and cut it into pieces. Wrap each *crépinette* in a piece of caul, coat with melted butter, roll in fresh breadcrumbs and cook gently under the grill (broiler).

## Poached ham in pastry à l'ancienne

Poach a York ham in water until it is two-thirds cooked, then drain. Remove the skin and glaze on one side with caramel, then let it get cold. Prepare 575 g (1¼ lb) lining pastry, about 225 g (8 oz) vegetable mirepoix and 3 tablespoons mushroom duxelles. Mix the mirepoix and the duxelles together, adding 1 chopped truffle.

Roll out the pastry to a thickness of about 4 mm (¼ in) and spread the vegetable mixture over an area in the centre about the same size as the ham. Place the ham on the vegetables, glazed side down, wrap it in the pastry and seal the edges. Put it in a buttered roasting tin (pan), sealed side down. Brush the top of the pastry with beaten egg yolk and garnish with shapes cut from the pastry trimmings. Make a hole in the top for the steam to escape and cook in a preheated oven at 180–200°C (350–400°F, gas 4–6) for about 1 hour. Place the ham on a serving dish. If liked, a few spoonfuls of Périgueux sauce can be poured in through the opening.

## Pork brochettes with prunes

Remove the stones (pits) from the prunes. Wrap each prune in a short piece of smoked streaky bacon. Cut some pork loin into cubes. Marinate these ingredients for 30 minutes in a mixture of groundnut (peanut) oil, salt and pepper with a little grated nutmeg and cayenne pepper. Drain the pork and the bacon-wrapped prunes, thread on to skewers and grill (broil) under a medium heat for about 10 minutes.

## Pork chops à la bayonnaise

Stud the chops with slivers of garlic. Season with salt, pepper, powdered thyme and bay leaf and sprinkle with oil and a dash of vinegar. Leave to marinate for 1 hour, then sauté briskly in lard. When the chops are browned on both sides, surround them with small new potatoes tossed in goose fat and cep mushrooms fried in oil. Cook in a preheated oven at 200°C (400°F, gas 6) for 20 minutes. Arrange on a hot dish and sprinkle with chopped parsley.

## Pork chops à la gasconne

Marinate the chops as for pork chops *à la bayonnaise*. Fry quickly in butter or goose fat. Place in a pan with 6 peeled and slightly blanched garlic cloves per chop and cook over a gentle heat for 20 minutes. When the chops are almost cooked add 8 stoned (pitted) blanched green olives per chop. Arrange the chops in a crown and put the garnish in the centre. Deglaze the pan with 4 tablespoons white wine, add a few tablespoons of meat juice (or stock) if required and reduce. Pour the sauce over the chops and sprinkle with parsley.

## Pork chops à l'alsacienne

Salt and pepper the pork chops and either sauté in a little butter or lard or braise them. Arrange in a turban on a heated serving dish and garnish as for loin of pork *à l'alsacienne*. Coat the chops with their deglazed cooking juices or, if braised, with the strained braising juices.

## Pork chops charcutière

This dish is found ready-cooked in some French pork butchers' shops, prepared as follows. Sauté the pork chops (they may be coated with breadcrumbs) in lard, then simmer in charcutière sauce with thinly sliced gherkins.

In restaurants the preparation is as follows. Flatten the chops slightly, season, coat with melted butter and breadcrumbs and gently grill (broil). Arrange them in a crown and fill the centre of the dish with mashed potato. Serve separately, in a sauceboat, a charcutière sauce to which chopped gherkins have been added at the last minute.

## Pork chops pilleverjus

Trim and slightly flatten 4 pork chops, season with salt and pepper, and fry in lard until both sides are golden. Place 4 tablespoons finely chopped onions, lightly cooked in butter, in the frying pan. Add a bouquet garni, cover and cook gently for about 30 minutes. Meanwhile, shred a spring cabbage heart and cook in butter. Moisten with a few tablespoons of boiling cream, then stir. Arrange the cabbage julienne in a dish, place the chops on top and garnish with boiled potatoes if required. Deglaze the pan juices with 1 tablespoon vinegar and 4 tablespoons meat glaze and pour over the chops.

## Pork chops with kiwi fruit

Fry 4 pork chops in butter. Meanwhile peel 8 kiwi fruit, cut them into thick slices or quarters, and sprinkle with a little lemon juice. Drain the chops and keep them hot in the serving dish. Add the fruit to the frying pan, cover the pan and heat in the pan juices. Arrange the fruit around the chops. Deglaze the pan with 100 ml (4 fl oz, 7 tablespoons) pineapple juice and an equal quantity of stock. Boil down to reduce the sauce to a thick syrup. Add a generous pinch of pepper and pour over the chops.

## Pork chops with Robert sauce

Season the chops with salt and pepper, grill (broil) gently and serve with Robert sauce and mashed potatoes or haricot (navy) beans.

Alternatively, sauté the chops in butter or lard; when half-cooked, add 100 g (4 oz, ⅔ cup) finely chopped white onions (for 4 chops). Drain the chops, arrange on a serving dish and keep warm. Deglaze the pan juices with 200 ml (7 fl oz, ¾ cup) white wine and reduce almost completely. Moisten with 300 ml (½ pint, 1¼ cups) demi-glace sauce or 200 ml (7 fl oz, ¾ cup) stock and boil for 5 minutes. Add 1 tablespoon concentrated tomato purée (paste) and thicken with 1 tablespoon beurre manié. Remove from the heat and add a pinch of caster (superfine) sugar and 1 tablespoon mustard to the sauce. Pour the sauce over the chops and serve very hot.

## Pork crépinettes

A crepinette is a small flat sausage, generally made of sausagemeat mixed with chopped parsley and wrapped in caul (*crépine*). Crépinettes may also be made with lamb, veal or poultry, prepared with a salpicon of meat and mushrooms, sometimes garnished with truffles and bound with white or brown stock.

Prepare some small flat sausages using either fine pork forcemeat or sausagemeat flavoured with chopped herbs and Cognac (a few diced truffles may also be added to the mixture). Divide the forcemeat into portions of about 100 g (4 oz, ½ cup) and wrap each one in a rectangular piece of previously soaked and dried pig's caul. Coat each crépinette in egg and breadcrumbs, brush with melted butter and grill (broil) under a moderate heat. (The crépinettes may be grilled or fried without a coating of breadcrumbs.) The classic garnish is a purée of potatoes or of haricot (navy) beans, but they may also be served with buttered green vegetables.

## Pork crépinettes Sainte-Menehould

Prepare some pork crépinettes with a salpicon of pig's trotters mixed with diced truffles, bound with a very reduced demi-glace and sandwiched between 2 layers of fine well-seasoned pork forcemeat. Dip in egg and coat with breadcrumbs and fry in butter over a gentle heat.

## Pork pâté à la hongroise (hot)

Cut 300 g (11 oz, 1½ cups) pork loin into strips and leave in a cold marinade for ingredients of pâtés and terrines for 5–6 hours. Peel and dice 150 g (5 oz,

¾ cup) onions, wash and slice 200 g (7 oz, 2½ cups) mushrooms, then sweat both vegetables in butter with salt, pepper and paprika. Bind with 2–3 table-spoons velouté sauce.

Line a pâté mould with pastry for pâté en croûte 'pavé du roy'. Coat the bottom with 200 g (7 oz, 1 cup) mousseline forcemeat containing chopped chives and paprika. Add the mushrooms and onions and press down gently. Drain the strips of pork, stiffen them slightly in hot butter, then put them on top of the vegetables. Cover with 200 g (7 oz, 1 cup) forcemeat and then with pastry (which can be pastry for pâté en croûte, shortcrust or puff pastry). Seal and glaze the pastry, cutting a vent for steam to escape and bake in a preheated oven at 180°C (350°F, gas 4) for 1½ hours. Pour some Hungarian sauce into the pâté through the chimney.

## Potjevfleisch

Trim and bone 200 g (7 oz) loin of pork, 200 g (7 oz) rabbit meat, 200 g (7 oz) chicken meat and 200 g (7 oz) leg of veal. Cut into pieces 5 × 2 cm (2 × ¾ in). Peel and blanch 5 large garlic cloves. Place in a bowl, then add 1 diced celery stick, 3 sprigs of thyme, ¼ bay leaf, 2 tablespoons juniper berries and 750 ml (1¼ pints, 3¼ cups) light beer. Add the pieces of meat, cover and leave to marinate for 24 hours in a cool place.

Soften 3 sheets of leaf gelatine in cold water. In a medium-sized terrine arrange the drained meat in three layers, each one covered with a sheet of gelatine. Strain the marinade and pour it on top of the meats. Cover the terrine and seal the lid with flour and water paste. Cook in a preheated oven at 150°C (300°F, gas 2) for 3 hours. Leave the terrine to cool and rest at room temperature then chill in the refrigerator until set. Arrange a slice of *potjevfleisch* on each plate and garnish with *fines herbes*. Serve with onion or rhubarb chutney or a herb salad.

## Prunes with bacon

Stone (pit) some semi-dried Agen prunes by splitting them lengthways. Insert a shelled pistachio in place of the stone, then roll up each prune in half a thin rasher (slice) of bacon. Secure the bacon around the stuffed prunes by means of a wooden cocktail stick (toothpick). Arrange the prunes in an ovenproof dish, and place in a preheated oven at 230°C (450°F, gas 8) until the bacon is crispy (about 8–9 minutes). Serve piping hot as a cocktail snack.

## Quiche lorraine

Make some lining pastry with 250 g (9 oz, 2¼ cups) plain (all-purpose) flour, 125 g (4½ oz, ½ cup) butter, a generous pinch of salt, 1 egg and 3 tablespoons very cold water. Roll it into a ball and chill in the refrigerator for a few hours. Then roll it out to a thickness of 5 mm (¼ in) and line a buttered and floured tart tin (pan), 23 cm (9 in) in diameter, bringing the edges of the pastry up to extend slightly beyond the tin edge. Prick it all over and cook blind in a preheated oven at 200°C (400°F, gas 6) for 12–14 minutes. Leave to cool.

Cut 250 g (9 oz) slightly salted pork belly into flat strips and blanch for 5 minutes in boiling water. Refresh and pat dry, then brown very lightly in butter. Spread the pork strips over the pastry case. Beat 4 eggs lightly and mix in 300 ml (½ pint, 1¼ cups) double (heavy) cream; add salt, pepper and nutmeg, then pour the mixture into the pastry case. Cook for about 30 minutes in a preheated oven at 200°C (400°F, gas 6). Serve very hot.

## Red kidney beans with red wine and bacon

Cook the beans with 500 g (18 oz) lean bacon in one piece for each 1 kg (2¼ lb) beans and a bouquet garni, 1 onion studded with cloves, garlic and carrot. Use a mixture of half water and half red wine. Part-drain them, leaving enough cooking liquor to lightly coat the beans, and put them into a sauté pan. Cut the bacon into dice, fry it in butter and add it to the beans. Finally, thicken the sauce with a knob of beurre manié.

## Rillettes de Tours

Rillettes is a preparation of pork, rabbit, goose or poultry meat cooked in lard, then pounded to a smooth paste and potted. It is served as a cold hors d'oeuvre.

. Select some pieces of fat and lean pork from various cuts, such as blade, neck, belly and leg. Separate the fat from the lean meat and remove any bones. Chop the bones, cut the lean meat into strips and coarsely chop the fat.

Put the fat into a large saucepan, arrange the chopped bones on top, then add the strips of lean meat. Tie 4 or 5 cloves and about 12 black peppercorns in a small piece of muslin (cheesecloth) and place it in the pan, then add salt, using 5 teaspoons per 1 kg (2¼ lb) meat. Cover the saucepan, bring to the boil, and simmer gently for 4 hours.

Remove the lid, turn up the heat and remove the bones, stripping off any adhering meat and returning it to the pan to continue cooking. Stir constantly until all the liquid has evaporated. Remove the bag of spices.

Pour the rillettes into stoneware pots, which have previously been scalded, stirring well so as to mix the fat and lean; leave to cool. The fat will rise to the top so there is no need to add lard. Cover with greaseproof (wax) paper and then foil and store in the refrigerator.

## Rillons

Rillons are a speciality of Touraine, made from pieces of belly or shoulder of pork. Cut some pieces of fat belly of pork into 6 cm (2½ in) cubes, without removing the rind. Sprinkle with salt – 1½ tablespoons salt per 1 kg (2¼ lb) meat – and leave for 12 hours.

Put one-third as much lard (shortening) as there is meat into a saucepan, heat and then brown the pieces of pork. Lower the heat and simmer gently for 2 hours. Finally, add 2 tablespoons caramel per 1 kg (2¼ lb) meat, heat through quickly and drain. The rillons may be served either very hot or thoroughly chilled.

## Roast loin of pork with various garnishes

Season a loin of pork with salt and pepper 2 hours before cooking. In an ovenproof dish heat a maximum of 15 g (½ oz, 1 tablespoon) lard (shortening) per 1 kg (2¼ lb) meat. Brown the meat on all sides, place the dish in a preheated oven at 200°C (400°F, gas 6) and cook for about 50 minutes per 1 kg (22 minutes per 1 lb). Baste the loin with its cooking juices and turn it several times during cooking.

Serve with the cooking juices, skimmed of fat, and any of the following garnishes: potatoes (*boulangère, dauphinoise,* or puréed), a vegetable purée (celery, turnips, lentils or chick peas), braised vegetables (celery, endive, cabbage, Brussels sprouts, chicory, artichoke hearts or lettuce) or fruit (apples, pears or pineapple). The skimmed cooking juices can also be used to make various sauces, such as *charcutière, piquante,* Robert or tomato.

## Roast pork with Jerusalem artichokes

Peel 800 g (1¾ lb) Jerusalem artichokes per 1 kg (2¼ lb) meat. Trim them into large bulb shapes and blanch for 5 minutes in boiling salted water. Rinse in cold water and drain. Melt 20 g (¾ oz, 1½ tablespoons) lard (shortening) in a pan and brown the piece of pork gently. Cook in a preheated oven at 200°C (400°F, gas 6) allowing 50 minutes per 1 kg (22 minutes per 1 lb). About 30 minutes before the end of the cooking time, add the artichokes and season with salt and pepper.

Serve the roast pork surrounded by the artichokes; the deglazed cooking juices should be served separately.

## Roast pork with lime sorbet and mint

To make the sorbet, dissolve 575 g (1¼ lb, 2½ cups) sugar in 200 ml (7 fl oz, ¾ cup) water, heat just sufficiently to dissolve the sugar completely and leave to cool. Squeeze enough limes to collect 500 ml (17 fl oz, 2 cups) strained juice. Add it to the syrup. Pour into ice trays and place in the freezer. After about 1 hour, whisk and leave for at least 1 further hour before whisking again. Continue until set completely.

Roast a 1 kg (2¼ lb) fillet of pork (pork tenderloin) for 70 minutes in a preheated oven at 220°C (425°F, gas 7) and leave to cool completely.

Slice the roast thinly and arrange on a serving dish; garnish with sprigs of fresh mint. Prepare a lettuce salad and sprinkle it with chopped mint. Serve the sorbet in small sundae glasses alongside the cold roast meat and the salad.

## Roast sucking pig

Clean out the sucking pig through an incision in the belly without boning it. Sew it up and tie up the trotters. Season the inside with *quatre epices* or four spices and sprinkle with brandy, oil, sliced carrots and onions, crushed garlic cloves, chopped parsley, thyme, bay leaf and pepper. Leave the pig to marinate in this mixture for 24 hours. Cook the pig on a spit over a high heat for about 1¾ hours: the skin should be golden and crisp. Baste the pig with a little of the marinade during cooking. Serve on a dish garnished with watercress.

## Salt pork with lentils

Soak 500 g (18 oz) slightly salted spare ribs, 1 slice slightly salted knuckle end of ham, 400 g (14 oz) slightly salted loin and 200 g (7 oz) slightly salted belly of pork streaked with fat in cold water for at least 2 hours. Rinse all the pieces of meat, place them in plenty of cold water and bring to the boil, then skim thoroughly and simmer for 1 hour. Wash and drain 500 g (18 oz, 2½ cups) Puy lentils, then cook for 15 minutes in plenty of water. Drain again and add to the meat with 1 large onion stuck with 2 cloves and 2 carrots, 2 leeks, a bouquet garni and a few black peppercorns. Simmer for 45 minutes, skimming from time to time. Add 1 cooking sausage and continue cooking for another 40 minutes. Remove all the meat and set aside in a warm place. Discard the bouquet garni and drain the lentils. Place on a large serving dish and arrange the meat on top.

## Sausages à la catalane

In a frying pan, fry 1 kg (2¼ lb) thick sausages in dripping until they are golden, then remove them and set aside. Add 2 tablespoons flour to the pan and stir until it is coloured, then add 1 teaspoon tomato purée (paste), 120 ml (4½ fl oz, ½ cup) white wine, and 120 ml (4½ fl oz, ½ cup) stock. Stir well, cook for 10 minutes, then press through a sieve. Blanch 24 peeled garlic cloves. Return the sausages to the frying pan, add the garlic, a bouquet garni and a piece of dried orange peel. Pour the sieved sauce on to the sausages, cover and cook gently for 30 minutes. Fresh breadcrumbs may be used instead of flour, if liked.

## Sautéed pork chops

Trim and flatten 4 pork chops and season with salt and pepper. Heat 25 g (1 oz, 2 tablespoons) butter or lard (shortening) in a frying pan and brown the chops on both sides. Cover the pan and cook for about 15 minutes. Remove the chops and arrange on a hot dish. Coat with the deglazed cooking juices and serve with any of the garnishes suggested for roast loin of pork.

## Shoulder of pork with five spiccs

In a mortar crush 2 garlic cloves and 2 shallots with 2 teaspoons sugar and the same amount of nuoc-mâm (a Vietnamese fish sauce) and soy sauce, ½ teaspoon Chinese five spice powder and a little black pepper. Fry the shoulder of pork, with its rind, on all sides, then add the spice mixture. Cover and cook for 30 minutes over a moderate heat, turning the meat halfway through the cooking time. Remove the lid and reduce, turn the meat in its cooking juices, then remove and slice; arrange the slices on a plate and pour over the reduced juices. Serve with plain boiled rice.

## Small ham and cheese quiches

Make some lining pastry (see short pastry) with 250 g (9 oz, 2¼ cups) plain (all-purpose) flour, 125 g (4½ oz, ½ cup) butter, a generous pinch of salt, 1 egg and 3 tablespoons very cold water. Roll it into a ball and chill in the refrigerator for a few hours. Then roll it out to a thickness of 5 mm (¼ in). Line 6 tartlet moulds, 10 cm (4 in) in diameter, with the pastry. Cut 150 g (5 oz, ⅔ cup) cooked ham into strips and spread over the pastry cases with 100 g (4 oz, ¼ cup) grated Gruyère cheese. Beat 4 eggs lightly and mix in 300 ml (½ pint, 1¼ cups) double (heavy) cream; add salt, pepper and nutmeg, then pour the mixture into the pastry case. Bake in a preheated oven at 180°C (350°F, gas 4) for about 18 minutes.

## Stuffed sucking pig à l'occitane

Clean out the sucking pig through an incision in the belly. Bone it, leaving only the leg bones. Season the inside with salt and *quatre épices* or four spices, sprinkle with brandy and leave for several hours.

Prepare a forcemeat: slice the pig's liver and an equal amount of calves' or lambs' liver, season and brown briskly in very hot butter. Drain and set aside.

In the same butter, still over a high heat, lightly brown the pig's heart and kidneys and 150 g (5 oz) calves' sweetbreads (trimmed, blanched, rinsed in cold water and sliced). Drain these ingredients and add to the liver. Add 40 g (1½ oz, 3 tablespoons) butter to the same pan and brown 200 g (7 oz, 1½ cups) finely chopped onions, then add 2 tablespoons chopped shallots and 75 g (3 oz, 1 cup) shredded mushrooms and cook for a few moments. Add a pinch of powdered garlic, cover with dry white wine and reduce, then add 400 ml (14 fl oz, 1¾ cups) stock and boil. Add 150 g (5 oz) fresh bacon rinds, cooked and cut into small pieces, and 100 g (4 oz, ¾ cup) blanched pitted green olives. Cook for a few minutes, then add the reserved liver mixture and heat without boiling. Mix well and leave to cool. Then add an equal amount of fine sausagemeat and bind with 4 eggs. Add chopped parsley and 60 ml (2 fl oz, ¼ cup) brandy, mix well and adjust the seasoning.

The day before the sucking pig is to be cooked, stuff it with this mixture. Sew it up, truss and marinate in a mixture of oil, brandy, sliced carrots and onions, crushed garlic cloves, chopped parsley, thyme, bay leaf and pepper.

On the day of cooking, lay the pig out in a large braising pan lined with bacon rinds and sliced carrots and onions (those from the marinade, with others if necessary). Do not hesitate to add plenty of vegetables, as they will be used as a garnish; small carrots and onions may be used whole. Brush the sucking pig with melted lard, cover and cook on the hob (stove top) until the vegetables begin to fry. Moisten with 300 ml (½ pint, 1¼ cups) dry white wine, reduce, then add a few tablespoons stock and a bouquet garni. Finish cooking in a preheated oven at 200°C (400°F, gas 6). The total cooking time should be about 2½ hours, when the skin will be slightly crisp.

Drain and untruss the sucking pig and lay out on a serving dish. Garnish with pork crépinettes with mixed herbs and small black puddings (blood sausages) cooked in butter. Add the sliced onions and carrots from the

braising pan and pour over the strained cooking juices. Serve with a celery
purée or mashed potatoes.

## Zampone

An Italian speciality from Modena, consisting of a boned and stuffed pig's
trotter (foot), sold ready to cook or precooked and served hot or cold. It is
stuffed with a forcemeat of pork, green (unsmoked) bacon, truffles and
seasoning, and then cured, smoked, boiled and often served with lentils.

The word comes from *zampa* (paw): a large trotter is called a *zampone*; a
small one a *zampino*.

Soak a ready-to-cook zampone in cold water for 3 hours; scrape the skin
well and prick it all over with a barding needle. Wrap it in a thin cloth, tie at
each end and in the centre, then put it into a flameproof casserole and cover
with cold water. Bring to the boil and poach for 3 hours. Serve either hot, with
mashed potatoes or lentil purée and braised spinach or cabbage; or cold,
sliced like a sausage, with parsley.

# Lamb & mutton

## Algerian lamb with prunes, tea and almonds

Bone 1 kg (2¼ lb) shoulder of lamb, remove the fat and cut the meat into large dice. Sprinkle with finely ground salt and cook it in a casserole with butter until golden brown. Drain. Add to the butter in the casserole 250 ml (8 fl oz, 1 cup) water, 1 cinnamon stick chopped into pieces, 50 g (2 oz, ½ cup) blanched almonds, 200 g (7 oz, 1 cup) caster (superfine) sugar and 2 tablespoons orange-flower water. Bring this mixture rapidly to the boil, stirring continuously. Replace the meat, cover the pan and allow to simmer over a low heat for 45 minutes. Meanwhile, soak 350 g (12 oz, 2 cups) stoned (pitted) prunes in very strong green tea. Add the prunes and tea to the casserole and cook for a further 10 minutes.

## Baekenofe

This dish, which is also known as *backenoff,* is an Alsatian stew made with an assortment of meats.

Cut 450 g (1 lb) shoulder of mutton, 450 g (1 lb) shoulder of pork and 450 g (1 lb) beef into large cubes and marinate overnight in 500 ml (17 fl oz, 2 cups) Alsace wine, 1 large finely chopped onion, 1 onion stuck with 2–3 cloves, 2 crushed garlic cloves, a bouquet garni and salt and pepper. The next day, peel and slice 2 kg (4½ lb) potatoes and 225 g (8 oz) onions. Grease a large casserole with lard, then fill with layers of the ingredients, as follows: a layer of potatoes, a layer of meat and a layer of onions. Repeat until all the ingredients have been used, ending with a layer of potatoes. Remove the bouquet garni and the onion stuck with cloves from the marinade and pour the liquid into the casserole. The liquid should just reach the top layer; if necessary, top up with water. Cover and cook in a preheated oven at about 160°C (325°F, gas 3) for 4 hours.

## Ballotine of lamb in aspic

Make a stuffing with a salpicon of pickled tongue, ham and stoned (pitted) black olives. Spread this mixture on a boned flattened shoulder of lamb, roll it up, wrap it in a piece of muslin (cheesecloth) and fasten with string. Cook the lamb in a casserole on a bed of vegetables with bacon and stock for about 1¾ hours, as in the recipe for braised ballotine of lamb. Drain and unwrap the ballotine (straining and reserving the cooking liquor), squeeze out the muslin and use it to wrap up the ballotine again. Fasten securely at both ends and in the middle and allow to cool for 12 hours under a weight. Unwrap and place in a dish. Warm the liquor and pour it over the ballotine, adding more warmed jellied stock, if necessary, to cover. Chill for at least 24 hours until firmly set before serving.

## Baron of lamb à la périgourdine

The baron is the cut of mutton or lamb that includes the saddle (loin) and both hind legs. Cook and shell 1 kg (2¼ lb) chestnuts. Cover the baron with a light even coat of butter and season with salt and pepper. Roast in a preheated oven at 200°C (400°F, gas 6) for 18–20 minutes per 450 g (1 lb). While the meat is cooking, fry some small tomatoes (preferably in goose fat) and keep warm. Repeat the process with the chestnuts. Arrange the baron on a warm plate surrounded with alternating tomatoes and chestnuts. Deglaze the dripping with boiling water and reduce until richly flavoured. Serve the meat juice in a sauce boat. The baron can also be served with potatoes lightly fried and enriched with truffle peelings.

## Blanquette of lamb à l'ancienne

This is prepared with shoulder, breast and best end (rib chops) of lamb. The stock for 1.8 kg (4 lb) lamb is made with 2 carrots cut into quarters, 2 medium onions (one stuck with a clove) and a vegetable bouquet garni consisting of 2 celery sticks and 2 small leeks (white part only). Cut the meat into 5 cm (2 in) cubes. Seal by frying the cubes in butter without browning. Cover with white stock or bouillon, season, quickly bring to the boil and skim. Simmer gently for 1½ hours. The garnish is made with 200 g (7 oz) baby onions, 200 g (7 oz) mushrooms (preferably wild) cooked in a thin white sauce, and 8 croûtons fried in butter.

Drain the meat and place in a sauté pan with the onions and mushrooms in sauce. Heat gently and, just before serving, bind the sauce with 50 g (2 oz, ¼ cup) butter and 50 g (2 oz, ½ cup) plain (all-purpose) flour for the roux, then 3 egg yolks, 150 ml (¼ pint, ⅔ cup) double (heavy) cream, the juice of ½ lemon, and a pinch of grated nutmeg. Place in a deep dish, sprinkle with parsley and garnish with the croûtons.

## Blanquette of lamb with beans and lamb's feet

Cut the meat from a shoulder of lamb into large cubes. Cover with iced water and keep for 12 hours in the refrigerator, changing the water once or twice. Soak 350 g (12 oz, 2 cups) dried white haricot (navy) beans for about 12 hours in cold water with an onion stuck with a clove, 4–5 whole carrots, a leek and a bouquet garni.

Rub 3 lamb's feet with lemon juice, blanch for 10 minutes in boiling water, refresh with cold water and trim. Make a paste of 1 tablespoon flour, lemon juice and water in a pan. Add the feet, together with 2 carrots, an onion, a bouquet garni and some peppercorns, and simmer for about 2 hours. When the feet are cooked, drain, skin and dice the flesh.

Cook the beans with the flavouring ingredients for about 1½ hours, skimming frequently at first, and add salt after 15 minutes.

Drain the pieces of lamb shoulder. Start cooking them in cold water and add a lamb stock (bouillon) cube, 2 carrots, an onion, a bouquet garni, peppercorns and a little salt. Simmer for about 1½ hours. When cooked, drain the pieces of lamb and arrange them in a large dish. Reduce the cooking liquor to 1 litre (1¾ pints, 4⅓ cups). In a separate pan, mix together 300 ml (½ pint, 1¼ cups) double (heavy) cream, 3 tablespoons Dijon mustard and 4 egg yolks. Pour the sieved reduced cooking liquor on to the mixture and heat gently, stirring constantly. Season with salt and pepper. As soon as the mixture approaches boiling, strain it over the pieces of lamb. Drain the beans and mix them and the diced feet with the blanquette.

## Boiled leg of lamb with caper sauce

This classic British dish was traditionally prepared with mutton. The meat must be cooked gently so that it becomes tender and succulent. Season a trimmed leg of lamb, wrap in a buttered and lightly floured muslin cloth (cheesecloth) and tie up with string. Put it into a pan of boiling salted water, together with 2 carrots cut into quarters, 2 onions (one studded with a clove), a bouquet garni and a garlic clove. Simmer gently but steadily, allowing 30 minutes per 1 kg (15 minutes per 1 lb) or until tender and cooked through. Drain, unwrap and place on a long serving dish.

For the sauce, prepare a roux with 40 g (1½ oz, 3 tablespoons) butter and 40 g (1½ oz, 6 tablespoons) plain (all-purpose) flour. Gradually stir in 300 ml (½ pint, 1¼ cups) milk and 300 ml (½ pint, 1¼ cups) cooking stock from the lamb. Bring to the boil, then simmer for 3 minutes. Stir in 4 tablespoons capers and seasoning to taste. This dish may be accompanied by a purée of turnips or celeriac (celery root), cooked with the leg of mutton, potatoes or white haricot (navy) beans. Broad beans are also a delicious accompaniment.

In Provence, leg of lamb is boiled in a reduced stock. The meat is served pink with the pot vegetables and aïoli. In Normandy, near Yvetot, leg of lamb is cooked in a vegetable stock flavoured with a tablespoon of Calvados. It is served with pot vegetables and a white sauce with capers.

## Braised ballotine of lamb

Ask the butcher to bone a shoulder of lamb. To prepare the stuffing, first finely chop 3 onions, and cook in 20 g (¾ oz, 1½ tablespoons) butter until soft. Mince together a bunch of parsley and 2 garlic cloves. Combine this mixture with the onions, 450 g (1 lb) sausagemeat and salt and pepper and work together by hand or in a food processor. Open out the boned shoulder, spread with the stuffing, then roll up and tie with string.

Dice 100 g (4 oz) carrots, 3 onions, 1 celery stick and 100 g (4 oz) bacon. Melt 25 g (1 oz, 2 tablespoons) butter in a large flameproof casserole and brown the stuffed lamb. Remove and set aside. Cook the vegetable mixture in the butter remaining in the pan until soft. Add a small sprig of thyme, then replace the vegetables. Add 200 ml (7 fl oz, ¾ cup) dry white wine, 200 ml (7 fl oz, ¾ cup) stock or meat juices, a bouquet garni, salt and pepper. Bring to the boil and cook, uncovered, for 5 minutes. Turn the shoulder over in the vegetables, cover the casserole and continue cooking in a preheated oven at 200°C (400°F, gas 6) for 1½ hours. Remove the bouquet garni. Untie the ballotine and serve very hot, either on its own or with spinach, mixed vegetables, noodles, pilaf or risotto.

## Braised leg of lamb à la bordelaise

Cook a leg of lamb in a mixture of butter and oil in a covered casserole in a preheated oven at 180°C (350°F, gas 4), allowing 40 minutes per 1 kg or

20 minutes per 1 lb, plus an additional 40 or 20 minutes. When the lamb is one-third done, add 575 g (1¼ lb) tiny potato balls and 250 g (9 oz) fresh cep or button mushrooms, lightly tossed in oil and season with salt and pepper. When the leg and garnish are cooked, sprinkle with noisette butter in which 4 tablespoons breadcrumbs and 1 tablespoon chopped parsley and garlic have been fried.

## Braised leg of lamb with spring onions

Calculate the cooking time for a leg of lamb at 40 minutes per 1 kg, 20 minutes per 1 lb, plus an additional 40 or 20 minutes. Cook the lamb in a covered flameproof casserole in a preheated oven at 200°C (400°F, gas 6) for 25 minutes, then drain. Melt some butter in the casserole. Lightly coat 1 kg (2¼ lb) spring onions (scallions) in sugar, then fry them in the butter. Place the leg of lamb on the onions and put the casserole back in the oven. When the onions have softened, add 2 tomatoes, peeled and cut into 8 pieces, and 500 ml (17 fl oz, 2 cups) white wine. Complete the cooking process, turning the leg to make sure it is browned all over and basting it as required with reduced beef stock.

Remove the leg of lamb from the casserole, draining off all the cooking liquor. Drain the spring onions. Cover both and keep hot. Thicken the cooking juices with beurre manié. Carve the lamb. Arrange the spring onions on plates and coat with the sauce. Arrange the lamb on the plates and serve.

## Braised mutton cutlets

Trim some thick cutlets and season with salt and pepper. Butter a shallow frying pan, line it with bacon rinds from which all the fat has been removed and add some thinly sliced carrot and onion. Arrange the cutlets in the pan, cover and cook gently for 10 minutes. Add enough white wine just to cover, then reduce with the lid removed. Moisten with a few spoonfuls of brown gravy or stock, add a bouquet garni and cook with the lid on for about 45 minutes. Drain the cutlets and keep them hot on the serving dish. Surround with boiled Brussels sprouts (the garnish may also consist of chestnuts, sautéed potatoes or a vegetable purée). Reduce the braising stock, strain it, and pour it over the cutlets.

## Braised shoulder of lamb

Bone a shoulder of lamb, trim it, season with salt and pepper, roll it up and tie with string. Crush the bones and brown them in butter with the trimmings. Trim the fat off some pork rind and line a braising pan with the rind. Peel and finely slice 2 carrots and 1 onion, cook in butter for 10 minutes, then add to the braising pan. Put the shoulder in the braising pan and season with salt and pepper. Add 150 ml (¼ pint, ⅔ cup) white wine and reduce. Add 250 ml (8 fl oz, 1 cup) thickened gravy, 100 ml (4 fl oz, 7 tablespoons) tomato purée, 1 bouquet garni and the bones and trimmings. Cover and cook in a preheated oven at 220°C (425°F, gas 7) for about 1–1½ hours, depending on the size of the joint. Drain it, glaze in the oven, then arrange it on a serving dish.

The usual garnish consists of green or white haricot (navy) beans, vegetable purées, artichoke hearts or haricot bean purée *à la bretonne*. It can also be served with mushrooms *à la bordelaise*, together with the cooking juices deglazed with red wine and demi-glace and flavoured with shallot, thyme and bay leaf.

## Breaded lamb cutlets

Season the cutlets (rib chops) with salt and pepper and coat them with a beaten egg, then with breadcrumbs. Sauté on both sides in clarified butter, then arrange in a crown in a serving dish and sprinkle with noisette butter.

## Chump end of lamb Belle Otéro

Bone a chump end of lamb weighing 2.25 kg (5 lb). Make a stock with 250 g (9 oz, 1½ cups) finely diced trimmings browned in butter with the bones, 1 carrot and 1 medium-sized onion (cut up into small pieces), and season with salt and pepper. After browning, add 100 ml (4 fl oz, 7 tablespoons) white wine. Reduce, then add 300 ml (½ pint, 1¼ cups) stock; simmer for 1 hour, then pass through a fine sieve.

Prepare the forcemeat. Finely dice 1 onion, 1 celery stick and 1 carrot, and cook gently in a knob of butter. Add 100 g (4 oz) whole truffles, and then 100 ml (4 fl oz, 7 tablespoons) port and 200 ml (7 fl oz, ¾ cup) of the strained stock. Season with salt and freshly ground pepper. Cook for 15 minutes. Take the truffles out and reduce the liquid. Prepare a duxelles with 500 g (18 oz, 6 cups) button mushrooms (cleaned and finely chopped, then wrung out in a cloth to extract all their juice) cooked for 10 minutes in butter with 4 chopped shallots, salt, pepper and nutmeg. To the duxelles, add 50 g (2 oz, ⅔ cup) cooked diced truffles and 65 g (2½ oz) foie gras cut into matchsticks. Bind with a little of the truffle cooking liquid and season with salt and pepper.

Stuff the lamb with this forcemeat, then arrange the remaining truffles on top, together with another 65 g (2½ oz) foie gras matchsticks. Roll and tie up the meat, wrap it in barding, then tie it up again. Roast for 50 minutes in a preheated oven at 220°C (425°F, gas 7). Serve the meat juices mixed with the truffle juices in a sauceboat. Untie the string, remove the barding and garnish the meat with bunches of buttered asparagus tips or braised artichoke hearts.

## Chump end of lamb Callas

Bone a chump end of lamb weighing about 2.75 kg (6 lb), trim the excess fat and season with salt and pepper. Prepare a mushroom julienne, cook it in butter and leave it to cool. Also prepare a julienne of fresh truffles. Put the truffle julienne down the centre of the meat with the mushroom julienne on each side. Roll and tie up the joint. Roast in a preheated oven at 220°C (425°F, gas 7), allowing 12 minutes per 450 g (1 lb). Deglaze the roasting pan with a little veal stock and sherry. Serve with buttered asparagus tips.

## Epigrammes

A dish consisting of two cuts of lamb, both cooked dry. These two pieces are a slice of breast and a cutlet or chop, dipped in egg and breadcrumbs and grilled (broiled) or fried.

Braise a breast of lamb, or poach it in a small quantity of light stock. Drain and bone the meat, and cool it in a press. Cut it into equal portions and coat with egg and breadcrumbs. Coat the same number of lamb cutlets with egg and breadcrumbs. Grill (broil) the cutlets and breast portions or fry them in butter and oil, and arrange in a round dish. Garnish the cutlet bones with paper frills, then put a few spoonfuls of reduced and sieved braising stock around the épigrammes. Garnish with glazed vegetables (carrots, turnips and baby onions), mushrooms, tomatoes fried in oil, or aubergine (eggplant) fritters, arranged in the centre of the dish.

## Falettes

Bone and season 2 breasts of mutton. Make a stuffing with 300 g (11 oz, 4 cups) chopped Swiss chard leaves, 200 g (7 oz, 2½ cups) spinach, 50 g (2 oz, 1 cup) fresh parsley, 2 garlic cloves and 1 large onion. Mix the ingredients with 100 g (4 oz, 4 slices) crustless bread soaked in milk and 100 g (4 oz, 2 cup) sausagemeat. Season with salt and pepper.

Flatten out the boned breasts on top of some bacon rashers (slices). Spread the stuffing along the length of each breast and roll up, including the bacon, then tie. Brown the falettes in a flameproof casserole with 200 g (7 oz,

1½ cups) sliced onions and 100 g (4 oz, 1 cup) sliced carrots. Deglaze the casserole with some white wine and add a generous quantity of mutton stock. Add ½ garlic clove and a bouquet garni, and cook, covered, in a preheated oven at 180°C (350°F, gas 4) for 2½ hours.

Meanwhile, soak 500 g (1 lb 2 oz, 2½ cups) haricot (navy) beans in cold water for 2 hours. Drain and boil in fresh water for 10 minutes. Drain and cool quickly by rinsing under the cold tap.

Sauté 100 g (4 oz, ¾ cup) sliced onions, 100 g (4 oz, ¾ cup) chopped Auvergne ham and 100 g (4 oz, ¾ cup) chopped tomatoes in a large saucepan until soft. Add the beans, a bouquet garni and enough mutton stock to cover the beans generously. Bring to the boil, reduce the heat and cover the pan. Then simmer gently for about 1½ hours.

Remove the falettes from the casserole and leave to cool briefly; then untie them, remove the bacon and cut them into slices. Strain and reduce the cooking liquid and pour it over the sliced falettes. Serve the beans separately.

## Grilled lamb cutlets

Season the cutlets (rib chops) with salt and pepper, brush them with melted butter or groundnut (peanut) oil, and cook either over a barbecue or under the grill (broiler). Arrange on a serving dish: the protruding 'handle' bone may be covered with a white paper frill. Garnish with watercress or with a green vegetable, which may be steamed (and tossed in butter or cream if desired), braised, puréed or sautéed. Serve with noisette potatoes.

## Grilled lamb cutlets à la paloise

Prepare some noisette potatoes and some French (green) beans in cream and keep hot. Season some lamb cutlets (chops) that have the bone end exposed with salt and pepper, coat them very lightly with olive oil and grill (broil) them quickly on both sides. Garnish the bone ends with white paper frills and arrange the cutlets in a crown on a large round serving dish. Place the beans in the centre and arrange the potatoes in clusters between the cutlets.

## Grilled loin of lamb

Trim the bones of a loin of lamb and lightly score its skin in a criss-cross pattern. Season with salt and pepper and brush with melted butter. Cook very slowly on both sides, either under the grill (broiler) or over a barbecue well away from the source of heat, until the meat is cooked through. Garnish with watercress or young vegetables and serve with maître d'hôtel butter.

## Grilled shoulder of lamb

Trim the bone, make incisions in the flesh on both sides, brush with melted butter or oil, and grill (broil) the lamb under a medium heat for 20–25 minutes. Sprinkle with breadcrumbs and melted butter and brown under the grill. Garnish with bunches of watercress.

## Halicot of mutton

Cut about 800 g (1¾ lb) neck or breast of mutton into pieces. Season and put into a casserole with 4 tablespoons oil. Add a large sliced onion, 1 teaspoon granulated sugar and 3 level tablespoons plain (all-purpose) flour. Stir thoroughly. Then add 3 tablespoons tomato purée (paste) diluted with a little stock. Completely cover the meat with more stock, stir well, add a small crushed garlic clove and a bouquet garni, and cook for 45 minutes. Skim the fat from the sauce and add 500 g (18 oz) potatoes cut into quarters or neat oval shapes, 400 g (14 oz) small turnips and 200 g (7 oz) small peeled onions. Add sufficient stock to cover the vegetables and continue to cook for about 40 minutes until the meat is tender.

## Kurdish milk lamb

Ask your butcher to dress a whole baby lamb ready for stuffing and spit-roasting. Finely slice the liver, heart, sweetbreads and kidneys, and fry quickly in butter, seasoning with salt and pepper. Add these to half-cooked rice pilaf with some cooked and chopped dried apricots and loosely stuff the lamb cavity with the mixture. Sew up the openings and truss the animal by tying the legs and shoulders close to the body to give it a regular shape. Pierce the lamb evenly with the spit, season with salt and pepper, and cook over a high heat (20 minutes per 1 kg, 15 minutes per 1 lb). Place a pan under the lamb to catch the juices. When the lamb is cooked, blend sufficient stock into the pan juices to make a gravy and keep it hot. Remove the lamb from the spit, untruss it and place it on a long serving dish. Garnish with watercress and lemon quarters and serve the gravy separately.

## Lamb brochettes

Cut some well-trimmed fillet or leg of lamb into 5 mm (¼ in) thick pieces. Thread the pieces of meat on to skewers, alternating with blanched bacon strips and sliced wild mushrooms (optional) tossed in butter. Season with salt and pepper. Brush the brochettes with melted butter, roll in white breadcrumbs, sprinkle again with butter, then grill (broil) under a high heat.

## Lamb (or mutton) chops Maintenon

Maintenon is the name given to a savoury dish made with mushrooms, onions and béchamel sauce, sometimes containing truffles, tongue and chicken breasts.

To make the Maintenon mixture, clean and slice 150 g (5 oz, 2 cups) mushrooms and sweat in 15 g (½ oz, 1 tablespoon) butter. Prepare a Soubise purée by puréeing 500 g (18 oz, 4½ cups) sliced onions, blanched and sweated in butter, and 500 ml (17 fl oz, 2 cups) thick béchamel sauce. Season with salt and pepper, and a little grated nutmeg. Add the mushrooms to the purée and bind with 2 egg yolks. Check the seasoning.

Quickly brown the chops in butter on one side only. Coat the cooked side of each chop with 1 tablespoon Maintenon mixture, shape into a dome, and coat with breadcrumbs. Lavishly butter a baking dish and arrange the chops on it. Sprinkle with melted butter and cook in a preheated oven at 240°C (475°F, gas 9) until golden. Serve with Périgueux sauce.

## Lamb curry

Mix 1 tablespoon grated fresh root ginger (or 1 teaspoon ground ginger), a pinch of saffron, 3 tablespoons oil, a large pinch of cayenne, salt and pepper. In this mixture, roll 1.5 kg (3¼ lb) neck or shoulder of lamb cut up into pieces, and leave to marinate for 1 hour. Peel and crush 3 large tomatoes. Brown the pieces of meat in a large saucepan containing 25 g (1 oz, 2 tablespoons) lard (shortening), then remove from the pan.

In the same fat, fry 4 large sliced onions until golden, then add the crushed tomatoes, the ginger mixture, 3 finely chopped garlic cloves and a bouquet garni. Leave to brown for 5 minutes. Peel and grate an acid apple, add to the pan and stir for 2–3 minutes. Replace the meat in the pan, stir, add a small cup of coconut milk or semi-skimmed milk, cover and leave to finish cooking gently for about 40 minutes. Adjust the seasoning.

Serve this curry very hot with boiled rice, cashew nuts, raisins, and pineapple and banana dice tossed in lemon juice, all in separate dishes.

## Lamb cutlets à la maréchale

In classic cuisine, *à la maréchale* describes small cuts of meat (such as lamb chops or noisettes, veal escalopes (scallops) or cutlets, calves' sweetbreads, or poultry suprêmes) that are coated with breadcrumbs and sautéed. They are garnished with bundles of asparagus tips and a slice of truffle on each item and served in a ring of thickened chateaubriand sauce or veal gravy.

Braise some asparagus tips in butter. Cut a truffle into thin strips and braise in butter for 2 minutes. Prepare a liquid maître d'hôtel butter. Season the cutlets with salt and pepper, coat them with breadcrumbs, and sauté them in clarified butter. Arrange the cutlets in a crown, garnish each one with a strip of truffle, and place the asparagus tips between the cutlets. Serve with the maître d'hôtel butter in a sauceboat. Very finely chopped truffle parings may be added to the breadcrumb coating.

## Lamb cutlets Du Barry

Boil or steam small florets of cauliflower until just tender. Prepare some Mornay sauce. Butter a gratin dish and arrange the florets, well separated, in it. Coat each floret with Mornay sauce, sprinkle with grated Parmesan cheese and pour over a little melted butter. Brown the cauliflower quickly in a preheated oven at 220°C (425°F, gas 7). Grill (broil) or sauté the cutlets (rib chops) until cooked through, then arrange in the dish with the cauliflower.

## Lamb cutlets Pompadour

Braise the cutlets, which should come from the fillet end and be trimmed of fat, and allow to cool. Mask with a well-reduced Soubise purée and leave until cold. Coat with fine breadcrumbs and then beaten egg. Lightly brown the cutlets in clarified butter and serve with lemon quarters.

## Lamb cutlets with figs and honey

Wash and wipe 1 kg (2¼ lb) fresh figs, but do not peel. Place them, stalks upwards, in a generously buttered ovenproof dish. Cover with a glass of water, add some pepper and a little ground cinnamon and grated nutmeg, and cook in a preheated oven at 200°C (400°F, gas 6) for 30–35 minutes. About 10 minutes before the end of the cooking time, melt 40 g (1½ oz, 3 table-spoons) butter in a frying pan and fry 4–8 lamb cutlets (depending on their size) for 3–4 minutes per side. Season with salt and pepper and arrange the cutlets in a warmed serving dish. Keep hot. Melt 2 tablespoons honey in a little hot water and add the pan juices from the cutlets to make a sauce. Adjust the seasoning. Arrange the figs around the meat. Coat the cutlets and the figs with honey sauce. Serve immediately.

## Lamb cutlets with hop shoots

Sauté some lamb cutlets in butter. Meanwhile, prepare hop shoots in cream by dropping the hop shoots into salted boiling water. Remove them while they are still firm. Drain, braise in butter in a covered pan, then add (200 ml (7 fl oz, ¾ cup) double (heavy) cream per 350 (12 oz) hop shoots. Arrange the lamb cutlets in a ring on a round dish, alternating with triangular croûtons fried in butter. Place the hops in the centre. Deglaze the cooking juices in the sauté pan with a little dry white wine and pour over the cutlets.

## Lamb fricassée

Fry some pieces of lamb (fillet, lean leg or shoulder) in butter without brown-ing and season with salt and pepper. Sprinkle with 2 tablespoons flour and stir over the heat. Add some white stock or consommé and a bouquet garni, and bring to the boil. Simmer with the lid on for 45–60 minutes. Fry some mushrooms in butter and glaze some button onions. Remove the lamb from the pan and keep warm, and stir the onions and mushrooms into the pan juices. Take off the heat and add an egg yolk to thicken. Pour the sauce into a large heated dish, add the lamb and sprinkle with chopped parsley. Serve hot.

## Lamb noisettes à la turque

Prepare some rice pilaf and sauté some diced aubergine (eggplant) flesh in oil. Fry the lamb noisettes in butter and arrange in a serving dish; garnish with the aubergine and the rice pilaf moulded in darioles. Keep hot. Dilute the pan juices with tomato-flavoured veal stock and pour over the noisettes.

## Lamb noisettes Melba

Stuff 8 small tomatoes with a salpicon of chicken and mushrooms bound with velouté sauce. Brown in the oven or under the grill (broiler) and keep warm. Fry 8 croûtons cut the same size as the noisettes. Sauté the noisettes in butter and arrange them on the croûtons on a serving dish. Keep warm.

Deglaze the sauté pan with 350 ml (12 fl oz, 1½ cups) stock and boil down to reduce by three-quarters. Blend 1 tablespoon arrowroot with 175 ml (6 fl oz, ¾ cup) Madeira, pour the mixture into the sauté pan and whisk until the sauce thickens. Add 20 g (¾ oz, 4½ teaspoons) butter, cut into small pieces, and continue whisking. Pour the sauce over the noisettes and arrange the stuffed tomatoes in a circle around them.

## Léa's roast leg of lamb

Crush 4 anchovy fillets in 4 tablespoons olive oil mixed with 2 level tablespoons mustard, sage, basil, rosemary and crushed garlic. Rub the meat with this mixture and marinate for 2 hours, turning from time to time. Calculate the cooking time for the lamb at 30–40 minutes per 1 kg, 15–20 minutes per 1 lb, plus an additional 30–40 or 15–20 minutes, according to how well cooked you require the meat to be when served. Drain and roast in a preheated oven at 200°C (400°F, gas 6).

Meanwhile, boil down the marinade with some butter, slowly adding half a bottle of champagne. Strain and thicken with softened butter.

## Leg of mutton en chevreuil

Prepare an en chevreuil marinade. Bone a fine leg of mutton and lard it with thin strips of bacon. Marinate the mutton for between 36 hours (in summer) and 3 days (in winter), turning it over several times. Wipe, then roast in a preheated oven at 200°C (400°F, gas 6). Serve with roebuck or poivrade sauce.

## Loin of lamb à la bonne femme

Lightly brown a dozen button onions in melted butter and set aside. Cut 250 g (9 oz) potatoes into large olive-shaped pieces. Coarsely chop 50 g (2 oz) unsalted streaky (slab) bacon. Blanch the bacon for 1 minute in boiling water, then drain, pat dry and lightly fry in butter with the potatoes. Shorten and trim the bones of a 1 kg (2¼ lb) loin of lamb. Brown the meat on all sides in butter over a fairly high heat, then place it in a large casserole, season with salt and pepper, and add the onions, bacon pieces and potatoes. Spoon 1–2 tablespoons melted butter over the meat, cover the casserole and cook in a preheated oven at 180°C (350°F, gas 4) for about 1 hour until the lamb is cooked. Serve the lamb in slices with the casserole vegetables and juices spooned round.

## Loin of lamb à la bordelaise

Cut 250 g (9 oz) potatoes into large olive-shaped pieces. Slice 225 g (8 oz) mushrooms (preferably cep mushrooms) and fry them quickly in a little oil. Shorten and trim the bones of a 1 kg (2¼ lb) loin of lamb, then brown on all sides in equal quantities of melted butter and oil. Place the meat in a large casserole with the mushrooms and potatoes, and season. Cover and cook the meat in a preheated oven at 180°C (350°F, gas 4) for about 1 hour, then add a small, crushed garlic clove mixed with several tablespoons stock and a little tomato purée (paste). Continue to cook until the lamb is tender.

## Loin of lamb Clamart

Shorten and trim the bones of a 1 kg (2¼ lb) loin of lamb, then brown the loin in butter in a flameproof casserole. Season with salt and pepper, then spoon over a little melted butter, cover and cook in a preheated oven at 180°C (350°F, gas 4) for about 1 hour. When the meat is cooked, add to the casserole 350 g (12 oz, 2½ cups) fresh garden peas cooked *à la française* and simmer for about 5 minutes.

## Loin of lamb en crépine

Soak a pig's caul (caul fat) in cold water. Braise a trimmed 1 kg (2¼ lb) loin of lamb in a preheated oven at 180°C (350°F, gas 4) for about 1 hour until just cooked. Leave until cold, then thinly coat it on both sides with finely minced (ground) pork stuffing to which diced truffles have been added. Roughly dry the caul, spread it out, place the loin on it, wrap it up and brush with melted butter. Slowly grill (broil) the wrapped meat on all sides to cook the stuffing.

## Loin of lamb La Varenne

Trim and completely bone a loin of sucking lamb. Flatten it slightly and season with salt and pepper. Dip it in beaten egg and cover with finely crumbled fresh breadcrumbs (press the breadcrumbs well in to make them stick). Cook the loin in clarified butter, allowing it to turn golden on both sides. Prepare a salpicon of mushrooms bound lightly with cream and coat the serving dish with it; place the loin on top. Moisten with noisette butter and serve piping hot.

## Loin of lamb Parmentier

Brown a trimmed loin of lamb in 25–40 g (1–1½ oz, 2–3 tablespoons) butter in a flameproof casserole. Add 400 g (14 oz, 2 cups) peeled, diced potatoes,

3 tablespoons melted butter and season with salt and pepper. Place the casserole in a preheated oven at 220°C (425°F, gas 7) and cook for about 45 minutes. Drain the meat and the potatoes and keep them hot in the serving dish. Deglaze the casserole with 4 tablespoons white wine and the same amount of stock (traditionally veal stock); reduce. Pour this sauce over the lamb and sprinkle with chopped parsley.

## Mignonettes of milk lamb

Season 8 noisettes of lamb with salt and pepper, sprinkle them with a little thyme and rosemary, and marinate them for 24 hours in grapeseed oil. Drain them and coat lightly with strong mustard. Add 1 tablespoon chopped shallot to 5 tablespoons white wine vinegar mixed with 5 tablespoons white wine and an equal quantity of beef stock. Boil down over a brisk heat until almost dry, add 575 ml (19 fl oz, 2½ cups) double (heavy) cream, and season with salt and pepper. Grill (broil) the noisettes briskly for about 2 minutes on each side. Put them in the sauce and cook, uncovered, until reduced.

## Minute sauté of lamb

Cut 800 g (1¾ lb) shoulder of lamb into small pieces and sauté in butter or oil over a brisk heat for 8 minutes. Season with salt and pepper. When the meat is well browned, add the juice of ½ lemon, turn into a hot dish and sprinkle with chopped parsley.

## Moussaka

Fry 1 large chopped onion, 2 crushed garlic cloves and 1 bay leaf in olive oil for about 15 minutes, until tender, but not browned. Add 450 g (1 lb) minced (ground) lamb and cook, stirring, until the lamb has browned. Add 1 teaspoon dried oregano, 1 teaspoon ground cinnamon and salt and pepper.

Peel and chop 450 g (1 lb) tomatoes and add to the meat mixture with 250 ml (8 fl oz, 1 cup) lamb or beef stock. Bring to the boil, then reduce the heat and cover the pan. Simmer gently for about 30 minutes.

Meanwhile, slice 2 large aubergines (eggplants). Lightly fry the aubergine slices in olive oil until lightly browned on both sides. Do this in batches, setting aside the slices on a plate as they are cooked. Layer the aubergine slices and minced meat mixture in a large ovenproof dish, ending with a layer of aubergines. Beat 2 eggs with 2 tablespoons flour, salt, pepper and a little grated nutmeg. Stir in 600 ml (1 pint, 2½ cups) yogurt. Pour this mixture over the top of the moussaka. Bake in a preheated oven at 180°C (350°F, gas 4) for about 1 hour, until the topping is set and golden brown. Allow to stand for 15 minutes before serving to give the layers time to settle.

## Mutton broth

Finely dice 1 carrot, 1 turnip, the white part of 2 leeks, 1 celery stick and 1 onion. Soften this brunoise in butter, then add 2 litres (3½ pints, 9 cups) white consommé. Add 300 g (11 oz) breast and collar of mutton and 100 g (4 oz, ½ cup) pearl barley blanched for 8 minutes in boiling water. Cover and cook gently for 1½ hours. Remove and dice the meat and put back in the soup. Sprinkle with chopped parsley just before serving.

## Mutton cutlets à la fermière

Season 6 thick cutlets with salt and pepper. Fry them lightly in butter in a shallow flameproof serving dish. Add 300 ml (½ pint, 1¼ cups) vegetable fondue, 6 tablespoons fresh green peas and 150 ml (¼ pint, ⅔ cup) white wine. Reduce, then add a bouquet garni and 200 ml (7 fl oz, ¾ cup) brown stock and cook covered for 20 minutes. Add 20 small potatoes and continue cooking with the lid on for a further 35 minutes. Serve in the cooking dish.

## Mutton cutlets à la Villeroi

Braise the cutlets and leave them to cool in their stock. Remove them with a slotted spoon and pat dry then coat them in Villeroi sauce and dip them in beaten egg and breadcrumbs. Fry until golden in clarified butter and serve with a Périgueux or a tomato sauce.

## Mutton cutlets champvallon

Peel 800 g (1¾ lb) potatoes and cut them into round slices. Peel and chop 125 g (4½ oz, ¾ cup) onions and 1 garlic clove. Brown 6 trimmed mutton cutlets (rib chops) in 20 g (¾ oz, 1½ tablespoons) butter, drain them and then soften the onions in the same butter with the lid on the pan. Place the onions in a buttered dish and arrange the chops on top. Sprinkle a little thyme, salt and pepper over the chops. Cover with 100 ml (4 fl oz, 7 tablespoons) stock and a further 20 g (¾ oz, 1½ tablespoons) melted butter. Place in a preheated oven at 240°C (475°F, gas 9) and cook for 20–25 minutes. Then arrange the potatoes over the chops, season with salt and pepper, and add the same amount of stock and melted butter as before. Return to the oven and cook for about 25 minutes.

## Mutton cutlets chasseur

Sauté 6 cutlets in butter in a shallow frying pan, then remove them with a slotted spoon and keep them hot. Place 1 tablespoon chopped shallots and 6 large thinly sliced mushrooms in the frying pan and stir for a few moments over a brisk heat. Sprinkle with 150 ml (¼ pint, ⅔ cup) white wine and reduce until almost dry. Pour in 250 ml (8 fl oz, 1 cup) thickened brown stock and 1 tablespoon tomato sauce, boil for a few moments, then add 15 g (½ oz, 1 tablespoon butter) and ½ teaspoon chopped chervil and tarragon. Place the cutlets on a serving dish and coat with this sauce.

## Mutton fillets in red wine

Cut the mutton fillets into small squares. Season with salt and pepper, then cook quickly in very hot butter, keeping them slightly pink inside. Drain them and set aside. In the same butter quickly cook (for 6 fillets) 125 g (4½ oz, 1½ cups) thinly sliced mushrooms and add them to the meat. Make a sauce by adding 300 ml (½ pint, 1¼ cups) red wine to the pan juices, reduce, then add several spoonfuls of brown veal gravy. Reduce once again, add some butter and strain. Mix the meat and the mushrooms with this sauce and serve hot.

## Navarin of lamb

Cut 800 g (1¾ lb) shoulder of lamb into 6 pieces and 800 g (1¾ lb) neck of lamb into 6 slices. Heat 2 tablespoons oil in a large flamepoof casserole. Brown the pieces and slices of lamb in it. Take out, drain and remove two-thirds of the fat. Put the meat back in the casserole and sprinkle with 1 teaspoon sugar. Stir well, sprinkle in 1 tablespoon flour and cook for 3 minutes while stirring all the time. Add 200 ml (7 fl oz, ¾ cup) white wine and season with salt, pepper and nutmeg. Cook over a moderate heat.

Peel, seed and crush 2 tomatoes. Peel and chop 2 garlic cloves. Add these ingredients to the casserole with a bouquet garni and enough water to cover the meat. As soon as it starts boiling, cover the casserole, reduce the heat and simmer for 45 minutes.

Peel and scrape 300 g (11 oz) new carrots and 200 g (7 oz) new turnips. Peel 100 g (4 oz) small white onions. Brown all these vegetables in 25 g (1 oz, 2 tablespoons) butter in sauté pan. Cut 300 g (11 oz) French (green) beans into short lengths and steam for 10–12 minutes. Add the carrots, turnips, onions and 300 g (11 oz, 2 cups) shelled petits pois to the casserole. Stir and cover again. Continue cooking for 20–25 minutes. Add the French (green) beans 5 minutes before serving and stir in very gently. Serve very hot.

## Noisettes Beauharnais

Braise some small artichoke hearts in butter. In another pan, sauté some lamb noisettes in butter, arrange them on fried croûtons then set aside and keep hot. Prepare some noisette potatoes and a béarnaise sauce, and pour the sauce over the artichoke hearts. Deglaze the meat pan with Madeira, boil down to reduce and add some chopped mushrooms. Arrange the noisettes on a serving dish with the artichoke hearts and the noisette potatoes and cover with the sauce.

## Noisettes chasseur

Sauté 8 lamb noisettes in a mixture of oil and butter, then drain. Add 100 g (4 oz, 1⅓ cups) finely sliced mushrooms and 1 tablespoon chopped shallots to the pan, deglaze with white wine and moisten with veal stock to which a little tomato sauce has been added. Arrange the meat on a hot dish, garnish with the mushrooms and pour the sauce over.

## Noisettes of the Tour d'Argent

Sauté some lamb noisettes in clarified butter and arrange them on a hot dish. Deglaze the cooking pan with a mixture comprising equal quantities of vermouth, sherry and veal stock. Thicken with butter. Put 1 teaspoon Soubise purée on each noisette and grill (broil) for a few seconds. Serve the sauce separately.

## Noisettes Rivoli

Prepare some pommes Anna and arrange them on a serving dish. Sauté some lamb noisettes in butter and place them on top of the potatoes. Deglaze the meat pan with Madeira and (if possible) with some demi-glace sauce, then add some finely diced mushrooms. Pour this sauce over the lamb.

## Oiseaux sans tête

Bone a shoulder of mutton or lamb and cut it into 8 slices. Beat them, trim the edges and season with salt and pepper. Make a stuffing from breadcrumbs (soaked in milk and squeezed dry) and plenty of finely chopped parsley, chives, chervil and tarragon and a raw egg. Put some of this stuffing in the centre of each slice of meat and roll it up. Put a small sprig of rosemary on top of each roll and wrap it in a piece of caul fat, preferably lamb's. Fry 250 g (9 oz, 3 cups) chopped mushrooms in a mixture of butter and oil, drain them and spread them over the bottom of an ovenproof dish. Arrange the rolls side by side on top of the onions. Cover with buttered greaseproof (wax) paper and cook in a preheated oven at 220°C (425°F, gas 7) for 25 minutes.

Just before serving, mix ½ teaspoon curry powder with a little crème fraîche. Pour this sauce over the rolls and serve.

## Pascaline

This method of preparing lamb was formerly traditional on Easter Day.

Truss a 6-month-old lamb to give a neat shape. Stuff with a forcemeat made of pounded lamb's flesh, yolks of hard-boiled (hard-cooked) eggs, stale breadcrumbs and chopped herbs, seasoned with *quatre epices* or four spices. Cover the lamb with thin strips of bacon, roast it over a brisk fire and serve it whole as a main dish following the soup, either with a green sauce or on a ragoût of truffles with ham coulis.

## Paupiettes of lamb à la créole

Cut 6 even slices from a leg of lamb. Flatten them well and season with salt and pepper. Peel and chop 6 large onions. Seed, then chop 1 large green (bell) pepper into very small dice. Gently cook half the onions and all the pepper in 25 g (1 oz, 2 tablespoons) butter. Add 350 g (12 oz, 1¾ cups) fine pork forcemeat and season with salt and pepper. Spread the forcemeat evenly over the slices of lamb, roll them up and tie with string. Brown the paupiettes in a casserole with 25 g (1 oz, 2 tablespoons) butter and the remaining onions, cook until brown, then add 3 peeled tomatoes (seeded and chopped), some chopped parsley, 1 small crushed garlic clove, 1 piece of lemon rind, some salt and pepper and a little cayenne. Cover and cook in a preheated oven at 200°C (400°F, gas 6) for 45 minutes.

Drain the paupiettes, arrange them in a circle on a serving dish and keep warm. Reduce the pan juices until thickened, add 1 tablespoon rum, strain and use to coat the paupiettes. Fill the centre of the dish with rice *à la créole*.

## Rack of lamb à la languedocienne

Lightly brown a rack of lamb, trimmed and bones shortened, in goose fat. Add 12 small onions tossed in butter with 12 small pieces of raw smoked ham, 6 blanched garlic cloves and 200 g (7 oz) ceps or small mushrooms sautéed in oil. Season with salt and pepper. Arrange the meat and its garnish in a flameproof dish and cook in a preheated oven at 150°C (300°F, gas 2) for about 45 minutes, basting frequently. If necessary, cover with foil towards the end of the cooking time. Sprinkle with chopped parsley and serve.

## Rack of lamb à la niçoise

Trim a rack of lamb and calculate the cooking time at 15 minutes per 450 g (1 lb). Brown the lamb lightly in butter in a flameproof casserole. Add a coarsely diced, peeled courgette (zucchini) fried quickly in olive oil, a large, peeled, seeded, chopped tomato fried in olive oil, and 20 or so small peeled and parboiled new potatoes tossed in olive oil. Season with salt and pepper and cook in a preheated oven at 230°C (450°F, gas 8) for the calculated time. Serve sprinkled with chopped parsley.

## Rack of lamb with thyme

Sweat 100 g (4 oz) lean bacon in a sauté pan. Add 3 racks of lamb (6–8 chops), trimmed but with the bone still attached to the fillet. Seal for 4–5 minutes, then season with salt and pepper. Remove the lamb and bacon from the pan. Pour away the fat. Deglaze with 550 ml (18 fl oz, 2¼ cups) vegetable stock. Reduce to a quarter. Place the lamb in a cast-iron braising pan, then cover with a large bunch of thyme, and bacon cut into small pieces to baste the meat. Cover. Make a long sausage with 200 g (7 oz) flour-and-water dough and put round the edge of the braising pan to seal it. Cook for 10 minutes in a preheated oven at 240°C (475°F, gas 9). Strain the juice and check the seasoning. Open the braising pan in front of the guests before cutting up the lamb. Serve the strained cooking juice with the lamb.

## Ragoût of mutton à la bonne femme

Cut 800 g (1¾ lb) mutton into cubes, season with salt and pepper, and fry quickly in oil with a chopped onion. Skim off some of the oil in which the meat was cooked, dust the meat with a pinch of caster (superfine) sugar and 2 tablespoons flour and mix. Then add a small crushed garlic clove and moisten with 1 litre (1¾ pints, 4⅓ cups) water or stock. Add 3 tablespoons tomato purée (paste) or 100 g (4 oz, ½ cup) fresh tomatoes, peeled and crushed, and a bouquet garni. Cook, covered, in a preheated oven at 220°C (425°F, gas 7) for 1 hour. Drain the meat and reserve the cooking stock (strained and skimmed).

Return the meat to the pan and add 400 g (14 oz, 2½ cups) potatoes cut into olive shapes, 24 glazed baby (pearl) onions, and 125 g (4½ oz, ½ cup) streaky (slab) bacon (diced, blanched and lightly fried). Pour the cooking stock over the ragoût. Bring to the boil, cover and finish cooking in the oven for 1 hour. Arrange in a timbale or in a round dish.

This ragoût may also be prepared with celeriac (cut into small pieces and blanched), kohlrabi, haricot (navy) beans, or chick peas. Alternatively it may be served with a macédoine of vegetables, a ratatouille or boiled rice.

## Ragoût of mutton with chick peas

Soak some chick peas in cold water for at least 12 hours, changing the water several times. Then place in a large pan of cold water allowing 2 litres (3½ pints, 9 cups) for every 500 g (18 oz, 3 cups) chick peas. Bring to the boil, skim, add some salt and simmer gently for about 2½ hours. Drain.

Prepare a mutton ragoût *à la bonne femme*, but add the chick peas (instead of potatoes) with the bacon. Cook for a further 30 minutes.

## Roast leg of lamb

Stud the leg near the projecting bones with 2–3 garlic cloves. Cook it on a spit or in a roasting tin (pan) in a preheated oven at 220°C (425°F, gas 7), allowing 20–22 minutes per 1 kg (9–10 minutes per 1 lb). Transfer it to a long serving dish and serve with a sauce made from the cooking juices, kept quite fatty, garnished with slices of lemon and chopped watercress. Roast leg of lamb is accompanied by French (green) beans in butter, white haricot (navy) beans, mixed vegetables or a vegetable purée.

This is the French method for roasting lamb, and the flesh will be pink. For fully cooked meat, reduce the oven temperature to 190°C (375°F, gas 5) when placing the joint in the oven and allow 45 minutes per 1 kg (20 minutes per 1 lb) and add 20 minutes to the total time.

## Roast leg of lamb à la boulangère

Season a 2.5 kg (5½ lb) leg of lamb with salt, pepper and garlic, and rub with butter. Roast in a preheated oven at 220°C (425°F, gas 7) for 40 minutes. Slice

675–800 g (1½–1¾ lb) potatoes and 300 g (11 oz) onions. Arrange them around the joint, baste with the meat juices and about 50 g (2 oz, ¼ cup) melted butter, and season with salt and pepper. Reduce the oven temperature to 200°C (400°F, gas 6) and cook the meat for a further 40–50 minutes, basting it four or five times. Finally, remove the lamb from the oven, cover the dish with foil and set it aside for a good 15 minutes for the meat to relax before carving.

## Roast leg of lamb en chevreuil

Prepare an en chevreuil marinade. Completely skin a very fresh leg of lamb and lard with lardons. Put it in the marinade. Leave it to steep for some time, depending on the tenderness of the meat and the temperature (2 days in summer, 3–4 days in winter). Dry the leg with a cloth, then roast. Serve a roebuck sauce or a poivrade sauce separately.

## Roast leg of lamb with 40 cloves of garlic

Desalt some anchovy fillets. Trim a leg of lamb as necessary. Stud it with slivers of garlic (2–3 cloves) and the anchovy fillets cut into fragments. Brush with a mixture of oil, thyme, powdered rosemary and pepper. Roast on a spit or in the oven as for roast leg of lamb, basting occasionally with a little of the herbs and oil. As the meat starts to cook, put 250 g (9 oz) unpeeled garlic cloves into a saucepan of boiling water. Boil for 5 minutes, then drain the garlic and put it into a saucepan with 200 ml (7 fl oz, ¾ cup) stock. Simmer for 20 minutes. Add a small cup of this liquor to the meat juices and pour over the meat. While completing the cooking, wash some watercress thoroughly in running water and chop coarsely. Arrange the leg on a serving dish, surrounded by the cloves of garlic and chopped watercress. Serve the meat juices in a sauceboat.

# Roast loin of lamb

Shorten and trim the bones of a loin of lamb. Brown it on all sides in butter, then place in a roasting tin (pan) and season with salt and pepper. Add a little more melted butter, then roast in a preheated oven at 220°C (425°F, gas 7), allowing 25 minutes per 1 kg (11 minutes per 1 lb). When cooked, place the lamb on a serving dish and keep hot. Add 150 ml (¼ pint, ⅔ cup) white wine to the meat juices and boil vigorously to reduce; add 2–3 tablespoons jellied stock to make a gravy. Sprinkle the meat with chopped parsley to serve.

Note: the loin may also be spit-roasted, allowing the same time. Cooked by either method, the meat will be rare.

# Roast milk lamb

Ask the butcher to dress a whole baby lamb ready for stuffing and spit-roasting. Truss the animal by tying the legs and shoulders close to the body to give it a regular shape. Pierce the lamb evenly with the spit, season with salt and pepper, and cook over a high heat (20 minutes per 1 kg, 15 minutes per 1 lb), basting with melted butter and meat juices during cooking. Place a pan under the lamb to catch the juices; blend sufficient stock into the pan juices to make a gravy and keep it hot. Remove the lamb from the spit, untruss it and place it on a long serving dish. Instead of using a spit, the lamb may be roasted in a preheated oven at 180°C (350°F, gas 4); allow 20 minutes per 450 g (1 lb) plus 20 minutes to the total time. Garnish with watercress and lemon quarters or surround with young vegetables and serve the gravy separately.

# Roast shoulder of lamb en ballotine

Bone a shoulder of lamb and lay it out flat. Season with salt and pepper, insert small pieces of garlic, if desired, then roll it up into a ballotine and fasten with string. Place the lamb in a roasting tin (pan) or on a spit, and roast in a preheated oven at 240°C (475°F, gas 9) for about 50 minutes. The skin should be crisp and the centre pink. Remove the string and serve the meat with the cooking juices in a sauceboat.

## Saddle of suckling lamb prepared as carpaccio

Carpaccio is an Italian antipasto (appetizer) consisting of very thin slices of raw beef served with a creamy vinaigrette. This dish of briefly roasted baby lamb is presented in a similiar style with very thin slices of meat and served with a pistou sauce.

Remove the fat from a saddle of suckling lamb and season with salt and pepper. Put the lamb in a roasting tin (pan) with 1 chopped shallot, 2–3 thyme sprigs, a little oil and some butter. Cook in a preheated oven at 220°C (425°F, gas 7) for 8–10 minutes, basting from time to time.

To prepare the pistou sauce, remove the leaves from 1 bunch of basil and crush them in a mortar with 3 peeled garlic cloves. Gradually work in 200 ml (7 fl oz, ¾ cup) olive oil.

Take the saddle out of the oven, still pink, and set aside to allow the meat to rest. Bone the fillets and cut them into long, thin slices.

Crush the bones finely and return them to the tin, then deglaze it with 120 ml (4½ fl oz, ½ cup) dry white wine and a little water. Reduce and add 2 teaspoons black and 2 teaspoons white coarsely ground peppercorns, 1 chopped tomato, 3 chopped garlic cloves, and half of the pistou sauce. Strain this syrupy juice and adjust the seasoning. Arrange the thin slices of lamb on large plates and coat with this sauce. Meanwhile, cook 200 g (7 oz) fresh noodles, drain, and then mix with 1½ teaspoons salted butter, 60 ml (2 fl oz, ¼ cup) double (heavy) cream and the remaining pistou sauce.

Reheat the plates of lamb in the oven. Place a pile of noodles in the centre of each plate and sprinkle the edge with grated Parmesan cheese.

## Sauté of lamb chasseur

Cut 800 g (1¾ lb) shoulder of lamb into 50 g (2 oz) pieces and brown in a mixture of 20 g (¾ oz, 1½ tablespoons) butter and 2 tablespoons oil. Add 2 peeled chopped shallots, some 200 ml (7 fl oz, ¾ cup) stock and 2 tablespoons tomato sauce. You could also add 175 ml (6 fl oz, ¾ cup) dry white wine to the stock if liked. Season with salt and pepper, add a bouquet garni, cover, then leave to simmer for 50 minutes. When the meat is cooked, add 250 g (9 oz, 3 cups) sliced mushrooms fried in oil. Heat all the ingredients through, put into a serving dish and sprinkle with chopped herbs.

This dish could also be made with veal: increase the stock to 300 ml (½ pint, 1¼ cups) and simmer for 1¼ hours.

## Sauté of lamb with artichokes

Sauté 800 g (1¾ lb) best end of neck (rack) of lamb or boned shoulder of lamb, cut into pieces. Season with salt and pepper, then lower the heat, cover the pan and continue cooking until tender. Put the meat in a dish and keep hot. Blanch 4 artichoke hearts, cut into large dice or thin slices and sauté in butter or oil. Add to the meat in the dish. Deglaze the cooking pan with 100 ml (4 fl oz, 7 tablespoons) white wine, reduce by half, then add 200 ml (7 fl oz, ¾ cup) gravy. Stir well and pour over the meat and artichokes. Sprinkle with chopped parsley. This dish could also be made with boned shoulder of veal.

## Sauté of lamb with aubergines

Cut 1.5 kg (3¼ lb) best end of neck (rack) of lamb into pieces. Season with salt and pepper and brown in a saucepan with a mixture of half butter and half oil. When the meat is cooked, arrange it on a dish and garnish with 3 aubergines (eggplants), peeled, cut into small dice and fried in oil. Deglaze the pan with white wine, then mix with brown gravy and tomato purée (paste) flavoured with a little garlic. Reduce, strain and pour over the meat and vegetables. Sprinkle with chopped parsley. This dish can also be made with shoulder of veal.

## Sauté of lamb with cep mushrooms

Cut 1.5 kg (3¼ lb) best end of neck (rack) of lamb into pieces. Season with salt and pepper and brown in a saucepan with half butter, half oil. When the meat is cooked, arrange it in a dish and garnish with 300 g (11 oz, 3½ cups) cep or morel mushrooms, which have been fried in butter or oil. Deglaze the pan juices with white wine, then mix with brown gravy and tomato purée (paste) flavoured with a little garlic. Reduce, strain and pour over the meat and mushrooms. Sprinkle with chopped parsley. This dish could also be made with shoulder of veal.

## Sauté of lamb with paprika

Cut 1.5 kg (3¼ lb) lamb cutlets (chops) or boned shoulder into cubes and sauté them in butter. When they are browned, add 150 g (5 oz, ⅔ cup) chopped onions to the frying pan. Season with salt and sprinkle with 2 tablespoons flour. Stir for a few minutes, then blend in 1 teaspoon paprika away from the heat. Moisten with 200 ml (7 fl oz, ¾ cup) white wine, reduce by half, then add 300 ml (½ pint, 1¼ cups) stock and 2 tablespoons tomato purée (paste). Add a bouquet garni and cook, covered, for 30 minutes. Remove the pieces of lamb with a slotted spoon and put them into a sauté dish with 250 g (9 oz, 3 cups) mushrooms, thinly sliced and quickly fried in butter. Add 200 ml (7 fl oz, ¾ cup) crème fraîche and 1 teaspoon paprika to the sauce, then reduce and strain and pour it over the lamb. Simmer gently with the lid on for 25 minutes.

## Sauté of lamb with tomatoes

Proceed as for sauté of lamb with artichokes, but replace the artichokes with 8 small tomatoes, which have been peeled, seeded and fried in olive oil. A little finely chopped garlic may be added. This dish could also be made with veal.

## Sautéed lamb cutlets

Season the cutlets (rib chops) with salt and pepper, then sauté on both sides in clarified butter, goose fat or olive oil. The sautéed cutlets may be served with any of the following garnishes: *à la financière, à la française, à la portugaise, à la romaine.*

## Shish kebab

Cut some shoulder or leg of mutton into cubes. Marinate the meat for 30 minutes in a mixture of olive oil and lemon juice seasoned with pepper and salt, thyme, powdered bay leaf and a little finely chopped garlic. Cut an equal quantity of belly of pork (fat pork) into cubes and blanch them. Thread the mutton and pork alternately on to skewers and grill (broil) them under a very high heat, or, preferably, over charcoal. Serve with quarters of lemon and either a green salad or saffron rice.

## Shoulder of lamb à l'albigeoise

Bone the shoulder and fill the bone cavity with a stuffing of half sausagemeat and half chopped pig's liver, seasoned with garlic, chopped parsley, salt and pepper. Roll up the shoulder into a ballotine and tie to secure. Weigh the stuffed joint. Brown the rolled shoulder in very hot fat, then place it in a roasting dish; surround with quartered potatoes (or whole small new potatoes) and 12 blanched garlic cloves, season with salt and pepper and sprinkle with a little melted fat. Cook the lamb in a preheated oven at about

200°C (400°F, gas 6), allowing 20 minutes per 450 g (1 lb), plus 20 minutes more. Sprinkle with chopped parsley to serve. This dish is traditionally cooked and served in an ovenproof earthenware dish.

## Shoulder of lamb à la boulangère

Bone a shoulder of lamb (or ask the butcher to do it for you) and season the inside with salt and pepper. Roll and tie the meat, then season the outside with salt and pepper. Complete the preparation and cook as for roast leg of lamb, allowing 25–30 minutes per 1 kg (2¼ lb). Add the garnish of potatoes and onions 30 minutes before cooking is complete.

## Shoulder of mutton en ballon

Bone a shoulder of mutton and season with salt and pepper, then spread it out flat. Prepare a stuffing with 200 g (7 oz) fine sausagemeat, 150 g (5 oz, 1⅔ cups) cep mushrooms chopped up with a small bunch of parsley, 1 shallot, 2 garlic cloves, 1 beaten egg, a little crushed thyme and salt and pepper. Make this stuffing into a ball and place it in the centre of the meat. Fold the meat into a ball around the stuffing and tie it neatly in shape with string.

Heat 3 tablespoons olive oil in a flameproof casserole, add the meat and brown all over. Then add 175 ml (6 fl oz, ¾ cup) white wine and the same amount of strong stock. Cover and cook in a preheated oven at 200°C (400°F, gas 6) for about 1¾ hours. Remove the string and cut the meat into segments, rather like a melon. Skim the fat off the cooking juices, then add 4 tablespoons thick tomato fondue; reduce if necessary. Sieve and serve with the meat.

## Shoulder of mutton en pistache

Roll up and tie a boned shoulder of mutton and place it in a flameproof casserole lined with a large slice of raw unsmoked gammon or ham, 1 sliced onion and 1 sliced carrot. Add salt, pepper and 2 tablespoons goose fat or lard. Cook over a very gentle heat for 20–25 minutes. Remove the mutton and ham and add 2 tablespoons flour to the casserole. Stir and cook for a few minutes, then add 200 ml (7 fl oz, ¾ cup) white wine and the same amount of stock. Mix thoroughly, strain and set aside.

Dice the ham and return to the casserole, together with the mutton. Add 50 garlic cloves (blanched and peeled), a bouquet garni and a piece of dried orange peel. Add the strained cooking liquid, cover the casserole and cook in a preheated oven at 220°C (425°F, gas 7) for about 1 hour. Remove and drain the shoulder, untie it and arrange on a warm plate. Cover with the sauce (bound with breadcrumbs if necessary) and serve with the garlic cloves.

## Shoulder of mutton with garlic

Bone a shoulder of mutton, roll it into a ballotine and tie neatly. Put it in a flameproof casserole with a slice of unsmoked ham, 1 chopped onion and 1 diced carrot. Season and add 3 tablespoons goose fat or lard (shortening). Cover the casserole and sweat for 20–25 minutes, basting occasionally.

Remove the mutton and the ham and set aside. Stir in 2 tablespoons plain (all-purpose) flour and cook for a few minutes then stir in 200 ml (7 fl oz, ¾ cup) white wine and 400 ml (14 fl oz, 1¾ cups) stock. Bring to the boil, then remove from the heat. Sieve the sauce and set aside.

Replace the mutton ballotine in the casserole. Dice the ham and sprinkle it over the mutton. Peel and blanch 50 garlic cloves, then add them to the casserole with a bouquet garni and a piece of dried orange peel. Pour in the sieved sauce and cover. Cook in a preheated oven at 220°C (425°F, gas 7) for 1 hour. Serve the ballotine sliced and arranged on a platter or plates, coated with the sauce and garnished with the garlic cloves. Serve a potato cake or gratin of potatoes with the mutton.

## Spelt broth

Place 1 kg (2¼ lb) shoulder or leg of mutton (on the bone) in a saucepan with 3 litres (5 pints, 3 quarts) water. Bring to the boil, then skim. Add 1 onion studded with 2 cloves and 2 carrots, 1 turnip, 1 leek, 1 stick celery, 1 garlic clove and 1 bouquet garni. Season with salt, add 4 small handfuls of spelt, then simmer for 3 hours. When ready, remove the meat and vegetables and serve together. The remaining swollen spelt makes a smooth, creamy broth.

## Spit-roast leg of lamb with parsley

Spit-roast a leg of lamb, placing a pan under the meat to catch the juices. Just before cooking is completed, cover it evenly with a layer of fresh breadcrumbs mixed with chopped parsley and chopped garlic. The lamb is ready when the surface turns golden. Put it on a long serving dish and garnish with chopped watercress and halved lemons. Serve the juices separately.

## Stuffed breast of mutton à l'ariégeoise

Make a cavity in a breast of mutton, season with salt and pepper, and fill with a fairly firm stuffing made with breadcrumbs soaked in stock and squeezed, fat and lean unsmoked bacon, chopped parsley and garlic, bound together with eggs and well seasoned. Sew up the opening in the breast. Put the meat in a buttered braising pan, lined with fresh pork rinds and sliced onions and carrots. Add a bouquet garni, cover and cook gently for 15 minutes. Moisten with 150 ml (¼ pint, ⅔ cup) dry white wine and reduce. Add 3 teaspoons tomato purée (paste) and 300 ml (½ pint, 1¼ cups) thickened brown gravy. Keep covered and cook in the oven for a further 45–60 minutes. Drain the mutton breast and arrange it on a long dish. Surround with a garnish consisting of balls of stuffed cabbage and potatoes cooked in stock and butter. Strain the cooking juices, skim off the fat, reduce and pour over the meat.

## Stuffed breasts of lamb

Open 2 breasts of lamb or mutton and remove all the rib bones without piercing the meat. Rub the flesh with garlic, and season both the inside and outside with salt and pepper. Prepare a forcemeat by mixing 300 g (11 oz, 2¾ cups) dry breadcrumbs (soaked in milk and well strained) with 2 beaten eggs, 150 g (5 oz, ⅔ cup) finely diced gammon or raw ham, 150 g (5 oz, 1⅔ cups) diced mushrooms, some chopped parsley and garlic, and salt and pepper. Spread the stuffing on one piece of meat and cover with the second one, with the skin sides outwards. Sew up all round the edge.

Line a lightly buttered casserole with pork rind from which the fat has been removed, then add 2 sliced onions and 2 sliced carrots. Place the meat in the casserole, add a bouquet garni, cover and cook gently on the top of the stove for about 20 minutes. Add 200 ml (7 fl oz, ¾ cup) dry white wine and boil down to reduce. Then add 100 ml (4 fl oz, 7 tablespoons) tomato sauce seasoned with garlic and diluted with 200 ml (7 fl oz, ¾ cup) stock. Cover and cook in a preheated oven at 220°C (425°F, gas 7) for about 45 minutes.

When the meat is cooked, remove the string, slice and arrange on the serving dish. Keep warm. Skim the fat from the cooking liquid, reduce if necessary to blend and thicken it, and pour over the meat. Serve piping hot.

## Stuffed milk lamb

Ask the butcher to dress a whole baby lamb ready for stuffing and spit-roasting. Finely slice the liver, heart, sweetbreads and kidneys, and fry quickly in butter, seasoning with salt and pepper. Add these to half-cooked rice pilaf and loosely stuff the lamb cavity with the mixture. Sew up the openings and truss the animal by tying the legs and shoulders close to the body to give it a regular shape. Pierce the lamb evenly with the spit, season with salt and pepper, and cook over a high heat (20 minutes per 1 kg, 15 minutes per 1 lb).

Place a pan under the lamb to catch the juices; blend sufficient stock into the pan juices to make a gravy and keep it hot. Remove the lamb from the spit, untruss it and place it on a long serving dish. Garnish with watercress and lemon quarters and serve the gravy separately.

## Stuffed shoulder of lamb à la gasconne

Bone a shoulder of lamb and season with salt and pepper. Soak 4 slices of bread in some milk. Chop up 3–4 slices of raw ham, 1–2 onions, 2–3 garlic cloves and a small bunch of parsley. Squeeze the bread and add to this mixture, together with 1 egg and some salt and pepper. Mix well and spread it over the meat. Roll up the shoulder into a ballotine and tie with string, then place in a roasting tin (pan). Brush with 1 tablespoon goose fat and brown quickly in a preheated oven at 240°C (475°F, gas 9).

Scald about 800 g (1¾ lb) green cabbage, cool in cold water and squeeze dry. Peel and dice 2 carrots; peel 1 onion and stick it with cloves. Transfer the joint to a braising dish, add the cabbage, diced carrots, onion and 1 bouquet garni, then half-cover the shoulder with stock (do not skim the fat off first). Cover and cook in a preheated oven at 190°C (375°F, gas 5) for 45 minutes. Then add 800 g (1¾ lb) peeled potatoes cut into quarters, or small whole potatoes, and cook for a further 20–25 minutes. Remove the onion and bouquet garni before serving.

## Stuffed shoulder of lamb à l'albigeoise

Bone a shoulder of lamb and season with salt and pepper. To make the stuffing, mix 350 g (12 oz) sausagemeat with 350 g (12 oz) chopped pig's liver, 2–3 garlic cloves, a small bunch of parsley (chopped) and some salt and pepper. Cover the shoulder with this stuffing, roll it up and tie it into a ballotine. Peel 800 g (1¾ lb) potatoes and cut into quarters. Peel 12 garlic cloves and scald for 1 minute in boiling water. Heat 2 tablespoons goose fat in a flameproof casserole, add the ballotine and brown all over, then add the potatoes and garlic, coating them well with the fat. Season with salt and pepper and cook in a preheated oven at 230°C (450°F gas 8) for at least 50 minutes (longer for a large shoulder). When the joint is cooked, sprinkle with chopped parsley and serve from the casserole.

## Tajine of mutton with prunes and honey

In a tajine (or saucepan) put 1 kg (2¼ lb) mutton cut into pieces, 5 tablespoons olive oil, a pinch of salt, 1 finely sliced onion, a pinch of ginger, a bouquet of coriander (cilantro), a pinch of saffron powder and 1 cinnamon stick. Cover with water, put on the lid and simmer over a very low heat for 2 hours (using a heat diffuser). When the meat is cooked, take off the lid and allow the sauce to reduce and thicken. Remove the coriander, meat and cinnamon. Add 450 g (1 lb) prunes to the sauce and cook for 20 minutes. Then pour in 5 tablespoons honey and simmer for a further 10 minutes. In a frying pan, brown 1 tablespoon sesame seeds. Return the meat to the tajine along with 1 teaspoon orange-flower water. Replace the lid, reheat and serve very hot. Just before serving, sprinkle with the fried sesame seeds.

## Tajine of spring lamb

Cut a boned shoulder of lamb into pieces. Chop 200 g (7 oz) onions and 3 garlic cloves. Heat 6 tablespoons olive oil in a tajine. Add the pieces of meat and onion and brown them. Cut 4 tomatoes into quarters. Peel 6 potatoes and cut into large cubes. Add to the tajine with the tomatoes, 1 teaspoon cinnamon and 1 teaspoon ground cumin. Season with salt and pepper and add 200 ml (7 fl oz, ¾ cup) water. Cover and simmer for 1 hour.

Shell and skin 250 g (9 oz) broad (fava) beans. Cut 4 preserved lemons into quarters, discarding their seeds. Add the beans and lemons to the tajine with 4 artichoke hearts, cut in half. Continue cooking for 30 minutes. Wash and remove the tough stalks from 1 bunch coriander (cilantro). Chop the leaves and sprinkle on the tajine just before serving.

## Yalanci dolmas (stuffed vine leaves)

Choose large sound vine leaves. Blanch for a maximum of 2 minutes, cool under running water and wipe dry. For about 50 dolmas, half-cook 125 g (4½ oz, ⅔ cup) long-grain or pilaf rice in meat stock. Peel and coarsely chop 400 g (14 oz) onions and cook gently in olive oil until soft but not brown. Mince (grind) 250 g (9 oz, 1 cup) mutton or lamb and gently brown it. Finally chop 1 tablespoon mint. Mix all these ingredients together. Place a small ball of stuffing on each vine leaf, fold up the tip and base of the leaf, roll into a cylinder and tie with kitchen thread.

Oil a sauté pan and place the dolmas in it, packing them closely together. Sprinkle with 4 tablespoons olive oil, the juice of 2 lemons and about 175 ml (6 fl oz, ¾ cup) stock flavoured with 1 tablespoon coriander seeds. Cover and simmer gently for about 30 minutes. Allow the dolmas to cool completely before removing the thread.

# Offal
# (variety meats)

# Amourettes

## Amourettes, to prepare

Amourette is the French term for the delicately flavoured spinal bone marrow of beef, mutton or veal. Amourettes may be prepared and dressed like calves' brains; they can also be cut into small pieces and used in fillings for croûtes, timbales, tarts and vol-au-vent or used as an ingredient for salads.

Clean the amourettes in cold water, remove the membranes, poach for a few minutes in a court-bouillon and allow them to cool.

## Amourettes au gratin

Line a buttered gratin dish with mushroom duxelles then add the cold cooked amourettes. Sprinkle with lemon juice. Cover with duxelles sauce and scatter with golden breadcrumbs. Pour over melted butter and brown in the oven.

## Amourette fritters

Marinate the amourettes in a mixture of olive oil and lemon juice seasoned with chopped parsley, salt and pepper for about 30 minutes. Drain, coat with fritter batter and cook in boiling hot oil until crisp and golden. Drain, then salt the fritters and serve hot with a well-seasoned tomato sauce.

# Brains

## Brain forcemeat

Cook a calf's brain in a court-bouillon. Drain, pat dry and press through a sieve. Add an equal volume of béchamel sauce. This forcemeat is used to fill barquettes, vol-au-vent, tartlets or hollowed-out croûtes.

## Calves' brain crépinettes

Crépinette is the term for a small flat sausage, generally made of sausagemeat mixed with chopped parsley and wrapped in caul (*crépine*). Crépinette may be made with lamb, veal, poultry or offal.

Soak a pig's caul in cold water for a few hours. Clean 2 calves' brains in cold water with a little vinegar then simmer in 1 litre (1¾ pints, 4⅓ cups) court-bouillon for about 10 minutes. Drain, wipe dry and allow to cool. Fry 400 g (14 oz, 4½ cups) chopped mushrooms, 1 chopped shallot, 1 chopped garlic clove and some parsley in a tablespoon of oil in a frying pan. Season with salt and pepper. Wipe the caul, stretch it gently so as not to tear it, and cut it into 5 pieces. Cut each brain into 5 slices. Put each slice in the middle of a piece of caul, cover with mushrooms and place a second slice of brain on top. Wrap in the caul. Roll the crépinettes in 40 g (1½ oz, 3 tablespoons) melted butter, then in some white breadcrumbs, and fry lightly in butter until brown.

## Calves' brains à l'allemande

Poach the brains in a court-bouillon, drain them and cut each into 4 slices. Coat these with flour and cook gently in butter. Arrange the slices on top of croûtons fried in butter and coat with allemande sauce.

## Calves' brains à la poulette

Soak 2 calves' brains in cold water with a little vinegar added, then clean them and poach for 6–7 minutes in a court-bouillon. Drain and leave to cool. Cut into thick slices and heat them very gently in some poulette sauce. Sprinkle with chopped parsley and serve very hot.

Lambs' brains, cut in half, are prepared in the same way.

## Ring of calves' brains à la piémontaise

Soak 2 calves' brains in cold water with a little vinegar added, then clean them and poach for 6–7 minutes in a court-bouillon. Drain and leave to cool. Cut into thick slices and heat very gently in some poulette sauce. Sprinkle with chopped parsley. Add some chopped mushrooms which have been cooked in butter. Butter a ring or savarin mould, fill with risotto, and press in lightly. Heat through in a preheated oven at 180°C (350°F, gas 4). Turn the ring out on to a warmed plate and arrange the mixture of brains and mushrooms in the centre. Garnish with slices of white truffle, if desired.

## Veal forcemeat ring with calves' marrow or brains

Prepare a veal forcemeat. Generously butter a ring or savarin mould and press the forcemeat into it. Poach gently in a bain marie in a preheated oven at 180°C (350°F, gas 4) for about 25 minutes, then cover and leave for about 30 minutes in the oven with the door open to set properly.

Meanwhile, lightly poach some calves' marrow or prepare calves' brains *à la poulette* and, separately, some lightly fried mushrooms cooked *au blanc*. Turn the veal ring out on to a heated serving dish. Pour the marrow or brains *à la poulette* into the centre of the ring and sprinkle with chopped flat-leaf parsley. Garnish the ring with the fried mushrooms and cover with more poulette sauce.

# Cheek

## Braised ox cheek

The day before they are required, clean 2–4 ox cheeks, removing all the gristle and fat. Cut the meat into large pieces and put them into an earthenware bowl with a marinade consisting of salt and pepper, 3 tablespoons olive oil, 175 ml (6 fl oz, ¾ cup) white wine, thyme and bay leaves; cover and leave overnight in a cool place.

Cut 4 carrots into small cubes. Cut 300 g (11 oz) salted belly pork (salt pork) into strips, blanch for 3 minutes, then refresh them. Blanch 300 g (11 oz, 2 cups) stoned (pitted) green olives for 3 minutes in boiling water. Melt 50 g (2 oz, ¼ cup) butter in a flameproof casserole and brown the drained meat, the strips of pork, the carrots and the olives. Pour in the marinade, then add a bottle of white wine, 4 crushed garlic cloves and 6 onions, peeled and quartered. Bring to the boil and cook for about 15 minutes, then cover the casserole and cook for a further 3 hours over a very low heat or in a preheated oven at 150°C (300°F, gas 2).

# Head

## Boiled pigs' ears

Singe 4 pigs' ears and clean the insides thoroughly; cook them in boiling salted water, using 1 teaspoon salt per 1 litre (1¾ pints, 4⅓ cups) water with 2 carrots, 1 onion studded with 2 cloves, and a bouquet garni. Simmer for about 50 minutes, then drain.

Boiled pigs' ears can be used in several ways. They can be chopped, dipped in batter and deep-fried; or spread with butter, dipped in fresh breadcrumbs and grilled (broiled), to be served with mustard or horseradish sauce and mashed potatoes or purée of celeriac (celery root). Pigs' ears *à la lyonnaise* are cut into large strips and sautéed in butter with sliced onion. They can also be served cold with vinaigrette, or browned in the oven with a white sauce.

## Braised pigs' ears

Singe 4 pigs' ears and clean the insides thoroughly. Blanch them for 5 minutes in boiling water, drain them and cut them in half lengthways. Grease a flameproof casserole, cover the bottom with pieces of pork rind, add 1 sliced onion and 1 sliced carrot, and arrange the pieces of ear on top in a flat layer; put a bouquet garni in the middle.

Cover the casserole and cook over a medium heat for 10 minutes, then add 200 ml (7 fl oz, ¾ cup) white wine and reduce until syrupy. Add 400 ml (14 fl oz, 1¾ cups) thickened veal juices or stock and cook, covered, in a preheated oven at 180°C (350°F, gas 4) for 50 minutes. Drain the ears and arrange them on a serving dish. Garnish with braised celery hearts or steamed cauliflower. Pour over the strained and reduced braising liquid.

## Calf's head à l'occitane

Cut half a well-soaked calf's head into 8 uniform pieces. Prepare a white court-bouillon: mix 3 tablespoons flour with 3 litres (5 pints, 13 cups) water in a saucepan. Season with salt and pepper, then add the juice of ½ lemon, an onion studded with 2 cloves, and a bouquet garni. Bring to the boil and immerse the head wrapped in muslin (cheesecloth) in this court-bouillon. Cook the tongue with the head. Simmer very gently for about 2 hours. Poach the brain separately in a highly flavoured court-bouillon.

Put 4 tablespoons chopped onion, lightly fried in butter, into a shallow ovenproof dish and add a small quantity of grated garlic towards the end of cooking. Arrange the pieces of calf's head on top with the sliced tongue and brain. Garnish with black olives, 2 peeled, seeded tomatoes crushed and tossed in oil, and 2 hard-boiled (hard-cooked) eggs cut into fairly thick slices. Season with salt and pepper. Pour 6 tablespoons olive oil and the juice of ½ lemon over the calf's head and sprinkle with chopped parsley. Heat in a bain marie, keeping the dish covered. Just before serving, baste the garnished head with the sauce in which it was cooked.

## Calf's head à la lyonnaise

Blanch some pieces of calf's head. Line an ovenproof dish with a layer of sliced onions softened in butter, plus some chopped parsley, then arrange the pieces of meat on top. Cover with lyonnaise sauce. Sprinkle with bread-crumbs, moisten with clarified butter and cook au gratin.

## Calf's head en tortue

Prepare a white court-bouillon and cook the calf's head and, separately, the tongue and sweetbreads. Cut all this offal (variety meat) into pieces and keep warm in their stock.

Make some tortue sauce. Cook in butter, without browning, 250 g (9 oz, 3 cups) diced mushrooms. Stone (pit) 150 g (5 oz, 1¼ cups) green olives, blanch for 3–4 minutes in boiling water and dice them. Also dice 7–8 gherkins. Strain the sauce and add the gherkins, olives and mushrooms. Heat thoroughly and adjust the seasoning by adding a pinch of cayenne.

Drain the pieces of offal and cover them with the sauce. Garnish the dish with small quenelles of veal forcemeat and croûtons fried in butter.

## Calf's head in a poupeton

Cook a whole calf's head in a court-bouillon, drain it and flatten it out on a large piece of pig's caul (caul fat). Remove part of the lean meat, as well as the ears and tongue, cut them into small dice and mix with a stuffing made from equal quantities of *à gratin* forcemeat and veal forcemeat; also add 150 g (5 oz, 1⅓ cups) chopped mushrooms. Season with salt and pepper and sprinkle with mixed spice, then add 2 liqueur glasses of brandy. Mix until all the ingredients are combined.

Spread the stuffing over the calf's head, then roll it up into a ballotine; wrap in the caul and tie up. Cook gently in a preheated oven at 180°C (350°F, gas 4) in some braising stock (made with Madeira, Bayonne ham, knuckle of veal, carrots, onions and a bouquet garni) until firm and cooked through. Drain and untie the *poupeton*. Slice and arrange the slices on a large serving dish. Pour over a few tablespoons of braising stock and glaze in the oven.

Surround with a garnish made up of braised lambs' sweetbreads or slices of calves' sweetbreads, cockscombs and kidneys stewed in Madeira, calf's-brain fritters and stuffed olives, blanched and dipped in Madeira demi-glace. Arrange 12 trussed crayfish, cooked in a court-bouillon with white wine, in rows on either side of the dish. Pour over a few tablespoons of braising stock, strained and reduced. Serve the rest of the sauce separately.

## Calf's head in crépinettes

Cut 500 g (18 oz) calf's head cooked in a white court-bouillon into medium-sized dice. Add one-third of its weight in diced mushrooms, lightly fried in butter, and 5 tablespoons diced truffles. Blend with concentrated Madeira sauce flavoured with truffle essence and allow to cool.

Divide the mixture into 50 g (2 oz) portions and enclose each of these in 100 g (4 oz, ½ cup) finely minced (ground) sausagemeat. Wrap each of these in a piece of pig's caul (caul fat), previously soaked in cold water, and roll into the shape of a flat sausage. Brush the crépinettes with clarified butter or melted lard, roll them in fine fresh breadcrumbs and sprinkle again with fat. Grill (broil) the crépinettes on both sides under a low heat and serve with Périgeux sauce.

## Calves' ears braised à la mirepoix

Clean the insides of 4 calves' ears thoroughly and blanch them for 8 minutes; refresh them, then drain, scrape and dry them. Put into a casserole and cover with 200 ml (7 fl oz, ¾ cup) vegetable mirepoix; add a bouquet garni, salt, pepper and 100 ml (4 fl oz, 7 tablespoons) white wine. Reduce the liquid completely, then pour in 300 ml (½ pint, 1¼ cups) brown veal stock, cover the dish, and cook in a preheated oven at 180°C (350°F, gas 4) for 1½ hours. Drain the ears. Remove the skin which covers the inside and the outside of the thin part of the ears; pull this part down and trim it. Arrange the ears in a round serving dish, possibly on slices of bread fried in butter. Skim the fat from the braising liquid and sprinkle over the ears.

## Mock turtle soup

Boil a boned calf's head in a white court-bouillon for 1½ hours, with carrots, an onion studded with cloves, celery, a bouquet garni, salt and pepper. Drain the head and discard the ears; trim the rest of the meat and put it under a press between 2 plates. When it is quite cold, cut it into small round or square pieces and reheat in a little of the stock.

While the calf's head is cooking, make a clear brown gravy in a stewpan, by adding some stock to slices of salt leg of pork, veal knuckle and a half-roasted chicken. When these meats are almost cooked and the gravy reduced, add the calf's head cooking juices and vegetables and continue to simmer gently for about 2 hours.

Strain, thicken with a little arrowroot diluted with cold stock, then add an aromatic infusion of basil, spring onion (scallion), marjoram, thyme and bay leaf in Madeira or port.

Strain the soup and pour it into a soup tureen; garnish with pieces of calf's head and, if desired, small quenelles made from sausagemeat mixed with mashed hard-boiled (hard-cooked) egg yolks.

## Pistachio brawn

Clean and scrape a pig's head; remove the tongue, brains and the fat portion of the throat. Cut off the ears at their base. Put the head, ears, tongue and 2 calves' tongues to soak in brine for 3–4 days. Drain. Wrap the head in a cloth, put it in a flameproof casserole together with the ears, also wrapped, and braise gently for 4–5 hours. After 2 hours, add the tongues.

Remove the best part of the skin and spread it on a linen cloth or napkin. Cut the flesh of the head into strips as thick and as long as possible, leaving out the parts tinged with blood. Sprinkle all the meats with *quatre épices* (four spices) and add about 10 chopped shallots. While still hot, arrange the meats and shallots on the skin, mixing the various meats and interspersing them with pistachios. Strips of raw truffle may also be added. Fold the skin over the contents, wrap it in the napkin and tie with string.

Return it to the cooking liquid, bring to the boil and simmer for 1 hour. Drain, remove the string and place the galantine in a brawn (headcheese) mould. Cool, putting a weight on top so it is well pressed. Chill before serving.

## Stuffed and fried pigs' ears

Braise the ears whole. Meanwhile, make a chicken forcemeat and some Villeroi sauce. Allow the ears to cool, then slit them and stuff with the chicken forcemeat. Dip them into the Villeroi sauce and leave for 30 minutes. Roll the ears in egg, then breadcrumbs, and fry them in very hot oil. Drain, arrange on the serving dish and serve with tomato sauce.

## Stuffed calves' ears du Bugey

Blanch, refresh, then carefully clean 1 calf's ear per guest. Rub the ears with lemon and sew each one into the shape of a cornet. Put them into a pan with 1.5 litres (2¾ pints, 6½ cups) well-flavoured beef stock, 1 litre (1¾ pints, 4⅓ cups) dry white wine, a bouquet garni, 1 sliced onion, 2 sliced celery sticks and 2 sliced carrots. Add plenty of salt and pepper and cook gently for about 2½ hours. Drain the ears and put them aside, covered with a damp cloth.

Dice 1 calf's sweetbread that has been braised in white wine, the meat from 1 cooked chicken wing and 1 fresh truffle. Fry 100 g (4 oz, 1⅓ cups) coarsely chopped wild mushrooms in butter; add salt and pepper. When they are half-cooked, add the truffle, the sweetbread and the chicken meat; continue to cook over a low heat. Add 200 ml (7 fl oz, ¾ cup) slightly soured cream, then take the pan off the heat and add 2 egg yolks. Blend everything well and leave to cool.

Spoon the cold mixture into the ear 'cornets'. Dip the ears in flour, then beaten egg, then breadcrumbs, and fry in butter, without allowing them to brown. Drain, arrange on a serving dish and sprinkle with fried curly parsley.

# Heart

## Casserole of calf's heart à la bonne femme

Clean the heart, season with salt and pepper, and brown it in butter in a casserole, traditionally made of earthenware. Add pieces of potato, small glazed onions and strips of streaky bacon that have been lightly fried in butter. Cook over a gentle heat for about 30 minutes.

## Grilled calf's heart on skewers

Clean the heart and cut it into large cubes. Clean some small mushrooms and marinate the heart and mushrooms in a mixture of olive oil, lemon juice, chopped garlic, chopped parsley, salt and pepper. Thread the cubes of heart and the mushrooms alternately on skewers, finishing each skewer with a small tomato. Cook under a hot grill (broiler).

## Matelote of ox heart

Divide the heart into two and soak the halves in cold water. Remove the blood clots and sinews, wash and wipe. Cut the heart into large dice and marinate for 6 hours in vinegar containing salt, pepper, thyme, cloves and a bay leaf. Drain and lightly brown the diced heart in a casserole with 20 g (¾ oz, 4½ teaspoons) butter and 100 g (4 oz, ½ cup) streaky bacon, cut into small pieces. Add 15 small onions and cook until golden brown. Stir in 1 tablespoon flour. Cover the contents of the pan with good red wine and add salt, pepper, a bouquet garni and 1 garlic clove. Cook gently for 3 hours. Half an hour before the end of cooking, add a few strips of bacon and about 15 mushrooms. Remove the bouquet garni and serve very hot.

## Roast calf's heart

Clean the heart, season with salt and pepper, cover with oil and 1 tablespoon lemon juice, and marinate for 1 hour. Drain and remove the heart, cut it into large slices and wrap each slice in a piece of pig's caul (caul fat). Put the slices on a spit or skewers and roast for 30–35 minutes. Make a sauce from the juices in the grill (broiler) pan mixed with a little white wine. Reduce and pour over the pieces of heart.

## Stuffed calf's heart

Clean the heart, season with salt and pepper, and stuff with forcemeat (fine or mushroom). Wrap it in a piece of pig's caul (caul fat) and tie with string. Brown the heart in butter in a casserole, traditionally made of earthenware. Add pieces of potato, small glazed onions and strips of streaky bacon that have been lightly fried in butter. Cook over a gentle heat for about 1 hour. Keep the heart hot on the serving dish and make a sauce with the pan juices and white wine. Reduce, then thicken with 15 g (½ oz, 1 tablespoon) beurre manié. Pour the sauce over the heart and serve with vegetables such as carrots, turnips and glazed onions, or a printanière of vegetables.

## Sautéed lambs' hearts

Clean the hearts, cut them into slices and sauté them briskly in butter or olive oil. Add parsley sauce and 1 tablespoon wine vinegar for each heart.

# Kidneys

## Calf's kidney à la bonne femme

Fry 50 g (2 oz, ⅓ cup) coarsely diced streaky (slab) bacon and 4 small onions in butter in a small flameproof casserole. Remove the bacon and onions from the casserole, and in the same butter toss a whole calf's kidney with most of the outer fat removed, just to stiffen it. Fry 12 small new potatoes in butter until they are three-quarters cooked, then add the diced bacon, the onions and the kidney, and season with salt and pepper. Continue the cooking in a preheated oven at 240°C (475°F, gas 9) for about 15 minutes. Just before serving, sprinkle with 3 tablespoons veal stock. Serve the kidney in the casserole. It may be garnished with mushrooms tossed in butter if desired.

## Calves' kidneys à la Bercy

Cut cleaned calves' kidneys crossways into slices 1 cm (½ in) thick and brush with melted butter. Season with salt and pepper and dip in white breadcrumbs. Grill (broil) quickly and serve with Bercy butter.

## Calves' kidneys Ali-baba

Remove most of the surrounding fat from 4 small calves' kidneys, season with salt and pepper, and coat them with strong mustard. Arrange in a lightly buttered ovenproof dish and cook in a preheated oven at 220°C (425°F, gas 7) for 7–8 minutes.

Meanwhile, put 500 ml (17 fl oz, 2 cups) double (heavy) cream into a saucepan, together with some grated lemon rind and ½ teaspoon ground pepper. Bring to the boil, add the kidneys and cook very gently for a further

8 minutes. Drain the kidneys, put on a plate, cut each into 8 pieces and arrange in a hot serving dish. Pour the juices that have collected on the plate into the sauce and put the pan over a high heat. Finish the sauce with a few drops of brandy and finally beat in 75 g (3 oz, 6 tablespoons) butter, cut into small pieces. Adjust the seasoning and pour the sauce over the kidneys.

## Calves' kidneys Collioure

Braise 4 calves' kidneys in a covered sauté pan on a bed of vegetables. When they are half-cooked, remove them from the pan and trim off the fat. Continue to cook the vegetables until they begin to brown, then deglaze the pan with 60 ml (2 fl oz, ¼ cup) white wine and boil down to reduce the cooking liquid by half. Put the kidneys into a small pan with 40 g (1½ oz, 3 tablespoons) butter, some chopped shallots and 12 well-pounded anchovy fillets. Simmer until cooked. Strain the cooking juices over the kidneys and heat through for a few moments. Serve sprinkled with chopped parsley.

## Calves' kidneys with chicken livers

Skin 4 calves' kidneys and remove the fat. Halve them and chop into small pieces. Slice 12 chicken livers. Using a tinned copper saucepan or a stainless steel saucepan with a copper base, fry the kidneys and the chicken livers in a knob of butter for about 5 minutes, taking care not to let them brown. While they are still pink, flame them with 5 tablespoons Armagnac and set aside, keeping them hot. Pour 150 ml (¼ pint, ⅔ cup) port and 500 ml (17 fl oz, 2 cups) red Gigondas wine into the cooking liquor. Boil down to reduce, then thicken with 15 g (½ oz, 1 tablespoon) beurre manié. When the sauce is ready (about 15 minutes), strain it. Arrange the kidneys and chicken livers in a warm serving dish, then coat with the sauce, adjust the seasoning and sprinkle with chopped parsley.

# Grilled calf's kidney

Remove some of the fat from a calf's kidney, slit it lengthways without cutting it through completely, and keep it open and flat by threading it on to 2 small metal skewers. Season with salt and pepper, brush lightly with oil and cook rapidly under a hot grill (broiler). Serve with Bercy butter, maître d'hôtel butter or anchovy butter.

# Lambs' kidneys à l'anglaise

Remove the skin of the kidneys and cut them in half without separating the halves completely. Remove the white central core and tubes. Thread the kidneys on skewers, pushing the skewer through each half of the kidney to keep them open. Season with salt and pepper, brush with melted butter and (if desired) roll them in fresh breadcrumbs. Grill (broil) the kidneys under a high heat for about 3 minutes on each side, then arrange in a long dish with grilled rashers (slices) of bacon, small boiled new potatoes and fresh watercress. Put a pat of maître d'hôtel butter on each half kidney.

# Lambs' kidneys sautéed with mushrooms

Clean and slice 8 large button mushrooms and sprinkle with lemon juice. Clean 8 kidneys, cut them in half, season with salt and pepper, and sauté them quickly in very hot butter. (Do not overcook; ensure that they remain pink.) Drain and keep hot in a serving dish.

Sauté the sliced mushrooms in the same butter, drain them and arrange around the kidneys. Keep hot. Pour 250 ml (8 fl oz, 1 cup) stock into the pan and boil down to reduce by one-third; add 100 ml (4 fl oz, 7 tablespoons) Madeira, port, champagne or Riesling and again reduce by one-third. Thicken with 1 teaspoon arrowroot, then add 40 g (1½ oz, 3 tablespoons) butter. Pour the sauce over the kidneys and sprinkle with chopped parsley.

## Lambs' kidney brochettes

Skin some lambs' kidneys, then cut in half and remove the white core. Brush with oil, season with salt and pepper and thread the kidneys on to skewers. Grill (broil) under a very high heat.

Alternatively, season the kidneys with salt and pepper, brush with melted butter, roll in white breadcrumbs, and thread on to skewers, alternating the kidneys with blanched strips of bacon. Sprinkle with melted butter and grill under a high heat.

Serve the kidneys with maître d'hôtel butter.

Sliced calves' or lambs' sweetbreads, small pieces of beef or lamb, and chicken livers can also be prepared in this way.

## Lambs' kidneys Turbigo

Cut the kidneys in half; remove the thin skin that surrounds them and the white central part. Season with salt and pepper and fry briskly in butter. Arrange them in a circle on a round dish, possibly on a bed of croûtons browned in butter, and keep hot.

Cook some small button mushrooms in the butter used to cook the kidneys and grill (broil) as many small chipolatas as there are kidney halves. Arrange the chipolatas between the kidney halves and place the mushrooms in the centre. Mix the cooking juices with white wine and tomato-flavoured demi-glace sauce; reduce and pour over the kidneys.

## Ox kidney with lardons

Slit an ox kidney (or preferably a heifer's kidney) in half and take out the central core. Cut the kidney into thin slices. Sprinkle 250 g (9 oz, 3 cups) washed sliced mushrooms with a little lemon juice. Cut 200 g (7 oz) rindless streaky (slab) bacon into thin strips; chop 2 shallots. Melt 25 g (1 oz,

2 tablespoons) butter in a sauté pan, add the sliced kidney and brown quickly over a high heat. Then add the mushrooms, the bacon lardons and the shallots, and cook until all the ingredients are lightly browned. Season with salt and pepper, lower the heat, cover the pan and cook for about 20 minutes. Then add a small glass of Madeira and 150 ml (¼ pint, ⅔ cup) crème fraîche and reduce the sauce over a high heat. Pour the preparation into a serving dish and sprinkle with chopped parsley.

## Pigs' kidneys

To reduce the rather strong taste of these kidneys, skin them, cut them open without separating the halves, take out the white central core, wash them under running water, cover them with milk and leave them in a cool place for 3–4 hours. They can then be grilled (broiled) or sautéed (with bacon lardons or mushrooms) in the same way as calves' kidneys.

## Roast calf's kidney with mustard

Remove some of the fat from a calf's kidney, season with salt and pepper, and spread with mustard. Place it in a small greased flameproof casserole and roast it in a preheated oven at 240°C (475°F, gas 9) for about 15 minutes. Drain the kidney and keep it hot. Pour the fat from the casserole, add 100 ml (4 fl oz, 7 tablespoons) Madeira and boil down to reduce by half. Off the heat, mix in 1 tablespoon mustard, then heat and whisk vigorously without boiling. Replace the kidney in the casserole and heat through before serving.

## Sautéed calf's kidney à la bordelaise

Poach 2 tablespoons diced beef marrow in salt water, drain and keep warm. Trim the calf's kidney, slice thinly, season with salt and pepper, and fry briskly in very hot butter, turning the pieces over as they cook. Drain, retaining the juice, and keep the kidney warm. Deglaze the frying pan with 100 ml (4 fl oz, ½ cup) white wine; add 1 tablespoon finely chopped shallots and boil off the liquid. Then add 250 ml (8 fl oz, 1 cup) veal stock and the juice from the kidney, and reduce by half. Thicken with a little arrowroot and adjust the seasoning. Replace the kidney in the sauce, add the beef marrow and stir. Arrange in a mound and sprinkle with chopped parsley.

## Sautéed calf's kidney with Madeira and three mustards

Remove some of the fat from a calf's kidney, season with salt and pepper, and cook for 10–15 minutes in a small pan with a little oil and butter (this is known as cooking *à la coque*). Drain all the fat away and flame the kidney with a generous liqueur glass of young good quality Armagnac. Drain the kidney and slice it thinly on a plate; keep hot.

Pour 100 ml (4 fl oz, 7 tablespoons) Madeira into the pan and boil to reduce the liquid by half. Pour any kidney juices on the plate into the sauce, boil rapidly for a few minutes, add the kidney and place the pan over a very low heat. Do not let it boil again.

Blend 50 g (2 oz, ¼ cup) butter with a mixture of Dijon, Champagne and Bordeaux mustards. Add this mixture, a little at a time, to the pan, stirring constantly, so that the sauce becomes smooth and creamy. This is the most critical process in the whole preparation and should be carried out away from the heat. Serve the kidney with sautéed potatoes.

## Sautéed calf's kidney with wholegrain mustard

Finely chop 1 large shallot and place in a pan with 1 bay leaf and a sprig of thyme. Add 200 ml (7 fl oz, ¾ cup dry white wine) and boil until reduced by half. Add 500 ml (17 fl oz, 2 cups) veal stock and 200 ml (7 fl oz, ¾ cup) double (heavy) cream. Reduce until the sauce has a coating consistency. Stir in

1 teaspoon Dijon mustard and strain the sauce through a fine sieve. Then stir in ½ teaspoon wholegrain Meaux mustard. Taste for seasoning and dot the surface of the sauce with a little butter to prevent a skin from forming, then set aside in a bain marie to keep hot.

Remove the fat from 1 calf's kidney, slice it in half lengthways and trim away any core or remaining fat, then cut the kidney halves crossways into thick slices. Season with salt and pepper. Brown the pieces of kidney in hot oil in a frying pan for 2 minutes on each side, then transfer to a sieve and leave to drain for about 10 minutes so that any blood drips away.

Reheat the kidneys in the sauce without boiling. Serve sprinkled with snipped chives. Serve with a potato galette, gratin dauphinois or tagliatelle and buttered spinach.

# Liver

## Calf's liver à l'anglaise

Cut some calf's liver into thin slices and fry them quickly on both sides in hot butter over a high heat, allowing 25 g (1 oz, 2 tablespoons) butter to 4 slices of liver. Drain the liver and keep hot in a serving dish. Fry some thin rashers (slices) of bacon in the same pan, and use to garnish the liver. Sprinkle with chopped parsley, a squeeze of lemon juice and the cooking juices. Serve with small potatoes.

## Calf's liver à l'espagnole

Season slices of calf's liver with salt and pepper. Coat with flour and sauté them in oil. To serve, arrange the liver slices on tomatoes that have been softened in olive oil with garlic. Garnish with fried onion rings and sprigs of fried curly parsley.

## Calf's liver à la bordelaise

Quickly fry slices of Bayonne ham in butter. Season slices of calf's liver with salt and pepper, coat with flour and fry in butter. Arrange on the serving dish, alternating with slices of the ham. Coat with bordelaise sauce.

## Calf's liver à la bourgeoise

Mix together in a shallow dish 4–5 tablespoons brandy and 2 tablespoons oil, then add some chopped parsley, salt, pepper and (optional) a small amount of cayenne pepper. Marinate some pieces of bacon fat in this mixture for at least 30 minutes and then use to lard a piece of calf's liver. Tie the liver and braise it in a mixture of red wine and stock. Sauté some mushrooms in butter and glaze some small onions. When the liver is cooked, remove it to a serving dish with the mushrooms and onions, and keep warm. Skim the fat from the cooking liquid, strain and reduce to make a thick smooth sauce. Pour it over the liver and serve.

## Calf's liver à la bourguignonne

Fry some slices of calf's liver in very hot butter over a high heat. Keep hot on a serving dish. Deglaze the pan with red wine and stock (in equal proportions), and reduce. Pour this sauce over the slices of liver and surround with bourguignonne garnish.

## Calf's liver à la lyonnaise

Cut the liver into thin slices and season with salt and pepper. Coat the slices with flour and sauté quickly in butter. Keep them warm on a serving dish. Peel and slice some onions and soften in butter. Bind them with a few spoonfuls of meat glaze and place on top of the liver. Moisten the liver with a dash of vinegar heated up in the same frying pan and sprinkle with chopped parsley. Serve with green beans in tomato sauce.

## Calf's liver brochettes

Prepare a marinade using 150 ml (¼ pint, ⅔ cup) olive oil, salt, pepper and chopped herbs. Cut the calf's liver into 2.5 cm (1 in) cubes. Seed some red and green (bell) peppers and cut the flesh into 2.5 cm (1 in) squares. Marinate the liver and peppers with some large quartered onions. After marinating, thread these ingredients on to skewers, placing a cube of liver between squares of red and green pepper, followed by an onion quarter, then another square of red pepper. Grill (broil) under a high heat.

## Calves' liver à la Bercy

Toss some slices of calves' liver in seasoned flour and grill (broil). Serve with Bercy butter.

## Calves' liver à la créole

Cut some fat bacon into very small strips and marinate them in a mixture of oil, lime juice, salt and pepper. Use them to lard some slices of calves' liver and then marinate the liver for 20 minutes in the same mixture. Drain them, coat them with flour and cook them in a frying pan in some lard (shortening). Remove the slices of liver from the pan and keep them warm in a buttered dish. For every 6 slices of liver, flavour the juices in the frying pan with 2 tablespoons chopped onion and 1 tablespoon chopped parsley. Brown the onion and parsley then add 1 tablespoon white breadcrumbs, salt, pepper and 1 tablespoon tomato purée (paste) diluted with 3–4 tablespoons white wine. Heat the sauce, stirring, and taste for seasoning. Coat the liver with the sauce.

## Calves' liver with bacon

Season slices of calves' liver with salt and pepper and then coat in flour, shaking them to remove any excess. Fry and then drain two thin slices of rindless bacon for each slice of liver. Cook the liver for about 10 minutes in the same frying pan, arrange on a plate, and garnish with the bacon and slices of lemon. Keep warm. Make a sauce in the frying pan using the meat juices and lemon juice or vinegar. Pour over the liver and sprinkle with parsley.

## Fried calf's liver à la florentine

Braise some spinach in butter. Peel some large onions, cut into thick slices and separate into rings. Dip the onion rings in batter and fry in very hot oil until golden brown. Drain and keep hot. Lightly grease a serving dish, cover it with drained spinach and keep it hot. Quickly fry some very thin slices of calf's liver in very hot butter and arrange on the spinach. Deglaze the pan with white wine, reduce, then pour the juice over the slices. Garnish the liver with the fried onion rings and (if liked) with lemon wedges.

## Lamb's liver brochettes

Make a marinade with 150 ml (¼ pint, ⅔ cup) olive oil, salt, pepper and chopped herbs. Cut the lamb's liver into 2.5 cm (1 in) cubes. Seed some red and green (bell) peppers. Cut the flesh into 2.5 cm (1 in) squares. After marinating, thread on to skewers, putting cubes of liver between squares of red pepper and green pepper. Grill (broil) under a high heat.

## Lamb's liver with garlic

Peel and chop very finely as many garlic cloves as there are slices of liver. Melt some butter in a frying pan and sauté the liver over a high heat, on both sides. Season with salt and pepper, drain and keep hot. Put the garlic in the frying pan, stirring well so that it does not brown. Immediately deglaze the pan with as many tablespoons of wine vinegar as there are slices of liver, and allow to reduce by half. Coat the liver with this sauce, sprinkle with chopped parsley and serve immediately.

## Pig's liver with mustard

Lard a pig's (pork) liver with strips of bacon and brush generously with strong mustard. Sprinkle with chopped parsley, crushed garlic and a little butter, and cook in a covered casserole in a preheated oven at 150°C (300°F, gas 2) for about 45 minutes. Cut and arrange the liver in slices on a hot dish. Deglaze the casserole with 1 tablespoon mustard and 2 tablespoons wine vinegar; coat the liver with this sauce.

## Roast calf's liver

Cover the liver with thick rashers (slices) of bacon, season with salt, pepper, a pinch of fennel and some chopped parsley, then moisten with brandy. Soak a pig's caul (caul fat) in cold water, wiping it dry and stretching it before use. Wrap the prepared liver in the caul and tie up with string. Cook on a spit or in a preheated oven at 200°C (400°F, gas 6) for 12–15 minutes per 450 g (1 lb). Dilute the pan juices with white wine or veal stock and pour over the liver.

# Sweetbreads

## Calves' sweetbreads à la financière

Soak the sweetbreads in cold water until they become white. Poach in salted water, drain and trim, removing skin and membranes. Place between 2 cloths in a meat press. Cut some truffles and some cooked tongue coated with aspic into matchstick shapes and use them to stud the sweetbreads. Braise the sweetbreads in a brown stock. Arrange them in croustades of puff pastry and cover with financière garnish.

## Calves' sweetbreads à la périgourdine

Clean some calves' sweetbreads, blanch them in boiling water, then cool and press them in the usual way. Stud them with small pieces of truffle and braise in brown stock. Drain and keep hot. Make a Périgueux sauce with the reduced cooking liquor. Coat the sweetbreads with some of the sauce and serve the remainder separately.

## Calves' sweetbreads princesse

Slice some calves' sweetbreads and braise them in white stock; drain and keep warm. Prepare an allemande sauce with the braising stock. In separate pans, cook some green asparagus tips in butter and heat through some slivers of truffle in butter. Arrange the slices of sweetbread in the serving dish and garnish with the slivers of truffle and bunches of asparagus tips. Serve the sauce separately.

## Calves' sweetbreads régence

Prepare the sweetbreads, stud them with truffles and braise them in white stock. Meanwhile, make some large chicken quenelles with truffles and sauté some slices of foie gras in butter. Prepare an allemande sauce using the reduced braising liquor from the sweetbreads. Arrange the sweetbreads on a hot dish and surround them with the quenelles and foie gras slices. Garnish with slivers of truffle tossed in butter and coat with the sauce.

## Choesels à la bruxelloise

Clean and blanch a choice calf's sweetbread, cool it under a press and cut it into thin slices. Cut an oxtail into pieces. Clean a heifer's kidney and cut it into pieces. Peel and finely slice 100 g (4 oz, 1¼ cups) onions. Heat 100 g (4 oz, ½ cup) clarified beef dripping in a frying pan, add the pieces of oxtail and sweetbread, and brown gently for 45 minutes. Then add 1 kg (2¼ lb) breast of veal cut into even-sized pieces, together with the thinly sliced onions. Brown again, still stirring, for 30 minutes. Add the pieces of kidney. When they have stiffened, add 300 ml (½ pint, 1¼ cups) lambic (Belgian beer), a bouquet garni, salt and a pinch of cayenne pepper. Cook very gently for 30 minutes. Finally, add a bottle of lambic and 500 ml (17 fl oz, 2 cups) mushroom stock and heat through.

## Croûtes Brillat-Savarin

Bake some small savoury pastry cases (pie shells) blind. Fill with a salpicon of calves' or lambs' sweetbreads and sautéed mushrooms (the original recipes include some cockscombs and kidneys), all bound with a reduced demi-glace or Madeira sauce.

## Feuilletés with calves' sweetbreads

Feuilletés refers to a piece of puff pastry cut into a finger or triangle and filled or garnished with cheese, ham or seafood.

Make the feuilletés with puff pastry and warm them in the oven. Clean the sweetbreads. Braise some calves' sweetbreads in well-seasoned white stock and use to fill the feuilletés. Serve very hot with cream sauce.

## Fried sweetbreads

Blanch, cool and press some sweetbreads. Cut each one into 3 or 4 slices and season with salt and pepper. Dip each slice in flour and fry in butter until brown. Alternatively, clean the sweetbreads well and dry them thoroughly. Put them into a sauté pan with some melted butter, add salt and pepper to taste, cover the pan and let them cook gently for 30–35 minutes.

Serve fried sweetbreads sprinkled with chopped parsley on a bed of pommes Anna, with a thick béarnaise sauce served separately.

## Grilled sweetbreads

Blanch, cool and press some sweetbreads. Brush them with oil or clarified butter, season with a few twists of the pepper mill and grill (broil) slowly, either whole or sliced, under a moderate heat. Serve with a green salad; with a seasonal vegetable, steamed and tossed in fresh butter; or with a purée of carrots, peas or turnips.

## Pâté with calves' sweetbreads (hot)

Braise 2 calves' sweetbreads in a thin white sauce until they are half-cooked. Clean and slice 300 g (11 oz, 3½ cups) mushrooms and lightly fry in butter (with some thin slices of truffle, if desired). Line a shallow oval pâté mould with butter pastry. Coat the bottom and sides with 250 g (9 oz, 1 cup) cream forcemeat. Pour half the mushroom and truffle mixture into the mould, cover with the sweetbreads, then add the remaining mushroom and truffle mixture. Sprinkle with melted butter. Cover the top with pastry and pinch all round to seal the edges.

Glaze the top with egg and garnish with shapes cut out from leftover pastry (rolled out thinly). Make a hole in the centre and insert a small smooth metal piping nozzle. Glaze the top again. Bake in a preheated oven at 190°C (375°F, gas 5) for about 1½ hours.

The same recipe can be followed using 6 lambs' sweetbreads.

## Poached sweetbreads

Blanch, cool and press some sweetbreads, put them into a sauté pan, barely cover them with white stock and simmer very gently for 35–40 minutes, according to their thickness. Drain the sweetbreads, set aside and keep them hot. Boil the cooking liquid to reduce it and pour this over the sweetbreads. Serve with buttered green beans, young broad (fava) beans, or a macédoine of spring vegetables.

## Roast sweetbreads

Blanch, cool and press some sweetbreads, and lard them if wished. Season with salt and pepper and wrap each one in a small piece of pig's caul (caul fat). Thread them on skewers and roast in a preheated oven at 220°C (425°F, gas 7) for about 30 minutes.

## Sauté of lamb à l'ancienne

Clean 250 g (9 oz) calves' sweetbreads, blanch them for 5 minutes in salted boiling water and drain. Cook them gently for about 5 minutes in 40 g (1½ oz, 3 tablespoons) butter in a saucepan without allowing them to brown. Clean 250 g (9 oz, 3 cups) small button mushrooms and add them to the sweetbreads; braise together for 10 minutes.

Remove all the contents of the pan; melt 25 g (1 oz, 2 tablespoons) butter in the same saucepan and brown about 1 kg (2¼ lb) best end of neck cutlets and pieces of boned shoulder of lamb (in equal proportions), seasoned with salt and pepper.

Drain the meat, pour the butter from the pan, then replace the meat together with the braised sweetbreads and mushrooms. Heat them, then sprinkle with 1 teaspoon flour. Mix together, then stir in 200 ml (7 fl oz, ¾ cup) Madeira and 200 ml (7 fl oz, ¾ cup) stock. Add a bouquet garni, cover the pan and cook gently for about 20 minutes. Reduce by half with the lid off, then add 200 ml (7 fl oz, ¾ cup) double (heavy) cream mixed with 2 tablespoons lemon juice, and reduce again until the sauce is creamy. Taste and adjust the seasoning.

Pour into a heated dish, sprinkle with chopped parsley and serve very hot, possibly with small croûtons fried in butter.

In the traditional preparation of this recipe, the quantity of sweetbreads was reduced and cockscombs and kidneys were added.

## Sweetbread fritters

Blanch, cool and press some sweetbreads. Cut into slices and dip them first in flour, then in a light fritter batter, and deep-fry at 180°C (350°F) until golden brown on both sides. Drain the fritters on paper towels. Serve with quarters of lemon and a well-reduced tomato fondue or a herb mayonnaise.

## Sweetbreads: blanched and pressed

Soak the sweetbreads in cold water until they become white, changing the water from time to time until it remains clear (at least 5 hours). Put them into a saucepan with cold salted water to cover and bring them slowly to the boil. At the first sign of boiling, remove and drain the sweetbreads and refresh them under cold running water. Then drain and wipe dry, remove the skin and fibres and press them between 2 cloths under a board with a weight on top. Leave for 1 hour.

## Sweetbreads braised in white stock

Blanch, cool and press some sweetbreads. (They may be larded, studded or left plain, depending on the recipe.) Put some bacon rinds and some finely sliced onions and carrots into a buttered flameproof casserole and lay the sweetbreads on top. Add salt and pepper and a bouquet garni. Cover the casserole and begin the cooking slowly over a gentle heat. Then moisten with a few tablespoons of white stock. Transfer the covered casserole to a preheated oven at 220°C (425°F, gas 7) and continue the cooking for 25–30 minutes, basting frequently with the stock. When the sweetbreads are cooked, they can be glazed very lightly by removing the lid and leaving the casserole in the oven for a further 5–6 minutes, basting with the fat in the stock. Serve with one of the following garnishes: anversoise, Nantua, princesse or Régence.

## Sweetbreads in breadcrumbs

Blanch, cool and press some sweetbreads. Cut them into slices, dip in beaten egg and then in breadcrumbs, and sauté them in butter. Alternatively, after dipping them in beaten egg, roll them in a mixture of minced (ground) cooked ham and mushrooms, or in a mirepoix or in grated Parmesan cheese. When cooked, serve with braised chicory (endive) or sweetcorn.

## Sweetbreads with grapes

Prepare either 1 large sweetbread or 2 medium ones, and lard them with 100 g (4 oz, ½ cup) strips of pork fat. Heat 50 g (2 oz, ¼ cup) butter in a saucepan and cook the sweetbreads gently until they are golden brown. Add 8 small onions, salt, pepper, 1 bouquet garni and 4 chopped mushrooms. Cover the pan and simmer until the sweetbreads are cooked (about 20 minutes). Arrange them in a dish and keep hot.

Deglaze the pan with 100 ml (4 fl oz, 7 tablespoons) fresh grape juice and add some white Muscat grapes and 4 tablespoons Madeira. Work 1 tablespoon flour with 50 g (2 oz, ¼ cup) butter to a smooth paste or beurre manié and use the mixture to thicken the sauce.

## Terrine of sweetbreads

Blanch and cool 4 sweetbreads. Stud them with slices of truffle and press them under a light weight for 24 hours. Brown a finely chopped mirepoix of onions, carrots, shallots and 1 garlic clove in some butter. Season the sweetbreads, then sauté them with the mirepoix, without allowing them to brown. Pour in 175 ml (6 fl oz, ¾ cup) white wine, 175 ml (6 fl oz, ¾ cup) Madeira and 6 tablespoons port. Add a bouquet garni and braise gently for 40 minutes. Take out the sweetbreads and reduce the cooking liquid by a quarter. Strain and set aside.

Prepare a fine forcemeat using 250 g (9 oz, 1 cup, firmly packed) minced (ground) fat pork, an equal quantity of minced noix of veal, 75 g (3 oz, ⅓ cup) minced cooked ham, 100 ml (4 fl oz, 7 tablespoons) crème fraîche, 1 egg, 1 tablespoon foie gras and season with salt and pepper. Line a terrine with thin strips of bacon. Fill the dish with alternate layers of sweetbreads and forcemeat, covering each layer of forcemeat with very thin rindless bacon rashers (slices). Pour a little of the strained reduced cooking liquid on to each layer. Finish with a layer of forcemeat topped with bacon rashers.

Cover the terrine and cook gently in a bain marie in a preheated oven at 180°C (350°F, gas 4) for 1½ hours. Before it becomes completely cold, cover with port-flavoured aspic jelly. Chill for 1–2 days before serving.

## Veal sweetbreads with hop shoots

Braise the sweetbreads in white stock. Strain and reduce the cooking juices to make a sauce. Drop some hop shoots into salted boiling water. Remove them while they are still firm. Drain them, braise in butter in a covered pan, then add (200 ml (7 fl oz, ¾ cup) double (heavy) cream per 350 g (12 oz) hop shoots). Coat the sweetbreads with the sauce and serve surrounded with hop shoots in cream sauce and small potatoes browned in butter.

## Vol-au-vent financière

Blanch 50 g (2 oz) sweetbreads, rinse under cold water, then dry. Remove the skin and cut into large chunks. Cut 200 g (7 oz) chicken quenelles into medum-sized cubes. Blanch 12 cockscombs and cook in butter for 2 minutes. Season with salt and pepper. Cut 300 g (11 oz) mushrooms into quarters and sauté in butter in a frying pan and then drain. In the same pan, sauté the sweetbreads, seasoned with salt and pepper, for 2 minutes. Remove and set aside with the mushrooms. Deglaze the pan with 100 ml (4 fl oz, 7 tablespoons) Madeira, reduce a little and return the mushrooms and sweetbreads to the frying pan. Cover and simmer for 3–4 minutes.

Make a golden roux with 40 g (1½ oz, 3 tablespoons) butter, 40 g (1½ oz, 6 tablespoons) flour and 500 ml (17 fl oz, 2 cups) chicken stock. Add salt, pepper, nutmeg, 1 chopped white truffle and 100 ml (4 fl oz, 7 tablespoons) Madeira. Cook gently for 10 minutes.

Place the sweetbreads, mushrooms and their juice, the diced quenelles, cockerels' kidneys and 12 shelled crayfish in a saucepan. Pour the sauce on top and allow to simmer for 4–5 minutes. Just before serving, remove from the heat and add 1 egg yolk mixed with 100 ml (4 fl oz, 7 tablespoons) double (heavy) cream. Fill the vol-au-vent with the stuffing and place the lids on top.

# Tails & feet

## Braised oxtail with horseradish croûtes

Cut 2 oxtails into chunks and trim off excess fat. Dust the pieces very lightly with a little well-seasoned flour, then brown them all over in a little butter, lard or oil in a large frying pan. Remove and set aside. Cook 2 large sliced onions, 2 diced celery sticks, 2 diced carrots, 2 bay leaves, 1 chopped garlic clove and 2 diced rindless bacon rashers (slices) in the pan, adding a little extra butter, lard or oil if necessary. When the vegetables are softened slightly remove the pan from the heat.

Layer the oxtail and vegetable mixture in a large deep casserole. Return the frying pan to the heat and deglaze it with a little brandy, stirring to remove all the cooking residue from the pan. Add a little water and bring to the boil, stirring. Pour this over the ingredients in the casserole. Add a bottle of red wine and plenty of salt and pepper. Cover the casserole and cook in a preheated oven at 160°C (325°F, gas 3) for about 3 hours or until the oxtail is completely tender.

Towards the end of the cooking time, beat a little creamed horseradish into softened butter. Cut slices off a baguette and spread them with the horseradish butter. Place on a baking sheet and bake until crisp and golden.

Taste the casserole for seasoning before serving. Stir in plenty of chopped fresh parsley and serve with the horseradish croûtes.

## Calves' feet à la Custine

Soak 2 pigs' cauls (pieces of caul fat) in cold water. Place the calves' feet in a large pan, cover them with cold water and bring to the boil. Boil for 5 minutes, remove the calves' feet, drain and leave to cool. Add 4 tablespoons flour, 4 tablespoons oil, the juice of 2 lemons, 4 litres (7 pints, 4 quarts) cold water, some salt and the calves' feet. Bring to the boil and simmer gently for about 2 hours (the feet must be very tender).

Mix 4 chopped shallots with 800 g (1¾ lb) chopped button mushrooms; season with salt and pepper and sprinkle with the juice of ½ lemon. Cook the resulting duxelles over a brisk heat until the mixture is dry. Add a small glass of Madeira.

Drain the calves' feet, remove the bones and dice the flesh finely. Mix it with the duxelles. Divide the forcemeat into 6 equal portions. Wipe the cauls, spread them out flat on the work surface and cut into 6 equal pieces. Shape the portions of forcemeat into rectangles and wrap each one in a piece of caul. Brown them lightly in hot butter. To serve, sprinkle with the butter in which they have been cooked.

## Daube of pigs' trotters

Cut 3 pigs' trotters (feet) in half and place the 6 halves in a stewpan, together with a slightly salted knuckle of veal and 2 slightly salted pigs' tails. Cover with cold water and leave to soak for 3 hours. Drain and rinse the meat, then place in a flameproof casserole. Cover with cold water. Bring to the boil, skim and cook gently for 10 minutes with the lid off. Drain the meat.

Rinse and wipe the pan. Add 3 tablespoons groundnut (peanut) oil and return to the heat. When the oil is hot, add 4 diced carrots, 3 diced onions, and 2 chopped celery sticks. Cook for about 6 minutes until the onions are transparent, stirring occasionally. Then add 3 or 4 crushed garlic cloves, a few chopped sage leaves, 1 tablespoon flour, 1 tablespoon tomato purée (paste) and 4 peeled diced tomatoes. Cook for 2 minutes. Add 3 tablespoons dry white wine, 2 pinches of caster (superfine) sugar and 3 pinches of salt. Bring to the boil. Add a bouquet garni and a pinch of cumin seeds tied in a muslin (cheesecloth) bag. Add the meat and remove from the heat. Cover the casserole with a lid and cook in a preheated oven at 140°C (275°F, gas 1) for at least 3 hours.

Arrange the meat on a heated serving dish, cover it with the sauce and vegetables and sprinkle with chopped parsley.

## Grilled oxtail Sainte-Menehould

Cut an oxtail into sections 6–7 cm (2½–3 in) long and cook them in stock prepared as for a pot-au-feu; stop cooking before the meat begins to come away from the bones. Drain the pieces, bone them without breaking them up, and leave them to cool, under a weight, in the stock (from which the fat has been skimmed). Drain and dry the pieces, spread them with mustard, brown them quickly in clarified butter, then roll them in fine fresh breadcrumbs. Grill (broil) gently and serve with any of the following sauces – diable, piquante, mustard, pepper, bordelaise or Robert – and mashed potatoes.

## Oxtail hotchpotch

Cut an oxtail into uniform pieces and put them into a casserole with 2 raw quartered pig's trotters (feet) and a raw pig's ear. Cover the meat with water and bring to the boil. Skim, and simmer for 2 hours. Then add a firm round cabbage (cut into quarters and blanched), 3 diced carrots, 2 diced turnips and 10 small onions. Simmer for a further 2 hours.

Drain the pieces of oxtail and trotters, and arrange them in a large round deep dish with the vegetables. Surround with grilled (broiled) chipolata sausages and the pig's ear cut into strips. Serve a dish of boiled potatoes sprinkled with chopped parsley separately.

## Oxtail soup

Put 1.5 kg (3¼ lb) oxtail, cut into small chunks, into a casserole, on a bed of sliced carrots, leeks and onions. Sweat in the oven for 25 minutes. Cover with 2.5 litres (4¼ pints, 11 cups) stock made by cooking 1.5 kg (3¼ lb) gelatinous bones for 7–8 hours in 3.25 litres (5½ pints, 14 cups) water and season with salt and pepper. Simmer gently, so that the boiling is imperceptible, for 3½–4 hours. Strain the soup and skim off the surplus fat. Clarify it by boiling for 1 hour with 500 g (18 oz, 2¼ cups) chopped lean beef and the white part of 2 leeks, finely sliced, first whisking both these ingredients with a raw white of egg. Strain the stock. Garnish with pieces of oxtail and 300 ml (½ pint, 1¼ cups) coarse brunoise of carrots, turnips and celery, sweated in butter and dropped into the stock. Add 1 tablespoon sherry.

## Sheep's trotters à la rouennaise

Blanch the trotters (feet) whole and braise them in a good strong stock until really tender. Drain, then remove all the bones.

Fill the boned trotters with sausagemeat mixed with 1 lightly browned chopped onion, chopped parsley and the stock left over from the braising, reduced and strained. Dip the trotters in egg and fresh breadcrumbs and deep-fry in sizzling fat. Alternatively, bake until crisp and golden, turning once. Serve immediately, garnished with fried curly parsley.

## Sheep's trotters with pieds-de-mouton mushrooms

Boil 10 trimmed blanched sheep's trotters (feet) gently for 4 hours in a mixture of water, white wine and lemon juice, with an onion studded with cloves, a bouquet garni, 2 garlic cloves, salt, pepper and curry powder. Place 800 g (1¾ lb) sliced mushrooms (use *pieds-de-mouton*, if available) in a strainer and plunge them for 3 minutes in boiling vinegar and water.

Place 300 ml (½ pint, 1¼ cups) boiling water, 6 tablespoons chopped parsley and 1 tablespoon chopped fennel in a saucepan. Cover the pan and boil for 45 minutes to reduce by three-quarters. Strain through muslin (cheesecloth) and twist the muslin to squeeze out the maximum quantity of liquid. Lightly brown 50 g (2 oz, ⅓ cup) chopped onions and 2 tablespoons chopped shallots in butter. Add the sheep's trotters, sauté them for 5 minutes, then add 2 tablespoons skimmed stock and a dash of lemon juice. Add 2 tablespoons chopped parsley, 1 tablespoon chives, 1½ tablespoons chopped fennel, salt and curry powder. Mix and cook for 1¼ hours, uncovered, over a gentle heat. Drain the cooked sheep's trotters, bone them completely and slice the flesh. Keep hot.

Make the sauce as follows: prepare a roux with 25 g (1 oz, 2 tablespoons) butter, 25 g (1 oz, ¼ cup) plain (all-purpose) flour, and 300 ml (½ pint, 1¼ cups) boiling salted water. Whisk and incorporate the reduced cooking liquid together with 1 tablespoon double (heavy) cream. Mix the trotters with the mushrooms, arrange them on a vegetable dish and coat with the sauce.

## Terrine of oxtail in tarragon jelly

Trim a 1.5 kg (3¼ lb) oxtail. Cut into three. Marinate for 24 hours with 2 carrots, 1 onion and small bunch of tarragon in 1 litre (1¾ pints, 4⅓ cups) red wine made from the Syrah grape. Put the oxtail, half a calf's foot and the boiled, filtered marinade in a large saucepan. Cover with water, add salt and bring to the boil. Skim regularly during the first 5 minutes, then add 1 bouquet garni with a few sprigs of tarragon, 1 small celery stick, the white part of 3 leeks, 1 garlic clove, 150 g (5 oz) green beans and 1 bunch of spring onions (scallions). Allow to simmer for 1½ hours, gradually removing the vegetables as they are cooked. Take the oxtail out and remove the bone. Filter the cooking liquid, reduce by half, add 100 ml (4 fl oz, 7 tablespoons) red port and 6 sheets of leaf gelatine, previously soaked in cold water. Filter again. Arrange the vegetables at the bottom of the terrine, pour some jelly on top, then a layer of meat. Repeat the process and finish with a layer of meat and jelly. Sprinkle with a few tarragon sprigs. Chill for 6 hours before serving.

# Tongue

## Boiled calf's tongue

Calf's tongue prepared in this way is always served with calf's head. Prepare and skin the tongue. Prepare a cooking stock: blend flour with cold water, using 1 tablespoon flour per 1 litre (1¾ pints, 4⅓ cups) water, until smooth. Strain the mixture and pour into a pan. Season with 1 teaspoon salt and add 1 tablespoon vinegar per 1 litre (1¾ pints, 4⅓ cups) water. Bring to the boil, then add 1 large onion stuck with 2 cloves and a bouquet garni. Add the tongue and the calf's head, weighing about 1 kg (2¼ lb), tied with string. Add 200 g (7 oz, 1 cup) chopped veal fat, bring back to the boil. Cook for 2½ hours.

The tongue may be served with a simple vinaigrette or with various other sauces, such as caper, fines herbes, Hungarian, *piquante*, ravigote or Robert.

## Braised calf's tongue

Prepare the tongue and brown it in 50 g (2 oz, ¼ cup) butter then drain. Brown 1 kg (2¼ lb) crushed veal knuckle bones in the oven. Blanch 1 boned calf's foot. Dice 2 large onions and 3 carrots; cook them in butter in a flameproof casserole until golden, then remove. Line the casserole with a large piece of pork rind with the fat removed, add the diced onions and carrots, the veal bones, boned calf's foot, the tongue, a bouquet garni and a crushed garlic clove.

Blend 2 tablespoons tomato purée (paste) with 300 ml (½ pint, 1¼ cups) white wine and the same quantity of stock (the wine may be replaced by Madeira, cider or beer); pour over the tongue. Add 2 tablespoons brandy, salt and pepper, cover and bring to the boil. Place in a preheated oven at 200°C (400°F, gas 6) and leave for about 2½ hours to finish cooking.

Drain the tongue and cut it into slices. Cut the flesh of the calf's foot into dice. Take out the bouquet garni, the remainder of the rind and the bones. Purée the stock and vegetables in a blender and spoon over the tongue.

## Calf's tongue à l'italienne

Prepare the tongue and brown it in 50 g (2 oz, ¼ cup) butter; drain. Brown 1 kg (2¼ lb) crushed veal knuckle bones in the oven. Blanch 1 boned calf's foot. Dice 2 large onions and 3 carrots, cook them in butter in a pan until golden, then remove. Line the pan with a large piece of pork rind with the fat removed, add the diced onions and carrots, the veal bones, the boned calf's foot, the tongue, a bouquet garni, some crushed tomatoes and a crushed garlic clove. Blend 2 tablespoons tomato purée (paste) with 300 ml (½ pint, 1¼ cups) white wine and the same quantity of stock (the wine may be replaced by Madeira, cider or beer); pour over the tongue. Add 2 tablespoons brandy, season with salt and pepper, cover and bring to the boil. Place the pan in a preheated oven at 200°C (400°F, gas 6) and leave for about 2½ hours to finish cooking. Blanch 200 g (7 oz, 1½ cups) green olives in boiling water, add them to the puréed braising stock and spoon them over the tongue.

## Devilled lambs' or sheep's tongues

Soak the tongues in plenty of cold water for 12 hours, renewing the water 2 or 3 times. Trim them, removing the fat parts, and dip in boiling water. Skin by making an incision in their skin at the base and on the top and pull the skin towards the tip. Wash and wipe the tongues, then sprinkle them with fine salt and leave them in a cool place for 24 hours. Wash them again, then wipe them.

Braise the tongues and leave to cool in their stock. Cut them in half and spread each half with mustard seasoned with cayenne pepper. Baste with butter. Dip in breadcrumbs, pour butter over them and grill (broil) slowly. Serve with devilled sauce.

## Devilled tongue

Cut braised or poached cold ox (beef) or calf's tongue crossways into fairly thick slices or cut sheeps' tongues in half lengthways. Spread with mustard, dip in melted butter and fresh breadcrumbs and grill (broil) gently until both sides are brown. Serve with devilled sauce.

## Lambs' or sheep's tongue brochettes

Prepare the tongues and brown in 50 g (2 oz, ¼ cup) butter; drain. Brown 1 kg (2¼ lb) crushed veal knuckle bones in the oven. Blanch 1 boned calf's foot. Peel and dice 2 large onions and 3 carrots, cook them in butter in a pan until golden, then take them out. Line this pan with a large piece of pork rind with the fat removed, add the diced onion and carrot, the veal bones, the boned calf's foot, the tongues, a bouquet garni and a crushed garlic clove.

Blend 2 tablespoons tomato purée (paste) with 300 ml (½ pint, 1¼ cups) white wine and the same quantity of stock; pour over the tongues. Add 2 tablespoons brandy, salt and pepper, cover and bring to the boil. Place the pan in a preheated oven at 200°C (400°F, gas 6) and leave for about 2½ hours to finish cooking, taking care that the tongues remain slightly firm. Allow them to cool completely, then cut lengthways into thin tongue-shaped slices. Marinate them for 30 minutes with some mushroom caps in a mixture of olive oil and lemon juice, with a crushed garlic clove. Cut some smoked streaky (slab) bacon into strips. Roll up the tongue slices and thread them on to skewers, alternating with the strips of bacon and the mushrooms. Soak once again in the marinade and grill (broil) slowly.

The marinade may be omitted: in this case, lightly brown the mushrooms and the strips of bacon in butter before skewering them, then baste the skewers with melted butter and coat with breadcrumbs. Sprinkle again with a little melted butter and grill (broil) gently. Serve with a tomato sauce or the puréed cooking mixture from braising the tongues.

## Lambs' or sheep's tongues au gratin

Braise the tongues and cut them in half lengthways. Put them in an ovenproof dish and mask with Mornay sauce. Garnish each half tongue with a cooked mushroom. Cover with Mornay sauce, sprinkle with breadcrumbs and pour on melted butter; brown slowly. Sprinkle with chopped parsley.

## Lambs' or sheep's tongues en crépinette

Braise the tongues and leave to cool in their stock. Cut them in half, enclose each half in fine pork forcemeat with truffles, then wrap in a piece of pork caul. Baste the crépinettes with melted butter. Dip in breadcrumbs and grill (broil) slowly. Serve with Périgueux sauce.

## Ox tongue à la bourgeoise

Prepare the tongue and brown it in 50 g (2 oz, ¼ cup) butter; drain. Brown 1 kg (2¼ lb) crushed veal knuckle bones in the oven. Blanch 1 boned calf's foot. Dice 2 large onions and 3 carrots, cook them in butter in a pan until golden, then remove. Line this pan with a large piece of pork rind with the fat removed, add the diced onion and carrot, the veal bones, the boned calf's foot, the tongue, a bouquet garni and a crushed garlic clove. Blend 2 tablespoons tomato purée (paste) with 300 ml (½ pint, 1¼ cups) white wine and the same quantity of stock; pour over the tongue. Add 2 tablespoons brandy, season with salt and pepper, cover and bring to the boil. Place the pan in a preheated oven at 200°C (400°F, gas 6) and cook for about 2½ hours.

Prepare a bourgeoise garnish with 500 g (18 oz) carrots cut to uniform size and half-cooked, about 20 small onions glazed and half-cooked, and 20 strips of larding bacon (slightly salted belly bacon) blanched and lightly fried in butter. About 15 minutes before the end of cooking, drain the tongue and strain the braising stock. Return the tongue to the braising pan, add the bourgeoise garnish and pour the strained braising stock over everything. Finish cooking in a preheated oven at 180–200°C (350–400°F, gas 4–6).

## Ox tongue à l'alsacienne

Prepare the tongue and braise it as for ox tongue à la bourgeoise. Prepare some sauerkraut *à l'alsacienne* with its aromatic garnish and a piece of blanched larding (belly) bacon. Line a braising pan with smoked bacon rinds and add the sauerkraut with its garnish and the bacon. Place the tongue in the middle, cover the pan and poach for 1 hour, or until done. Boil some potatoes; poach some Strasbourg sausages for 10 minutes in boiling water. Arrange the sauerkraut on a hot dish. Slice the tongue and bacon, place them on the sauerkraut and surround them with the potatoes and the sausages.

## Pickled ox tongue

Soak a trimmed ox (beef) tongue in cold water for 24 hours, then drain and wipe it. Prick it lightly all over, rubbing the surface with salt mixed with saltpetre. Put the tongue in a stoneware container. Prepare a brine by adding 2.25 kg (5 lb, 6¼ cups) coarse salt, 150 g (5 oz) saltpetre, 300 g (11 oz, 1¾ cups) brown sugar, a sprig of thyme, a bay leaf, 12 juniper berries and 12 peppercorns to 5 litres (9 pints, 5½ quarts) water. Boil for a few minutes, then leave it to become cold. Cover the tongue with this brine, place a wooden board with a weight on top over it, and leave it to steep in a cool place for 6 days in summer, or 8 days in winter.

Drain the tongue and soak it for a few hours in fresh water to draw out the salt, then cook in water without any seasonings or condiments for 2½–3 hours, depending on its size. Drain the tongue, then strip the skin off completely while still hot. Cover it with buttered paper to prevent blackening and leave it to cool. Wrap the tongue in very thin pieces of fat bacon, tie it up and wrap in muslin (cheesecloth), tying it at each end. Poach the tongue in a large quantity of simmering water for about 10 minutes. Drain immediately, remove the muslin and brush the tongue with red food colouring. Hang it up and leave to cool. Prepared in this way, the tongue will keep for several weeks in a cool dry place.

## Valenciennes stuffed ox tongue

Trim a smoked tongue and cut it into thin slices. Prepare a mixture consisting of two-thirds foie gras and one-third fine-quality butter; work it with a glass of port, some finely chopped fresh truffles, salt and pepper. Coat the slices of tongue with this preparation and reshape the tongue; wrap it in muslin (cheesecloth) and keep it in a cool place. To serve, unwrap the tongue, glaze it with clear aspic and arrange it on a bed of aspic.

# Tripe & intestines

## Andouillettes à la lyonnaise

An andouillette is a type of sausage made from pork intestines (*chaudins*), often with the addition of pork stomach and calf's mesentery, precooked in stock or milk and packed into a skin.

Lightly prick the andouillettes. Soften some onion slices in butter without browning. Fry the andouillettes in a pan with a little lard, and add the softened onion 5 minutes before the end of the cooking time. Just before serving, pour some vinegar into the pan (1 tablespoon per 2 portions of andouillette), heat and serve the andouillettes very hot with the juices from the pan. Sprinkle with chopped parsley.

## Andouillettes à la tourangelle

Lightly slit 6 andouillettes, pour over some Armagnac and let them steep for 24 hours. Slice 500 g (18 oz, 5–6 cups) button mushrooms and sprinkle with lemon juice. Butter an ovenproof dish, add the mushrooms, season and top with the andouillettes. Pour over a glass of dry Vouvray wine and cook in a preheated oven at 180°C (350°F, gas 4) for 40 minutes, turning and basting the andouillettes several times. Add a little more wine or water if needed.

## Boudin antillais

Boudin antillais is a Caribbean sausage, also called *boudin cochon*, that is grilled (broiled), fried in lard or simply heated in very hot (not boiling) water. It is often eaten as an appetizer to accompany punch. The filling is fairly liquid and can be sucked out from one end of the skin.

For 6–8 sausages, add 2 tablespoons vinegar to 1.5 litres (2¾ pints, 6½ cups) fresh pig's blood; this prevents the blood from coagulating. Moisten 250 g (9 oz, 2½ cups) stale white breadcrumbs (without crusts) with 120 ml (4½ fl oz, ½ cup) milk. Turn some clean pig's intestines inside out, wash and dry them, rub with lemon juice, and turn right side out. Finely chop 250 g (9 oz) onions and brown gently for 7–8 minutes in 100 g (4 oz, ½ cup) lard (shortening). In a food processor purée the breadcrumbs and blood, adding the drained onions. Then add 5 large garlic cloves, finely chopped, a small chilli pepper, about 20 chopped chives or the same quantity of spring onions (scallions), salt to season and 1 tablespoon flour. Work together well and adjust the seasoning. The mixture must be highly flavoured.

Knot the end of one of the pieces of intestine and, using a funnel, fill the intestine with the mixture, pushing it with the hand towards the knotted end. When the sausage is about 10 cm (4 in) long, twist the intestine several times to seal it. Repeat for the other sausages.

Place them together in boiling water seasoned with chives, bay leaves, peppers and sandalwood and allow barely to simmer for about 15 minutes, or until no more fat comes out when they are pricked. Drain the sausages and allow to cool completely.

## Boudin noir

Add 1 tablespoon wine vinegar to 1 litre (1¾ pints, 4⅓ cups) pig's blood to prevent it from coagulating. Chop 400 g (14 oz) onions and gently cook them in 100 g (4 oz, ½ cup) lard without browning. Dice 800 g–1 kg (1¾–2¼ lb) fresh pork fat and soften in a pan very gently without frying, until it becomes translucent. Add the onions and a bouquet garni and cook for about 20 minutes. Remove from the heat and, stirring constantly, add the blood, 2–3 tablespoons salt, 175 ml (6 fl oz, ¾ cup) white wine, ½ teaspoon freshly ground pepper and ½ teaspoon allspice. Sieve to remove remaining lumps of fat at this stage, if required, then add 200 ml (7 fl oz, ¾ cup) crème fraîche.

Turn some clean pig's intestines inside out, wash and dry them, rub with lemon juice, and turn right side out. Knot the end of one of the pieces of intestine and, using a funnel, fill the intestine with the mixture, pushing it with the hand towards the knotted end. When the sausage is about 10 cm (4 in) long, twist the intestine several times to seal it. Repeat with the remaining ingredients.

Plunge the boudin into boiling water and poach for about 20 minutes without boiling. As the puddings rise to the surface, prick them with a pin to release the air, which would otherwise burst them. Drain them and leave to cool under a cloth.

## Boudin noir à la normande

Chop about 800 g (1¾ lb) dessert (eating) apples for 1 kg (2¼ lb) sausage, sprinkle with lemon juice (if desired) and fry in butter in a large pan. Poach the black pudding, slice into portions and fry in butter in a separate pan. Add the slices to the apple and fry together for a few seconds. Serve piping hot.

## Boudin noir bearnais

Gently cook 1 kg (2¼ lb) minced (ground) pig's throat, or fatty pork, for 30 minutes in the bottom of a large stock pot or heavy based saucepan. Peel 1 kg (2¼ lb) onions and 250 g (9 oz) garlic and add to the meat, together with 5 tablespoons chopped thyme and a bunch of chopped parsley. Simmer for 1½ hours. In a large saucepan, boil half a pig's head seasoned with coarse salt, with 1 kg (2¼ lb) leeks, 500 g (18 oz) onions stuck with cloves, 4 red sweet (bell) peppers and 500 g (18 oz) carrots. When the head is cooked, bone it, chop the meat and vegetables, discarding the cloves from the onions, and add to the stock pot. Adjust the seasoning and add some allspice. Add 5 litres (8½ pints, 5½ quarts) blood. Stir well. Put in containers, cover and sterilize in a pan of boiling water for 2 hours. Serve sliced cold or grilled (broiled).

## Tripes à la mode de Caen

Line the bottom of a marmite or flameproof casserole with 500 g (18 oz, 2½ cups) finely sliced onions and 500 g (18 oz, 3 cups) sliced carrots. On top of these put 2 calves' feet, boned and cut into pieces, together with their long bones split in half lengthways. Add a mixture of 2 kg (4½ lb) ox (beef) tripe, consisting of the psalterium (or manyplies), rennet (or reed), reticulum and rumen, cut into 5 cm (2 in) pieces. Insert among the tripe 4 garlic cloves, a large bouquet garni (mostly thyme and bay leaf) and 300 g (11 oz) leeks, tied in a bunch. Season with 3 teaspoons coarse salt, 1 teaspoon freshly ground pepper and a pinch of *quatre epices* or four spices. Cover with a few slices of beef fat, then pour in enough cider, mixed with a few tablespoons of Calvados, to cover.

Begin cooking on the stove without a lid, then cover and seal with a flour-and-water luting paste. Cook in a preheated oven at 140°C (275°F, gas 1) for about 10 hours. Before serving, remove the layer of fat, drain the tripe and take out the bouquet garni, all the bones and the leeks. Put the tripe into a serving dish and pour over the cooking stock, strained and skimmed of fat. Keep as hot as possible until serving. Serve on heated plates or in small earthenware bowls, with steamed potatoes.

## Tripe soup à la milanaise

Cut into julienne strips 500 g (18 oz) calf's tripe, which has been blanched, cooled and drained. In a flameproof casserole heat 100 g (4 oz, ½ cup) bacon cut into small cubes, a medium-sized onion and the shredded white part of a leek. Add the julienne strips of tripe and brown for a few minutes on the stove. Sprinkle with 1 tablespoon flour. Add 2 litres (3½ pints, 9 cups) stock or water and bring to the boil. Cut the heart of a medium- sized cabbage into small pieces, blanch for 6 minutes in boiling water, then drain. Peel and seed 2 tomatoes and crush the pulp. Add to the boiling soup the cabbage, the tomatoes, 5 tablespoons peas and a few small sprigs of broccoli. Season with salt and pepper and cook rapidly for at least 1½ hours.

# Poultry

# Chicken

## Agnès Sorel tartlets

Fill tartlet cases with a layer of creamed chicken purée, containing chopped truffles if desired. Surround with a border of small rounds of cold cooked chicken breast and pickled ox (beef) tongue. Put a mushroom cap cooked in a white court-bouillon on each tartlet. Warm in a preheated oven at 160°C (325°F, gas 3) for 10 minutes. To serve, pour cream sauce over the mushrooms.

## Agnès Sorel timbales

Butter a dozen dariole moulds. Put a very thin layer of chopped truffles in half of them and in the other half a similar layer of chopped cooked pickled ox (beef) tongue. Prepare 500 g (18 oz) mousseline forcemeat made with chicken and flavour it with a few spoonfuls of soubise purée; the mixture should be thick. Cover the base and sides of the moulds with the chicken mousseline. Fill the centre with a salpicon of chicken and truffles, bound with a little reduced Madeira sauce, then cover the tops of the moulds with a final layer of chicken mousseline. Place the moulds in a shallow pan and cook in a bain marie for 12–15 minutes. When ready to serve, turn out of the moulds and arrange on a dish; serve with Madeira sauce separately.

## Attereaux of chicken livers à la mirepoix

*Attereau* is a hot hors d'oeuvre consisting of various raw or cooked ingredients that are threaded on to a skewer, dipped in a reduced sauce, coated with breadcrumbs and fried. The skewer used, also called an *attereau*, is made of wood or metal. The word comes from the Latin *hasta* (spear).

Sauté some chicken livers in butter, drain and allow to cool. Dice some cooked ham and clean some small button mushrooms. Assemble the attereaux with these ingredients, threading the mushrooms on lengthways. Roll them in a suitable sauce and a mirepoix and then coat them with breadcrumbs. Plunge them into very hot fat, drain and season with salt and pepper. Serve with fried parsley.

## Ballotine of chicken in aspic

Cut off the feet and pinions (wing tips) of a chicken. To bone, cut through the middle of the back from the neck to the tail and then, using a small knife, working one side of the backbone at a time, gently ease the flesh away from the bone, taking care not to pierce the skin. Then remove the bones from the legs and wings. Spread the chicken out flat on the table. Remove the breast meat and as much as possible of the legs and wings and dice this together with 150 g (5 oz) cooked ham, 150 g (5 oz) pickled tongue and 150 g (5 oz) bacon. Combine this meat with 225 g (8 oz) sausagemeat, 225 g (8 oz) lean minced (ground) veal, 2 eggs, 7 tablespoons Cognac, 150 g (5 oz) chopped truffles or pistachios, a generous pinch of mixed spice and salt and pepper. Knead the mixture well with wet hands. Shape the stuffing into an oblong, place on the boned chicken and shape the ballotine by drawing the skin all around the stuffing. Rinse and squeeze out a piece of muslin (cheesecloth) and use to roll up the ballotine tightly. Tie with string at both ends, slightly compressing the ballotine, then tie in the middle and between the middle and each end.

Prepare a jelly (aspic) stock using 2 calf's feet, 300 g (11 oz) pork rind, 800 g (1¾ lb) knuckle of veal, 2 carrots, 1 onion, 2 leeks (white part only), a bouquet garni, about 3.5 litres (6 pints, 3½ quarts) chicken stock (or water), and 400 ml (14 fl oz, 1¾ cups) Madeira, adding the chicken carcass and giblets (except the liver) and other giblets if desired. Simmer the ballotine gently in the stock for 1¾ hours. Remove from the stock and allow to cool.

Unwrap the ballotine. Rinse the muslin in warm water, squeeze out thoroughly, and wrap up the ballotine again. Tie up and allow to cool for 12 hours under a weight. Clarify the stock, adding gelatine to thicken if necessary, and coat the cold ballotine with the half-set aspic, then chill and serve when completely cold.

## Ballotine of chicken in chaud-froid sauce

Prepare the ballotine as for ballotine of chicken in aspic, but coat with chaud-froid sauce instead of aspic.

## Bouchées à la reine

Prepare and bake some bouchée cases. Prepare a salpicon *à la reine* for the filling as follows. Dice some chicken breasts poached in stock; and dice some truffle and poach in white wine. Cut some trimmed button mushrooms into four; sprinkle with lemon juice and cook very gently in butter so they retain their original colour. Prepare a white sauce with the stock from the chicken, add some cream, and, if desired, some egg yolk. For 500 ml (17 fl oz, 2 cups) stock, use 40 g (1½ oz, 3 tablespoons) butter, 40 g (1½ oz, ⅓ cup) plain (all-purpose) flour, 100 ml (4 fl oz, 7 tablespoons) double (heavy) cream, and 1 egg yolk. Using this sauce, bind the chicken, truffles and mushrooms.

Heat the bouchée cases in a preheated oven at 180°C (350°F, gas 4) for 5 minutes. Fill them with the hot mixture and replace the lids. If the truffles are omitted from the filling, equal quantities of chicken breast and mushrooms should be used. A salpicon of calves' sweetbreads, quenelles and brains braised in white sauce may be added to the filling.

## Boudin à la Richelieu

Butter some small oval ovenproof moulds. Line the bottom and sides with a finely ground chicken forcemeat. Add a mixture similar to that used to fill bouchées *à la reine* but cut up more finely. Finally, cover with more forcemeat and smooth the surface. Place the moulds in a bain marie and cook in a preheated oven at 180°C (350°F, gas 4) for about 25 minutes. Unmould the puddings and allow to cool. Arrange them in a circle on a platter and serve with Périgueux sauce or suprême sauce with diced truffle or truffle peelings.

## Boudin blanc, grilled

Prick some *boudins blancs* with a fork, roll each one in oiled greaseproof (wax) paper, and grill (broil) gently. Remove the paper and serve hot with mashed potatoes, apple sauce or celery purée.

## Boudin blanc with prunes

Soak some prunes in a little lukewarm water or weak tea, then remove the stones (pits). Prick some *boudins blancs* with a fork, arrange in an ovenproof dish and surround with the prunes. Sprinkle with melted butter and cook in a preheated oven at 240°C (475°F, gas 9) until golden brown.

## Braised ballotine of chicken

Cut off the feet and pinions (wing tips) of a chicken. To bone, cut through the middle of the back from the neck to the tail and then, using a small sharp knife, working one side of the backbone at a time, gently ease the flesh away from the bone, taking care not to pierce the skin. Then carefully remove the bones from the legs and wings. Spread the chicken out flat on the table. Remove the breast meat and as much as possible of the legs and wings and cut it into cubes.

Prepare a stuffing from finely minced (ground) pork and veal – about 225 g (8 oz) of each – mixed with 100 g (4 oz) diced cooked ham, 2 eggs, 7 tablespoons Cognac, a generous pinch of allspice, and salt and pepper. Braise the ballotine on a mirepoix in a flameproof casserole. Add 200 ml (7 fl oz, ¾ cup) each of dry white wine and stock, and a bouquet garni. Bring to the boil and cook, uncovered, for 5 minutes, then turn the ballotine in the vegetables. Cover tightly and braise in a preheated oven at 200°C (400°F, gas 6) for 1½ hours. Remove the bouquet garni and serve hot or leave to cool completely in the covered casserole and then chill.

The same method can be used to make hot or cold ballotines of turkey or pigeon, adding foie gras and truffles, if required, in proportions corresponding to the size of the bird.

## Bresse chicken liver terrine

Select 8 Bresse chicken livers (preferably white ones; ordinary chicken livers can be used instead, but will give a darker result); rub through a sieve together with 150 g (5 oz, ¾ cup) beef marrow. Add 50 g (2 oz, ½ cup) plain (all-purpose) flour. Mix thoroughly, then, one by one, add 6 eggs and 4 yolks, 2 tablespoons double (heavy) cream, and 750 ml (1¼ pints, 3¼ cups) milk. Season with salt, pepper and ground nutmeg. Add a generous pinch of chopped parsley and ½ crushed peeled garlic clove. Place the mixture in a greased mould and cover with foil. Then cook in a bain marie in a preheated oven at 180°C (350°F, gas 4) for about 45 minutes or until set. Turn out of the mould just before serving.

Prepare a sauce by reducing some cream, port and fresh tomato purée, enriched with a little butter. Pour the sauce over the dish and garnish with a few slices of truffle. Serve warm or cold.

## Camerani soup

Slowly cook in butter 200 g (7 oz, 1½ cups) finely shredded mixed vegetables, including a small turnip. Add 2 chicken livers, peeled and diced very finely, season with salt and pepper, and brown over a brisk heat. Meanwhile, cook 125 g (4½ oz) Naples macaroni in fast boiling salted water. Drain, bind together with butter and season. In a serving dish, buttered and sprinkled with grated Parmesan, arrange alternate layers of the macaroni and the chicken liver mixture, also sprinkled with Parmesan. Heat gently for a few minutes before serving.

## Cannelloni à la béchamel

Chop 2 large onions and soften them in 25 g (1 oz, 2 tablespoons) butter. Chop 3 slices of cooked ham and about 250 g (9 oz) cooked chicken; add these to the onions and season with salt and pepper.

Make a béchamel sauce using 50 g (2 oz, ¼ cup) butter, 50 g (2 oz, ½ cup) plain (all-purpose) flour, 500 ml (17 fl oz, 2 cups) milk, salt, pepper and some grated nutmeg. Add 75 g (3 oz, ¾ cup) grated Parmesan cheese and the chopped meat and onions. Fill cooked fresh pasta rectangles with this mixture, then roll them up. Alternatively, use bought cannelloni tubes cooked according to the packet instructions. Butter an ovenproof gratin dish and arrange the cannelloni in it. Cover with the remaining béchamel sauce. Sprinkle with 50 g (2 oz, ½ cup) grated Parmesan cheese and a few knobs of butter. Heat through and brown in a preheated oven at 240°C (475°F, gas 9) or under a hot grill (broiler).

## Caribbean chicken with pineapple and rum

Season a large chicken inside and out with salt and pepper. Brown in a flameproof casserole in chicken fat, butter or oil and dust with a pinch of ginger and cayenne. Chop 2 large onions and 1 shallot and soften them in the fat around the chicken. Pour 3 tablespoons rum over the chicken and set light to it. Then add 60 ml (2 fl oz, ¼ cup) syrup from canned pinapple and 1 tablespoon lemon juice. Cover and cook in a preheated oven at 180°C (350°F, gas 4) for 45 minutes. Dice 6 slices canned pineapple and add them to the casserole. Add salt and pepper and cook for about 10 more minutes.

## Chartreuse à la parisienne en surprise

Chartreuse is the name given to a preparation of vegetables (particularly braised cabbage) and meat or game, moulded into a dome and formed of layers of alternating colours.

(from a recipe by Carême) Cook 8 truffles in champagne. When they are cold, pare and cut them in the direction of the greatest length. Peel (shell) 100 crayfish tails – these can be replaced by very thin, 1 cm (½ in) squares of carrot – and begin to form a crown on the bottom of a buttered mould. Trim the truffles and place them on the crayfish tails. Add chicken fillets previously stiffened with butter and trimmed. Set on top of this border a crown of crayfish tails to form a parallel with the crayfish border underneath.

Chop the trimmings of the truffles very finely and scatter them on the bottom of the mould. Cover these with a 2.5 cm (1 in) thick layer of quenelle mixture made with chicken instead of veal. Cover the border too. Fill the middle with a blanquette of chicken, veal or lamb sweetbreads, slices of game fillets or with a ragoût *à la financière* or *à la Toulousaine*. The mould should not be quite filled.

Form a layer of forcemeat 13 cm (5 in) in diameter and 1 cm (½ in) thick on a round of buttered paper. Place this on top of the filling (stuffing-side down). To remove the paper, put on it, for a second only, a hot lid which melts the butter. Secure the forcemeat lid to the forcemeat surround with the point of a knife.

Cover the top of the chartreuse with a circle of buttered paper and put it in a bain marie for 1½ hours.

To garnish, place a ring of small white mushrooms on the chartreuse, and in the centre put a rosette of 8 filets mignons *à la Conti* (fowl or game, according to the nature of the basic ragoût) in the form of a crescent, topped by a mushroom.

## Chaud-froid of chicken with tarragon

Take a chicken of about 2.5 kg (5½ lb) with its own giblets. Place the giblets and 500 g (18 oz) chicken wings in a saucepan, cover with cold water, and bring to the boil; drain and rinse in cold water. Peel 3 onions, 2 carrots and 1 turnip. Place in a saucepan with the white part of 1 leek, 3 cloves, a large bouquet garni, the giblets and chicken wings. Cover with plenty of water (about 3.5 litres, 6 pints, 3½ quarts), add salt and pepper, and cook quite gently (without a lid in order to reduce the stock) until the flesh falls off the giblets and chicken wings. Season the whole chicken inside with salt and pepper, and add 3 or 4 sprigs of tarragon. Truss the bird, place it in the stock; cover the pan and leave to cook very gently for about 1½ hours. When the chicken is cooked, leave it to cool in the stock, then drain it on a rack. Strain the stock, discarding the giblets and wings and skim off excess fat. Return it to the pan and add a bunch of tarragon, then boil until reduced to about 1 litre (1¾ pints, 4⅓ cups).

To prepare the chaud-froid sauce, soften 5 leaves of gelatine in 120 ml (4½ fl oz, ½ cup) cold water. Then dissolve the gelatine in the water. Make a very pale roux with 125 g (4½ oz, ½ cup) butter and 100 g (4 oz, 1 cup) plain (all-purpose) flour, leave it to cool, then gradually add the boiling stock and stir briskly over the heat. Simmer gently for 10 minutes, then add a small glass of brandy and the same of port, and 400 ml (14 fl oz, 1¾ cups) double (heavy) cream, spoonful by spoonful. Finally stir in the dissolved gelatine. Leave the chaud-froid sauce to cool, stirring to prevent a skin from forming.

Skin the chicken and cut it into pieces, then put them into the refrigerator. When chilled, coat the pieces of chicken with several layers of chaud-froid sauce, putting them in the refrigerator between each application of sauce. To collect the sauce which drains away, arrange the chicken on a rack over a tray or piece of foil. Dilute the sauce with a little cold stock for the last two applications. Garnish the pieces of chicken with tarragon leaves.

## Chicken à blanc

Joint a raw chicken: cut into four if it is small; separate the wings, legs and breast if it is larger (the thigh bones can be removed if desired). Sprinkle the pieces with salt and pepper. Heat 40 g (1½ oz, 3 tablespoons) butter in a sauté pan or flameproof casserole and cook the pieces gently until firm but not coloured (first the thighs, which take longer to cook, then the wings and breast, which are more tender). Then cover and cook gently for about 40 minutes. Remove the pieces in the same order that they went in. Pour off the cooking fat; deglaze the pan with white stock, wine, cream, mushroom stock or other suitable liquid.

## Chicken à brun

Joint a raw chicken: cut into four if it is small; separate the wings, legs and breast if it is larger (the thigh bones can be removed if desired). Sprinkle the pieces with salt and pepper. Heat 40 g (1½ oz, 3 tablespoons) butter in a sauté pan or flameproof casserole and fry the chicken pieces over a brisk heat until brown all over. Cover and finish cooking, removing the wings and breast first, as these cook more quickly. Pour off the cooking fat, then add the sauce or required garnish and return the pieces of chicken to the pan. Reheat, but do not allow to boil.

## Chicken à l'ancienne

Sauté a chicken *à blanc*. Deglaze the pan with 100 ml (4 fl oz, 7 tablespoons) white stock or mushroom stock, reduce by two-thirds, then add 150 ml (¼ pint, ⅔ cup) chicken velouté sauce. Boil for 5 minutes, then add 150 ml (2 oz, 4 tablespoons) butter cut into small pieces; whisk and allow it to melt. Strain the sauce. Add 2 tablespoons chopped truffle and 3 tablespoons of port. Arrange the chicken in the serving dish with the sauce poured over.

## Chicken à l'italienne

Sauté a chicken *à brun* in equal quantities of oil and butter. Deglaze the pan with 150 ml (¼ pint, ⅔ cup) white wine and reduce; add 150 ml (¼ pint, ⅔ cup) sauce italienne. Pour over the chicken and sprinkle with parsley.

## Chicken à l'ivoire

Poach a chicken in white stock. Prepare 500 ml (17 fl oz, 2 cups) ivoire sauce, made by adding 2 tablespoons reduced veal stock or meat glaze to 200 ml (7 fl oz, ¾ cup) suprême sauce. Make 24 small chicken quenelles. Trim 24 button mushrooms and sprinkle with lemon juice. Place in a sauté pan with a little butter. Just cover with chicken consommé and cook for about 10 minutes. Drain the chicken and arrange on a serving dish, surrounded by the mushrooms and quenelles. Coat with ivoire sauce; serve the remaining sauce in a sauceboat.

## Chicken à la bourgeoise

Season a chicken with salt and pepper and cook in butter in a covered dish in a preheated oven at 180°C (350°F, gas 4) for 30 minutes. Then add 100 g (4 oz, ⅔ cup) diced fat bacon that has been lightly fried and 20 small carrots fried in butter. Cook for about another 35 minutes, basting the chicken with its own juice from time to time. Place the chicken and the garnish in a dish and keep warm. Deglaze the cooking pot with 7 tablespoons each of white wine and 20 glazed small onions, cooked in butter. Pour the sauce over the chicken and sprinkle with chopped parsley.

## Chicken à la bourguignonne

For a chicken weighing about 2 kg (4½ lb), use 100 g (4 oz) bacon, cut into larding strips and then blanched. Peel 20 small onions, and clean and slice 20 mushrooms. Put the cleaned and trussed chicken in a hot flameproof casserole and gently colour the outside in 25 g (1 oz, 2 tablespoons) butter. Remove the chicken and fry the bacon, onions and mushrooms in the same casserole. Remove the bacon, onions and mushrooms and add 2 tablespoons mirepoix, stirring well. Deglaze the casserole with 400 ml (14 fl oz, 1¾ cups) red wine and an equal quantity of chicken stock; boil down to reduce by half and add a bouquet garni. Return the chicken to the casserole, bring the liquid to the boil, then cover with the lid and cook gently for 20 minutes. Add the prepared garnish of bacon, mushrooms and onions, together with salt and pepper. Bring to the boil, cover and simmer gently for a further 45 minutes, or until cooked.

Drain the chicken and its garnish and arrange on a warm serving plate. Remove the bouquet garni. Add 1 tablespoon beurre manié to the juices in the casserole, stirring well for 2 minutes. Taste and adjust the seasoning and pour the sauce over the chicken.

### Chicken à la Chantilly

Make a stuffing with some boiled rice, truffle peelings and diced foie gras. Stuff the chicken, sew up the aperture and brown the bird in a flameproof casserole with some butter. Take care not to overcook. Season with pepper, cover the pan and cook for about 1 hour. Cook some truffles slowly in port and sauté some slices of foie gras in butter. When the chicken is cooked, drain it and arrange on a serving dish, surrounded by the truffles and foie gras. Keep it hot. Add some chicken velouté to the pan juice; reduce by half and add several tablespoons of whipped cream. Coat the chicken with the sauce.

### Chicken à la chivry

Poach a chicken in a white stock. Slowly cook some green asparagus tips in butter and prepare some green peas *à la française*. Cook some artichoke hearts in a court-bouillon and use half of them to garnish the asparagus tips and the other half to garnish the peas. Arrange the vegetables around the chicken and coat with chivry sauce.

### Chicken à la d'Albufera

Half-cook some rice in a white stock and add a salpicon of truffles and foie gras. Use to stuff a chicken and poach in the white stock. Arrange it on a dish, surrounded with an Albufera garnish – pickled ox (beef) tongue, sliced and sautéed calves' sweetbreads and mushrooms. Coat with Albufera sauce.

### Chicken à la lyonnaise en crapaudine

Spatchcock a chicken by splitting and flattening it. Season with salt and pepper and coat with mustard. Leave for 30 minutes, then roll it in fresh breadcrumbs. Sprinkle with melted butter and grill (broil) gently until cooked through. Serve with a mustard and cream sauce.

# Chicken à la minute

Sauté a chicken *à brun* and arrange it in a serving dish. Pour over the very hot butter in which it was cooked and a little lemon juice. Sprinkle generously with chopped parsley.

# Chicken à la néva

Prepare a chicken weighing about 3 kg (6½ lb) and carefully remove the breastbone. Stuff the bird with a mixture of 800 g (1¾ lb, 3¼ cups) fine chicken forcemeat, small cubes of raw foie gras and truffles. Truss the bird, poach it in white stock and leave to cool in the liquid. When the chicken is quite cold, wipe it dry and coat it with a white chaud-froid sauce prepared with some of the cooking liquor. Garnish the chicken with mushroom slices, glaze with aspic and allow to set firmly. Place the chicken in the centre of a long serving dish.

Prepare some Russian salad mixed with a thick mayonnaise; divide the mixture into two halves and shape each half into a dome. Garnish each dome with mushroom slices and place them on the serving dish at each end of the chicken. Garnish the edges of the dish with chopped aspic.

# Chicken à la niçoise

Sauté a chicken *à brun* in oil alone; drain it then set aside and keep warm. Deglaze the sauté pan with 100 ml (4 fl oz, 7 tablespoons) white wine and 150 ml (¼ pint, ⅔ cup) tomato sauce. Add 1 crushed garlic clove and boil to reduce. Put the chicken back in the sauce and reheat without boiling, then arrange it in a warm serving dish, surrounded with artichoke quarters cooked in butter, braised courgettes (zucchini) and stoned black olives (pitted ripe olives). Pour the sauce over the chicken and sprinkle with chopped herbs.

## Chicken à la parisienne

Remove the breastbone from a chicken, stuff it with 500 g (18 oz) forcemeat (cream or fine), truss it and poach in veal stock. Drain and leave to cool. Take off the chicken breasts. Remove the forcemeat, cut it into dice and mix with about 400 g (14 oz) cold chicken mousse. Replace this mixture in the chicken and round it out well to reshape the breast of the bird. Coat the chicken with chaud-froid sauce.

Cut the breasts into thin slices, coat them with chaud-froid sauce, garnish with truffle and pickled tongue and place them on the chicken. Glaze with aspic jelly. Arrange the chicken on the serving dish. Mix some vegetable macédoine with mayonnaise and pour into small dariole moulds. When set, turn them out on to the serving dish around the chicken, placing a thick slice of truffle on each dariole. Garnish the spaces between with chopped aspic.

## Chicken à la piémontaise

Stuff a large roasting chicken with risotto mixed with 100 g (4 oz, 1 cup) diced white Piedmont truffles. Roast it in butter in a flameproof casserole, then drain it and place it on a warm serving dish. Deglaze the casserole with white wine and thicken the sauce with a little beurre manié; serve this in a sauceboat. Serve the chicken on a round dish surrounded with the risotto sprinkled with freshly grated Parmesan cheese.

## Chicken à la polonaise

Sauté chicken pieces in butter in a flameproof casserole for about 20 minutes. When cooked, pour over the juice of a lemon and cover with about 25 g (1 oz, ½ cup) fresh breadcrumbs mixed with 125 g (4½ oz, ½ cup) noisette butter. Serve very hot accompanied by red cabbage, braised chestnuts or braised celeriac (celery root).

## Chicken à la portugaise

Cook a large roasting chicken in butter in a flameproof casserole in the oven until it is three-quarters cooked. While it is cooking, peel and seed 8 tomatoes, chop the flesh and cook in butter with 1 tablespoon chopped onion. Add this to the chicken and finish cooking, only half-covering the casserole.

Place the chicken in a serving dish and keep warm. Deglaze the casserole with a little white wine, reduce, season with salt and pepper to taste and pour this sauce over the chicken. Sprinkle with chopped parsley and serve at once.

## Chicken à la reine

Prepare 500 g (18 oz) panada forcemeat with butter and use it to stuff a chicken weighing about 1.8 kg (4 lb). Poach it gently in white stock. Bake some puff-pastry tartlet cases and fill them with chicken purée with cream; garnish with sliced truffles. Make a suprême sauce with the chicken stock. Arrange the chicken on a large hot serving dish and place the tartlets round it. Serve the suprême sauce separately.

## Chicken à la viennoise

Quarter a young chicken weighing 800–900 g (1¾–2 lb), sprinkle the joints with salt and pepper, then coat with egg and breadcrumbs. Cook in a frying pan in 60 g (2 oz, ¼ cup) clarified butter, turning once, or deep-fry in fat at a temperature of 180°C (350°F) until golden and cooked through. Drain on paper towels and serve with fried parsley and lemon quarters.

## Chicken ambassadrice

Use a velouté sauce to bind a mixture of chopped lamb's sweetbreads, truffles and mushrooms; stuff a good-sized chicken with this mixture. Cook the chicken until tender in a flameproof casserole with a purée of vegetables cooked in meat stock. Arrange the fowl on a round dish and surround it with tartlets filled with sautéed chicken livers (formerly cockscombs and kidneys would have been added). Place a thin slice of truffle on each tartlet. Deglaze the casserole with Madeira and veal stock, and coat the fowl with this sauce.

## Chicken Annette

Sauté a chicken *à brun* and prepare a base of pommes Anna. Arrange the drained chicken pieces on top of this and keep warm. Deglaze the cooking pan with 100 ml (4 fl oz, 7 tablespoons) white wine; add 1 chopped shallot, reduce, moisten with 150 ml (¼ pint, ⅔ cup) chicken stock, reduce a little more, then thicken with 1 tablespoon beurre manié. Add a squeeze of lemon juice and some chopped mixed herbs such as parsley, chervil and tarragon. Pour this sauce over the chicken.

## Chicken au blanc

Poach a boiling chicken in white stock for 1¼–1¾ hours, depending on its size and tenderness. The legs and wings should come away in the hand without using a knife. Reduce a bowlful of the cooking liquor and add an equal volume of allemande sauce. Coat the chicken with the sauce and serve piping hot with rice and carrots cooked in stock.

## Chicken au gratin with sauerkraut

Peel and dice 1 leek (white part) and 2 carrots. Stick an onion with 2 cloves. Tie up in a small piece of muslin (cheesecloth) 1 tablespoon juniper berries, 1 teaspoon peppercorns and 2 peeled garlic cloves. Wash 1.5 kg (3¼ lb) raw sauerkraut well, then squeeze and disentangle it with your fingers.

Grease a large flameproof casserole with 40 g (1½ oz, 3 tablespoons) goose fat and pile half the sauerkraut in it. On top, arrange the vegetables and a large bouquet garni augmented with 1 celery stick and the muslin bag of spices. Cover with the remaining sauerkraut. Over the contents, pour 200 ml (7 fl oz, ¾ cup) dry white wine and 300 ml (½ pint, 1¼ cups) chicken stock. Season lightly with salt, cover and bring to the boil. Then transfer to a preheated oven at 190°C (375°F, gas 5) and cook for 1 hour.

Season a 1.5 kg (3¼ lb) chicken with salt and pepper inside and out, and place it in the middle of the sauerkraut. Return to the oven for a further 2 hours. Then take the chicken out, cut it up and bone it. Grease a gratin dish with goose fat. Press the sauerkraut and pile it in the dish, having removed the bag of spices, the cloves and the bouquet garni. Cover with the chicken, moisten with 300 ml (½ pint, 1¼ cups) crème fraîche, sprinkle 100 g (4 oz, 1 cup) grated Gruyère cheese on top and brown in a very hot oven.

## Chicken boivin

Sauté a chicken *à brun*; halfway through, add some small new onions softened in butter, blanched artichoke quarters and some tiny new potatoes. Finish cooking, then arrange the drained chicken and its garnish in a serving dish. Deglaze the cooking pan with some pot-au-feu broth, some meat glaze and a little lemon juice. Whisk in some butter. Pour this sauce over the chicken.

## Chicken bonne femme

Trim a chicken weighing 1.8–2 kg (4–4½ lb), season with salt and pepper, then truss. Brown the chicken slowly on all sides in butter in a flameproof casserole or heavy-based saucepan. Blanch 100 g (4 oz, ⅔ cup) finely diced unsmoked streaky (slab) bacon. Add the diced bacon and 20 small onions to the casserole. Cover and cook gently for 15 minutes. Add 500 g (18 oz) potato balls or small new potatoes and continue cooking slowly, basting the chicken from time to time, until tender. Garnish with the cooked vegetables and serve.

## Chicken casserole

Clean a chicken weighing 1.8 kg (4 lb) and truss it. Heat 50 g (2 oz, ¼ cup) butter in a flameproof casserole and brown the chicken on all sides. If a poulard (capon) is not used, cover the chicken breast with strips of fat bacon to keep it moist. Sprinkle with salt and pepper and cover the casserole; cook in a preheated oven at 230°C (450°F, gas 8) for about 1 hour. Serve the chicken with its own gravy, accompanied by glazed small (pearl) onions or carrots.

## Chicken clos-jouve

Joint a large Bresse chicken into 6 pieces and bone them. Make a concentrated stock with the crushed chicken bones, the green part of 1 leek, 1 onion, 1 calf's foot (partially boned) and some thyme and bay leaf. Strain, deglaze with port, then moisten with stock and white wine until the ingredients are just covered; cook for 1½ hours until the stock resembles a rich demi-glace.

Prepare a forcemeat with the white parts of 3 leeks (shredded), 125 g (4½ oz, 1¼ cups) horn of plenty (or cultivated) mushrooms browned in butter, the liver of the chicken and 150 g (5 oz, ⅔ cup) foie gras (both diced), 100 ml (4 fl oz, 7 tablespoons) double (heavy) cream and 1 egg yolk. Season the forcemeat with salt and pepper and use it to stuff the boned chicken pieces. Tie them up (not too tightly), brown in butter in a flameproof casserole, then reduce the heat, cover the pan and cook gently – turning once – until cooked through (about 35 minutes). Remove the chicken and arrange on a serving dish; keep warm. Add the demi-glace to the casserole, heat through, adjust the seasoning and pour over the pieces of chicken.

## Chicken cooked in beer

Cut a 1.25 kg (2¾ lb) chicken into pieces and fry them in butter in a casserole until golden. Add 2 peeled, chopped shallots and fry lightly. Add 60 ml (2 fl oz,

¼ cup) Dutch gin and flambé it. Now add 400 ml (14 fl oz, 1¾ cups) beer, 60 ml (2 fl oz, ¼ cup) crème fraîche, 1 bouquet garni, salt and a little cayenne pepper. Cover and simmer. Clean and finely slice 250 g (9 oz) mushrooms and add the contents of the casserole. After 45 minutes of cooking, take the chicken pieces out of the casserole, drain and arrange on a serving dish. Put aside in a warm place. Remove the bouquet garni, add 60 ml (2 fl oz, ¼ cup) crème fraîche and reduce by half. Mix a little of the sauce with an egg yolk and stir, then pour back into the casserole and beat vigorously. Pour the sauce over the chicken and sprinkle with finely chopped parsley.

## Chicken crépinettes

Crépinette is the term for a small flat sausage, generally made of sausagemeat mixed with chopped parsley and wrapped in caul (*crépine*). Prepare a forcemeat of 3 parts minced (ground) chicken and 1 part fat bacon. Shape into small sausages, wrap them in caul and cook them as for pork crépinettes.

## Chicken croûtes ambassadrices

Fill some small croûtes with chicken purée. Top each with a thin slice of truffle and 1 teaspoon vegetable mirepoix.

## Chicken curry

Prepare the curry powder first (see Basics: condiments). Draw, singe and clean a medium-sized chicken, then cut it into quarters and divide each quarter into 3–4 pieces (make sure the chicken bones are cut cleanly, without splintering). In a flameproof casserole containing lard (shortening) or butter, cook 2 medium onions, 100 g (4 oz, ¾ cup) raw ham or gammon and 2 peeled dessert (eating) apples, all chopped and seasoned with crushed garlic, thyme, bay leaf, cinnamon, cardamom and powdered mace. Then add the chicken pieces and cook until they are firm, stirring them in the mixture without letting them get too coloured.

Add the curry powder. Add 2 tomatoes, peeled, crushed and seeded, and mix well. Moisten with 250 ml (8 fl oz, 1 cup) coconut milk (or almond milk). Simmer with the lid on for about 35 minutes. Ten minutes before serving, add 150 ml (¼ pint, ⅔ cup) double (heavy) cream and the juice of 1 lemon. Continue to reduce the sauce to the desired consistency.

Arrange the chicken pieces in a dish and serve with rice prepared as follows: boil 250 g (9 oz, 1½ cups) rice for 15 minutes in salted water, stirring often; drain and wash several times in cold water. Empty on to a metal plate, wrap in a cloth and dry in a preheated oven at 110°C (225°F, gas ¼) for 15 minutes.

Chicken curry can also be made using the recipe for lamb curry.

## Chicken dauphinoise

Insert some slivers of truffle beneath the skin of a good large Bresse chicken. Sprinkle with salt and pepper inside, then stuff with its own liver and 100 g (4 oz, ½ cup) foie gras, both diced, mixed with a little chopped truffle. Truss the bird and put it in a pig's bladder, sprinkle again with a little salt and pepper, add 3 tablespoons brandy and the same quantity of Madeira, then tie up the bladder.

Make some stock with the giblets, pour it into a flameproof casserole, add the chicken in the bladder and bring to the boil. Cook gently for 45 minutes. Remove the chicken from the pan, being careful not to pierce the bladder, untie it and drain the cooking liquid into a bowl. Remove the forcemeat from the chicken and press it through a sieve. Cut the chicken into joints and arrange on a warm dish. Thicken the cooking liquid with the sieved forcemeat and serve separately in a sauceboat.

## Chicken demi-deuil braised in white stock

Poach a chicken in white stock, place on a serving dish and keep hot. Prepare 8 tartlets or croustades and fill them with a salpicon of calves' or lambs' sweetbreads braised in white stock, and mushrooms gently cooked in butter – all mixed with suprême sauce. Garnish each tartlet with a slice of truffle heated in Madeira. Arrange the tartlets around the chicken and coat it with suprême sauce.

## Chicken Demidof

Stuff a large chicken with a mixture comprising one-third *quenelle* stuffing and two-thirds *à gratin* forcemeat. Prepare a very thick matignon vegetable fondue using 125 g (4½ oz) carrots, 50 g (2 oz) celery, 25 g (1 oz) sliced onion, half a bay leaf, a sprig of thyme, a pinch of salt and a pinch of sugar. Soften the vegetables in butter, moisten with 100 ml (4 fl oz, 7 tablespoons) Madeira and reduce until almost dry.

Place the chicken in a roasting tin (pan) and brown in a preheated oven at 220°C (425°F, gas 7). Remove it from the oven and cover it with the vegetable fondue, then wrap it in a pig's caul or bard it with streaky (slab) bacon or pork fat. Tie it up and braise in a covered casserole, adding a small quantity of chicken stock, at 180°C (350°F, gas 4) for about 2 hours, or until the chicken is cooked through. Add more hot stock to the casserole occasionally to prevent it from drying up. Uncover the casserole to brown the chicken for the final 15–20 minutes cooking time.

Arrange the chicken on a serving dish and surround with artichoke hearts cooked in butter and topped with the vegetable fondue. Garnish each artichoke heart with an onion ring (covered in batter and deep-fried) and a slice of truffle. Deglaze the cooking vessel used for the chicken with Madeira and pour over the chicken.

## Chicken en capilotade

Capilotade is the term for a ragoût, originally from classic French cookery, made of cooked meat leftovers (poultry, beef or veal) that are stewed until they disintegrate.

Take a chicken (boiled, braised, poached or roasted) and remove the bones. Cut the meat into small pieces and place in a well-reduced cold sauce (chasseur, Italian, Portuguese or Provençal). Cover and leave to simmer gently until the meat forms a hash. Then pour into a deep dish.

Alternatively, the chicken and sauce can be poured into a gratin dish, sprinkled with breadcrumbs and knobs of butter, then cooked in a preheated oven at 240°C (475°F, gas 9) or under a hot grill (broiler) until the surface is well browned. Serve with rice *à la créole*.

## Chicken fricassée à la berrichonne

Scrape some new carrots and fry in butter with a small onion, then drain. Using the same butter, brown a chicken cut up into portions. Add 250 ml (8 fl oz, 1 cup) boiling water or clear chicken stock, then the carrots, a bouquet garni, salt and pepper. Cover and cook gently for 30 minutes. Drain the chicken and keep warm. Mix together 2 egg yolks, a pinch of salt, 2 table-spoons cream and 1 tablespoon vinegar and add to the cooking liquor; heat but do not allow to boil. Roll the chicken pieces in the sauce and serve.

## Chicken in a salt crust

In a bowl mix together 1 kg (2¼ lb, 9 cups) plain (all-purpose) flour, the same weight of coarse sea salt and 100 ml (4 fl oz, 7 tablespoons) cold water. Knead this dough and roll it out on a pastry board. Sprinkle the inside of a chicken with salt and pepper and insert a sprig of rosemary, a bay leaf, its own liver and the livers of 2 other chickens. Place the chicken on the dough, wrap it up and seal it, place on a baking sheet and cook in a preheated oven at 160°C (325°F, gas 3) for 1½ hours. Break off the hard salty crust and discard; remove the chicken and carve. Serve with a salad dressed with walnut oil.

## Chicken in aspic with champagne

Season a chicken weighing about 1.8 kg (4 lb) with salt and pepper, inside and out. Brown it in butter in a flameproof casserole. Add finely diced vegetables, including carrot, turnip, leek, celery, onion, mushroom stalks and a bouquet garni. Cover the pan and place in a preheated oven at 220°C (425°F, gas 7) for 45 minutes, turning the chicken over so that it cooks on all sides.

Remove the lid, add half a bottle of champagne, stir and check the seasoning. Then leave the chicken to finish cooking without the lid.

Prepare some liquid aspic jelly using aspic crystals or gelatine, as preferred, and the rest of the champagne. Strain the juice in which the chicken was cooked and add it to the jelly.

Leave the bird to cool completely, then cut it up and arrange the pieces in the serving dish. Coat them twice with the syrupy jelly, leaving it to set in the refrigerator between coats.

## Chicken jambalaya

Poach a chicken in stock, then drain. When it is quite cold, remove the skin and bones, weigh the meat, and dice it finely. Sauté half this weight of raw diced ham in 50 g (2 oz, ¼ cup) butter over a low heat, with the pan covered. While it is cooking, prepare some rice *à la grecque* using 300–400 g (12–14 oz, 2 cups) uncooked rice and the stock from the chicken. When the ham is cooked, add the diced chicken together with some cayenne, salt and pepper so that the mixture is highly seasoned. Finally, add the rice, mix everything together thoroughly, and serve very hot.

## Chicken koulibiac

Koulibiac is the name of a Russian pie filled with fish, vegetables, rice and hard-boiled (hard-cooked) eggs. The classic recipe has been adapted in many ways – this is one variation.

Make 675 g (1½ lb) puff pastry. Boil a chicken in stock. Hard-boil (hard-cook) 3 eggs, shell them and cut into quarters. Chop 250 g (9 oz, 3 cups) mushrooms, 2 shallots and a small bunch of parsley, and cook in 50 g (2 oz, ¼ cup) melted butter until all the moisture has evaporated.

Put 100 g (4 oz, ⅔ cup) rice into the pan with 2½ times its volume of the strained chicken stock and a bouquet garni. Season with salt and pepper, mix, cover the pan, bring to the boil and cook for about 16 minutes. Add the cooked mushroom mixture and leave to get cold. Dice 400 g (14 oz, 2 cups) cooked chicken meat and the hard-boiled eggs and carefully mix them into the mushroom-flavoured rice.

Roll out two-thirds of the dough into a rectangle 3 mm (⅛ in) thick. Leaving a narrow border free, pile the chicken and rice mixture into the centre. Roll out the remaining dough and cover the pie. Pinch the edges to seal them, garnish with strips of pastry and brush with beaten egg. Cook in a preheated oven at 230°C (450°F, gas 8) for about 30 minutes. Serve the koulibiac very hot, with melted butter.

## Chicken liver brochettes à l'italienne

Clean some chicken livers and cut each in half. Roll up each piece of liver in a thin slice of smoked bacon, then thread them on to skewers, with pieces of onion and sage leaves in between each piece. Moisten lightly with oil and season with salt, pepper and a little dried thyme. Leave to stand for 30 minutes. Grill (broil) the brochettes under a fierce heat for about 10 minutes, brushing with oil as necessary. Serve with lemon halves and a green salad.

## Chicken liver croustades

Make some small pastry cases. Clean the chicken livers (turkey or duck livers can also be used), separate the pieces, season with salt and pepper, and fry quickly in very hot butter. Drain. Fry some sliced mushrooms and chopped shallots in butter, then season. Warm the empty croustades in the oven.

Add enough Madeira sauce to the mushroom pan to make a filling for the croustades, then add the livers. Alternatively, deglaze the liver and mushroom cooking juices with Madeira, then thicken with a small amount of beurre manié. Heat up this mixture and use to fill the pastry cases. Serve very hot. The croustades can be garnished with slices of truffle poached in Madeira.

## Chicken liver flan chavette

Bake a flan case (pie shell) blind. Thickly slice 500 g (18 oz) trimmed chicken livers. Season and sauté quickly in hot butter. Drain and keep warm. Sauté 200 g (7 oz, 2⅓ cups) sliced mushrooms in the same butter. Season, drain and keep warm with the chicken livers.

Make a sauce by adding 200 ml (7 fl oz, ¾ cup) Madeira to the juices in the pan in which the chicken livers and mushrooms were cooked. Reduce a little. Add 350 ml (12 fl oz, 1½ cups) thin béchamel sauce and 200 ml (7 fl oz, ¾ cup) single (light) cream and reduce the sauce until it has a creamy consistency. Strain it, then add the chicken livers and mushrooms. Simmer gently without allowing the sauce to boil.

Prepare some very soft scrambled eggs (using 8–10 eggs) and then add 2 tablespoons grated Parmesan cheese and 2 tablespoons butter.

Arrange the chicken livers and mushrooms in the bottom of the flan case. Top with the scrambled egg mixture and sprinkle with grated cheese. Pour some melted butter over the top and brown quickly in a preheated oven at 240°C (475°F, gas 9) so that the scrambled eggs are not overcooked.

## Chicken liver fritots

Trim about 500 g (18 oz) chicken or duck livers and purée by rubbing through a sieve or using a food processor or blender. Peel 4 shallots and chop them finely. Separately, chop a small bunch of parsley and a small peeled garlic clove. Gently braise the chopped shallots in 25 g (1 oz, 2 tablespoons) butter. Mix together the liver purée, garlic, chopped parsley and braised shallots in a bowl together with 100 g (4 oz, 2 cups) fresh breadcrumbs, 2 beaten eggs, 2 tablespoons Madeira, 2 tablespoons cream, 1 tablespoon plain (all-purpose) flour and some salt and pepper. Knead together to obtain a smooth mixture and leave to rest for 1 hour. Divide the mixture into small pieces (about the size of a tangerine), roll them into balls and flatten them slightly then dip into batter. Deep-fry in very hot oil and drain on paper towels. Serve the fritots with a highly seasoned tomato sauce, slices of lemon and some fried chopped parsley sprigs.

## Chicken liver fritters

Remove the gall from the chicken livers (if present) and marinate for 30 minutes in oil seasoned with salt, pepper and chopped mixed herbs to taste. Then dry and dip in batter. Deep-fry in hot oil and serve garnished with fried parsley.

## Chicken liver timbale

Prepare some chicken livers and mushrooms as in the recipe for chicken liver croustades. Cook some shell-shaped pasta or macaroni *al dente*. Drain well. Add the chicken livers to the pasta, together with the mushrooms and some Madeira sauce (or a Madeira sauce thickened with blended arrowroot or beurre manié) and cream. Adjust the seasoning and serve very hot in a timbale mould or large dish.

## Chicken Maryland

Cut a raw chicken into joints and dip the pieces into cold milk. Drain them, coat with flour and fry in butter until golden. Continue cooking over a very low heat, turning once, until cooked through. Meanwhile, place the carcass and giblets in a saucepan with garlic, onion, a little stock and some milk. Bring to the boil and simmer for a few minutes, then strain the liquid and pour over the fried chicken pieces. Garnish with fried bacon rashers (slices) and serve with corn fritters or grilled (broiled) corn-on-the-cob.

## Chicken medallions à l'égyptienne

Remove the breasts from a raw chicken and trim and flatten them into round or oval medallions. Cut some large aubergines (eggplants) into rounds about 1 cm (½ in) thick and sprinkle with lemon juice. Prepare some rice pilaf. Fry the chicken medallions and aubergine rounds separately in olive oil, then arrange them alternately round a serving dish. Fill the centre of the dish with rice pilaf. Deglaze the pan in which the chicken was cooked with white wine, add this juice to a thick and well-seasoned tomato fondue, and serve separately in a sauceboat (gravy boat).

## Chicken medallions Beauharnais

Remove the breasts from a large chicken and cut each into 2 or 3 slices of equal thickness; flatten them slightly and trim them into round or oval medallions. Season with salt and pepper and sauté in butter. Prepare an equal number of artichoke hearts and cook them in butter.

Fry some bread croûtes, the same size as the medallions, in butter. Arrange an artichoke heart on each croûton, cover with Beauharnais sauce, made by mixing 200 ml (7 fl oz, ¾ cup) béarnaise sauce with 25 g (1 oz, 2 tablespoons) tarragon butter, and top with a chicken medallion.

## Chicken medallions Fédora

Prepare some medallions from the breast of a chicken. Peel some cucumbers, cut them into uniform pieces, and cook them in butter. Keep warm. Cut some slices of bread to the same size and shape as the medallions and fry them in butter. Cook the medallions gently in butter, and keep them warm.

Deglaze the pan in which the chicken was cooked with a mixture of wine and stock; boil until almost completely evaporated. Add some cream and reduce again until the sauce is smooth. Place a medallion on top of each croûton and arrange them in a circle on the serving dish. Coat with the sauce and place the pieces of cucumber in the centre of the circle.

## Chicken mireille

Heat 65 g (2½ oz, 5 tablespoons) butter in a sauté pan and gently cook a large Bresse chicken, cut into 8 pieces, until the meat turns white. As soon as the pieces are firm, but not coloured, add 500 ml (17 fl oz, 2 cups) dry white wine and reduce until almost all the liquid has evaporated. Add 1 kg (2¼ lb) fresh morels, carefully cleaned, washed and patted dry, then 1 litre (1¾ pints, 4⅓ cups) double (heavy) cream; cook gently for 35 minutes.

Remove the pieces of chicken and the morels and arrange on a hot serving dish. Reduce the cooking liquid to 500 ml (17 fl oz, 2 cups). Thicken it with 1 egg yolk, whisking over the heat but not allowing it to boil. Pour this sauce over the chicken.

## Chicken mousse

Poach 500 g (18 oz) chicken meat and pound in a mortar or purée in a food processor or blender and season the mixture well using curry powder or ground nutmeg. Sprinkle with salt and pepper, then blend in 2–3 egg whites, one after the other. Rub this forcemeat through a sieve and refrigerate for

2 hours. Then place the bowl in a container of crushed ice and gradually add 600 ml (1 pint, 2½ cups) double (heavy) cream, stirring the mixture with a wooden spoon. Adjust the seasoning, pour the mousse into a lightly oiled plain mould, and poach gently in a bain marie in a preheated oven at 190°C (375°F, gas 5) for about 20 minutes. Set aside and wait about 10 minutes before turning out the mousse on to a platter. Serve the mousse warm, coated with a sauce for chicken.

## Chicken pâté pantin

A pâté pantin is a variety of pâté en croute, rectangular or oblong in shape, that is not cooked in a mould.

Prepare a chicken ballotine. Half-cook it in a light chicken stock, drain it and leave it to cool. Roll out about 575 g (1¼ lb) brioche dough and divide it into 2 equal portions. Coat one of the halves with very thin strips of bacon, place the chicken in the centre and turn up the edges of the dough all around the sides. Place some more thin strips of bacon on top of the filling and cover with the second piece of dough. Seal the edges and make a small hole in the centre of the top to allow steam to escape. Place the pâté pantin on a baking sheet and cook in a preheated oven at 190°C (375°F, gas 5) for about 70 minutes. Serve hot.

## Chicken petit-duc

Cook some morels and truffle slivers in a frying pan with some butter. Sauté a chicken *à brun*, then drain it and set it aside and keep warm in a serving dish. Deglaze the pan in which the chicken was cooked with 3 tablespoons Madeira, boil to reduce and then moisten with 150 ml (¼ pint, ⅔ cup) demi-glace sauce. Garnish the chicken with the morels and truffles slivers and pour over the Madeira sauce.

## Chicken pie

Cut a raw chicken weighing about 1.25 kg (2¾ lb) into pieces. Sprinkle the pieces with 100 g (4 oz, ⅔ cup) finely chopped onions and shallots, 150 g (5 oz, 1¾ cups) sliced mushrooms and some chopped flat leaf parsley. Season with salt and pepper. Line a buttered pie dish with 200 g (7 oz) very thin slices of veal seasoned with salt and pepper. Place the chicken in the pie dish, first the thighs, then the wings and finally the breasts. Cover the chicken with 150 g (5 oz) bacon cut into very thin rashers (slices). Add 4 hard-boiled (hard-cooked) egg yolks cut in half. Pour in some chicken stock to three-quarters fill the pie dish.

Press a strip of puff pastry around the rim of the pie dish, brush with water, then cover the whole dish with a layer of pastry. Seal the edges, then flute with the back of a knife. Brush the whole surface with beaten egg and make a hole in the centre. Bake for 1½ hours in a preheated oven at 190°C (375°F, gas 5). Just before serving, pour 2–3 tablespoons concentrated chicken stock into the pie.

## Chicken pilaf

Prepare some pilaf rice. Select a chicken weighing about 1.25 kg (2¾ lb) and divide it into 8 pieces. Season with salt and pepper and cook in a flameproof casserole containing 50 g (2 oz, ¼ cup) butter. Remove with a draining spoon and set aside. Add to the casserole 1 tablespoon chopped onion, 175 ml (6 fl oz, ¾ cup) dry white wine, 200 ml (7 fl oz, ¾ cup) chicken stock, 1 tablespoon well-reduced tomato sauce, a crushed garlic clove and a bouquet garni. Cook this sauce for 5 minutes, stirring, then strain and return it to the casserole with the pieces of chicken; reheat thoroughly. Shape the pilaf rice into a ring on the serving dish and pour the chicken and its sauce into the centre. Serve hot.

## Chicken princesse

Poach a chicken in white stock and keep warm in a serving dish. Bake some barquette cases blind and cook some green asparagus tips in butter. Prepare an allemande sauce with the cooking liquid. Put the asparagus tips in the barquettes and sprinkle with slivers of truffle heated in butter. Use to garnish the dish. Pour some of the sauce over the chicken and serve the rest separately.

## Chicken rosière

Stuff a large roasting chicken with panada forcemeat made with cream, truss and bard it, then cook in white stock, like chicken with tarragon. Prepare separately some slices of calves' sweetbreads cooked in white stock, and a mushroom purée. Untie the chicken, remove the barding fat, cut into joints and arrange in a round dish, surrounded by the calves' sweetbreads and the forcemeat, cut into slices. Pour over all this a sauce made from the cooking liquid, strained and reduced. Serve the mushroom purée separately.

## Chicken velouté soup

Thicken a generous 750 ml (1½ pints, 3¼ cups) chicken consommé with a white roux made with 40 g (1½ oz, 3 tablespoons) butter and 40 g (1½ oz, 6 tablespoons) plain (all-purpose) flour. Add a small young chicken and simmer gently until the bird breaks up with a fork. Drain and bone the chicken, reserve some breast meat for a garnish and reduce the remainder to a purée in a food processor or blender, adding a little of the cooking liquid. Mix with the rest of the cooking liquid. Remove from the heat and thicken the soup with 3 egg yolks beaten with 100 ml (4 fl oz, 7 tablespoons) double (heavy) cream. Whisk in 75 g (3 oz, 6 tablespoons) butter. Cut the reserved meat into very fine strips and add to the soup. Reheat but do not boil.

Game can be used instead of chicken to make a game velouté soup.

## Chicken waterzooï

Poach a chicken until three-quarters cooked (about 40 minutes) in a white stock containing an onion stuck with 2 cloves, a bouquet garni, 1 celery stick and 1 leek, both sliced. Slice 1 leek, 1 carrot and 1 celery stick and cook in a covered flameproof casserole with some of the chicken stock for 30 minutes. Cut the chicken into 8 pieces and arrange them on the vegetables. Add sufficient stock to cover the chicken and cook for a further 30 minutes.

Remove the chicken pieces and the vegetables with a slotted spoon. Add 200 ml (7 fl oz, ¾ cup) double (heavy) cream to the casserole and reduce to a smooth sauce; adjust the seasoning. Replace the chicken and vegetables and serve, accompanied with bread and butter or buttered toast.

## Chicken with artichokes

Sauté a chicken *à brun*, adding some artichoke quarters (blanched in salted water) halfway through the cooking period. Drain the chicken and its garnish, arrange in a serving dish and keep warm. Deglaze the cooking pan with white wine and stock; reduce, thicken with a little beurre manié and pour this sauce over the chicken and artichokes. Sprinkle with parsley.

## Chicken with bamboo shoots

Place a chicken in a large pan and cover with water. Bring to the boil. Immediately remove and drain the chicken. Cool the stock by standing the container in cold water. Skim the stock, replace the chicken and bring back to the boil. Add 5–6 shiitake mushrooms, 1–2 scented Chinese mushrooms, 100 ml (4 fl oz, 7 tablespoons) soy sauce, 3 tablespoons sugar, salt and pepper, and continue cooking. After 1 hour, drain 225 g (8 oz) preserved bamboo shoots, rinse in cold water, then cut into thick sticks, add to the pan and simmer gently until the chicken is cooked – about 20 minutes for a tender bird or 1 hour for a boiling fowl. Drain the chicken, remove the skin and cut all the meat into thin strips. Arrange the chicken on a serving dish and surround with the mushrooms and bamboo shoots. Just before serving, trim 3–4 spring onions (scallions) and fry quickly in oil. Add 2 tablespoons soy sauce and use to garnish the dish. The stock, highly seasoned with pepper and with fine rice stick vermicelli added, can be served at the end of the meal.

## Chicken with basil

Sauté the chicken *à brun*. Drain it and arrange on a warm dish. Deglaze the cooking pan with 200 ml (7 fl oz, ¾ cup) dry white wine. Add 1 tablespoon chopped fresh basil and whisk in 50 g (2 oz, 4 tablespoons) butter. Pour this sauce over the chicken.

## Chicken with ceps

Sauté a chicken *à brun* in equal quantities of butter and oil. Three-quarters of the way through the cooking time, add 300 g (11 oz, 4 cups) ceps or other mushrooms, sliced and sautéed in oil, then 2 chopped shallots. Finish cooking. Arrange the drained chicken and mushrooms in a serving dish. Deglaze the casserole with 100 ml (4 fl oz, 7 tablespoons) white wine; reduce, then pour it over the chicken and mushrooms. Sprinkle with chopped parsley. A small crushed garlic clove can be added to the sauce.

## Chicken with cider

Peel, quarter and core 500 g (18 oz) sour apples; cut half of them into thin slices. Season the inside of a large chicken with salt and pepper, stuff it with the apple slices and sew up the opening. Baste the chicken with melted butter and brown in a flameproof casserole for about 20 minutes. Meanwhile, chop 3 shallots and brown them lightly in butter. When the chicken is golden brown, surround it with the remaining apples and add a little crumbled thyme, 2 crushed cloves, salt, freshly ground pepper, the shallots and ½ bottle of cider, already heated. Bring to the boil, partly cover and cook for about 40 minutes. Remove the chicken and keep it hot. Add 200 ml (7 fl oz, ¾ cup) double (heavy) cream to the casserole and reduce by a third. Cut the chicken into portions and serve coated with the sauce.

## Chicken with cream

Sauté a chicken *à blanc*; drain and keep warm on a serving dish. Pour off the cooking fat from the pan, add 150 ml (¼ pints, ⅔ cup) dry cider and reduce until all the liquid has evaporated. Mix in 200 ml (7 fl oz, ¾ cup) double (heavy) cream and reduce just enough to make the sauce very smooth; adjust the seasoning. Pour the sauce over the chicken and sprinkle with parsley. The chicken can be flamed in Calvados, or white wine used instead of cider.

## Chicken with hazelnuts

Cut a chicken into 4 pieces. Sprinkle the pieces with salt and freshly ground pepper, dip them in flour, then brown them in butter. Moisten with stock made from the giblets and cook with the lid on for 30 minutes. Keep hot. Lightly toast 150 g (5 oz, 1 cup) shelled hazelnuts under the grill (broiler), then grind them and blend with 150 g (5 oz, ⅔ cup) butter. Reduce the cooking liquid from the chicken, then add the nut butter and 4 tablespoons crème fraîche; cook for 5–6 minutes over a low heat. Pour this sauce, to which some whole nuts can be added, over the chicken.

## Chicken with lemon

Cut a chicken into portions. Squeeze 2 lemons and add salt, pepper and a dash of cayenne to the juice. Marinate the chicken pieces in this for at least 1 hour, then drain, reserving the marinade. Brown the chicken pieces in butter in a flameproof casserole. Reduce the heat, sprinkle the chicken with crumbled thyme, cover and leave to cook gently for 30 minutes. Drain the chicken and keep hot. Add the marinade to the casserole with 100 ml (4 fl oz, 7 tablespoons) double (heavy) cream. Stir well and heat, stirring constantly as the sauce thickens. Adjust the seasoning. Coat the chicken with this sauce.

## Chicken with morels

Wash 4–5 morels and split them in two lengthways. Dredge 6–8 chicken fillets with flour and fry briskly in 25 g (1 oz, 2 tablespoons) butter in a shallow pan with 1 chopped shallot. When golden brown, season with salt and pepper and add the morels. Cover the pan and cook gently for 7–8 minutes, then add 6 tablespoons Sauvignon wine and finish the cooking with the lid off. (A little grated nutmeg will further improve the flavour.) Add 1 tablespoon double (heavy) cream and cook for another 10–12 minutes. Serve in a hot dish.

## Chicken with oysters

Sauté a chicken *à blanc*. Poach 12 oysters in their own liquid. Drain the cooked chicken and keep warm on a serving dish. Deglaze the cooking pan with 100 ml (4 fl oz, 7 tablespoons) white wine and the liquid from the oysters; reduce by half and add 100 ml (4 fl oz, 7 tablespoons) chicken velouté sauce. Add a little lemon juice, then 40 g (1½ oz, 3 tablespoons) butter, whisking all the time. Put the oysters around the chicken and pour over the sauce.

## Chicken with plantains

Sauté a chicken *à brun* in a flameproof casserole; when golden, add 1 large chopped onion, 5 peeled tomatoes and 250 g (9 oz) streaky bacon cut into pieces. Cook for 1 hour, occasionally adding a little cold water to prevent the fat from blackening; season with salt and pepper. While the chicken is cooking, cut 12 peeled plantains in half and boil them in a saucepan of water for 30 minutes. Drain them and place in the casserole with the chicken; simmer for a further 15 minutes. Serve very hot.

## Chicken with preserved lemon

Cut a chicken into portions and sprinkle with salt and pepper. Finely slice 300 g (11 oz) onions; crush 3 garlic cloves. Grate at least 1 teaspoon fresh root ginger. Oil a flameproof casserole and spread the sliced onions over the bottom, then sprinkle with the crushed garlic, a pinch of powdered saffron, the grated ginger and 1 tablespoon coriander seeds. Add a bouquet garni. Garnish with 8 slices of preserved lemon.

Arrange the chicken portions on top, sprinkle with 6 tablespoons olive oil, season with salt and pepper, and one-third cover the chicken pieces with chicken stock. Cover the casserole and cook over a moderate heat for about 1½ hours, or until the flesh comes easily away from the bones. Remove and drain the chicken, throw away the bouquet garni and reduce the pan juice until it is oily. Coat the chicken portions with the juice and serve very hot, with rice *à la créole*.

## Chicken with rice à la Bourbon

Fry a large roasting chicken with a little lard (shortening) in a flameproof casserole, until just golden. Add 1 finely chopped onion, 2 whole carrots, 1 tablespoon tomato purée (paste) and a bouquet garni. Season with salt and pepper, half-cover with stock and cook gently for 1¼–1½ hours, according to the size of the bird.

Blanch 250 g (9 oz, 1¼ cups) rice for 5 minutes, then drain and cool. Add twice its volume of stock to the rice and cook until soft, but do not allow the grains to disintegrate (about 18 minutes). Pack into a greased ring mould and unmould on to a round serving dish. Cut the chicken into pieces and arrange in the middle. Strain the chicken cooking liquid and pour it over the chicken.

## Chicken with rice and suprême sauce

Truss a large chicken as for roasting and cook it in white stock, like chicken with tarragon, but for only 40 minutes. Blanch 250 g (9 oz, 1¼ cups) rice for 5 minutes, drain, rinse and drain once more. Drain the half-cooked chicken, strain the stock, then return the chicken to the casserole; add the drained rice and the stock – it should come to about 3 cm (1¼ in) above the rice. Add 25 g (1 oz, 2 tablespoons) butter and cook gently for 20 minutes. Make a suprême sauce with the rest of the stock. Put the chicken on a dish, pour over a little of the sauce and surround with rice. Serve the remaining sauce separately.

## Chicken with sherry

Cut a 1.25 kg (2¾ lb) chicken into quarters. Lightly brown 50 g (2 oz, ¼ cup) butter in a flameproof casserole and thoroughly brown the chicken pieces in it. Season with salt and pepper, cover and cook for about 35 minutes, adding 1 finely chopped shallot 10 minutes before the end of cooking. Remove the chicken pieces and keep hot on a serving dish. Blend 1 teaspoon arrowroot with 150 ml (¼ pint, ⅔ cup) medium sherry. Pour this mixture into the casserole and stir well while heating. Add a pinch of cayenne pepper, then pour the sauce over the chicken pieces and serve.

## Chicken with tarragon

Clean a large roasting chicken and put a bunch of tender tarragon sprigs inside it. Truss as for roasting, rub lightly with half a lemon and bard the breast and back with thin slices of rindless bacon. Place in a flameproof casserole and just cover with white stock, adding a small bunch of tarragon. Cover, bring quickly to the boil, then cook gently for about 1 hour (when pricked, the juice which comes out of the chicken should be clear). Drain the chicken, untie it and remove the barding fat and the tarragon from inside. Garnish with blanched tarragon leaves and keep hot on a serving dish.

Thicken the cooking liquid with a little arrowroot or beurre manié; strain it and add 2 tablespoons chopped fresh tarragon. Pour a little of this sauce over the chicken and serve the remainder in a sauceboat.

Alternatively, the casserole can be deglazed with a glass of white wine and a little thickened and strained veal stock to which a handful of chopped tarragon leaves has been added.

## Chicken with tarragon in aspic

Cook a large roasting chicken in white stock as in the recipe for chicken with tarragon. Drain it, untruss it and pat dry; leave it to cool, then place it in the refrigerator.

Skim the fat off the cooking liquid and strain it, then heat it, adding 20 g (¾ oz, 3 envelopes) powdered gelatine completely dissolved in cold water. In a saucepan, whisk together 100 g (4 oz, ¾ cup) lean minced (ground) beef, 1 egg white and a handful of tarragon leaves, roughly chopped. Add the cooking liquid, whisking all the time, and bring to the boil. Simmer gently for 30 minutes, then strain the liquid, add 100 ml (4 fl oz, 7 tablespoons) Madeira and leave to cool.

When the aspic is nearly set, coat the chicken with several layers, placing it in the refrigerator after each application. Garnish the chicken with blanched tarragon leaves, arranged in a decorative pattern, before the last application of aspic. Finally, place the chicken on a serving dish surrounded with any remaining set aspic cut into cubes.

## Chicken with vinegar

Peel and dice 2 carrots, 1 turnip, the cleaned white parts of 2 leeks and 1 celery stick; stud 1 large onion with 2 cloves. Brown the giblets of the chicken, plus those of 2 others, in a little butter. Place all these giblets into a pan with 1 litre (1¾ pints, 4⅓ cups) cold water and bring to the boil; then add all the vegetables, a bouquet garni, 4 shallots, 2 peeled crushed garlic cloves, 175 ml (6 fl oz, ¾ cup) dry white wine, some salt, pepper and a small pinch of cayenne pepper. Simmer gently for 45–60 minutes.

Heat 40 g (1½ oz, 3 tablespoons) butter in a flameproof casserole and cook the chicken, cut into 6 pieces, for about 10 minutes until golden brown; cover and simmer for another 35 minutes.

Reduce the liquid in which the giblets were cooked by half, then strain it and add 175 ml (6 fl oz, ¾ cup) white wine vinegar; reduce again by one-third. Purée the chicken liver. When the chicken is cooked, pour the vinegar sauce into the casserole, stir well and cook together for 5 minutes; thicken with 1 tablespoon beurre manié. Dilute the liver purée with 1 tablespoon vinegar and blend into the sauce, away from the heat. Serve very hot.

## Chicken yassa

The day before the meal (or at least 2 hours in advance) cut up a chicken into 4 or 6 pieces; marinate them in the juice of 3 limes with half a chilli pepper, finely chopped, 1 tablespoon groundnut (peanut) oil, 3 large onions (sliced), salt and pepper. Remove the chicken pieces and grill them, preferably over hot embers, browning them well all over. Remove the onions from the marinade and brown them with a little oil in a sauté pan, then moisten with the marinade and 2 tablespoons water. Add the chicken pieces, cover the pan and simmer for about 25 minutes. Serve the chicken very hot coated with the sauce, in the centre of a ring of rice *à la créole*.

## Cockscombs en attereaux à la Villeroi

Prick the combs lightly with a needle and put them under cold running water, pressing them with the fingers to dispel the blood. Place in saucepan, cover with cold water and cook until the water reaches a temperature of 40–45°C (104–113°F), when the skin of the combs begins to detach itself. Drain the combs and rub them one by one in a cloth sprinkled with fine salt.

Remove the outer skin; put the combs in cold water and, when they are white, plunge them into a boiling white court-bouillon. Cook for 35 minutes. Drain and dry them, then cover with Villeroi sauce. Leave to cool on a grid. Cover the combs with beaten egg, sprinkle with breadcrumbs and fry in clarified butter.

## Consommé à la madrilène

Prepare a chicken consommé for 5 people. When clarifying, add 300 ml (½ pint, 1¼ cups) chopped fresh tomato pulp. Strain the soup through a very fine strainer, add a pinch of cayenne and leave to cool completely, then refrigerate. Serve cold in cups. The soup can be garnished with finely diced red (bell) pepper which has been cooked in stock.

## Consommé à la parisienne

Use chicken consommé. Garnish the consommé with shredded vegetables lightly cooked in butter, rounds of plain royales and chervil leaves.

## Consommé à la reine

Make some chicken consommé and some plain royale. Then poach some chicken breasts in court-bouillon and shred the meat finely. Thicken the consommé with tapioca. Garnish the soup with the royale cut into dice or lozenges and the shredded chicken.

## Consommé à l'impériale

Use chicken consommé. Poach some very small cockscombs and cock's kidneys in stock. Cook 1½ tablespoons rice in the consommé, adding 1–2 tablespoons garden peas cooked in water, the cockscombs and kidneys, and finely shredded savoury pancakes.

## Consommé à l'infante

Use chicken consommé. Fill 20 small profiteroles with a purée of foie gras mixed with a thick chicken velouté. Thicken the consommé with arrowroot and serve with the profiteroles.

## Consommé au diablotins

Use chicken consommé. To garnish the soup, prepare a number of very small *diablotins*. Lightly thicken the consommé with tapioca and garnish with the *diablotins*.

## Consommé Bizet

Use chicken consommé. Make some very small chicken quenelles mixed with chopped tarragon leaves and poach them in the consommé. Clarify the consommé and thicken it lightly with tapioca. Garnish with quenelles and sprinkle with chervil leaves. Serve immediately with very small profiteroles filled with a *brunoise* of vegetables, which have been braised in butter.

## Consommé Brillat-Savarin

Use chicken consommé. Thicken with cornflour (cornstarch) or leave it thin, as liked. Garnish with 1½ tablespoons finely shredded poached chicken breast, 1½ tablespoons savoury pancakes cut into very small diamonds, and 1½ tablespoons mixed finely shedded lettuce and sorrel. Sprinkle with chervil.

## Consommé Colbert

Use chicken consommé. Garnish the consommé with 3 tablespoons finely shredded vegetables cooked in butter and poach 1 egg in the consommé for each person. Sprinkle with chervil leaves.

## Consommé Dalayrac

Use chicken consommé. Thicken the consommé with tapioca. Garnish with shredded chicken, mushrooms cooked in a court-bouillon and truffles.

## Consommé Leverrier

Use chicken consommé. Thicken the consommé with tapioca and garnish with royales cut into star shapes and chervil leaves.

## Consommé Pépita

Use chicken consommé. Prepare a tomato royale and cut it into dice. Peel a green (bell) pepper, chop it finely and cook in a little consommé. Season 4 teaspoons tomato purée (paste) with paprika and add it to the consommé, along with the royale and the pepper. (The royale may be omitted.)

## Consommé princesse

Use chicken consommé. Cook 15 green asparagus tips in butter. Prepare 15 small chicken forcemeat quenelles and poach them in stock. Add them to the consommé with the asparagus tips and some chervil leaves.

## Consommé with chicken pinions

Use chicken consommé. Poach in a simple consommé 4 chicken pinions and 2 necks cut into 3–4 sections and tied in a muslin (cheesecloth) bag. When cooked, clarify the stock, cut the meat into pieces and add to the consommé.

## Coq au vin

Cut up a chicken of about 1.8 kg (4 lb) into 6 pieces. Gently fry 90 g (3½ oz, ⅔ cup) diced lean bacon and about 20 small onions (pearl onions) in 40 g (1½ oz, 3 tablespoons) butter in an earthenware or cast iron pot. When these are lightly browned, add the chicken pieces, 1 finely chopped garlic clove, a bouquet garni and about 20 morels or other mushrooms. Sauté, covered, over a brisk heat until golden. Remove the lid and skim off the fat. Pour a little good brandy over the chicken, set light to it, then pour on 500 ml (17 fl oz, 2 cups) old Auvergne wine (a Chambertin or a Mâcon). After cooking over a brisk heat for about 1¼ hours, take out the chicken, thicken the sauce with beurre manié, and pour it over the chicken.

## Coq en pâte

Despite its name, this dish is usually prepared with a fine roasting chicken. When the chicken has been dressed and singed, remove the breastbone and stuff it copiously with a mixture of foie gras and large pieces of truffle (seasoned with salt and spices, and moistened with a little Cognac) and a small quantity of fine forcemeat. Truss the chicken, tucking the legs into the sides. Brown on all sides in butter – about 20 g, (¾ oz, 1½ tablespoons). Cover the chicken with a *matignon* of braising vegetables – about 300 g (11 oz, 2 cups) – and wrap it in a pig's caul soaked in cold water and dried.

Make some lining pastry using 500 g (18 oz, 4½ cups) plain (all-purpose) flour, 300 g (11 oz, 1⅓ cups) butter, 1 egg, 100 ml (4 fl oz, 7 tablespoons) water and 1½ teaspoons salt. Place the chicken on an oval sheet of pastry and cover it with a similar sheet. Pinch the edges together. (Nowadays, the chicken is usually put in an oval terrine which exactly contains it and then simply covered with the chosen short pastry.) Brush the pastry with egg and cut several slits in the top to allow steam to escape.

Cook in a preheated oven at 190°C (375°F, gas 5) for about 1½ hours, protecting the top of the pastry with foil once it is browned. *Coq en pâte* is traditionally accompanied by a Périgueux sauce served separately.

## Coquelets en crapaudine à l'américaine

Split and flatten 2 young cocks as spatchcocks. Chop 2–3 garlic cloves and some parsley. Add salt, 3 tablespoons oil, a good quantity of pepper, 2 teaspoons ground ginger and a pinch of cayenne. Cover the cocks inside and outside with this mixture, then marinate them for 1 hour. Grill (broil) briskly and serve them with a green salad or mixed salad.

## Country-style coq au vin

Cut 1 cockerel into pieces and season well. Peel 12 small pickling or pearl onions. Scald 125 g (4½ oz) lean bacon rashers (slices). Melt 50 g (2 oz, ¼ cup) butter and 1 tablespoon oil in a casserole. Add the bacon and onions and fry until golden. Remove and drain thoroughly. Brown the pieces of cockerel in the fat in the casserole, turning them over several times. Return the bacon and onions to the casserole. Heat 1 tablespoon Cognac, pour into the casserole and ignite. Pour in 750 ml (1¼ pints, 3¼ cups) red wine, 1 bouquet garni and 2 crushed garlic gloves. Bring slowly to the boil, cover and simmer for 1 hour.

Thinly slice 200 g (7 oz) button mushrooms and fry in 25 g (1 oz, 2 tablespoons) butter. Add to the casserole and cook for another 20–25 minutes. A few minutes before serving, cream 50 g (2 oz, ¼ cup) butter with 1 tablespoon flour. Gradually stir in a little cooking liquid from the casserole, then pour this mixture slowly into the casserole. Cook, stirring, for 5 minutes, then add 3 tablespoons of cockerel blood and allow to thicken, without boiling, for 5 minutes, stirring constantly. Serve with steamed potatoes or fresh pasta.

## Cream of chicken soup

Put a small chicken into a saucepan with 1 litre (1¾ pints, 4⅓ cups) white consommé, bring to the boil and skim. Add a bouquet garni and the white parts of 2 leeks and 1 celery stick. Simmer gently, covered, until the meat comes away from the bones. Drain the chicken, retaining the stock, and remove the skin and bones. Keep the breast fillets and reduce the remaining meat to a purée using a food processor. Press through a sieve. Shred the breast fillets finely and keep them hot in a little consommé. Add 750 ml (1¼ pints, 3¼ cups) béchamel sauce to the chicken purée and bring to the boil. Add a few spoonfuls of the chicken stock and whisk. Adjust the seasoning and sieve again. Add 100 ml (4 fl oz, 7 tablespoons) single (light) cream and whisk while heating. Add the finely shredded breast fillets just before serving.

## Chicken à la reine

Prepare 500 g (18 oz) panada forcemeat with butter and use it to stuff a chicken weighing about 1.8 kg (4 lb). Poach it gently in white stock. Bake some puff-pastry tartlet cases and fill them with chicken purée with cream; garnish with sliced truffles. Make a suprême sauce with the chicken stock. Arrange the chicken on a large hot serving dish and place the tartlets round it. Serve the suprême sauce separately.

## Devilled spring chicken

Spatchcock a spring chicken. Sprinkle with salt and pepper, brush lightly with clarified butter on both sides and half-roast it in a preheated oven at 240°C (475°F, gas 9). Mix 2 tablespoons mustard with a little cayenne and brush this over the chicken. Coat generously with fresh breadcrumbs and sprinkle with a little clarified butter. Finish cooking under the grill (broiler), on both sides. Serve with gherkins (sweet dill pickles), lemon halves and a devilled sauce.

## Feuilletés of chicken or duck liver

Feuilleté is the term for a piece of puff pastry cut into the shape of a finger or triangle and filled or garnished with cheese, ham or seafood.

Make the feuilletés with puff pastry and warm them in the oven. Clean the chicken or duck livers. Separate the lobes and cut into very thin escalopes (scallops). Season with salt and pepper and sauté them briskly in butter; then use a draining spoon to remove them and set aside. Sauté a small quantity of finely chopped shallots, fines herbes, and a few tiny button mushrooms or wild mushrooms, thinly sliced if large, in the butter remaining in the pan. Use the draining spoon to remove the mushrooms, then boil the cooking juices until virtually dry. Return the mushrooms and livers to the pan, then add sufficient Madeira sauce to coat all the ingredients. Cook until the livers are heated through. Cut the middle out of the feuilletés, reserving the tops as lids. Fill the feuilletés with the mushroom and liver mixture and replace the pastry lids; serve piping hot.

## Fricassée of chicken à la berrichonne

Joint a chicken. Brown 350 g (12 oz, 3 cups) new carrots in 50 g (2 oz, ¼ cup) butter in a sauté pan. Drain them, and then brown the chicken pieces in the same butter. Add 250 ml (8 fl oz, 1 cup) chicken stock, the carrots, a bouquet garni and some salt and pepper. Bring to the boil, reduce the heat, cover the pan and cook gently for 45 minutes. Remove the chicken pieces and keep them hot. Mix 2 egg yolks and a pinch of caster (superfine) sugar with 200 ml (7 fl oz, ¾ cup) double (heavy) cream, 1 tablespoon white wine vinegar, and a few drops of the chicken stock. Pour the mixture into the pan and mix thoroughly with the pan juices. Heat without boiling so that the sauce thickens a little. Serve the chicken coated with the sauce and sprinkled with finely chopped parsley.

# Fricassée of chicken Cardinal La Balue

Cut a chicken into 8 portions, season and brown in 40–50 g (1½–2 oz, 3–4 tablespoons) butter in a flameproof casserole. Put the casserole in a preheated oven at 220°C (425°F, gas 7) and cook for about 40 minutes. Prepare a stock with 1 sliced carrot, 1 sliced onion, a bouquet garni, 150 ml (¼ pint, ⅔ cup) white wine, 750 ml (1¼ pints, 3¼ cups) water and some salt and pepper. Cook for about 30 minutes.

Clean 12 crayfish, wash them and cook them for 5 minutes in the stock. Drain the crayfish and shell the tails. Pound the shells and press through a fine sieve to make a purée. Mix the purée with 50 g (2 oz, ¼ cup) butter.

Drain the cooked chicken pieces and place them in another casserole, with the thighs at the bottom. Add the crayfish tails, cover and put the casserole in the oven, which should be either turned off or at a very low heat, so that the chicken does not become tough. Pour 500 ml (17 fl oz, 2 cups) double (heavy) cream into the casserole in which the chicken was cooked, heat up and deglaze the pan. Heat for a few minutes to reduce the cream (but do not boil), then add the crayfish butter and whisk. Arrange the chicken pieces on a heated serving dish and coat with sauce. Serve very hot.

# Fricassée of chicken with Anjou wine

Cut a large chicken into medium-sized portions and season with salt and pepper. Peel 24 button onions and 24 button mushrooms. Brown the chicken portions in butter, then add the onions and mushrooms. Add sufficient white Anjou wine to just cover the chicken, cover the pan and simmer gently for 30–35 minutes.

Add 200 ml (7 fl oz, ¾ cup) double (heavy) cream and adjust the seasoning. Serve very hot, with small steamed new potatoes or a mixture of carrots and glazed turnips. A small turkey can be prepared in the same way.

## Fried spring chicken

Cut a spring chicken into 6 pieces (2 wings, 2 legs and 2 pieces of breast). Mix 2 tablespoons oil with 1 tablespoon lemon juice, some salt and pepper, a little cayenne, 1 finely chopped garlic clove, 1 tablespoon very finely chopped parsley, and, if liked, ½ teaspoon ground ginger. Marinate the chicken pieces in this mixture for 30 minutes. Drain them, coat in breadcrumbs, then deep-fry in very hot oil (180°C, 350°F). When they are golden (13–15 minutes), drain on paper towels, sprinkle with fine salt and serve with lemon quarters.

## Galantine of chicken

Cut the wing tips off a 2 kg (4½ lb) chicken. Slit the bird along the back and, with a small, sharp-pointed knife, bone it completely without tearing the flesh. This operation, which at first sight seems awkward, is actually fairly simple: follow the joints of the chicken and work inwards towards the carcass, shaving off the flesh as close to the bone as possible. This separates the carcass from the body of the chicken. Now remove the bones from the legs and wings, still being careful not to tear the skin. Spread out the bird and cut away the breast and the flesh of the thighs and wings, then cut these pieces into squares.

Now prepare the forcemeat: finely mince (grind) 250 g (9 oz, 1 cup) boned loin of pork and 250 g (9 oz, 1 cup) shoulder of veal. Cut 150 g (5 oz, ¾ cup) fat bacon, 150 g (5 oz, ¾ cup) ham, and 150 g (5 oz, ¾ cup) pickled tongue into 1.5 cm (½ in) cubes; mix with the chicken squares, 150 g (5 oz, 1¼ cups) blanched pistachios, the minced meat, 2 beaten eggs, 6 tablespoons brandy, salt, pepper and ½ teaspoon allspice. Wet your hands in order to work this mixture and blend it together. Shape it first into a ball and then into a rectangular block.

To prepare the galantine, place the block of forcemeat over the central third of chicken and enclose it by folding over the parts of the chicken skin that project at the sides and ends, stretching it without tearing. Soak a coarse linen cloth in water, wring it out, then spread it flat on the table. Place it so that a flap about 25 cm (10 in) long hangs over the edge of the table. Put the galantine lengthways on the cloth, breast upwards, about 10 cm (4 in) from the edge of the table and wrap it as tightly as possible. Tie both ends of the cloth then tie the galantine with string in 3 more places to keep it in shape.

Prepare an aspic stock with 2 partly boned calf's feet, 500 g (18 oz) fresh pork skin, 2 kg (4½ lb) knuckle of veal, 2 large sliced carrots, a large onion studded with cloves, 2 shredded leeks, a bouquet garni enriched with celery, 5 litres (8½ pints, 5½ quarts) white stock, 400 ml (14 fl oz, 1¾ cups) Madeira (optional), salt and pepper. Cook the stock for 1½ hours, then add the galantine, bring rapidly to the boil and simmer for 2¾–3 hours. Remove the galantine. Let it stand for 15 minutes before unwrapping it. Remove the cloth, rinse in lukewarm water and wring thoroughly. Spread it on the table and carefully wrap the galantine in it as before, taking care to keep the slit part of the chicken underneath. Tie up the galantine. Press it on a slab, covering it with a wooden board with a weight on top. Allow to cool for at least 12 hours; it can be kept for several days if it is stored in a cool place.

The galantine is served garnished with its own clarified aspic jelly.

## Grilled chicken à la tyrolienne

Spatchcock a 1 kg (2¼ lb) chicken. Season with salt and pepper, brush with flavoured oil and grill (broil) for 25–30 minutes. Meanwhile, peel and slice 2 large onions and separate into rings. Dust the rings with flour and deep-fry in oil at 180°C (350°F). Cut 4 medium-sized tomatoes into quarters, seed and lightly fry in 25 g (1 oz, 2 tablespoons) butter. Arrange the grilled chicken on a hot dish, surrounded by the onions and tomatoes. Season with salt and pepper and garnish with parsley.

## Hungarian soup with liver dumplings

Cut 150 g (5 oz) calves' or chicken liver into dice and sauté briskly in 15 g
(½ oz, 1 tablespoon) lard (shortening). Season with salt and pepper. Braise
50 g (2 oz, ⅓ cup) thinly sliced onions in butter. Put these ingredients
through a food processor or blender, together with 1 tablespoon chopped
parsley, 1 large egg, 50 g (2 oz, ¼ cup) butter, salt, pepper, 1 teaspoon paprika
and a generous pinch of grated nutmeg. Shape the mixture into small
dumplings and simmer them in stock for 15 minutes. Prepare 1.5 litres
(2¾ pints, 6½ cups) chicken consommé and serve with the dumplings.

## Minute fricassée of chicken

Joint 2 chickens in the usual way and put them in a saucepan with 175 g (6 oz,
¾ cup) good-quality melted butter. Fry the chicken without browning, add
2 tablespoons flour and season with salt, pepper and grated nutmeg; then add
sufficient water to make a lightly thickened sauce. Add 6 blanched button
onions and a bouquet garni and cook over a brisk heat, ensuring that the
chicken pieces do not burn and the sauce is gradually reduced. After
25 minutes, test one of the thighs to see that it is cooked. Add 250 g (9 oz,
3 cups) button mushrooms and skim the fat off the sauce. Blend in 4 egg yolks
to thicken the sauce and add a dash of fresh lemon juice.

## Mme Maigret's coq au vin

(from a recipe by Georges Simenon) Prepare and finely slice 1 carrot, 1 leek
and 1 onion. Cut a chicken of 2 kg (4½ lb) into pieces. Put the vegetables, a
bouquet of parsley and the chicken legs into a pot. Pour over 300 ml (½ pint,
1¼ cups) water and cook gently for 30 minutes to obtain a chicken stock.

Meanwhile, cut 2 carrots in slices and chop 4 shallots and 2 garlic cloves.
In another pot brown the remaining chicken pieces in 2 tablespoons lard

(shortening) over a brisk heat. Take these out and put in the carrot slices and the chopped shallots and garlic. Reduce the heat and lightly brown for 10 minutes. Put the chicken pieces back into the pot. Sprinkle with 1 tablespoon flour and stir.

Pour over the chicken stock – there should be about 100 ml (4 fl oz, 7 tablespoons) after reduction – with the same quantity of Riesling. Season with salt and pepper, a little grated nutmeg and dried thyme. Cook for about 1½ hours (depending on the age of the chicken). Take out the chicken pieces and place them on a warm dish. Thicken the sauce away from the heat with an egg yolk thinned with 100 ml (4 fl oz, 7 tablespoons) single (light) cream. Finally, add the juice of a lemon and 2 teaspoons sloe brandy. Pour the sauce over the dish and serve.

## Omelette à la Célestine

Prepare two small flat omelettes. Place one on a round plate, garnish with slices of poached chicken breast and cover with a thick cream sauce containing chopped parsley. Place the second omelette on top and sprinkle with melted butter.

## Paupiettes of chicken with cabbage

Blanch some large leaves of green cabbage for 15 seconds. Drain and wipe them. Remove the legs, wings and breast from an uncooked chicken and season them with salt and pepper. Wrap the chicken pieces in cabbage leaves to make 5 large paupiettes or parcels and tie them up tightly with string. Brown some chopped carrots and onions in goose fat or dripping in a pan, add the paupiettes and cook them until they brown. Add 400 ml (14 fl oz, 1¾ cups) water, cover the pan and cook for about 1½ hours.

The chicken pieces may be boned and skinned before use, if preferred.

## Poule au pot à la béarnaise

For a chicken weighing 2 kg (4½ lb) make a forcemeat with 350 g (12 oz, 1½ cups) fine sausagemeat, 200 g (7 oz) chopped Bayonne ham, 200 g (7 oz, 1¼ cups) chopped onions, 3 crushed garlic cloves, a small bunch of parsley (chopped) and 4 chopped chicken livers. Season with salt and pepper and work these ingredients together well to make a smooth paste. Stuff the chicken and carefully sew up the openings at the neck and parson's nose (tail) with trussing twine.

Pour 2.5 litres (4½ pints, 11 cups) cold consommé into a sauté pan and place the chicken in the pan. Bring to the boil and skim the scum that rises to the surface. Then add 100 g (4 oz, 3 cup) chopped carrots, 75 g (3 oz, 9 cup) chopped turnips, 75 g (3 oz) leeks (white part only, cut into chunks), 2 baby (pearl) onions browned in a dry frying pan, 50 g (2 oz) celery hearts (cut into small pieces and blanched) and 100 g (4 oz) cabbage (blanched in salted water, cooled and rolled into tight balls). Simmer these ingredients for 3 hours, occasionally adding a little consommé to compensate for the evaporation. Cut the chicken into portions, slice the forcemeat and serve with the vegetables.

## Poulet sauté archiduc

Joint a chicken and sauté the pieces in butter. When half-cooked, add 2 tablespoons chopped onions softened in butter and ¼ teaspoon paprika. Drain the chicken pieces and keep hot. Deglaze the juices in the pan with 100 ml (4 fl oz, ½ cup) dry white wine and heat to reduce. Add 150 ml (¼ pint, ⅔ cup) double (heavy) cream and reduce further. Finally, add a trickle of lemon juice and 50 g (2 oz, ¼ cup) butter. Strain the sauce (if desired) and use it to coat the chicken pieces. Sliced cucumber, steamed in butter, may be served at the same time.

# Risotto with chicken livers

Make a risotto *à la milanaise*, but omit the final garnish of white truffle. While the risotto is cooking, prepare 150 ml (¼ pint, ⅔ cup) very thick tomato fondue. Sauté 200 g (7 oz, 1 cup) diced chicken livers and 250 g (9 oz, 3 cups) sliced cultivated mushrooms in butter in a flameproof casserole. Season with salt and a grinding of black pepper and stir in a small grated garlic clove. Mix the tomato fondue, the chicken livers and the mushrooms with the risotto and serve immediately. If you like, 75 g (3 oz, ¾ cup) grated Parmesan cheese may be added.

# Roast chicken

Clean a chicken, weigh it and calculate the cooking time, allowing 15 minutes per 450 g (1 lb), plus 15 minutes. Sprinkle with salt and pepper both inside and outside. Truss the bird, then brush it lightly with clarified butter. Place it on its breast in a roasting tin (pan) and cook in a preheated oven at 200°C (400°F, gas 6) for half the cooking time. Then turn it on to its back to finish cooking. Baste it from time to time with its juices. Transfer the chicken to a warmed platter, deglaze the roasting dish with boiling water and serve, offering the gravy separately.

# Roast chicken Rossini

Using lining or shortcrust pastry, line 1 tartlet tin (pan) per serving and bake them blind. Roast a chicken weighing 1.8 kg (4 lb) and keep hot in a serving dish. Cut 2 slices of truffle per serving and sauté the slices in butter. Place 1 slice of foie gras and 2 slices of truffle in each tartlet case. Deglaze the roasting pan with Madeira and demi-glace sauce made from the truffle cooking liquor and pour the sauce over the chicken. Surround the chicken with the filled tartlets.

## Roasted poached capon with pumpkin gratin

Season the body cavity of a 3–3.5 kg (6½–8 lb) capon. Place 1 peeled onion and a large bunch each of tarragon and parsley in the cavity, then truss the capon securely. Place in a large pan and pour in enough chicken stock to cover. Heat gently until simmering, then cover and simmer gently for 30 minutes. Drain the capon well and transfer it to a roasting tin (pan).

Dot the capon with 50 g (2 oz, ¼ cup) butter and roast it in a preheated oven at 240°C (475°F, gas 9) for 30 minutes. Reduce the temperature to 220°C (425°F, gas 7) and cook for a further 30 minutes. Baste the bird well, then add 2 diced carrots, 1 chopped onion, the chopped green part of 1 leek, 1 diced celery stick, 1 crushed garlic clove and 1 bouquet garni to the container. Turn the vegetables in the juices and cook for a further ½–1 hour, basting frequently, until the capon is cooked. Cover the top loosely with foil, if necessary to prevent the capon from becoming too brown.

Meanwhile, peel and seed a 3 kg (6½ lb) pumpkin and cut it into wedges. Cook the pumpkin in boiling salted water with 1 bouquet garni and 3 peeled garlic cloves for 12 minutes, or until tender. Drain the pumpkin thoroughly.

Press the garlic cloves over the bottom of a large gratin dish. Coarsely mash the pumpkin with a fork, adding salt to taste, a little grated nutmeg and a pinch of cayenne pepper. Spread the pumpkin out evenly in the dish. Pour 400 ml (14 fl oz, 1¾ cups) double (heavy) cream over the pumpkin and sprinkle with 90 g (3½ oz, 1 cup) grated Gruyère cheese. Place the pumpkin gratin in the oven with the capon for the final 15–20 minutes cooking, until it is golden and bubbling.

Transfer the capon to a serving platter. Skim off and reserve excess fat, then add 100 ml (4 fl oz, 7 tablespoons) dry white wine to the vegetables remaining in the roasting tin. Boil until well reduced and nearly dry. Pour in 250 ml (8 fl oz, 1 cup) chicken stock and bring to the boil, then boil for a few minutes, scraping all the cooking juices into the liquor. Strain through a fine sieve and return to the pan. Bring to the boil and boil until reduced slightly and full flavoured. Whisk in a knob of butter and a little of the reserved cooking fat. Serve this sauce with the carved capon and the pumpkin gratin.

## Royale of chicken purée

Poach 50 g (2 oz) white chicken meat and pound it finely. Add 2 tablespoons béchamel sauce and the same amount of cream and press it through a sieve. Bind with 4 egg yolks, pour into dariole moulds and cook in a bain marie in a preheated oven at 200°C (400°F, gas 6) for 30 minutes.

## Salpicon of cockscombs

Prick the combs lightly with a needle and put them under cold running water, pressing them with the fingers to dispel the blood. Cover with cold water and cook until the water reaches a temperature of 40–45°C (104–113°F), when the skin of the combs begins to detach itself. Drain the combs and rub them one by one in a cloth sprinkled with fine salt.

Remove the outer skin; put the combs in cold water and, when they are white, plunge them into a boiling white court-bouillon. Cook for 35 minutes. Drain and dice the cockscombs. Heat them for a few minutes in Madeira or any other dessert wine. Add a few tablespoons of chicken velouté, white sauce or a very reduced Madeira sauce.

## Sautéed chicken à la biarrote

Cut a 1.4 kg (3 lb) chicken into pieces and sauté until brown on all sides and cooked through. Deglaze with 100 ml (4 fl oz, 7 tablespoons) dry or medium white wine. Reduce the liquid, then add 100 ml (4 fl oz, 7 tablespoons) tomato sauce and a small crushed garlic clove. Using a separate pan, sauté 100 g (4 oz,

2 cups) ceps, 100 g (4 oz, ⅔ cup) diced potatoes and 1 diced aubergine (eggplant) in olive oil. Fry a thinly sliced onion, separating the rings. Arrange the chicken in a heated serving dish, coat with the sauce and arrange the garnish in bouquets around it.

## Sautéed chicken à la bohémienne

Season a medium-sized chicken with paprika and sauté in a flameproof casserole or large heavy-based saucepan until brown. Cover the pan and continue cooking very slowly either on top of the stove or in a preheated oven at 180°C (350°F, gas 4). Cut 4 red or green (bell) peppers into thick strips. Peel 2 tomatoes and slice them thickly. Finely dice 1 onion and then blanch it. Prepare 1 tablespoon chopped fennel. Add all these ingredients, together with a pinch of crushed garlic, to the pan when the chicken is half-cooked (after about 30 minutes). At the end of the cooking time, when the chicken is tender, deglaze the casserole with 100 ml (4 fl oz, 7 tablespoons) dry white wine. Add 60 ml (2 fl oz, ¼ cup) thickened veal stock or well-reduced bouillon. Finally, add a dash of lemon juice. Pour the sauce over the chicken and serve with a dish of saffron rice.

## Sautéed chicken à la fermière

Sauté a chicken in some butter until brown. Thinly slice 2 carrots, 2 onions, the white part of 2 leeks and 3 or 4 celery sticks. Cook them slowly in 25 g (1 oz, 2 tablespoons) butter, ensuring that the vegetables remain fairly firm. Add the vegetables 15 minutes before the chicken is cooked. Place all the ingredients in an ovenproof casserole and add 2 tablespoons diced ham. Cover and cook in a preheated oven at 220°C (425°F, gas 7) for about 10 minutes. The cooking liquid can be deglazed at the last moment with 100 ml (4 fl oz, 7 tablespoons) thick gravy or thick veal stock.

## Sautéed chicken à la zingara

Season a 1.25 kg (2¾ lb) chicken with salt and pepper, cut it into 4 pieces and dust with paprika. Brown the pieces in oil in a flameproof casserole, reduce the heat, cover and continue cooking. After 30 minutes add 4 tablespoons strips of ham and the same quantity of pickled tongue and mushrooms; add a little truffle and a small sprig of tarragon. Arrange the cooked chicken on a serving dish with its garnish (without the tarragon), and keep hot.

Deglaze the casserole with 60 ml (2 fl oz, ¼ cup) Madeira and 2 tablespoons tomato fondue. Reduce until almost dry, then add 150 ml (¼ pint, ⅔ cup) demi-glace sauce and heat through. Toast 4 slices of sandwich bread; quickly fry in butter 4 small round slices of ham; place the ham on the pieces of toast and arrange alongside the chicken. Coat the chicken with the sauce and sprinkle with chopped parsley. Serve very hot.

## Sautéed chicken Alexandra

Joint a chicken and sauté the joints in butter until cooked. Remove and keep them hot. Add 100 ml (4 fl oz, ½ cup) white stock to the sauté pan and cook briskly to reduce it, then add 1½ tablespoons soubise purée, moisten with 100 ml (4 fl oz, ½ cup) white stock and reduce again. Finally stir in 2 tablespoons double (heavy) cream and 40 g (1½ oz, 3 tablespoons) butter, then strain the sauce. Arrange the chicken in a dish, coat with the sauce and garnish with buttered asparagus tips.

## Sautéed chicken chasseur

Sauté a chicken in a mixture of oil and butter. Season, cover and cook for about 35 minutes. Add 150 g (5 oz, 1⅓ cups) thinly sliced raw mushrooms and cook for about 10 minutes more. Drain the chicken and keep it hot. Brown 1 or 2 chopped shallots in the pan juices and add 100 ml (4 fl oz,

7 tablespoons) white wine and 1 tablespoon well-reduced tomato sauce. Reduce by half and then add 1 tablespoon marc and 1 tablespoon chopped tarragon. Bring to the boil and coat the chicken with the sauce. Sprinkle with parsley and serve very hot.

## Sautéed chicken Demidof

Remove the giblets from a chicken and cut off the breast, wings and legs. Brown the remaining carcass and giblets in oil in a sauté pan, dust with flour and brown again. Moisten with 150 ml (¼ pint, ⅔ cup) dry white wine and bouillon and cook gently for 30 minutes. Pour this cooking liquid through a strainer and reserve.

Cut 2 carrots, 1 turnip, 2 celery sticks and 1 onion into thin julienne strips. Flour the chicken portions and brown them in a saucepan. Add the vegetable julienne and the cooking liquid, cover and cook gently for 30 minutes. Add a slice of smoked ham and a diced truffle. Cook for a further 15 minutes, then deglaze with Madeira and demi-glace sauce.

## Sautéed chicken Doria

Brown a small chicken in 1 tablespoon oil and 25 g (1 oz, 2 tablespoons) butter in a flameproof casserole. Add salt and pepper, cover the casserole and continue cooking over a low heat for 30 minutes. Brown 675 g (1½ lb, 6 cups) peeled chopped cucumber in butter in a separate pan and add to the chicken. Cook for a further 20 minutes. Finish cooking the chicken, uncovered, in a preheated oven at 220°C (425°F, gas 7) for a further 20–30 minutes, or until brown and tender. Remove the chicken, drain and carve. Arrange the chicken slices on the serving dish surrounded by the cucumber. Keep hot. Make a sauce by deglazing the casserole with the juice of a lemon and pour it over the chicken and cucumber.

## Sautéed chicken Stanley

Cut a chicken into 6 pieces and sauté them in butter in a flameproof casserole without allowing them to brown. After 30 minutes, add 2 large finely sliced onions, cover and finish cooking over a low heat (about 20 minutes). Cook some mushrooms in butter. Arrange the chicken and mushrooms in a serving dish and keep warm. Deglaze the casserole juices with 200 ml (7 fl oz, ¾ cup) double (heavy) cream, reduce by a quarter and press through a sieve. Add ½ teaspoon curry powder and a pinch of cayenne pepper, then whisk in 40 g (1½ oz, 3 tablespoons) butter. Cover the chicken with this sauce and, if desired, garnish with a few strips of truffle.

## Sautéed chicken with mangoes

Cut a chicken into pieces and sauté in butter for about 20 minutes. Soften a chopped onion and a peeled crushed tomato in a mixture of 2 tablespoons oil and 20 g (¾ oz, 1½ tablespoons) butter with a pinch of ground ginger. Add the crushed pulp of 2 or 3 mangoes, a squeeze of lemon juice, the chicken pieces, a cup of water, salt, pepper and a pinch of cayenne. Cover and cook for about 30 minutes over a medium heat.

## Sautéed chicken with tarragon

Sauté a chicken *à brun*, then drain it and keep warm in a serving dish. Deglaze the cooking pan with 150 ml (¼ pint, ⅔ cup) white wine; add 1 chopped shallot, reduce, then add 150 ml (¼ pint, ⅔ cup) thickened gravy (or chicken or veal stock thickened with a little arrowroot). Finally, add 1 tablespoon lemon juice and 2 tablespoons tarragon leaves, blanched and chopped. Pour this sauce over the chicken.

This dish can also be prepared in the same way as chicken with cream, replacing the parsley with tarragon.

## Scrambled eggs à la reine

Make some very thick cooked chicken purée and some suprême sauce. Bake a large vol-au-vent case and keep it hot. Make some scrambled eggs, cooking them gently until creamy. Fill the vol-au-vent case with alternate layers of chicken purée and scrambled eggs. Serve the vol-au-vent hot, offering the suprême sauce in a sauceboat.

## Shaped chicken cutlets Helder

Make a velouté from chicken carcasses (the white meat that has been removed is shaped into cutlets). Add tomato to the velouté and reduce over a gentle heat. Add some butter then strain the sauce. Season the cutlets with salt and pepper, brush with melted butter and put them into a buttered casserole. Sprinkle with a little lemon juice, cover and cook in a preheated oven at 240°C (475°F, gas 9) for 6–10 minutes. Braise some diced carrots in butter and boil some diced artichoke hearts and mushrooms. Arrange the cutlets on a warm serving dish and garnish with the vegetables. Coat with the tomato sauce.

## Soft-boiled or poached eggs à la reine

Make some tartlet cases using puff pastry or shortcrust pastry (basic pie dough) and cook them blind. Prepare some cooked chicken purée and some suprême sauce. Soft-boil (soft-cook) or poach 1 egg per tartlet. Reheat the tartlets and fill them with the purée; arrange an egg on each one and mask with the suprême sauce.

## Spring chickens à la piémontaise

Prepare a risotto *à la piémontaise*, using 250 g (9 oz, 2¼ cups) rice. Chop 75 g (3 oz) onions, soften in butter, then mix with 400 g (14 oz, 2 cups) finely minced (ground) sausagemeat and the minced livers of 4 spring chickens (poussins). Season the chickens with salt and pepper, stuff with the forcemeat, truss, and cook in a casserole containing 50 g (2 oz, ¼ cup) butter in a preheated oven at 180°C (350°F, gas 4) for about 50 minutes. Place the risotto in a ring on a heated serving dish, arrange the chickens in the centre and keep warm. Deglaze the casserole with 300 ml (½ pint, 1¼ cups) white wine and 3 tablespoons tomato purée (paste). Reduce by half, thicken with 1 tablespoon beurre manié, add 2 tablespoons freshly chopped parsley and pour this sauce over the chickens.

## Spring chickens à la sicilienne

Boil some pasta shapes in salted water. Drain, reheat for a few minutes in very hot butter, then mix with a purée of pistachio nuts. Sprinkle with salt and pepper and leave to cool. Stuff the chickens with this mixture and truss them, then spit-roast over a pan to catch the juices, basting frequently. Three-quarters of the way through cooking, sprinkle with fresh breadcrumbs and allow to colour. Serve the cooking juices as a gravy separately.

## Steamed stuffed chicken with ragoût of broccoli

Peel 100 g (4 oz) carrots and 100 g (4 oz) turnips. Chop very finely and cook in boiling water. At the same time, cook separately 100 g (4 oz) unpeeled courgettes (zucchini) in boiling water, making sure they remain firm. Drain thoroughly and dice.

Braise 500 g (18 oz) calves' sweetbreads until brown and cut into small dice. Strain the braising juices and reduce to a quarter of their original quantity. Pour 100 ml (4 fl oz, 7 tablespoons) of the reduced juices on to the sweetbreads, finely chopped carrots, turnips and courgettes.

Using a wide kitchen knife, flatten 4 chicken fillets between 2 pieces of cling film (plastic wrap). Sprinkle a little pepper on top, then put a small amount of sweetbread mixture in the centre. Roll individually into small cylinders and wrap in cling film. Steam for 20 minutes.

Cook 575 g (1¼ lb) broccoli for a few minutes in boiling salted water. Fry 1 finely chopped onion and 150 g (5 oz, ⅔ cup) lardons of smoked streaky (slab) bacon in 20 g (¾ oz, 1½ tablespoons) butter, until golden, then add the broccoli. Season with salt and pepper and keep warm. Unwrap the chicken fillets and cut them in half. Arrange 2 half chicken fillets on each plate and pour over the braising juice. Arrange the broccoli and the smoked bacon around the fillets.

## Stuffed chicken à la mode de Sorges

Fill the inside of a chicken with a forcemeat made up of its liver chopped and mixed with stale breadcrumbs, chopped bacon, parsley, chives, shallots, garlic, salt, pepper, mustard and the bird's blood (if available), all bound together with an egg yolk. Truss it as for roasting.

Brown all over in goose fat, then place it in a flameproof casserole and cover with boiling water; season with salt and pepper. Bring to the boil, skim, then add 3 carrots and 2 turnips (peeled), the white part of 3 leeks tied together in a bundle, 1 celery heart, 1 onion stuck with a clove and a few leaves of Swiss chard tied in a bundle. Simmer very gently for about 1¼ hours. Drain the chicken, untruss it and place it on a dish, surrounded with the vegetables, cutting the carrots and turnips into pieces.

Prepare some Sorges sauce to be served separately: make a highly seasoned vinaigrette, add chopped parsley, chives and shallots, then bind with the yolks of 2 eggs boiled for 3 minutes. Continue cooking the egg whites for 2 minutes in the chicken stock, dice them and add to the sauce. As they do in Périgord, serve the strained chicken cooking stock first as a soup, either poured over slices of toast or garnished with large boiled vermicelli.

## Suprême of chicken

The breast and wing of a chicken or game bird are referred to as the suprême.

To prepare suprêmes from a whole bird, pull the leg of the bird away from the body; slice down to where the thigh joins the carcass. Cut through the joint and remove the whole leg. Repeat with the other leg and set both legs aside for use in another recipe. Separate the flesh on either side of the breastbone, cutting down towards the wing joints. Then sever the joints of the wings from the body, without separating them from the breast meat. Finally, cut through each wing at the second joint to remove the pinion (wing tip). Carefully ease off the skin.

## Suprême of chicken with Sauternes and preserved lemon

Season 4 prepared chicken suprêmes. Use a flameproof casserole in which the suprêmes will fit snugly, overlapping slightly if necessary. Cook the suprêmes gently in a mixture of butter and olive oil, skin-side down, until browned. Turn the suprêmes over and half cover the casserole, then continue to cook gently until the chicken is cooked through.

Meanwhile, clean 500 g (18 oz) chanterelles and sweat them gently in a covered frying pan. Drain and set aside. Finely chop 3 shallots. Remove the chicken from the pan. Remove the fat and stir in half the shallots. Add 200 ml (7 fl oz, ¾ cup) Sauternes and reduce by half. Stir in 300 ml (½ pint, 1¼ cups) single (light) cream and a pinch of mignonette – a mixture of ground black and white pepper – then reduce for 2 minutes. Sieve the sauce.

Return the sauce to the pan and stir in a dash of lemon juice and the finely diced zest of 1 preserved lemon. Replace the chicken and reheat thoroughly but gently, without boiling. In another pan, cook the remaining shallot in butter with the chanterelles. Season. Arrange the suprêmes on plates, with their sauce. Add the chanterelles and garnish with lemon zest and parsley.

### Suprêmes of chicken à blanc

Season the suprêmes with salt and pepper, brush with clarified butter, arrange in a buttered casserole and sprinkle with a little lemon juice. Cover the casserole and cook in a preheated oven at 220°C (425°F, gas 7) for about 15 minutes. Drain the suprêmes and arrange them on a serving dish with the chosen garnish.

The following garnishes can be used: diced aubergines (eggplants) sautéed in butter, braised lettuce or chicory (endive), cucumber slowly cooked in butter, spinach in butter or gravy, artichoke hearts slowly cooked or sautéed in butter, French (green) beans or macédoine of vegetables in butter, peas *à la française*, asparagus tips in butter or cream, or a vegetable purée.

### Suprêmes of chicken à brun

Season the suprêmes with salt and pepper, coat them in flour and cook them in clarified butter in a sauté pan until golden on both sides. Arrange on a serving dish with the chosen garnish. The same garnishes may be used as for suprême of chicken à blanc.

### Suprêmes of chicken à l'anglaise

Season the suprêmes with salt and pepper, then coat them with beaten egg and breadcrumbs. Cook in clarified butter until golden and cooked through. Arrange on a bed of pommes Anna, surround with grilled (broiled) tomatoes and garnish each suprême with a grilled (broiled) rasher (slice) of bacon.

### Suprêmes of chicken à la financière

Sauté some suprêmes of chicken in clarified butter. Arrange them on fried croûtons or puff pastry croustades. Coat with financière sauce and surround with a financière garnish.

## Suprêmes of chicken à la florentine

Season some suprêmes of chicken or young turkey with salt and pepper and brush with melted butter. Melt some butter in a flameproof casserole, add the suprêmes and flavour with a little lemon juice. Cover the casserole and place it in a preheated oven at 220°C (425°F, gas 7). Cook for 12–15 minutes. Meanwhile, cook some spinach in butter and spread it in the base of an ovenproof dish. Arrange the suprêmes on top, coat with Mornay sauce, sprinkle with grated cheese and melted butter, and brown in a preheated oven at 240°C (475°F, gas 9).

## Suprêmes of chicken à la périgourdine

Cook some suprêmes *à brun* and arrange them on a serving dish. On each suprême place a slice of foie gras fried quickly in butter and a thin slice of truffle. Coat with Périgueux sauce.

## Suprêmes of chicken ambassadeur

Sauté the suprêmes in butter. Fry some croûtons in butter and cover them with the suprêmes, each garnished with a thin slice of truffle. Surround the croûtons with mushrooms cooked in cream and with buttered asparagus. Coat lightly with suprême sauce.

## Suprêmes of chicken with mushrooms

Cook some suprêmes *à blanc*. Garnish them with mushrooms that have been slowly cooked in butter and coat them with suprême sauce mixed with the pan juices.

Alternatively, cook the suprêmes *à brun*, then garnish them with sautéed mushrooms and coat with Madeira sauce or a demi-glace sauce flavoured with Madeira.

## Tajine of chicken with quince

Cut a prepared chicken into 8 pieces. Peel and chop 3 onions. Brown the chicken in a flameproof casserole in 3 tablespoons olive oil. Add the onions, stir, season and add a pinch of paprika, a generous pinch of ground ginger, a few parsley and coriander (cilantro) leaves and 175 ml (6 fl oz, ¾ cup) chicken stock. Cook gently for 30 minutes with the casserole half-covered.

Meanwhile, cut 2 large quinces into 8 pieces, remove and discard the seeds and fry them in oil or butter over a high heat until golden. Place the pieces of chicken and quince in a tajine (an earthenware dish). Pour the cooking liquid over the top and cover the dish with a piece of perforated greaseproof (wax) paper. Cook in a preheated oven at 220–230°C (425–450°F, gas 7–8) for about 30 minutes. Serve very hot.

## Tarte cauchoise

Prepare some shortcrust pastry (basic pie dough). Roll into a ball and leave to rest in a cool place for at least 1 hour. Line a flan tin (tart pan) and bake blind. Soften 800 g (1¾ lb, 5 cups) finely chopped onion in butter. Beat 1 egg, mix in 200 ml (7 fl oz, ¾ cup) double (heavy) cream, then add salt, pepper and a little grated nutmeg. Allow to thicken on a gentle heat, without boiling, then add the onions. Fill the flan case with cooked chicken leftovers or finely chopped cooked veal or ham and cover them with the onion mixture. Dot with flecks of butter and cook in a preheated oven at 200°C (400°F, gas 6) for 15–20 minutes.

## Truffled chicken à la périgourdine

Wash and peel 1 kg (2¼ lb) truffles, reserving the outer skins and trim to the size and shape of pigeon's eggs; chop the trimmings finely. Melt 250 g (9 oz) chicken fat and the same quantity of unsmoked bacon over a low heat and

Pot-au-feu
**Recipe on page 48**

Terrine of veal with spring vegetables
**Recipe on page 82**

Veal grenadins with salsify
**Recipe on page 87**

Cassoulet (2)
**Recipe on page 96**

Navarin of lamb
**Recipe on page 142**

Rack of lamb with thyme
**Recipe on page 146**

Tajine of spring lamb
**Recipe on page 159**

Sautéed calf's kidney with wholegrain mustard
**Recipe on page 182**

Vol-au-vent financière
**Recipe on page 195**

Chicken waterzooï
**Recipe on page 246**

Roasted poached capon with pumpkin gratin
**Recipe on page 268**

Suprême of chicken with Sauternes and preserved lemon
**Recipe on page 277**

Jellied fillets of Rouen duck à l'orange
**Recipe on page 297**

Hare mousse with chestnuts
**Recipe on page 338**

Partridge Monselet
**Recipe on page 347**

Quails in vine leaves
**Recipe on page 369**

strain through a sieve, pressing down well to extract as much flavour as possible. Pour this fat into a saucepan containing the truffles, the truffle trimmings, some salt, pepper and mixed spices, half a bay leaf, a small sprig of thyme and a little grated nutmeg. Simmer, covered, for 15 minutes, then remove from the heat and leave to cool.

Stuff a large roasting chicken with this mixture, making sure the openings are well sewn up and completely closed. Place the chicken in a terrine and cover it with the reserved outer skins of the truffles; leave the chicken like this for 3 or 4 days in a cool place. On the last day, remove the truffle skins and cook them in butter with an onion and a carrot (both chopped) and some sprigs of parsley. Secure the chicken on a spit; cover with strips of unsmoked bacon and, on top of this, the vegetable mixture. Wrap securely in a double thickness of oiled greaseproof (wax) paper and spit-roast for 1½ hours. Five minutes before serving, unwrap the chicken and allow it to brown. Take it off the spit, untruss it and serve with Périgueux sauce.

## Turban of poultry

Line a buttered ring mould with thin slices of raw poultry cut from the breast, so that the slices slightly overhang both edges. Mask with a thin layer of poultry forcemeat, then fill the mould with a salpicon of cooked poultry, mixed with truffles and mushrooms, and bound with allemande sauce. Cover with a thin layer of forcemeat and fold the overhanging slices over the top. Cook in a bain marie in a preheated oven at 180°C (350°F, gas 4) for about 40 minutes, then leave to stand for 10 minutes before turning out of the mould on to a round dish. Fill the centre of the turban with braised slices of calves' sweetbreads and sautéed morels. Coat with suprême sauce.

# Duck

## Aiguillettes of duckling with honey vinegar

Aiguillette is the French name for a long narrow fillet, taken from either side of the breastbone of poultry (mainly duck) and game birds. This separates easily from the underside of the breast meat and is a popular chef's item for small dishes.

Cut 2–3 aiguillettes per serving (there are 2 per duckling). Season with salt and pepper. Cook a chopped shallot in butter over a gentle heat. When it begins to brown, add 1 tablespoon liquid honey (preferably acacia honey); boil for about 2 minutes until it thickens. Grill (broil) the aiguillettes separately and arrange them on a warm dish. Pour the sauce over the top and serve immediately with straw potatoes, rice or a mixture of sautéed carrots and turnips.

## Amiens duck pâté

To prepare the pastry, spread 500 g (1 lb 2 oz, 4½ cups) plain (all-purpose) flour out on a board or work surface, make a well in the centre and put in 1 teaspoon table salt. Break an egg into the well and mix with the salt, then add 1 tablespoon olive oil. Soften 125 g (4½ oz, ½ cup) lard (shortening) by kneading if necessary, then mix it with the liquid part in the centre of the flour. Then blend the flour and lard, without moistening at all. When the pastry is well blended, spread it out and sprinkle with about 1½ tablespoons cold water. Roll the pastry together into one lump and leave to rest in a cool place for at least 2 hours before use. (This pastry has the advantage of rising very little during cooking.)

To make this pâté, use only a young duckling, which can be cooked very quickly. Pluck, draw and singe the bird, carefully removing any innards that may remain. Cut off the wing tips just below the first joint from the shoulder. Cut off the feet at the joint. Season the inside and outside with spiced salt. Cut up a side of streaky (slab) bacon and fry over a low heat in a little cooking fat. Remove it and brown the duck in the fat over a low heat, turning it so that it browns all over. Drain the duck and leave to cool before making the pâté.

*À gratin* forcemeat is always used for this pâté. The ingredients may vary, depending on what is available, and may include veal or poultry liver, in addition to the liver from the duck. Melt 150 g (5 oz, ⅔ cup) finely chopped fat over a low heat and use it to brown 500 g (1 lb 2 oz) veal or poultry liver, which has been suitably trimmed and coarsely diced. When the liver is well browned, add 1 chopped onion and 2 chopped shallots, and season with 1 tablespoon spiced salt, some chopped thyme and bay leaves. Cover and leave for a few minutes on a low heat. Remove and allow to cool, then pound the mixture in a mortar and pass through a fine sieve.

Divide the pastry into two equal portions and roll one half into an oval about 1 cm (½ in) thick so it is a little longer and wider than the duck. Place this pastry in the centre of a metal baking sheet or ovenproof pie dish that has been lightly moistened with a little cold water. Next, spread a quarter of the forcemeat in the middle of the pastry and lay the duck, on its back, on top; season the duck with more spiced salt and a little cayenne pepper. Completely cover the duck with the remaining forcemeat. Roll out the remaining pastry in an oval shape and place over the duck, sealing it well at the edges. Crimp up the sides, garnish the top with some pieces of pastry cut into fancy shapes and make an opening in the centre for the steam to escape. Finally, glaze the pastry with beaten egg. Bake the pâté in a preheated oven at 220°C (425°F, gas 7) for 1¼–1½ hours, depending on the size.

## Ballotine of duck

Bone a 2.5 kg (5½ lb) duck. Open the duck and carefully remove all the flesh, leaving the skin intact. Dice the breast meat. Draw the sinews from the rest of the meat and finely chop with an equal weight of unsmoked fatty bacon, half this weight of lean veal, and 75 g (3 oz, 1½ cups) fresh breadcrumbs soaked in milk. Combine these ingredients in a food processor with 4 egg yolks. Season with salt, pepper and allspice. Add to this stuffing 150 g (5 oz) fresh foie gras, cut into large cubes and quickly fried in butter, 1 diced truffle and the diced breast meat. Add 2 tablespoons Cognac and mix well.

Wet and squeeze out a piece of muslin (cheesecloth) and spread on the table. Place the duck skin, opened flat, on the muslin and spread evenly with the stuffing. Roll into a neat ballotine and tie at both ends and in the middle.

Boil the ballotine immersed in a rich stock for 2–3 hours, arrange on a serving dish, and garnish as desired (châtelaine, chipolata, forestière, Godard, Lucullus, with braised chestnuts, or lettuce) and serve with other vegetables braised or cooked in butter. Baste the ballotine with a few spoonfuls of reduced sieved pan juices. Serve the remainder of this liquid separately.

To serve the ballotine cold, increase the foie gras to at least 200 g (7 oz). Once the cooked ballotine has been unwrapped, rewrap it very tightly in the same muslin, rinsed and wrung out, and allow to cool between two plates under a weight. Refrigerate overnight, then glaze with aspic jelly made from the well-reduced stock and chill to set before serving.

## Braised duck

Singe and truss a duck weighing about 2 kg (4½ lb). Put it into an ovenproof braising pan lined with fresh bacon rind and with a carrot and an onion cut into rounds and tossed in butter. Add a bouquet garni, season and cook, covered, for 15 minutes, browning the duck all over. Moisten with 100 ml

(4 fl oz, 7 tablespoons) white wine, reduce and add 300 ml (½ pint, 1¼ cups) chicken stock. Boil, then transfer to a preheated oven at 220°C (425°F, gas 7) and cook, covered, for 1 hour. Drain the duck, untruss it, place on a serving dish and surround with garden peas. Pour over some of the braising juices, reduced and strained, and serve the remainder in a sauceboat.

The same method is used for duck *à l'alsacienne*, which is surrounded with braised sauerkraut and a garnish of streaky (slab) bacon and Strasbourg sausages; duck *à la chipolata*, which is garnished with braised chestnuts, small glazed onions, lean rashers (slices) of blanched bacon and chipolata sausages cooked in butter; and duck with olives, which uses green olives, stoned (pitted) and blanched.

## Braised Rouen duck

The excellent Rouen duck, in particular the Duclair (named after a village in Normandy), is mainly sold locally. Very fine flesh, tinged with red, with a special flavour due to the fact that the bird is smothered, not bled, so that the blood remains in the muscles. Rouen duck may be braised, although this is an unusual way of cooking it. It may be prepared *à la bigarade*, with a bitter orange sauce; with cherries – use stoned (pitted) morello cherries and dilute the pan juices with Madeira; with champagne – dilute the pan juices with 300 ml (½ pint, 1¼ cups) dry champagne and, if liked, a few tablespoons of thickened veal stock; or *au chambertin* – finish off the cooking with 125 g (4½ oz) blanched and fried larding bacon and mushrooms tossed in butter.

## Chaud-froid of duckling

Cook a fine duckling weighing about 1.8 kg (4 lb) in a preheated oven at 230°C (450°F, gas 8), keeping it slightly underdone (40–45 minutes). Remove the skin, detach the legs and cut the fillets into long thin slices. Prepare a white sauce or fumet from the carcass and the skin (and possibly some of the giblets), and use it to make an orange-flavoured chaud-froid sauce. Skin the duck and cut it into pieces, then put them into the refrigerator. When chilled, coat the pieces of duck with several layers of chaud-froid sauce, putting them in the refrigerator between each application of sauce. To collect the sauce which drains away, arrange the duck on a rack over a tray or piece of foil. Dilute the sauce with a little cold stock for the last two applications.

## Chinese duck smoked over tea leaves

Draw a duck weighing about 1.4 kg (3 lb). Rub the inside and outside of the carcass with salt, then with sugar. Place the duck in a deep ovenproof dish sprinkled with 3 tablespoons fresh root ginger cut into thin strips, 2 table-spoons crushed cinnamon, and 2 tablespoons star anise. Sprinkle with 175 ml (6 fl oz, ¾ cup) Chinese rice wine or dry sherry. Add 100 ml (4 fl oz, 7 table-spoon) water, cover and cook in a bain marie for 2 hours. Drain the duck and leave to cool on a plate. Heat a deep cast-iron pan and pour in 75 g (3 oz, ¾ cup) green tea leaves. Place over a moderate heat until a light white smoke is given off. Then put the duck in the hot pan, cover and leave it to absorb the smoke for 4 minutes, then remove from the heat. Heat a little groundnut (peanut) oil in a large deep frying pan and brown the duck on all sides over a brisk heat for 5 minutes. Carve and serve piping hot, garnished with braised broccoli.

## Cold duck foie gras escalopes with grapes and truffles

Prepare and cook the raw liver, then cut it into equal-sized slices. On each of these escalopes (scallops) place l large slice of truffle dipped in aspic jelly and leave to set, then glaze the whole escalope with aspic. Arrange the escalopes in a crown shape in a shallow glass bowl. In the middle of the crown, heap a dome of fresh peeled seeded grapes which have been steeped in a little liqueur brandy. Coat everything lightly with clear port-flavoured aspic. Cover and then chill well before serving.

This recipe can also be made with goose foie gras.

## Cold duck pâté

This is made using a boned duck, stuffed with *à gratin* forcemeat to which foie gras and truffles have been added, either *en pantin* (a variety of pâté en croute, retangular or oblong in shape, that is not cooked in a mould), like cold lark pâté, or in a mould, like cold timbale of woodcock.

## Croûtes à la rouennaise

Fry 4 slices of bread in butter. Prepare 150 g (5 oz) *à gratin* forcemeat using Rouen duckling livers, grill (broil) 4 large mushroom caps and make 2 tablespoons very thick bordelaise sauce. Spread the croûtes with the forcemeat and heat them through for 10 minutes in the oven. Garnish each with a grilled mushroom cap, filled with 1½ teaspoons bordelaise sauce.

## Dodine of duck

Dodine is a dish of boned, stuffed and braised poultry (particularly duck) or meat.

Bone a duck without damaging the skin, keeping the breast meat intact as far as possible. Remove all the flesh from the skin. Cut the breast meat into thin slices (*aiguillettes*) and marinate them for 24 hours in 2 tablespoons brandy, a pinch of ground fennel seeds, salt and pepper. Chop the remaining flesh and mix it with 250 g (9 oz, 1 cup) chopped fat bacon, 250 g (9 oz, 1 cup) chopped lean pork, 250 g (9 oz, 1 cup) chopped veal, 250 g (9 oz, 3 cups) chopped button mushrooms, 50 g (2 oz, ½ cups) ground almonds and a chopped small bunch of parsley. Work 2 tablespoons truffle parings (or diced truffles), 1 egg, salt and pepper into the mixture. Cook a knob of the mixture in a sauté pan and taste it, then adjust the seasoning if necessary.

Spread out the skin of the duck and cover it with half of the stuffing. Arrange the slices of breast on top and cover with the remaining stuffing. Fold the skin towards the centre at the neck and the tail, roll and tie up the dodine. Either wipe a soaked pig's caul and tie it around the dodine or tie the dodine in shape with string. Pork fat or streaky (slab) bacon may be used to bard the dodine. Braise the dodine in a little white wine in a preheated oven at 180°C (350°F, gas 4), basting it several times. Cook for 1½–1¾ hours, until the juices that run out when it is pricked are clear.

If the dodine is to be served hot, cut the thread and remove any parts of the caul that have not melted. Skim the fat from the cooking juices and add 2 tablespoons port and a few tablespoons of stock. Reduce by half. Cut the dodine into slices, garnish with watercress and serve with the sauce.

If the dodine is to be served cold, allow it to cool completely before cutting the thread. Serve with a green or mixed salad.

## Duck à l'agenaise

Singe a duck weighing about 2 kg (4½ lb). Season the inside with salt and pepper, stuff with a dozen or so stoned (pitted) prunes soaked in Armagnac and sew up. Brown the duck in a pan containing 25 g (1 oz, 2 tablespoons) butter, sprinkle with a glass of Armagnac and set alight. Cover the pan and cook for about 40 minutes. Meanwhile, poach the grated zest of ½ orange for 5 minutes in half a bottle of Bordeaux wine, together with 2 cloves, a little grated nutmeg, 5 or 6 crushed peppercorns, a sprig of thyme and a bay leaf. In a saucepan, brown 100 g (4 oz, ½ cup) very small lardons of smoked bacon, 2 tablespoons diced carrot, 1 tablespoon diced celery and a large chopped onion, adding a knob of butter if required. Sprinkle with 1 tablespoon flour, then add the strained orange-flavoured wine. Season with salt and pepper, stir well and cook slowly for 20 minutes. Drain the duck and keep it hot. Pour the wine sauce into the juices from the duck and add a small glass of Armagnac and about 20 stoned (pitted) prunes. Reheat the sauce. Garnish the duck with prunes and cover with the sauce.

## Duck à l'orange Lasserre

Prepare a Nantes duck weighing about 2 kg (4½ lb), brown it in butter, then cook gently for 45 minutes. Sprinkle with 100 ml (4 fl oz, 7 tablespoons) Grand Marnier and leave to cook for a further 5 minutes. Remove the duck from the pan and keep hot. Strain the liquor and pour it into a saucepan, adding 1 tablespoon each vinegar and caster (superfine) sugar, the juice of 3 oranges and 100 ml (4 fl oz, 7 tablespoons) each of mandarin and apricot liqueur to make the sauce. Peel 6 oranges down to the flesh, cut them into slices, removing all fibres and seeds, and place them in a frying pan with a few spoonfuls of the sauce. Heat without boiling. Now carve the duck, arrange it on a hot dish and surround with slices of orange. Cover with some of the sauce and serve the remainder in a sauceboat (gravy boat).

## Duck foie gras with grapes

Skin and seed 8 large white Muscat grapes for each slice of foie gras. Cut the foie gras into fairly thick slices and season them with salt and pepper. Sauté them rapidly in butter then drain and keep hot. Deglaze the pan with a small glass of Sauternes, Monbazillac or a liqueur wine (or use half wine and half thickened veal stock, if you prefer), then add the grapes and shake them about in the pan. Taste and adjust the seasoning. Pour the sauce and the grapes on to the foie gras and serve.

## Duck foie gras with white pepper and green leeks

Prepare a foie gras weighing 300–400 g (11–14 oz). Boil some young green leeks in salted water and purée them with a little cream. Put this purée in a small greased cake tin (pan). Season the foie gras with salt and coarsely ground pepper and arrange it on the leek purée. Cover the tin with foil and bake in a preheated oven at 140°C (275°F, gas 1) for 35 minutes. Leave to cool for 45 minutes (the last 15 minutes in the refrigerator).

## Duck in bitter orange sauce

Cut the rind of 1 Seville orange (or 1 sweet orange) and ½ lemon into thin strips; blanch, cool and drain. Fry the duck in butter for about 45 minutes, until the flesh is just pink. Drain, untruss and arrange on a serving dish. Deglaze the cooking stock with 100 ml (4 fl oz, 7 tablespoons) white wine. Add 300 ml (½ pint, 1¼ cups) veal stock or a fairly light demi-glace sauce; otherwise use well-reduced chicken stock. Prepare some vinegar caramel, using 2 sugar lumps dissolved in 2 tablespoons vinegar and add to the sauce. Boil for a few moments. Add the juice of the orange and the lemon half, reduce, strain and add the orange and lemon rind. The duck can be garnished with peeled Seville orange segments, if liked.

## Duck or goose foie gras mousse

Press a poached foie gras through a fine sieve, and place the purée in a bowl. For each litre (1¾ pints, 4⅓ cups) purée, add 250 ml (8 fl oz, 1 cup) melted aspic jelly and 400 ml (14 fl oz, 1¾ cups) chicken velouté sauce. Beat the mixture lightly over ice. Season, then add 400 ml (14 fl oz, 1¾ cups) partly whipped double (heavy) cream. Line a round mould with aspic jelly and garnish with slices of truffle, the thinly sliced whites of hard-boiled (hard-cooked) eggs and tarragon leaves. Then fill with the mousse up to 1.5 cm

(¾ in) from the top of the mould. Cover the mousse with a layer of aspic jelly, allow to cool, then chill in the refrigerator.

Turn out the mousse on to a serving dish and surround it with chopped aspic jelly. The foie gras mousse can also be served in a silver dish or a crystal bowl, at the bottom of which a layer of aspic jelly has been left to set. Smooth the top of the mousse, which should be slightly dome-shaped. Garnish with slices of truffle and glaze lightly with any remaining aspic jelly.

## Duck saupiquet

Grill (broil) or roast 300 g (11 oz) sliced duck breasts and arrange them in a hot dish. Gently cook 2 small chopped garlic cloves in 2 tablespoons vinegar and 2 tablespoons white wine. Leave to cool, then purée in a food processor with 1½ tablespoons cream cheese, 100 g (4 oz) cooked duck's liver and 1 tablespoon olive oil flavoured with herbs. Cover the duck with this sauce.

## Duck suprêmes with truffles

This is made with the breast fillets (suprêmes) of a Rouen duck. Roast the duck in a preheated oven at 200°C (400°F, gas 6) for about 30 minutes, so it is still slightly pink. Cut the fillets into large slices and arrange them in a timbale mould with thick slices of truffle which have been tossed in butter. Keep hot. Roughly chop the remaining carcass and trimmings, moisten with Madeira, port or sherry, and reduce. Add a few tablespoons of reduced demi-glace and boil briefly, then strain. Return the sauce to the boil, then add 1 tablespoon flamed brandy and 2 tablespoons butter. Pour the sauce over the fillets.

## Duck Voisin

Voisin, the name of a famous Parisian restaurant regarded as one of the foremost in the capital between 1850 and 1930, is still used for this timbale of duckling fillets with truffles in aspic. The starting point, a salmi, is a stew (usually of game birds) made first by part roasting and then stewing the bird.

Roast a duckling so that the meat remains slightly pink – about 30 minutes in a preheated oven at 230°C (450°F, gas 8). Let it get completely cold, then remove the fillets. Break up the carcass and trimmings and stew these with a mixture of flavouring vegetables in stock to prepare a salmi. Strain the salmi, remove the fat, and add to it an equal quantity of meat aspic. Reduce and strain. Place a layer of this sauce in a timbale mould; when it has set, place on top a layer of finely sliced duckling fillets. Coat them with more of the sauce, then cover with a layer of sliced truffle. Continue to fill the timbale with alternating layers of duck and truffle, coating each layer with a little half-set aspic. Finish with a layer of aspic. Chill in the refrigerator until set. Turn out and serve very cold.

## Duck with crystallized turnips and cider

Make a stock with the roast giblets from a 2 kg (4½ lb) duck, 1 sliced onion and 1 sliced carrot. Add 1 litre (1¾ pints, 4⅓ cups) cider, 1 apple and 2 large turnips, peeled and cut into pieces. When the liquid has reduced to half its original volume, add 1 litre (1¾ pints, 4⅓ cups) clear stock and cook gently for 20 minutes. Pour the liquid through a strainer. Roast the duck in a preheated oven at 200°C (400°F, gas 6). It should lie on each leg for 10 minutes and then on its back for 5 minutes. Remove the duck from the oven and allow to rest.

In a sauté pan, heat 50 g (2 oz, ¼ cup) butter, add a pinch of sugar and 24 small turnips and fry until golden. Put the duck in a cast-iron casserole with the turnips and stock and simmer for 10 minutes. Thicken the sauce with 50 g (2 oz, ¼ cup) butter and add 1 bunch of coriander (cilantro), chopped, and a dash of cider.

# Duck with mangoes

Pluck, draw, singe and truss a duck. Season with salt and pepper and coat lightly with fat. Roast in a preheated oven at 220°C (425°F, gas 7) with chopped onions, carrots, celery, a little thyme, a bay leaf and 2 tablespoons water. After about 35 minutes for a 1.12 kg (2½ lb) duckling, when the flesh is still pink, pour off the cooking juices into a pan and add 5 tablespoons white wine or stock. Keep the duck warm.

Choose mangoes that are not too ripe, peel them, and remove the stones (pits) over a plate to collect the juice. Put the fruit and juice in a saucepan with a little apricot or peach liqueur, cover and cook gently for a few minutes over a low heat. Strain the fruit, reserving the juice, and put to one side.

Make a dry caramel by heating 2 tablespoons granulated sugar, stirring with a wooden spoon. Add 1 tablespoon vinegar to the caramel, followed by the strained mango juice and then the pan juices. Cook the sauce gently for a few minutes. Carve the duck and garnish with the warm cooked mangoes. Serve coated with the sauce.

# Duck with olives

Stone 250 g (9 oz, 1½ cups) green olives, blanch them for 10 minutes in boiling water, refresh them under cold water and drain. Rub salt and pepper on the inside and the outside of a duck weighing about 2 kg (4½ lb) and truss it. Slice 200 g (7 oz) slightly salted bacon into small strips, blanch for 5 minutes in boiling water, refresh and dry, then fry in 40 g (1½ oz, 3 tablespoons) butter. Drain.

Fry the duck until golden in the same butter, then remove it. Still using the same butter, brown 2 onions and 2 carrots, both finely chopped. Add 250 ml (8 fl oz, 1 cup) meat stock, 1 tablespoon tomato purée (paste), a pinch of crumbled thyme and bay leaf, and 1 tablespoon chopped parsley. Season with salt and pepper and cook gently for about 20 minutes, then strain.

Pour this sauce into a large flameproof casserole, add the duck and the bacon, cover the pot and bring to the boil on top of the stove. Transfer the casserole to a preheated oven at 230°C (450°F, gas 8) and cook for 35–40 minutes, then add the olives and continue cooking for at least another 10 minutes. Arrange the duck on a hot serving dish, cover it with the sauce, and arrange the olives all around it.

## Duck with peas

Cut 200 g (7 oz) larding bacon into large dice, and blanch. Brown these, together with 12 small onions, in butter in a casserole. Remove the onions and diced bacon from the pan and replace with a trussed Nantes duck. Brown the duck on all sides and then drain, retaining the juices. Dilute the pan juices with 100 ml (4 fl oz, 7 tablespoons) dry white wine and 250 ml (8 fl oz, 1 cup) veal or chicken stock and put the duck into this liquor. Add 1 litre (1¾ pints, 4⅓ cups) shelled fresh garden peas, the onions, the bacon, and a bouquet garni. Season and add 2 teaspoons sugar. Simmer gently with the lid on for 35–40 minutes. Drain the duck and arrange on a serving dish, surrounding it with the peas. Reduce the pan juices and pour over the duck. Arrange a lettuce, shredded into a chiffonnade or cut into quarters, on the peas. Alternatively, cook the duck in the same way but leave it slightly underdone. Add 1 litre (1¾ pints, 4⅓ cups) fresh garden peas cooked *à la française* and simmer gently for a few minutes.

## Duck with pineapple

Prepare a young duck, season its liver with salt and pepper and replace inside the carcass. Slowly brown the duck in butter in a flameproof casserole for 20 minutes, add salt and pepper, and then flame it in rum. Add a few tablespoons canned pineapple syrup, 1 tablespoon lemon juice and 1 tablespoon black peppercorns. Cover the dish and finish cooking (50 minutes altogether). Brown some pineapple slices in butter and add them to the casserole 5 minutes before the end of the cooking time. Check the seasoning. Cut the duck into pieces and arrange on a warm plate. Garnish with the pineapple and pour the cooking juices over the top.

## Ducklings à la d'Albufera

Dress and truss 2 young ducklings. Cut 12 pieces of smoked Bayonne ham into heart shapes. Put into a saucepan 50 g (2 oz, ¼ cup) best butter, the pieces of ham, then the ducklings, a bouquet garni, an onion stuck with 2 cloves and half a glass of Málaga (or another Muscat) wine. Cover the contents of saucepan with a circle of buttered paper. In a restaurant this is cooked by placing the pan on a *paillasse* (brick hearth with charcoal fire), with flames above and below but not too fierce, so that the ducklings cook without frying. At home, cook in a preheated oven at 200°C (400°F, gas 6). After 20 minutes, turn the ducklings and remove the onion and the bouquet. After a further 20 minutes, strain them, untruss and place on a serving dish. They should be well browned. Garnish with thin slices of ham. Skim off the fat from the juices in the pan and add 2 tablespoons financière sauce with the fat removed. Add 2 punnets of lightly fried very small mushrooms and coat with the sauce.

## Duckling with lavender honey and lemon

For 4 people, allow 2 ducklings, each weighing about 1.5 kg (3¼ lb), and their giblets. Soften 2 tablespoons mirepoix in a shallow frying pan. Add the giblets and turn them over in the mirepoix. Barely cover with a mixture of half white wine and half water. Season with salt and pepper. Cover and leave to cook gently for about 30 minutes. Strain. Season the ducklings with salt and pepper. Fry them lightly in butter for 20 minutes, taking them out while they are still pale pink. Discard the cooking butter and deglaze the pan with the juice of 2 lemons; then add 1 small teaspoon lavender honey to make a sauce. Leave to reduce almost completely. Then add 2 tablespoons strained duck giblet juices and finally stir in a knob of butter. Adjust the seasoning.

Cut the breast of the ducklings into long thin slices; grill (broil) the legs briefly on both sides. Coat with the seasoned sauce.

## Fillets of wild duck in bitter orange sauce

Take the breast fillets from 2 wild ducks and place in an earthenware dish with salt, coarsely ground pepper, parsley, thyme, 1 bay leaf, chopped shallots, lemon juice and 3 tablespoons good oil. Marinate the duck in the mixture for 45 minutes, turning frequently. Lay the fillets on a spit rack, then skewer them loosely and sprinkle with the marinade. Cook until they are firm to the touch. Remove the skewers and place the duck in a sauté dish containing a melted knob of butter and the juice of ½ lemon. Serve with bitter orange sauce

## Glazed duck with foie gras

Season a fine duck foie gras with salt and pepper, then marinate it in port for at least 24 hours. Draw a 2.5 kg (5½ lb) duck through the neck, remove the breastbone and open out the tail end. Put the liver into the duck and truss it up. Brush the duck with oil and cook in a covered casserole in a preheated oven at 200°C (400°F, gas 6) for 1 hour 20 minutes. While the duck is cooking, prick the skin frequently with a fork so that it does not burst. Remove from the casserole and leave to cool. Add the port marinade and some aspic jelly made with the duck's giblets to the pan juices. Glaze the duck with this clarified aspic and chill.

Poach some prunes in water, some cherries in a red-wine jelly, and some apple quarters in butter. Flavour all these fruits with ginger and glaze with the remaining duck aspic. Stuff some stoned (pitted) green olives with foie gras or ham mousse. Peel the segments of a large orange. Arrange the duck in the serving dish with all the fruits, making the orange segments into a rosette.

## Jellied fillets of Rouen duck à l'orange

Cook a 2 kg (4½ lb) duck for 35 minutes in a preheated oven at 240°C (475°F, gas 9) so that it remains slightly pink. Remove the legs and cut the breast fillets diagonally into slices, leaving them attached at the base. Coat the breast fillets with a brown chaud-froid sauce *à l'orange*. Glaze with aspic and chill.

Prepare a mousse (as for chicken mousse) using the flesh off the legs, adding diced truffles. Fill tiny dome-shaped moulds (or a parfait mould) with the mousse and place in the refrigerator to set.

From a loaf, cut croûtons to the size of the moulds and butter them, then toast or fry until crisp and golden. Cool. Turn the set mousses out on to the croûtons. Arrange the fillets of duck on plates, taking care to keep the tops of the slices neatly closed together. Pour a few spoonfuls of half-set aspic on to the plates and arrange some orange segments as a garnish. Garnish the duck fillets with shreds of pared orange zest and add a mousse-topped croûton to each plate. Chill before serving.

## Magrets of duck

The magret is a portion of meat from the breast of a duck (mallard or Barbary, traditionally fattened for foie gras). Magrets are presented with the skin and underlying layer of fat still attached.

Place 4 chopped shallots and 300 ml (½ pint, 1¼ cups) red wine in a small saucepan and reduce over a high heat until the wine has been absorbed. Then add 120 ml (4 fl oz, ½ cup) single (light) cream and reduce again until syrupy.

Lower the heat. Remove from the heat and gradually whisk in one or two pieces of butter cut from 350 g (12 oz, 1½ cups), returning the saucepan to the heat for a few moments and then removing it. Continue in this way until all the butter has been incorporated. Keep the sauce warm in a bain marie.

Quickly brown 6 duck breasts (magrets) in a heavy-based saucepan, placing the fatty side down. Turn them over as soon as they are golden, cook the other side similarly and reduce the heat. Leave to cook for about 15 minutes. Remove the breasts from the pan and keep warm in a serving dish. Skim off the cooking fat and deglaze the pan with 7 tablespoons red wine. Reduce for a few minutes, then remove from the heat and thicken the sauce with 1 tablespoon of the butter sauce prepared earlier. Pour this sauce over the duck breasts and serve the remainder of the butter sauce separately.

## Magrets with green peppercorns

Brown the duck breasts in butter or goose fat in a frying pan. Add ½ glass of stock, salt and some green peppercorns and cook, keeping the meat rare. Off the heat, add 2 tablespoons double (heavy) cream. Keep warm.

Cook some rice in the Oriental way (lightly brown the rice in butter or goose fat, then add stock and cook until the rice is tender and all the stock has been absorbed) and add an equal quantity of chopped mushrooms. Prepare a thick béchamel sauce (half the volume of the rice). Add the rice and mushrooms and form into flat cakes. Brown the cakes in a little hot oil. Serve the duck breasts with the rice cakes and coat with the sauce.

## Mallard with green peppercorns

Select a mallard duck weighing about 1.4 kg (3 lb). Season the inside and outside with salt and pepper and place in a roasting pan. Sprinkle with 2 tablespoons oil and cook for 30 minutes in a preheated oven at 200°C

(400°F, gas 6). Then cover the dish with foil to keep the duck hot. Peel 2 good-sized Granny Smith apples, cut them into halves, and remove the seeds and cores. Cook in a preheated oven at 180°C (350°F, gas 4) for about 10 minutes. For the sauce, pour 5 tablespoons white wine and 1 tablespoon Armagnac into a saucepan, and reduce by about two-thirds. Add the juice from a can of green peppercorns and 4 tablespoons stock (duck or other poultry). Reduce again for 2–3 minutes. Add 200 ml (7 fl oz, ¾ cup) single (light) cream, season with salt and cook until the sauce is smooth. Check the seasoning and at the last moment add 4 teaspoons port and 1½ tablespoons green peppercorns. Cut off the breast fillets of the duck and place on a serving dish. Cover with the sauce and garnish with the apple, cut into quarters.

## Ravioli of daube of duck with red wine

Cook 1 duck in a casserole in 60 ml (2 fl oz, ¼ cup) oil with 2 chopped onions and 2 thinly sliced carrots. Add 1 litre (1¾ pints, 4⅓ cups) red wine, salt, pepper and 1 bouquet garni halfway through the cooking. Reserve the duck in a warm place and finish the sauce by thickening it with a mixture of 25 g (1 oz, ¼ cup) plain (all-purpose) flour and 25 g (1 oz, 2 tablespoons) butter. Joint and debone the duck. Chop coarsely. Incorporate 20 g (¾ oz) chopped, stoned (pitted) olives and a little sauce. Brush 10 x 10 cm (4 x 4 in) squares of pasta with egg white. Put the stuffing on the moistened sides of half the squares and cover with the remaining squares, moistened sides down. Press the edges together. Cook the ravioli for 2 minutes in simmering salted water. Pour the remaining sauce on top and garnish with chervil. Serve immediately.

## Roast duck

Season the duck with salt and pepper both inside and out, truss and roast in the oven or on a spit. A duckling weighing about 1.25 kg (2¾ lb) should be cooked in a preheated oven at 220°C (425°F, gas 7) for 35 minutes, or for 40–45 minutes on a spit.

## Roast duck with maple syrup

Peel 2 Williams (Bartlett) pears, cut in half lengthways and remove the cores. In a frying pan, combine 50 g (2 oz, ¼ cup) caster (superfine) sugar with 250 ml (8 fl oz, 1 cup) dry white wine and the juice of 2 lemons and 2 oranges. Bring to the boil. Add the pears, 250 ml (8 fl oz, 1 cup) pure maple syrup and a pinch of ground allspice. Simmer until the pears have softened, then remove them from the liquor and set aside in a warm place. Reserve the liquor.

Meanwhile, wash 2 ducks. Prick the skin of the breasts with a fork and season with salt and pepper. Place in an ovenproof casserole and roast in a preheated oven at 200°C (400°F, gas 6) for 15 minutes. Peel and chop 2 carrots, 2 onions, 3 celery sticks, 1 salsify and 2 garlic cloves. Add to the ducks with 2 cloves, 2 bay leaves and 1 bunch of thyme, chopped. Reduce the oven temperature to 150°C (300°F, gas 2). Skim the excess fat from the casserole and baste the ducks every 10 minutes with the reserved maple syrup mixture. As soon as the vegetables begin to turn slightly brown, pour in 500 ml (17 fl oz, 2 cups) chicken stock. Continue cooking (1½ hours in all), basting regularly with the juices in the casserole.

When the ducks are cooked, remove them from the dish and put aside in a warm place. Remove as much fat as possible from the liquid in the dish, leaving the duck juices. Put the vegetables and juice in a smaller saucepan and heat. Add 1 tablespoon tomato purée (paste) and cook for 2–3 minutes. Add a further 500 ml (17 fl oz, 2 cups) chicken stock and any remaining maple syrup mixture. Simmer for 15 minutes and strain. Bone the ducks. Place the pieces of duck on a serving dish and garnish with slices of pear, arranged in a fan shape. Pour the cooking juices over the pieces of duck.

## Roast duck with peaches

Roast the duck. Meanwhile, peel some medium-sized peaches and poach them whole in a light syrup. When the duck is roasted, drain it and keep it hot. Dilute the pan juices with a little peach syrup and reduce to the consistency of a sauce. Add the peaches to the sauce to flavour them, heat them through and arrange them around the duck. Serve the sauce in a sauceboat (gravy boat).

## Rouen duck en chemise

Remove the breastbone from a Rouen duck. Prepare a stuffing by frying 1 heaped tablespoon chopped onion with 125 g (4½ oz, ⅔ cup) diced bacon, without browning the onion. Add an entire duck's liver and 2 or 3 additional duck or chicken livers cut into thin fillets, salt and pepper, a pinch of allspice and some chopped parsley. Cook all the ingredients in butter, cool, and blend in a food processor. Stuff the duck with this mixture, truss and roast in a preheated oven at 240°C (475°F, gas 9) for 8–12 minutes. Leave to cool.

To follow the traditional method, place the duck, head downwards, in a large pig's bladder that has been soaked in cold water. Tie the opening with string and poach in clear braising stock for 45 minutes. Arrange the duck, still in the bladder, on a serving dish.

Alternatively, the duck can be cooked wrapped in a piece of muslin (cheesecloth) or a white table napkin with both ends tied, like a galantine. It is then served unwrapped, surrounded with orange quarters. Serve rouennaise sauce separately.

## Rouen duck in port

Cook a trussed Rouen duck in butter for 30–40 minutes, so that the flesh remains slightly pink. Drain the duck and arrange it on a long dish. Prepare the sauce as follows: dilute the pan juices with 250 ml (8 fl oz, 1 cup) port, add

250 ml (8 fl oz, 1 cup) thickened brown veal stock, boil for a few moments, add some butter and strain. Pour a few spoonfuls of the sauce over the duck and serve the rest separately. The port can be replaced by Banyuls, Frontignan, Madeira, sweet sherry or any other dessert wine.

## Rouen duck (or duckling) soufflé

This very stylish dish is made with 2 birds, the larger to be served and the smaller to make the forcemeat. Roast a trussed Rouen duck in a preheated oven at 200°C (400°F, gas 6) for 10–15 minutes; the meat should still be very rare. Remove the breast fillets, which should be kept for the final garnish, and remove the breastbone, so that the carcass forms a hollow case. Season the inside with salt, pepper and spices, and sprinkle with a spoonful of brandy. Fill the carcass with a forcemeat made from the raw meat of the smaller duck, boned and prepared as for mousseline forcemeat, 150 g (5 oz) raw foie gras and the livers of the 2 ducks. Stuff the carcass so it is re-formed into its original shape. Cover the duck with buttered greaseproof (wax) paper and tie it so that it will hold the forcemeat during cooking. Place the stuffed duck on a baking sheet, coat with melted butter and roast in a preheated oven at 150°C (300°F, gas 2) for 30–35 minutes. Remove the greaseproof paper and arrange the duck on a serving dish.

Make some tartlet cases from short pastry (basic pie dough), bake blind, heap with a salpicon of truffles and mushrooms bound with concentrated Madeira sauce, and cover each with a slice of duck breast fillet and a thick slice of truffle heated in butter. Arrange the tartlets around the duck. Serve with rouennaise sauce or Perigueux sauce.

Instead of being used to fill the tartlets, the duck fillets can be cut into thin slices and embedded in the mousseline forcemeat in the duck carcass.

The same filling can be used to make Rouen duck mousses and

mousselines. The former are made in large charlotte moulds and the latter in small individual moulds. They are poached in a bain marie in the oven. The forcemeat can also be used for duck soufflé *en timbale*: put it in buttered soufflé timbale moulds and bake as for other soufflés.

## Steamed duck foie gras with Sauternes

Prepare some stock with duck bones, 1 bottle of Sauternes, 2 carrots, 1 turnip, 2 celery sticks, 2 shallots and the white part of 1 leek (all sliced). Season with salt and pepper. Trim the foie gras and remove the tubes, season and chill (with the strained stock) for 24 hours. Pour the stock into a steamer, place the foie gras in the steamer basket and cook for about 15 minutes. Cut the foie gras into slices, pour over a little of the stock and serve hot or cold.

## Stuffed duck à la rouennaise

Draw, singe and truss a duck weighing 1.5 kg (3¼ lb). Prepare a forcemeat: melt a little butter and oil in a saucepan and in this brown 25 g (1 oz, 2 tablespoons) chopped onion, 2 duck livers, a few sprigs of parsley and 100 g (4 oz, ⅔ cup) chopped bacon fat. When all the ingredients are golden brown, take the pan off the heat and leave it to cool.

Stuff the duck with the cold forcemeat, season, and bard it. Put it in a roasting tin with a little butter and some roughly chopped vegetables – 1 onion, 2 carrots, 1 celery stick. Cook for 1 hour in a preheated oven at 240°C (475°F, gas 9). Towards the end of the cooking time, remove the barding. Take the bird out of the pan and keep hot. Strain the cooking juices and pour off the fat. Return the duck to the pan, sprinkle it with Madeira, bring to the boil, add the cooking juices, bring to the boil again, cover the pan and leave to cook for a few minutes. Put the duck on a hot dish and serve with rouennaise sauce or the cooking juices, strained and thickened with a little beurre manié.

## Terrine of duckling

Bone a duckling weighing about 1.25 kg (2¾ lb) without damaging the breast meat. Cut the latter into even strips, together with 300 g (11 oz) bacon fat. Put the meat into a bowl with salt, pepper, ½ teaspoon *quatre epices* or four spices, 4 tablespoons brandy, a chopped bay leaf and the leaves from a small sprig of fresh thyme. Thoroughly soak the meat in this mixture and marinate for 24 hours in a cool place. Put the rest of the duck in the refrigerator. Soak an intact pig's caul (caul fat) in cold water, then squeeze and wipe it dry.

Prepare a duxelles with 250 g (9 oz, 3 cups) button mushrooms, 2 or 3 shallots, salt and pepper. Finely chop 350 g (12 oz) fresh belly of pork, 1 onion, the remaining duck meat and the blanched zest of an orange. Mix the duxelles and the chopped meat in a bowl with 2 eggs, pepper and salt. Work the mixture until well bound, adding the marinade in which the strips of bacon fat and duck were steeped.

Line the terrine with the caul. Arrange half of the forcemeat in an even layer. Cover with alternating strips of the marinated duck and bacon fat. Cover with the rest of the forcemeat. Press down the caul on the contents of the terrine and trim. Place a bay leaf and 2 small sprigs of fresh thyme on top and then put on the lid.

Place the terrine in a bain marie, bring to the boil on the hob (stove top), then cook in a preheated oven at 180°C (350°F, gas 4) for 1½ hours. Remove from the oven and allow to cool. When lukewarm, take off the lid and replace with a weighted board. Allow the terrine to cool completely.

An aspic flavoured with port can be poured into the terrine and allowed to set. To preserve the terrine, cover with a fine layer of melted goose fat.

# Goose

## Foie gras, prepared and poached

To prepare a foie gras, carefully remove all the tubes and skin from the liver, using the point of a thin-bladed knife. First make an incision in each lobe starting from the larger end, where the main vein is located. Separate it. Still using the knife, pull on the vein. It will come away by itself, showing the rest of the network, which can then be easily removed. Once the lobes are open, season them with ½ teaspoon salt and ¼ teaspoon freshly ground pepper per 450 g (1 lb). Close up each lobe, wrapping it tightly in muslin (cheesecloth), and chill overnight.

To poach the foie gras, next day, place the liver in a terrine, cover it with goose fat and poach it, allowing 4 minutes per 100 g (4 oz) foie gras when the fat starts to simmer. When it is cooked, cool and drain the liver on a wire rack, then chill for at least 24 hours. Remove the muslin before serving the foie gras cold, possibly with a hot truffle cooked *en papillote*.

The taste of the liver can be enhanced by marinating it for 48 hours in port mixed with 10% Armagnac.

## Baked foie gras

Prepare a foie gras weighing about 575 g (1¼ lb), season with coarse salt and keep in a cool place for 24 hours. Wash the liver, wipe it and marinate for 48 hours with ground paprika, spices and Armagnac. Drain the liver, place it in an ovenproof dish and half fill it with melted goose fat. Bake in a preheated oven at 190°C (375°F, gas 5), turning once, for about 15 minutes per 450 g (1 lb). To test, pierce with a skewer: the juice should be only just pink.

## Ballotine of goose with Savigny-lès-Beaune

For this dish, the goose legs are stuffed and shaped into ballotines, then braised. They are served with a chestnut custard, stuffed onions and the fried goose suprêmes.

Take a young goose weighing about 3.5 kg (8 lb) and cut off the wings and legs. Bone the legs and remove the meat from the wings to make the forcemeat. Remove the suprêmes from the carcass and chill in the refrigerator until required.

To make the stuffed goose legs en ballotines, mince (grind) the reserved wing meat and the liver very finely. Place in a bowl over a dish of ice and work the mixture until smooth. Then blend in an egg white followed by 300 ml (½ pint, 1¼ cups) double (heavy) cream. Add salt, pepper and a pinch of cayenne pepper, and 50 g (2 oz, ½ cup) boiled diced chestnuts. Stuff the boned legs with this mixture, shape them into ballotines and tie them. Spread some sliced onion over the base of an ovenproof dish and lay the carcass of the goose on top. Then place the ballotines on top of the carcass and braise them in a preheated oven at 180°C (350°F, gas 4) for 45–60 minutes, basting frequently so that they remain moist. (The remainder of the stuffing can be used to make godiveau.)

To make the chestnut custard, mix 300 ml (½ pint, 1¼ cups) single (light) cream, 3 eggs, 150 g (5 oz, ½ cup) chestnut purée and 100 g (4 oz, 1 cup) boiled diced chestnuts. Butter 8 small dariole moulds and divide the mixture among them. Cook in a bain marie in a preheated oven at 170° C (325° F, gas 3). Leave for a few minutes before unmoulding.

To make onions stuffed with garlic purée, blanch 8 Spanish onions in fast-boiling salted water, refresh them and drain them carefully. Remove some of the inner flesh of the onions, leaving the outer layers intact. (Use the removed onion for another recipe.) Peel 500 g (18 oz) garlic cloves, cook them in milk, drain them and rub them through a fine sieve. Reheat them with a little cream. Stuff the onions with the garlic purée, filling them to the top.

Remove the fat from the liquor in which the ballotines were braised and deglaze the pan with a bottle of Savigny-lès-Beaune. Reduce by one-third, then strain the sauce and thicken with 200 g (7 oz, scant 1 cup) butter. Taste and adjust the seasoning.

Fry the goose suprêmes in the goose fat until the outside is golden brown but the inside is still pink. Place a thin slice of suprême on each plate, add a slice of ballotine, a stuffed onion and a chestnut custard. Pour the sauce around the food without covering the sliced meat. Serve the remaining sauce separately.

## Confit of goose

Clean the inside of a fat goose thoroughly and remove the bones, keeping the carcass whole. Cut into quarters. Place in a container and season very liberally with coarse salt, then leave in a cold place for 24 hours to allow the salt to penetrate thoroughly into the flesh. Cook in a large copper cauldron with 2 kg (4½ lb) goose fat for 2 hours. Make sure the fat simmers while cooking, but do not allow it to boil. While the fat is still hot, strain it into a stoneware pot and place the pieces of goose in the fat so they are completely covered. Leave to cool and then cover the pot. To obtain an authentic *confit*, store in a cellar for 5–6 months. For *confit* of duck, follow the same method.

## Confit of goose à la béarnaise

Heat a quarter of preserved goose in its own fat and keep hot in a serving dish. Peel and slice some potatoes and fry them in the *confit* fat. Chop some parsley and garlic together, add to the potatoes and reheat. Surround the *confit* with the potatoes and serve very hot.

## Confit of goose à la landaise

Peel 6 small onions and dice 75 g (3 oz, ½ cup) Bayonne ham. Heat 1 tablespoon goose fat in an earthenware casserole and cook the onions and ham for 5 minutes, then add 1 litre (1¾ pints, 4⅓ cups) freshly shelled peas. Sprinkle with 1 tablespoon flour and stir for a few moments with a wooden spoon. Moisten with 150 ml (¼ pint, ⅔ cup) water; add pepper and ½ teaspoon sugar (salt is not needed because the ham is already salty). Add a bouquet garni with chervil, cover and leave to cook for about 30 minutes. Then add a quarter of preserved goose and leave until cooked, the total cooking time depending on the tenderness of the peas.

## Confit of goose à la sarladaise

Prepare as for *confit* of goose *à la béarnaise*, but add slices of truffle when the potatoes are cooked.

## Confit of goose with green cabbage

Braise potato quarters with green cabbage arranged on top. Press a piece of preserved goose, with a little of its fat, into the cabbage layer and reheat. Arrange the *confit* on a dish surrounded by the potatoes and cabbage.

## Foie gras Souvarov

Season a goose foie gras weighing 500 g (18 oz) with salt and pepper and steep for 24 hours in Cognac. Drain off the excess liquid, then seize (quickly and lightly brown the surface) the foie gras in 25 g (1 oz, 2 tablespoons) butter. Place it in a terrine just large enough to contain it, surrounded by quartered truffles. Half-cover it with reduced demi-glace sauce flavoured with truffle. Cover the terrine and seal the lid with a strip of dough. Cook for 40 minutes in a preheated oven at 200°C (400°, gas 6). Serve in the terrine.

## Goose à l'alsacienne

Braise some sauerkraut with a small piece of lean bacon. Stuff a goose with sausagemeat seasoned with salt, pepper, a pinch of allspice and a little chopped onion and parsley. Sew up the vent. Calculate the cooking time at 40 minutes per 1 kg, 20 minutes per 1 lb, in a preheated oven at 180°C (350°F, gas 4), basting it frequently.

When the goose is half-cooked, add a little of the goose fat to the sauerkraut and continue cooking. Poach Strasbourg sausages gently in barely simmering water. Spread the sauerkraut over a long serving dish and place the goose in the centre. Cut the bacon into pieces and arrange them around the bird, alternating the bacon with the sausages. Keep everything hot. Skim the fat from the goose cooking juices and deglaze the pan with white wine and an equal quantity of stock. Boil down to reduce. Serve the sauce separately.

## Goose à l'instar de Visé

Take a 3.5 kg (8 lb) goose that has not yet started laying and poach it in white stock with 2 heads (bulbs) garlic for 1½ hours. Drain it, cut into pieces and place in a sauté pan. Moisten with goose fat and simmer, covered, until done.

Meanwhile, prepare a velouté sauce using the goose fat (for the roux) and the cooking juices from the goose. Cook over a low heat for 1 hour. Thicken the velouté with 4 egg yolks, then pass it through a fine sieve. Add a few tablespoons of cream and a purée of the garlic that was cooked with the goose.

Drain the pieces of goose and add to the sauce. Heat well and serve.

## Goose à la bourguignonne

Dice 100 g (4 oz) blanched lean bacon and fry it in 25 g (1 oz, 2 tablespoons) butter. Using the same pan, fry 20 small onions and then 20 sliced mushrooms. Remove them and brown the goose all over in the same butter.

Remove the goose, deglaze the pan with 500 ml (17 fl oz, 2 cups) red wine, boil down to reduce it by half and then add 400 ml (14 fl oz, 1¾ cups) demi-glace sauce (or reduced stock). Boil for 5 minutes and add a bouquet garni. Put the goose back into the pan. Start the cooking over a high heat, then reduce the heat, cover the pan and cook gently for 30 minutes. Add the bacon, onions and mushrooms and continue to cook over a moderate heat, with the pan still covered, for 45–60 minutes. Remove the bouquet garni, and either serve the goose and its accompaniments in the cooking dish or arrange it on a large serving dish and pour the sauce over it.

## Goose en daube Capitole

Stuff the goose with a fine forcemeat mixed with foie gras and diced truffles. Truss and braise the goose on a mirepoix of flavouring vegetables in stock for about 1½ hours, depending on size. When it is almost cooked, remove the string used for trussing and pour the braising liquid through a fine strainer. Put the goose back into the pan with 250 g (9 oz) small mushrooms, an equal quantity of stoned (pitted) blanched olives and 250 g (9 oz) small fried chipolatas. Pour the cooking juices over the goose and finish cooking in a preheated oven at 180°C (350°F, gas 4).

## Foie gras en brioche (hot)

Soak a pig's caul (caul fat) in cold water. Prepare some unsweetened brioche dough. Take a firm foie gras weighing 675–900 g (1½–2 lb) and stud it with truffles which have been seasoned and moistened with brandy. Season the foie gras with spiced salt, moisten it with brandy and leave to marinate for a few hours. Drain the pig's caul, wipe it dry and wrap the foie gras in it. Cook in a preheated oven at 190°C (375°F, gas 5) for 18–20 minutes, then cool.

Line the bottom of a plain greased timbale mould with a fairly thick layer of brioche dough, then add the liver and cover it with another, thinner, layer of dough. Cover the mould with a piece of buttered greaseproof (wax) paper and tie with string to prevent the dough from spilling out. Leave the dough to rise for 2 hours in a warm place, then bake in a preheated oven at 200°C (400°F, gas 6) for 50–60 minutes. To see if the brioche is done, pierce with a needle, which should come out clean. Turn out the brioche and serve.

## Foie gras purée

Prepare some thick chicken velouté sauce and double its volume of foie gras, cooked and pressed through a fine sieve. Stir together over heat, then bind with egg yolk. This purée can be used as it is for filling bouchées, barquettes, tartlets or brioches. It can also be mixed with white breadcrumbs to stuff artichoke hearts or mushroom caps, or used plain to garnish cold hors d'oeuvre and eggs.

## Goose foie gras with sultanas

Prepare a foie gras weighing about 575 g (1¼ lb) in the usual way. Cook in a saucepan over a gentle heat for 5–6 minutes, drain and remove the fat. Fry 1 chopped onion in goose fat, sprinkle with a little flour and add the liver cooking juices, a little white wine, 1 chopped tomato, a bouquet garni and some stock. Cook for 30 minutes, then strain. Put the liver in a heavy-based casserole with this sauce, add some sultanas (golden raisins) that have been soaked in warm Madeira until swollen, and leave to simmer for 20 minutes. Serve with croûtons fried in goose fat and drain well.

## Goose hearts en papillotes

Cut 4 large squares of foil. Place 3 carefully cleaned goose hearts in the centre of each square together with 100 g (4 oz) cleaned and sliced cep mushrooms.

Season generously with salt and pepper and fold the foil into parcels, sealing the edges thoroughly. Place them on a grill over very hot embers. Cook for about 20 minutes on each side.

## Goose in the pot

The day before it is required, stuff a young goose weighing about 3.5 kg (8 lb) with the following mixture: the chopped liver and heart, 2–3 diced apples and 3–4 desalted anchovy fillets pounded to a paste. Leave the goose in a cool place for 24 hours. The following day make a stock with 20 unpeeled garlic cloves, a bouquet garni and an onion studded with 2 cloves. Stud the goose all over with garlic and poach it in the stock for 1½ hours, skimming the pan when it comes to the boil.

Stew some dessert apples and add to them 2 desalted, pounded anchovies and 1 cup of the strained cooking stock. Prepare some small gougères: for every 2 eggs used for the dough, add 100 g (4 oz) Gruyère cheese and 1 puréed anchovy fillet.

Serve the goose very hot, accompanied by the apple and garnished with the gougères.

## Goose rillettes

These are made in the same way as *rillettes de Tours* (see Pork), using boned birds whose liver has been made into foie gras. The rillettes can be potted by shredding the meat and pouring it, still boiling hot, with any remaining cooking fat and liquor, into sterilized jars. Use goose fat to seal the pots.

## Potted foie gras with truffles

Remove the tubes from a goose foie gras and divide it in half. Trim the lobes and reserve the trimmings. Stud the liver with pieces of truffle. Season with spiced salt, pour over some brandy and leave to marinate for 5–6 hours. Prepare a forcemeat made of 375 g (13 oz) lean pork meat, 450 g (1 lb) fatty pork, the foie gras trimmings, 150 g (5 oz, 1 cup) diced truffles, 3 tablespoons Madeira and 2 tablespoons spiced salt.

Line the bottom and sides of an oval terrine or ovenproof dish with thin slices of pork fat, then cover the inside with a thin layer of the forcemeat. Place half the remaining foie gras on top of the forcemeat and press down. Cover with another layer of forcemeat, then place the foie gras on top. Finish with the rest of the forcemeat. Cover with a thin slice of pork fat. Press well to flatten the ingredients and place half a bay leaf and a sprig of thyme on top. Cover the terrine, seal the lid with a flour and water paste and place in a bain marie. Bring to the boil, then place in a preheated oven at 180°C (350°F, gas 4) and bake for 1¼–1½ hours, depending on the size of the terrine.

Cool, uncover, then leave under a light weight until the next day. Turn out the potted foie gras by standing the dish in hot water for a few seconds. Remove the pork fat and dry the top of the foie gras with a cloth, pressing down a little to firm it. Pour a thin layer of lard (shortening) mixed with goose fat (rendered during cooking) over the bottom of the terrine and leave it to set. Replace the foie gras and pour some more lard and goose fat mixture (just warm) over the top. Chill for at least 12 hours and serve in the terrine.

## Roast goose with fruit

Stuff a goose and roast it as for roast goose with sage and onion stuffing. While it is cooking, poach some quartered pears in boiling syrup until translucent. Peel and core some small apples and sprinkle them with lemon juice. Fill the centres with redcurrant jelly. Half an hour before the goose is cooked, place the apples around it and baste with the goose fat that has collected in the pan. Complete the cooking. Place the goose on a long serving dish and arrange the apples and the drained pear quarters around it. Keep hot in the oven. Deglaze the cooking pan with a little of the pear syrup, reduce the liquid by half and pour it into a sauceboat (gravy boat).

## Roast goose with sage and onion stuffing

Roast 1 kg (2¼ lb) large unpeeled onions in the oven. Let them get cold, then peel and chop them. Soak an equal weight of crustless bread in milk, then press out as much milk as possible. Mix the bread with the chopped onion and season with 1½ teaspoons salt, a pinch of pepper, a little grated nutmeg and 3 tablespoons chopped fresh sage.

Stuff the goose with this mixture and sew up the vent. Calculate the cooking time at 40 minutes per 1 kg, 20 minutes per 1 lb, in a preheated oven at 180°C (350°F, gas 4). Drain off excess fat during roasting. Place it on a long serving dish, pour over the deglazed cooking juices and serve with unsweetened or very slightly sweetened apple sauce.

## Truffled foie gras with Madeira

Trim a foie gras and remove the tubes. Stud with truffle sticks and season with spiced salt. Pour brandy over it and leave to marinate for a few hours. Wrap the foie gras in a pig's caul (caul fat) or in thin strips of bacon fat and place in a braising pan lined with fresh pork skin, sliced onions and carrots tossed in butter. Cover and simmer for 7–8 minutes. Add 250 ml (8 fl oz, 1 cup) Madeira, port or sherry and simmer for several minutes. Add 200 ml (7 fl oz, ¾ cup) concentrated brown veal stock (containing some dissolved gelatine if the foie gras is to be served cold) and cook in a preheated oven at 190°C (375°F, gas 5) for 45 minutes.

Drain the foie gras, unwrap it and place it on a serving dish. Strain the cooking juices and skim off all the fat. Pour over the foie gras and serve hot.

To serve cold, place the drained and unwrapped foie gras in a terrine just large enough to hold it. Pour over the strained cooking juices and leave to cool for 12 hours (of which at least 2 hours should be in the refrigerator). Remove the layer of solidified fat on the surface of the sauce and serve the foie gras from the terrine.

## Truffled pâté de foie gras

Prepare 1 kg (2¼ lb) pâté pastry dough, made with butter or lard (shortening), and leave to rest for 12 hours. Prepare 2 firm foies gras in the usual way. Stud the lobes with peeled truffles cut into sticks, seasoned with spiced salt and moistened with brandy. Season the livers well. Soak them in brandy and Madeira for 2 hours. Prepare 1 kg (2¼ lb) pork and foie gras forcemeat.

Line a hinged pâté mould (round or oval) with some of the dough, then spread a layer of forcemeat over the bottom and sides of the mould. Put the foie gras into the mould, pressing it well. Cover with a domed layer of forcemeat. On top of this lay a slice of pork fat, half a bay leaf and a small sprig of thyme. Cover the pâté with a layer of dough and seal the edges. Garnish the top with decorative pastry motifs shaped with pastry (cookie) cutters (lozenges, leaves, crescents) or strips of plaited dough. In the middle put 3 or 4 round pieces of dough shaped with a fluted pastry cutter. Make a hole in the middle of these so the steam can escape during baking. Brush with egg. Bake in a preheated oven at 190–200°C (375–400°F, gas 5–6) until the dough is cooked thoroughly and golden brown.

Cool. When it is lukewarm, pour into it either half-melted lard, if it is to be kept for some time, or Madeira-flavoured aspic if it is to be used at once.

Pâté de foie gras must be made at least 12 hours before using. The mould can be lined with a forcemeat made entirely of foie gras instead of with pork and foie gras forcemeat.

# Turkey

## Braised turkey legs

This recipe uses the legs of young turkeys; the wings or suprêmes can be used for another dish. Bone the legs, fill with a suitable poultry stuffing, then roll them into small ballotines. Braise in white or brown stock, then drain and glaze in the oven. Arrange on a serving dish and coat with the cooking stock. Serve with a vegetable purée, braised vegetables (such as carrots or celery), rice or creamed potatoes.

## Daube of turkey à la bourgeoise

This dish is made with a very tender turkey hen, rather than a young turkey cock. Braise the bird in a suitable brown stock; when three-quarters cooked, drain. Strain the braising stock. Replace the bird in the braising pan and surround with a bourgeoise garnish. Add the strained braising stock, cover the pan and finish cooking over a gentle heat.

## Giblets à la bourgeoise

Dice 100 g (4 oz) thick streaky (slab) bacon and blanch for 5 minutes in boiling water. Strain and leave to cool. Prepare 800 g (1¾ lb) turkey or chicken giblets. Peel 100 g (4 oz) small onions, 300 g (11 oz) baby carrots and a garlic clove. Brown the diced bacon in a sauté pan in 25 g (1 oz, 2 tablespoons) butter, lard or goose fat, then strain and remove from the pan. In the same fat cook the onions until golden, strain and remove. Next brown the giblets (except the liver) in the pan, then add the crushed garlic. Stir well, sprinkle on 25 g (1 oz, ¼ cup) flour, and mix in until coloured. Add 100 ml (4 fl oz,

7 tablespoons) dry white wine and let it reduce for a few minutes. Season lightly and add a bouquet garni, the bacon, onions and carrots, and 1.15 litres (2 pints, 5 cups) water or poultry stock to cover the giblets. Cover and bring to the boil, then reduce the heat and simmer for 30 minutes. Add the liver and stir gently, then continue cooking for about 10 more minutes until the liver is cooked. Place the giblets and vegetables in a dish and pour over the sauce.

## Giblets à la bourguignonne

Prepare as for giblets *à la bourgeoise* but replace the carrots by 100 g (4 oz, 2 cups) button mushrooms and the white wine by red Burgundy.

## Paupiettes of turkey à la Crécy

Flatten some slices of turkey breast, roll them into paupiettes using a suitable forcemeat or stuffing. Arrange them in a buttered flameproof casserole lined with pieces of pork skin or bacon rinds and sliced onions and carrots browned in butter. Place a bouquet garni in the middle. Season with salt and pepper. Cover and cook over a gentle heat for 10 minutes.

Add some dry white wine or (depending on the accompaniments) Madeira – 200 ml (7 fl oz, ¾ cup) per 10 paupiettes. Reduce almost entirely, then add some thickened stock to cover the paupiettes by two-thirds. Cover and braise in a preheated oven at 200°C (400°F, gas 6), basting frequently, for 45–60 minutes. Drain the paupiettes and return to the pan with the strained braising liquor. Add 1 kg (2¼ lb) glazed carrots and heat through. Serve the paupiettes coated with their sauce and surrounded with the carrots.

## Poupeton of turkey Brillat-Savarin

Prepare a turkey as for a ballotine, boning it out without damaging the skin. Stuff it with a smooth mixture of fine veal forcemeat, *à gratin* forcemeat, lambs' sweetbreads braised *à blanc* and diced foie gras and truffles. Roll the turkey into a ballotine; wrap it in a pig's caul (caul fat), then in muslin (cheesecloth) and tie it up.

Line a greased flameproof casserole with diced raw ham and slices of carrot and onion. Place the turkey in this and cook gently, covered, for 15 minutes, then add 3 tablespoons Madeira. Reduce by half, add some gravy (or chicken stock) and continue cooking, covered, in a preheated oven at 190°C (375°F, gas 5) for 1½ hours. Skim the fat from the cooking liquid, strain, season and serve in a sauceboat.

The *poupeton* can also be served cold, as it is or in aspic.

## Roast turkey

Season and truss a small turkey and bard the breast and back with bacon. Roast either on a spit, allowing 20 minutes per 450 g (1 lb), or in a preheated oven, allowing 25 minutes per 450 g (1 lb) at 160°C (325°F, gas 3). Remove the bacon before the bird is completely cooked so that it browns. Serve with the skimmed strained cooking juices and garnish with watercress.

## Roast turkey stuffed with chestnuts

Scald and peel 1 kg (2¼ lb) chestnuts. Half-cook them in stock, drain and wrap in a large piece of soaked pig's caul, if available. Enclose them in the boned turkey, tie it up neatly and roast in the usual way.

## Roast turkey stuffed with dessert apples

Season the turkey and, if desired, insert some slices of truffle between the skin and the flesh. Remove the gall bladder from the liver and pound the liver with a small can of goose foie gras mousse, 40 g (1½ oz, 3 tablespoons) butter and 2 tablespoons port. Peel and remove the seeds from 800 g (1¾ lb) dessert (eating) apples, cut them into thick slices and brown them in a frying pan in 75 g (3 oz, 6 tablespoons) butter. Mix half the apples with the liver mixture and use to stuff the turkey. Keep the remaining apples hot. Place a very thin strip of bacon on the breast and on the back of the bird and tie up firmly.

Cook the turkey in a preheated oven at 200°C (400°F, gas 6) for 2 hours for a 3 kg (6½ lb) bird. The bird is cooked if the juices released when the skin is pricked are clear. Remove the bacon and quickly brown the turkey breast, if necessary, in a very hot oven. Carve. Put the remaining hot apples into a dish, sprinkle with the cooking juices and serve with the sliced turkey.

## Stuffed braised turkey pinions

Singe and clean 6 turkey pinions and remove the bones without tearing the skin. Stuff with finely minced (ground) pork forcemeat or a poultry or quenelle forcemeat. Wrap each pinion in a thin rasher (slice) of bacon and tie with kitchen thread. Line a buttered sauté pan with bacon rinds, 50 g (2 oz, ¼ cup) chopped onions and 50 g (2 oz, ⅓ cup) thinly sliced carrots; add a bouquet garni and the pinions. Season, cover and cook gently for 15 minutes. Moisten with 200 ml (7 fl oz, ¾ cup) dry white wine or Madeira and cook uncovered until the liquid has evaporated. Add 400 ml (14 fl oz, 1¾ cups) poultry or veal stock, bring slowly to the boil, then cover and cook in a preheated oven at 180°C (350°F, gas 4) for 40 minutes. Drain the pinions, remove the bacon, brown the pinions quickly in a preheated oven at 240°C (475°F, gas 9) and arrange on a serving dish. Remove the fat from the cooking liquor, reduce and strain it, and pour over the pinions.

Serve with one of the following garnishes: *Choisy, financière, forestière, Godard, jardinière, languedocienne, macédoine, milanaise* (à la milanaise), *piémontaise* (à la piémontaise), rice pilaf or risotto. Braised pinions may also be garnished with braised or boiled vegetables, coated with butter or cream.

## Stuffed roast turkey

Stuff the turkey with a sage and onion stuffing prepared as follows: bake the onions in their skins in the oven, peel and chop them, then toss in butter. Season with plenty of chopped fresh sage. Mix with an equal quantity of fresh breadcrumbs and half their quantity of chopped suet. Bind with a little milk. Roast the turkey in the usual way, weighing it and calculating the cooking time with the stuffing. Put it on a serving dish surrounded with slices of bacon or grilled sausages. Serve with gravy made from the cooking juices and bread sauce.

## Stuffed turkey grand-duc

Slit open a turkey along the back, bone it and make a stuffing with the following mixture: 500 g (18 oz) chicken rubbed through a fine sieve, 500 ml (17 fl oz, 2 cups) double (heavy) cream, 250 g (9 oz) foie gras poached in port wine and rubbed through a sieve. Mix all these ingredients thoroughly and season with salt and pepper. Add 12 truffles, peeled and cooked for 10 minutes in a little liqueur brandy, and 24 chicken hearts with the blood vessels removed, which have been soaked in water, steeped in white Malaga wine, drained, dried in a cloth, stuffed with a purée of York ham and poached for 15 minutes in truffle essence.

Carefully reshape the stuffed turkey. Cover with slices of raw ham or bacon, and enclose in a large layer of lining pastry, taking care to keep the shape of the bird as far as possible. Bake in a preheated oven at 180°C (250°F, gas 4) for 2½ hours. During cooking, cover the turkey with greaseproof (wax) paper folded into four, so that it will cook all the way through without browning the pastry too soon. Serve the turkey freshly cooked on a warmed serving platter, accompanied with a demi-glace sauce flavoured with truffle essence in a sauceboat.

## Truffled turkey

Draw the turkey, leaving the skin of the neck very long so that the opening in the bird can be secured firmly when trussing. Insert beneath the skin some large slices of truffle that have been seasoned and soaked in brandy.

Prepare the stuffing as follows: dice 500 g (18 oz) fresh pork fat and mix with 250 g (9 oz) uncooked foie gras. Reduce to a purée in a mortar or a blender and add any parings from the truffles. Season with salt, pepper and a pinch of dried fennel. Press the stuffing through a sieve, add a little crushed thyme and bay leaf, and cook very gently in a heavy-based saucepan, stirring, for about 10 minutes. Add 2 tablespoons brandy and cool completely.

Stuff and truss the turkey and wrap it in a sheet of buttered greaseproof (wax) paper. Leave it in a cool place for at least 24 hours. Bard the truffled turkey, wrap it again in the buttered paper and roast, uncovered, in a preheated oven at 160°C (325°F, gas 3), allowing 20–25 minutes per 450 g (1 lb). Unwrap the turkey, remove the barding and replace in the oven to brown. Place on the serving dish and keep hot. Deglaze the pan, reduce the gravy and serve separately. Alternatively, serve with a Périgueux sauce to which the cooking juices have been added.

## Turkey mole

Joint a small turkey into small portions and marinate them overnight in a mixture of the juice of 4 oranges, 100 ml (4 fl oz, 7 tablespoons) tequila, 2–4 chopped garlic cloves, 1 chopped onion, some chopped fresh oregano, a sprinkling of ground cinnamon and 6 whole cloves.

The following day, grill (broil) a mixture of fresh chillies until just soft – try 250 g (9 oz) mulatto chillies, 300 g (11 oz) ancho chillies, 150 g (5 oz) pasilla chillies and 50 g (2 oz) chipotle chillies. Remove the cores and seeds, then rinse the chillies and chop finely. Fry the chillies in a little oil, then add

6 chopped garlic cloves, 150 g (5 oz, 1¼ cups) chopped blanched almonds, 100 g (4 oz, 1 cup) unsalted peanuts 100 g (4 oz, ¾ cup) sesame seeds and 100 g (4 oz, ⅔ cup) raisins. Remove from the heat.

In a dry frying pan, lightly roast 6 black peppercorns, 10 coriander seeds, 4 cloves, 1 teaspoon aniseeds and 1 teaspoon ground cinnamon. Cool, then grind these spices and add them to the chilli mixture. Fry 450 g (1 lb) peeled, chopped tomatoes and 250 g (9 oz) peeled chopped tomatillos until all their excess liquid has evaporated, then purée them with the chilli mixture, adding a little turkey stock to make a smooth, thick paste. Transfer the paste to a pan and add a little salt, then cook over a low heat, stirring, until the oil rises to the surface. Add 200 g (7 oz, 7 squares) bitter chocolate and stir until it has melted into the sauce. Dilute the sauce with extra stock if necessary, then set it aside off the heat.

Drain the turkey portions, reserving the marinade, and place in a large deep roasting tin (pan). Roast in a preheated oven at 200°C (400°F, gas 6) for 30 minutes. Pour the marinade over and continue cooking for a further 40 minutes, turning and rearranging the turkey occasionally. The turkey should be thoroughly cooked and the marinade evaporated to a glaze. Arrange the turkey on a dish and sprinkle with sesame seeds. Serve with the reheated mole sauce.

## Turkey pinion fritters

Stuff and braise small turkey pinions as in the recipe for stuffed braised turkey pinions. Strain the hot cooking liquor, then pour it back over the pinions and leave until cool. Remove the pinions from the liquor, pat dry, then marinate for 30 minutes in olive oil, lemon juice, salt, pepper and chopped parsley.

Drain and dry the pinions, then dip them in batter and fry in very hot deep fat until crisp and golden. Drain and sprinkle with salt. Serve the pinion fritters on a doiley or napkin, garnished with fried parsley and lemon quarters or, more originally, with fresh mint leaves. A well-seasoned tomato sauce may be served with this dish.

## Turkey pinions à la fermière

Prepare and braise the pinions as in the recipe for stuffed braised turkey pinions. Cooked chopped onions and parsley may be added to the finely minced (ground) pork forcemeat. Arrange the drained pinions in a casserole with a fermière vegetable garnish. Remove the fat from the reserved cooking liquor, then reduce and strain it into the casserole over the vegetables. Cover and cook in a preheated oven at 200°C (400°F, gas 6) for about 25 minutes or until piping hot.

## Turkey wings Sainte-Menehould

Braise some small turkey wings with herbs and flavourings, but do not let them get too soft (about 50 minutes). Drain and leave to cool. Pour a little melted butter or lard over them, roll them in fresh breadcrumbs and chill for 1 hour. Coat with melted butter and bake in a preheated oven at 230°C (450°F, gas 8) until golden (about 15 minutes). Serve with mustard or Sainte-Menehould sauce.

# Game

# Grouse

## Roast grouse

Mash 50 g (2 oz, ¼ cup) butter with 2 tablespoons lemon juice, salt and pepper. Wipe 2 plump or 4 small prepared grouse and place some of the butter inside each bird. Cover the breasts of the birds with bacon and tie in place, then wrap each bird in foil. Place the birds, breast side down, on a rack resting in a baking tin (pan) and roast in a preheated oven at 200°C (400°F, gas 6) for about 25 minutes for small birds and 35 minutes for the larger ones. While the birds are roasting, fry the grouse livers in butter, then mash together to make a paste. Fry 2–4 slices of bread, crusts removed, in a mixture of butter and oil until crisp and golden. Spread these croûtons with the liver paste. Unwrap the birds, baste each one well with hot fat, then dust the breasts with flour, baste again and return to the oven for about 5 minutes until well browned. Serve the grouse resting on the croûtons, garnished with watercress. Serve hot game chips and rowan or redcurrant jelly separately. The birds should be moist enough to serve without gravy.

# Guinea fowl

## Ballotine of guinea fowl Jeanne d'Albret

Bone 2 raw guinea fowl without damaging the skin and reserve the breasts whole. Make a forcemeat with the flesh of the thighs and their trimmings, plus 300 g (11 oz) lean Bayonne ham, 300 g (11 oz) fat bacon and 200 g (7 oz) mushrooms. Reduce these ingredients to a paste by puréeing them in a food processor or blender or mince (grind) them finely in a mortar, then bind together with 2 eggs. Press through a sieve. Spread a piece of muslin (cheesecloth) on the table, place on it 2 strips of fat bacon, and spread the skin of the guinea fowls over them. Spread half of the forcemeat over the guinea fowl skins. Slice the breasts into thin strips and arrange half of them on top of the forcemeat then add a slice of foie gras and place 2 truffles on either side of it. Make two more layers using the rest of the sliced breasts and the remaining forcemeat.

Roll the bird up to make a ballotine enclosing the stuffing, using the muslin to lift the meat. Tie it up securely with string at both ends and in the middle. Place in a braising pan together with a good white stock and a crushed calf's foot, the bones and carcasses of the guinea fowls, 1 carrot, a small bouquet garni, the white part of a leek and 100 g (4 oz) of bacon rind or pork rind. Cook for 1½ hours.

The following day, strain the stock through a cloth and clarify it using 2–3 eggs to obtain a full-flavoured aspic jelly. Turn out the ballotine on to a long dish and glaze with the half-set aspic. Make a crown with a piece of truffle and some chopped aspic and garnish the ballotine with cubes of aspic jelly and truffles.

## Breast of guinea fowl with potatoes Alex Humbert

Prepare 800 g (1¾ lb) potatoes by the Alex Humbert method: slice thinly and soak in cold water for about 10 hours, then cook for approximately 20 minutes in 150 g (5 oz, ⅔ cup) clarified butter seasoned with salt and pepper. Drain off the excess butter and brown the potatoes in the oven.

Remove the breast meat from 2 guinea fowl, each weighing about 1.5 kg (3¼ lb), slicing along the breastbone. Season with salt and pepper. Heat 100 g (4 oz, 7 tablespoons) butter in a large flameproof casserole and brown the guinea fowl breasts on both sides (8 minutes in all), then remove. Add 4 chopped shallots to the casserole. Cook them for a few seconds and then mix in 50 g (2 oz, 1 cup) fresh breadcrumbs to absorb all the cooking butter. Brown slightly and stir in 3 tablespoons wine vinegar, then add 6 chopped basil leaves. Put to one side and keep warm.

On to each of 4 warmed plates, pour 2 tablespoons previously made brown gravy, place some of the potatoes in the centre and cover with a guinea fowl breast cut into 5 or 6 slices. Give one twist of the pepper mill and add a little salt. Finally, sprinkle with the breadcrumb mixture and serve.

## Guinea fowl Catalan style

Blanch 30 peeled garlic cloves for 1 minute, having first removed any green parts. Peel 3 lemons and remove all the pith. Cut 2 into quarters and slice the third one. Blanch them for 1 minute. Roast a guinea fowl, barded with a few thin slices of salted or smoked breast of pork. Cut the guinea fowl into pieces. Deglaze the roasting tin (pan) with 100 ml (4 fl oz, ½ cup) Rancio or dry Banyuls. Add the crushed carcass of the bird and 200 ml (7 fl oz, ¾ cup) veal stock. Simmer for 10 minutes, strain through a chinois, pressing in order to extract all the juices. Pour this sauce on to the garlic and lemons, and return to the heat for a few minutes. Season with salt and pepper. Place the pieces of guinea fowl in the sauce and cook over a low heat for 10 minutes. Serve with steamed or roasted new potatoes or with rice.

## Guinea fowl salad with fruit

Roast half a guinea fowl weighing about 1 kg (2¼ lb) in a preheated oven at 200°C (400°F, gas 6) for approximately 30 minutes. Leave to cool completely. Wash and dry some radiccio leaves, and cover the serving dish with them. Peel and finely slice 1 Granny Smith apple and 2 peaches. Sprinkle with lemon juice. Arrange these items on the bed of lettuce, together with the finely sliced meat of the guinea fowl and 25 g (1 oz, ¼ cup) blackcurrants. Blend 150 ml (¼ pint, ⅔ cup) plain yogurt with 1 tablespoon cider vinegar, seasoned with salt and pepper. Cover the guinea fowl with this dressing.

## Guinea fowl with chestnuts

Cut 2 small guinea fowl in half lengthways. Brown them in hot butter in a flameproof casserole, together with 150 g (5 oz, ¾ cup) diced belly of pork and 3 chopped shallots. Cook gently for approximately 40 minutes, turning occasionally, then dilute the meat juices with 250 ml (8 fl oz, 1 cup) red Burgundy. Add a bouquet garni and 300 g (11 oz) cooked chestnuts. Cook gently for a further 10 minutes. Remove the bouquet garni, bind the sauce with 75 g (3 oz, 6 tablespoons) butter, adjust the seasoning and serve hot straight from the casserole.

## Stuffed guinea fowl Jean Cocteau

Draw a guinea fowl weighing about 1 kg (2¼ lb) and put the liver and gizzard to one side. Soak 100 g (4 oz, 1¾ cups) fresh breadcrumbs in hot milk, then strain them. Mix with 1 raw egg, 1 chopped hard-boiled (hard-cooked) egg, a pinch of salt, pepper, nutmeg and cinnamon, 1 tablespoon chopped tarragon, chives, chopped parsley and chervil, then the liver and gizzard, also chopped. Stuff the guinea fowl with this forcemeat and season the outside lightly with salt and pepper. Sew it up, bard it and tie firmly, then fry in a flameproof casserole containing 15 g (½ oz, 1 tablespoon) butter and 1 tablespoon oil. When the guinea fowl begins to turn a golden colour, remove it from the casserole and place on a dish, then sprinkle with 100 ml (4 fl oz, ½ cup) heated Cognac and set alight.

In the same casserole place 3 carrots and 3 onions chopped into large pieces and 2 crushed garlic cloves. Leave to cook for a few moments, then return the guinea fowl to the casserole. Moisten with 250 ml (8 fl oz, 1 cup) each white wine and Cognac. Add 100 ml (4 fl oz, ½ cup) water, cover the casserole and cook for 45 minutes over a gentle heat.

Use a fork to prick 4 *boudins blancs* and 4 black puddings (blood sausages), place them with 1 tablespoon oil in a flameproof dish and grill (broil). Peel, quarter and core 4 apples and brown them in a sauté pan with a little butter. Season very lightly with salt. When the guinea fowl is ready, carve it and arrange on a warm dish. Cover with the strained cooking liquid, sprinkle with chopped herbs and surround with the grilled puddings and apple quarters.

# Hare

## Civet or jugged hare, to prepare

Skin and gut (clean) the hare. Carefully collect the blood and put to one side along with the liver, having removed the gall bladder; add 1 tablespoon vinegar. Detach the thighs and forelegs and chop each thigh in half, splintering the bones as little as possible; cut the saddle into 4 pieces. Place all the pieces in a deep dish and season with salt, pepper, thyme and powdered bay leaf. Add a large finely sliced onion, 3–4 tablespoons oil and at least 1 tablespoon Cognac. After marinating for 24 hours, the hare is ready to be cooked *à la flamande, à la française* or *à la lyonnaise.*

## Civet of hare

Prepare a hare as described in the basic preparation and marinate overnight in red wine containing 3 onions (halved), a sliced carrot and a sprig of thyme. The following morning, drain the hare in a colander. Heat 250 ml (8 fl oz, 1 cup) oil and 40 g (1½ oz, 3 tablespoons) butter in a frying pan and lightly brown the pieces of hare on each side, as well as the onions and carrots from the marinade. Then place the pieces in a saucepan and sprinkle with flour. Moisten with the wine from the marinade, a trickle of Cognac and 1 tablespoon tomato purée (paste); add 2 garlic cloves crushed in their skins, a bouquet garni, a quarter of a bay leaf (crushed), salt and pepper. Mix well and leave to simmer for 2 hours.

Separately, cook 20 small onions in a little water to which 1 teaspoon caster (superfine) sugar has been added. Cut 250 g (9 oz) small mushrooms into quarters (or leave tiny button mushrooms whole) and brown them in some butter. Dice 150 g (5 oz) smoked bacon, blanch it, then cook it gently in a frying pan.

When the hare is cooked, arrange the pieces in a dish and keep hot. Chop up the hare's liver and mix it with the blood. Add it to the cooking liquor and bring to the boil. Pass through a fine strainer to form a sauce. Add the garnish of onions, mushrooms and pieces of bacon. Adjust the seasoning, pour the sauce over the hare and serve accompanied by fresh noodles.

## Civet of hare à la flamande

Marinate a hare as described in the basic preparation of *civet* of hare. Drain the pieces of marinated hare, brown them in about 40 g (1½ oz, 3 table-spoons) butter in a flameproof casserole, dust them with 2 tablespoons flour and again lightly brown them, turning them with a wooden spoon. Press the liver through a sieve along with the blood and add to it 1 litre (1¾ pints, 4⅓ cups) red wine; then add 200 ml (7 fl oz, ¾ cup) wine vinegar. Pour this mixture into the casserole; add some salt, pepper, 25 g (1 oz, 3 tablespoons) moist brown sugar and a large bouquet garni. Cover and cook for 15 minutes.

During this time, peel and finely slice 500 g (18 oz) onions and brown them in some butter. Add them to the casserole after the 15 minutes have elapsed and leave to finish cooking gently with the lid on. Cooking time depends on the age of the animal; the tip of a knife should pass easily into the flesh when it is cooked.

Remove the cooked hare, drain and place the pieces in a sauté dish. Strain the cooking liquid to remove the onions, pour it into the sauté dish, cover and simmer for 5 minutes. Fry some croûtons in butter and spread them with redcurrant jelly. Serve the *civet* in a deep dish, garnished with the croûtons. If desired, the ends of the croûtons can be dipped in the sauce and then in chopped parsley.

## Civet of hare à la française

Marinate a hare as described in the basic preparation of *civet* of hare. Cut 200 g (7 oz) streaky (slab) bacon into strips, blanch them in boiling water for about 5 minutes, drain, then colour slightly in a shallow frying pan containing 40 g (1½ oz, 3 tablespoons) butter.

Remove the bacon from the frying pan and drain it on paper towels then in the same butter brown 2 large onions cut into quarters; sprinkle with 2 tablespoons flour and, using a wooden spoon, stir until it is golden brown. Add the drained pieces of hare to this roux and continue to stir (the pieces of hare may be sealed in butter beforehand, if desired). Cover with red wine and add a bouquet garni and a crushed garlic clove then cover the casserole and cook gently for 45 minutes.

Meanwhile, prepare 24 mushroom caps and brown them in some butter. When the hare is cooked, remove and drain the pieces and place them in a casserole. Add the strips of bacon and the mushrooms. Add the marinade to the cooking juices in the frying pan, mix well, then pour it over the hare. Cover and cook in a preheated oven at 200°C (400°F, gas 6) for about 1 hour, depending on the age of the hare.

Prepare 24 glazed onions; fry in butter some croûtons cut into triangles. Five minutes before the hare has finished cooking, thinly slice the liver and add it to the casserole. Thicken with the blood by mixing it in with 2–3 tablespoons double (heavy) cream. Serve the *civet* in a deep dish, garnished with the glazed onions and fried croûtons.

## Civet of hare à la lyonnaise

This is prepared as for *civet* of hare *à la française* except that the mushrooms are replaced by chestnuts, which are cooked in consommé and caramelized in their cooking liquid when it has been well reduced.

## Civet of saddle of hare with fresh pasta

Peel and dice 3 carrots and 1 onion; peel and chop 2 shallots; peel and crush 2 garlic cloves. Coarsely chop 2 foreparts of hare, brown the pieces in a pan containing 20 g (¾ oz, 1½ tablespoons) butter, add the diced onion and carrot, and brown for about 10 minutes. Then add 100 ml (4 fl oz, 7 tablespoons) wine vinegar, 500 ml (17 fl oz, 2 cups) red wine, the garlic and the shallots. Lightly season with salt and pepper and bring to the boil. Add a bouquet garni and simmer gently for 2 hours, skimming from time to time.

Take out the vegetables and process in a blender. Pour the remaining cooking liquid through a strainer, pressing well to extract all the juices; add the blended vegetables to the strained pan juice, return to the heat and simmer for 30 minutes. Strain again, leave to cool and place in the refrigerator; after about 6 hours, the fat will have collected on the surface and can be skimmed off. Then return to the heat and reduce for a further 5 minutes; away from the heat add a small glass of hare's blood while stirring with a hand whisk. Then add 50 g (2 oz, ¼ cup) butter, plus salt and pepper. At the last moment, finish the sauce with 1 teaspoon cranberries.

Season 2 saddles of hare with salt and pepper; heat some oil in a frying pan and cook the saddles over a brisk heat, turning them over. Cut the hare into thin slices and serve coated with the sauce, with fresh pasta.

## Fillets of hare, to prepare

Separate the saddle from the forequarters of a hare as far behind the ribs as possible, and place the saddle on its back. With a pointed knife, cut away the meat on both sides of the backbone. Ease off the flesh to halfway up the backbone, then place the blade of a very heavy knife against the backbone and, by tapping on the blade, complete the separation of the fillets. Do the same on the other side. Separate the fillets from each other, then lard them with fat bacon. Season with salt, pepper and a pinch of cayenne; pour over a dash of brandy and leave to marinate until the time for cooking.

## Fillets of hare on croûtes

Prepare the fillets and place them in a buttered roasting dish. Pour over melted butter and cook them in a preheated oven at 240°C (475°F, gas 9), covering them with foil once they are browned. Serve on bread croûtes fried in butter and coat with financière or Périgueux sauce, or , if you prefer, a fruit sauce (cranberry or redcurrant).

## Hare à la royale

Collect the blood from a good-sized skinned hare, reserve the liver, heart and lungs, and remove the head. Carefully grease the bottom and sides of a very large stewpot with goose fat. Make a bed of bacon rashers (slices) in the pot, place the hare (on its back) on top and cover with bacon rashers. Add 1 sliced carrot, 20 garlic cloves, 40 shallots, 4 onions studded with cloves, and a bouquet garni. Pour in 250 ml (8 fl oz, 1 cup) wine vinegar and a bottle and a half of Burgundy. Season with salt and pepper. Put the pot over a low heat, cover it and cook for 3 hours.

Finely chop 125 g (4½ oz) bacon, the hare's offal (variety meat), 10 garlic cloves and 20 shallots. Mix all these together very thoroughly. Remove the stewpot from the heat. Lift out the hare very carefully and put it on a dish, leaving the bacon and vegetables in the stewpot. Tip the contents of the pot into a strainer, pressing to extract as much liquid as possible. Add this to the chopped bacon, offal and vegetables and pour in half a bottle of heated Burgundy. Pour this mixture into the stewpot, replace the hare and cook over a low heat for 1½ hours. Skim off the surface fat. About 15 minutes before serving, add the blood, well whisked and diluted with Cognac. When cooking is complete, arrange the hare on a serving dish and pour the sauce around it. Serve the same type of wine that was used to cook the hare.

## Hare cutlets with mushrooms

Finely chop a boned hare. Add one-third of its weight of bread soaked in cream and an equal quantity of chopped mushrooms, parsley and shallots. Season with salt and pepper, add a pinch of *quatre-épices* or four spices, and blend all the ingredients into a firm paste. Divide the mixture into portions of 50–65 g (2–2½ oz), roll into balls, then flatten into cutlets. Coat with flour and fry in clarified butter. Serve with a game sauce, such as poivrade.

## Hare en cabessal

Skin and gut a hare, reserving the liver and blood. Pound the liver with a garlic clove, then add the blood and 1 tablespoon vinegar. On the day before cooking, place the hare in a marinade of red wine, oil, carrots, thinly sliced onions and shallots, thyme, a bay leaf, a clove, salt and pepper. Prepare a stuffing with 500 g (18 oz) fillet of veal, 250 g (9 oz) raw ham, 250 g (9 oz) fresh pork, 2 garlic cloves and 2 shallots. Chop the ingredients finely, season with salt and pepper, and bind with an egg. Remove the hare from the marinade, wipe and stuff.

Sew up the opening in the belly. Bard the hare all over with larding bacon, then tie it with string so that it forms a round. Place it in a round dish with a little goose or pork fat, some pieces of larding bacon and a few small onions. Add a small glass of brandy and a bottle of good-quality red or white wine, then a roux made with flour and goose fat. Cover the dish and cook in a preheated oven at 150°C (300°F, gas 2) for 4 or 5 hours. When three-quarters cooked, add the pounded liver and blood. Check the seasoning. When cooking is complete, the sauce should be substantially reduced.

When serving, remove the string, the larding bacon and the bones (which should come away easily from the flesh). Serve with croûtons of bread fried in goose fat, which may be rubbed with garlic if desired.

## Hare mousse

Remove the sinews from 450 g (1 lb) hare meat and chop the meat very finely in a food processor. (A few chopped truffle skins may be added.) Sprinkle with 1¼ teaspoons table salt and a large pinch of white pepper. Gradually incorporate 2–3 egg whites, still in the processor, then rub the mixture through a sieve. Stir the sieved mixture in a shallow frying pan over a low heat until it is quite smooth, then transfer it to a bowl; refrigerate for 2 hours.

Stand the chilled bowl in a container of ice cubes and gradually add 750 ml (1¼ pints, 3¼ cups) double (heavy) cream, stirring vigorously with a wooden spoon. Put it back in the refrigerator for 1 hour. Butter some dariole moulds and fill with the mousse. Put the moulds in a bain marie, bring to the boil, cover with foil, and cook them in a preheated oven at 200°C (400°F, gas 6) for 25–30 minutes (a fine needle inserted in the mousse should come out clean). Serve with a Périgueux sauce.

## Hare mousse with chestnuts

Finely mince (grind) 500 g (18 oz) hare meat, having first removed all the nerves, and sprinkle with salt and white pepper. Slowly add 2 or 3 egg whites, then pass through a sieve. Put the meat in a sauté pan and stir over a low heat with a wooden spoon to obtain a smooth mixture. Then put the meat in a bowl and place it in the refrigerator for 2 hours.

Meanwhile, braise 400 g (14 oz) chestnuts and chop 300 g (11 oz) of them. Reserve the remaining whole chestnuts. Place the bowl of meat in a container filled with ice cubes and briskly but gradually incorporate 500 ml (17 fl oz,

2 cups) thick crème fraîche and the chopped chestnuts. Put back in the refrigerator for 1 hour.

Butter dariole moulds and put the hare mousse in them, pressing it down lightly. Place the moulds in a bain marie and bring it to the boil over the heat. Cover with foil and cook in a preheated oven at 200°C (400°F, gas 6) for 25–30 minutes. Serve on a bed of lightly cooked cabbage, on a truffle sauce, if liked. Garnish with sliced truffle and the reserved whole chestnuts.

## Hare pâté

Bone a hare and set aside the fillets (including the filets mignons) and the thigh meat. Remove the sinews from these cuts, lard the meat, and season with salt, pepper and a little mixed spice. Then marinate them in brandy together with an equal weight of thin slices of lean unsmoked ham, fat bacon and quartered truffles. Prepare a game forcemeat with the rest of the meat; rub it through a sieve and then thicken it with the hare's blood.

Butter an oval hinged mould and line with lining pastry. Cover with very thin slices of fat bacon and spread a layer of forcemeat over the bottom and up the sides. Add a layer of marinated hare fillets and cover with a layer of forcemeat. Continue to fill the mould with layers of hare and forcemeat, finishing with a layer of forcemeat. Cover with slices of fat bacon, then a layer of pastry, inserting a chimney in the centre for the steam to escape during cooking. Seal the edges. Shape the crust with a pastry crimper and garnish with pastry shapes. Brush with beaten egg and cook in a preheated oven at 190°C (375°F, gas 5), allowing 35 minutes per 1 kg (15 minutes per 1 lb).

Let the pâté cool in the mould. When it is cold, pour a few spoonfuls of Madeira-flavoured aspic through the central hole (or, if the pâté is to be kept for any length of time, a mixture of melted butter and lard). Prepare the pâté at least 24 hours before serving.

## Hare with cherries

Choose a hare weighing between 1.5 and 2 kg (3½–4½ lb) and cut into pieces. Brown the pieces in olive oil in a flameproof casserole until they are golden, then remove. In the same oil, brown a large onion and a shallot, both chopped, and a finely diced carrot. Sprinkle in 1 tablespoon flour and stir until it turns golden brown, then replace the pieces of hare. Moisten with ½ bottle of red Burgundy and add a bouquet garni, a crushed garlic clove, a clove, salt and pepper. Cover and leave to cook gently for 1 hour.

Remove the stalks and stones (pits) from 1 kg (2¼ lb) cherries, cook them with 250 g (9 oz, generous 1 cup) sugar and a little water, then remove and drain. Caramelize the syrup slightly, then add 100 ml (4 fl oz, 7 tablespoons) wine vinegar, bring to the boil and reduce to obtain a syrupy mixture. Roll the cherries in this syrup. Arrange the pieces of hare in the serving dish, coat with the strained cooking stock and distribute the cherries around the dish.

## Hare with chocolate

Skin a hare, detach the saddle and thighs, season these with salt and pepper, and marinate for 3 days in oil. Break up the rib cage, the forelimbs and the offal (variety meats), and marinate these for 3 days in a marinade made with 2 bottles of red wine, 2 onions, a garlic head (bulb) broken into cloves, 2 carrots and a leek (coarsely chopped), thyme, bay leaves, grated nutmeg, pepper, the juice of 1 lemon, chopped root ginger, cinnamon and cloves.

After 3 days, strain the marinade and sauté the pieces of carcass in olive oil until brown. Remove the fat. Add a little of the marinade and a calf's foot. Cook very gently for 4 hours, then remove the fat. Strain the sauce obtained and thicken it with 50 g (2 oz) bitter (bittersweet) chocolate and 100 g (4 oz, ½ cup) butter. Heat the juice of 1 lemon with 3 tablespoons poultry blood without boiling, and add to the sauce. Cook the saddle and thighs in butter in a casserole (the meat should remain pink). Cut into portions. Pour over the sauce and serve with spiced pears sautéed in butter.

## Roast hare en saugrenée

Let the hare hang, unskinned, in a cool place for 24 hours, then joint it and reserve the blood and liver. Place the joints in a dish containing 250 ml (8 fl oz, 1 cup) cider, 4 tablespoons olive oil, 1 onion and 1 carrot (finely chopped), 6 juniper berries, 12 shallots and a pinch of spice. Leave to marinate for 12 hours.

Blanch the shallots from the marinade and put them in a roasting dish with a slice of fat bacon. Place the hare on top and roast in a preheated oven at 200°C (400°F, gas 6) for 30–40 minutes. Prepare the hearts of 2 celery heads, wash them, blanch them in salted water and drain. Braise the celery for 40 minutes in a buttered dish, moistened with stock.

Place the cooked hare in a warm dish. Deglaze the roasting dish with 1 small ladle of stock and 1 tablespoon brandy. Remove from the heat and thicken carefully with the puréed liver of the hare and the reserved blood. Pour this sauce over the hare. Serve the celery separately.

## Roast saddle of hare

The saddle is a cut of meat consisting of the two joined loins. The saddle of a hare or rabbit extends from the lower ribs to the tail. It is a fleshy piece of meat that can be roasted whole, often larded or barded and marinated. It can also be cooked with mustard or with cream (sautéed in a casserole); braised and served with mushroom purée, chestnuts and poivrade sauce; or sautéed and garnished with cherries, with a soured (sour) cream sauce. When it is not cooked whole, the saddle is cut into two or three pieces and made into a civet, stew or sauté with the rest of the animal.

Insert some small strips of fatty bacon into the saddle. Sprinkle it with salt and pepper, brush with oil and roast it in a preheated oven at 240°C (475°F, gas 9) for about 20 minutes (the meat should still be pink). The saddle can also be spit-roasted.

Garnish the serving dish with fluted half slices of lemon and watercress. Serve the saddle either with its own cooking juices – by deglazing the roasting tin (pan) with white wine – or with a poivrade sauce; the tin can also be deglazed using a mixture of equal proportions of white wine and double (heavy) cream.

## Saddle of hare à l'allemande

Insert some small strips of fatty bacon into the saddle and sprinkle it with table salt. Cut 1 carrot and 1 onion into slices; chop 1 shallot, 1 celery stick and 1 garlic clove. Put some of these vegetables into a deep bowl and lay the saddle on top. Pour in 250 ml (8 fl oz, 1 cup) oil, sprinkle with coarsely chopped parsley, powdered thyme, 1 bay leaf cut into pieces and 12 peppercorns, and add 1 small onion studded with 2 cloves. Cover the saddle with the remaining vegetables and pour in just enough white wine to cover everything. Leave to marinate for 6 hours, turning the meat once.

Oil a roasting tin (pan) and place in it the vegetables from the marinade; place the saddle on top and cook in a preheated oven at 240°C (475°F, gas 9) for 20–25 minutes (the meat should still be pink). Drain the saddle and keep it hot. Pour the marinade into the roasting tin, add 200 ml (7 fl oz, ¾ cup) double (heavy) cream, and boil to reduce by half. Adjust the seasoning with the juice of ½ lemon; strain and pour over the saddle. Serve with unsweetened apple sauce and redcurrant jelly.

# Partridge

## Boned partridge Brillat-Savarin

Open out the partridge and remove as much bone as possible. Flatten the partridge and season with salt and pepper. Seal by frying rapidly in butter. Cover both sides with a forcemeat of foie gras and truffle. Wrap the partridge in a piece of pig's caul, coat with breadcrumbs, and grill (broil) gently. Place on a bed of lentil purée and serve with a well-reduced Madeira sauce, containing game stock.

## Chartreuse of partridge

Braise some cabbage in goose dripping, together with an old partridge (the latter provides more flavour). Cut some turnips and carrots into very thin 1 cm (½ in) squares. Prepare a veal quenelle forcemeat and use it to line a small round casserole. Cover the bottom and sides with the carrot and turnip squares to form a decorative chequered pattern. Place enough of the cabbage in the pan to comes a third of the way up the side. Put a piece of slightly salted bacon (which has been poached for at least 2 hours) on top of the cabbage. Roast one or two partridges to seal them. Cut them into pieces and place on top of the bacon. Cover with the remaining cabbage. Cover the pan and cook in a bain marie in a preheated oven at 180°C (350°F, gas 4) for 30–40 minutes. Remove from the oven, cool briefly and turn out on to a serving dish.

## Partridge à la coque

Gut (clean) and singe a young partridge, season with salt and pepper, spread foie gras in the cavity and truss. Fill a saucepan with salted water and lay a stick across the top. Bring the water to the boil and hang the partridge by its feet from the centre of the stick so that it is suspended in the water. Boil briskly for 20 minutes, then remove the bird and allow it to cool. When cold, keep it in the refrigerator until ready to serve.

## Partridge à la Souvarov

Stuff a partridge with fois gras and truffles cut into large dice, seasoned with salt and pepper and sprinkled with a dash of brandy. Truss the bird and brown it in butter, then place it in a small oval terrine, surrounded by diced or whole truffles, peeled and seasoned with salt and pepper. Moisten with 100 ml (4 fl oz, 7 tablespoons) Madeira-flavoured game fumet to which the pan juices, diluted with Madeira, have been added. Sprinkle with a dash of brandy. Cover the terrine, seal the lid with a strip of dough and cook in a preheated oven at 190°C (375°F, gas 5) for 45 minutes. Serve in the terrine.

Woodcock and chicken can be prepared in the same way, but fry chicken in butter until it is three-quarters done, then finish in the oven for 30 minutes.

## Partridge à la vigneronne

Pluck, clean and truss a partridge. Cook it in butter in a saucepan for about 30 minutes, then drain and untruss it. Put into the saucepan 24 skinned and seeded grapes, 3 tablespoons game fumet and 1 tablespoon flamed brandy. Cover the pan and cook gently for 5 minutes, then replace the partridge on top, heat through and serve.

## Partridge croustades

Completely bone 4 young partridges. Reserve the breast fillets and marinate them for 24 hours in 750 ml (1¼ pints, 3¼ cups) red wine. Mince (grind) the meat from the thighs with the liver and season with salt and pepper. Place the bowl of minced meat over a dish of ice and gradually work in 2 eggs, followed by 150 ml (¼ pint, ⅔ cup) crème fraîche. Refrigerate the resulting mousse and then shape it into small quenelles.

Prepare a game stock with the partridge trimmings, the carcass and the marinade. Boil until reduced by half, then add 300 ml (½ pint, 1¼ cups) demi-glace sauce. Strain this stock, bring it to the boil, add the quenelles of partridge mousse and poach them for 6 minutes.

Make 4 rectangular croustades with puff pastry. Fry 4 sliced cep mushroom caps in butter and season with salt and pepper. When the quenelles are cooked, remove from the stock and keep hot. Reduce the stock to make about 400 ml (14 fl oz, 1¾ cups) sauce, removing any scum that rises to the surface. At the last minute, thicken the sauce with 50 g (2 oz, ¼ cup) foie gras. Fry the partridge fillets in butter, season with salt and pepper and cook for 2 minutes only on each side, so that they are still pink.

Fill the croustades with the quenelles, the fried mushrooms and the partridge fillets. Add a little sauce and place in a preheated oven at 150°C (300°F, gas 2) for 3 minutes. Serve the remaining sauce separately.

## Partridge cutlets Romanov

Soak 2 pigs' cauls (caul fat) in cold water. Pluck 4 young partridges, singe them, gut (clean) them and set aside the livers and hearts. Bone the breasts and remove the skin. Remove the feet, but keep them whole except for cutting off the claws. Marinate the breasts in a mixture of 4 tablespoons port, 1 tablespoon brandy, salt and pepper.

Prepare a forcemeat by finely mincing (grinding) 100 g (4 oz, 1 cup) pork, 100 g (4 oz, 1 cup) fat bacon, 50 g (2 oz, ½ cup) chicken livers and the hearts and livers of the partridges. Sauté 2 chopped shallots in butter, then place in a bowl and mix with an egg yolk, some spiced salt and a little truffle juice.

Prepare the sauce by first browning the partridge bones in a saucepan together with 1 onion and 1 carrot. Then add some powdered thyme, a peeled, crushed tomato, 250 ml (8 fl oz, 1 cup) white wine, the marinade and a ladleful of veal stock. Add 6 juniper berries and cook for 1 hour (the liquid should then be syrupy).

Spread the cauls out on the worktop, wipe them and cut each into 2 rectangles measuring 20 × 15 cm (8 × 6 in). Spread a thin layer of forcemeat on each rectangle and put a partridge foot at the end. Place a partridge breast (both fillets from one bird) on the forcemeat and add a thin slice of foie gras and a slice of truffle. Cover with a thin layer of forcemeat. Fold the caul over the stuffing and shape it into a cutlet, using the partridge foot as the bone. When four 'cutlets' have been prepared, roast them in a preheated oven at 230°C (450°F, gas 8) for 15–20 minutes (they should still be slightly pink).

Arrange the cutlets on a dish and garnish the ends of the feet with a little white paper frill. Strain the cooking juices, add 150 ml (¼ pint, ⅔ cup) double (heavy) cream, and thicken with 100 g (4 oz, ½ cup) butter. Adjust the seasoning and pour the sauce over the cutlets. Serve with either chestnut purée or fried fresh cep mushrooms.

## Partridge en pistache

Stuff a partridge with a forcemeat of its liver, breadcrumbs, raw ham, parsley and garlic, all chopped and bound with 1 egg. Truss the partridge, bard it, season with salt and pepper and place in a flameproof casserole containing 3 tablespoons heated goose fat. Cook until the partridge becomes a good golden colour, then remove it.

Brown 1 tablespoon diced raw ham in the casserole, dust with 1 tablespoon flour and cook for a few minutes. Add 3 tablespoons dry white wine, then 100 ml (4 fl oz, 7 tablespoons) giblet or chicken stock. Add 1 tablespoon tomato purée (paste), a bouquet garni and a small piece of dried orange peel. Cook for 10 minutes. Remove the ham and bouquet garni. Strain the sauce.

Return the partridge to the casserole, together with the ham and bouquet garni, then pour on the sauce. Bring to the boil, cover and cook for 10 minutes. Then add 12 garlic cloves (blanched in boiling salted water, drained and peeled) and simmer for a further 30 minutes. Remove the bouquet garni and serve the partridge straight from the casserole.

## Partridge Monselet

Trim a partridge and stuff it with foie gras to which a truffle salpicon has been added. Truss it, season with salt and pepper, and brown in a small heavy flameproof casserole. Cover and cook in a preheated oven at 160°C (325°F, gas 3). After about 15 minutes, add 2 thin slices of artichoke hearts which have been tossed in lemon and butter. Cook for about a further 15 minutes. Cut a truffle into small dice and add to the casserole. Add 2 tablespoons warmed brandy and set alight. Serve in the casserole.

## Partridge Monselet with chanterelles

Stuff 2 cleaned partridges with foie gras, adding a little diced black truffle. Truss and season well, then brown the birds all over in butter in a small flameproof casserole. Cover the casserole and continue to cook gently for 15 minutes. Turn 4 lightly cooked artichoke hearts in a little lemon juice and melted clarified butter, then add them to the casserole and cook for a further 15 minutes. Add a finely diced black truffle. Heat 2 tablespoons brandy, add to the casserole and flambé. Lightly cook some chanterelles in butter in a separate pan. Arrange the partridges with the artickoke bottoms and sliced foie gras used as stuffing, with the cooking juices poured over. Add the chanterelles and serve at once.

## Partridge salad with cabbage

Select a large Savoy cabbage with a good heart. Remove about 8 of the leaves and wash them in plenty of water after removing the thick midribs. Blanch for 5 minutes in boiling salted water, cool and drain. Pluck 6 partridges, gut them and retain the livers. Cut the birds into quarters and use the breasts only (the thighs can be made into a terrine). Bone the breasts and season them with salt and pepper. Wipe 500 g (18 oz, 6 cups) small firm cep mushrooms with a damp cloth and chop them roughly.

Brown 6 slices of belly of pork in a frying pan and add the partridge breasts and livers. Cook for 6 minutes and then add the mushrooms. Cover the pan and braise for a further 5 minutes. Remove the contents of the pan and keep hot. Deglaze the pan with 100 ml (4 fl oz, 7 tablespoons) sherry vinegar, add some crushed peppercorns, boil down to reduce and then thicken the sauce with 100 ml (4 fl oz, 7 tablespoons) hazelnut oil. Dip the cabbage leaves in the sauce and lay them out on the serving dish. Arrange the slices of pork, the partridge and livers, and the sliced mushrooms on the top and sprinkle with chopped chives.

## Partridges en vessie

Soak 4 small pigs' bladders in salt water and vinegar for 24 hours, then squeeze thoroughly. Gut (clean) 4 young partridges. Prepare a forcemeat with 250 g (9 oz, 1 cup) fine sausagemeat, the finely minced (ground) partridge livers, 150 g (5 oz, 2½ cups) breadcrumbs soaked in milk and squeezed thoroughly, 2 tablespoons crème fraîche, salt, pepper and an egg. Stuff the birds with the mixture, adding a large sprig of thyme to each portion.

Truss the partridges and place each in a pig's bladder. Add a pinch of coarse salt and a dash of brandy and port to each bladder, squeeze to release any air, tie them up with string and prick with a needle. Cook for 30 minutes in simmering veal stock and leave to cool in the liquid for 12 hours. Remove the partridges from the bladders, untruss and serve cold.

## Partridge with cabbage

Clean a large cabbage, cut it into 8 pieces and blanch for 8 minutes in boiling water. Drain the cabbage and allow to cool. Place the cabbage in a buttered heavy-based saucepan with a 500 g (18 oz) piece of lean bacon, an onion studded with 2 cloves and a bouquet garni. Add 175 ml (6 fl oz, ¾ cup) stock, cover and cook gently for 1 hour.

Pluck, gut (clean) and truss 2 partridges. Lard the breasts with thin rashers (slices) of bacon. Brown them in a preheated oven at 230°C (450°F, gas 8), then add them to the saucepan containing the cabbage, together with 1 boiling sausage and 2 sliced carrots. Continue cooking for at least another hour (or more, if the partridges are old). Untruss the birds and slice the bacon and the sausage. Place the cabbage in a deep dish; cut the partridges in half and arrange them on top. Garnish with the slices of bacon, sausage and carrot. Pour the cooking liquid over the top.

Alternatively, the cooked partridges can be arranged *en gâteau*: cover the bottom of a round buttered timbale with the sliced carrots, sausage and bacon, then add a layer of cabbage, the partridges and finally the rest of the cabbage. Press down the cabbage, warm in a preheated oven at 160°C (325°F, gas 3) for 5 minutes and turn it out on to a round dish. Pour a few tablespoons of game fumet, demi-glace sauce or brown veal stock around the 'gâteau'.

## Partridge with lentils

Roast 2 partridges in 50 g (2 oz, ¼ cup) lard in a preheated oven at 180°C (350°F, gas 5) for 20 minutes. Then place them in a heavy-based saucepan with 100 g (4 oz, 1 cup) bacon pieces, 2 sliced onions, 2 sliced carrots,

175 ml (6 fl oz, ¾ cup) white wine, 175 ml (6 fl oz, ¾ cup) stock, some salt and a bouquet garni. Simmer gently for 1½ hours. In the meantime, boil in water until tender 250 g (9 oz, 1¼ cups) lentils (previously soaked for 2 hours and drained) with 200 g (7 oz) fat bacon, 4 small onions, 2 carrots (cut into quarters), 1 boiling sausage weighing 200 g (7 oz) and a pinch of salt. Arrange the lentils in a deep dish, place the partridges on top and surround with the sliced sausage. Spoon over the cooking juices.

## Partridges with grapes

Pluck, singe and gut (clean) some young partridges. Season them with salt and pepper. Also season some large grapes with salt and pepper. Place 2 grapes and half a Petit-Suisse cheese (or 1 tablespoon cream cheese) inside each bird. Quickly brown the birds in 50 g (2 oz, ¼ cup) butter in a heavy-based saucepan for 6 minutes. Cover the pan and cook gently for a further 10–15 minutes (the wings should be white and the thighs pink near the bone). Drain the partridges and keep them hot.

Skim the fat from the cooking juices, add some green grapes and 3 tablespoons Armagnac and simmer over a low heat. Add a glass of red Banyuls wine and boil for 5 minutes to reduce. Strain the sauce and thicken with a Petit Suisse cheese (or 2 tablespoons cream cheese). Season generously with salt and pepper. Spoon over the partridges and serve with dauphine potatoes and red cabbage *à la flamande*.

## Stuffed partridges in aspic

Bone some young partridges from the back. Cut them open and season with salt and pepper. Stuff each bird with 100 g (4 oz, ½ cup) truffled game forcemeat wrapped around a piece of raw foie gras and a small peeled truffle. Season with salt, pepper and mixed spice and sprinkle with brandy. Close up the partridges, truss them and wrap each one in thin bacon barding or a piece of pig's caul (caul fat).

Prepare an aspic stock with Madeira, the partridge carcasses and trimmings, knuckle of veal and fresh bacon rind. Cook the partridges in this stock, then drain, remove the barding, untruss, wipe and arrange them in an oval terrine. Leave them to cool, then chill them. Clarify the aspic, adding gelatine if necessary for a good set, and cover the partridges completely with it. Chill again until ready to serve.

# Pheasant

## Pheasant, to prepare

Chill the pheasant in the refrigerator for a few hours before you begin to prepare it, as this makes it easier to pluck. Begin by twisting the large wing feathers to remove them. Then pluck the remaining feathers in the following order: the body, legs, neck and wings. Draw the bird in the same way as a chicken, cut through the skin down the length of the neck and remove the trachea (windpipe) and the oesophagus (gullet), pulling out the crop at the same time; leave the neck as it is or sever it at the base, without cutting through the skin. Make an incision at the tail end of the bird and pull out the intestines, gizzard, liver, heart and lungs. Remove the gall bladder from the liver immediately. Season the inside of the carcass with salt and pepper. Bard if necessary and truss the bird with the legs pressed as tightly as possible against the breast, especially if the bird is to be roasted.

## Ballotine of pheasant in aspic

(from Carême's recipe) Take a Strasbourg foie gras. Soak in cold water and blanch. Cut each half into 4 fillets and trim. Pound 2 of these fillets in a mortar with the trimmings and the meat of a red partridge with an equal weight of pork fat. Season the mixture very well. Add 2 egg yolks and some cultivated mushrooms tossed in butter. Pound all of these ingredients together thoroughly. Press the stuffing through a quenelle sieve.

Carefully bone a well-hung fat pheasant. Place it on a cloth and season generously with salt and pepper. Arrange half the stuffing on top of it and then 3 fillets of foie gras, interspersing these with halved truffles. Add as much spiced salt as required. Cover the whole with half the remaining stuffing. Put the rest of the foie gras and the halves of truffle on top. Season and cover with the rest of the stuffing.

Fold the pheasant into shape. Wrap in a cloth. Tie and cook in aspic stock flavoured with Madeira, to which have been added the bones and trimmings of the pheasant and partridge. Leave the ballotine to cool under a light weight. Glaze with aspic in the usual way.

## Casserole of pheasant

Brown a trussed pheasant in 25 g (1 oz, 2 tablespoons) butter in a flameproof casserole. Cover and continue to cook gently for 45 minutes. Add some Cognac (or other brandy) and 2 tablespoons boiling water or stock. Season with salt and pepper. Cook for a further 5–10 minutes. Cut the pheasant into joints and serve with, for example, puréed celery.

Alternatively, halfway through the cooking time add 12 mushroom caps and some small shaped potato pieces to the casserole. Then deglaze with cream, reducing the sauce by half.

A third method is to add 250 ml (8 fl oz, 1 cup) single (light) cream to the casserole two-thirds of the way through the cooking time and basting the pheasant frequently with the cream. Just before serving, add a squeeze of lemon juice to sharpen the sauce.

## Chaud-froid of pheasant

Cook a prepared trussed pheasant in butter in an ovenproof casserole, taking care that the meat remains pinkish. Joint (cut) the bird into 4 or 6 pieces. Skin the pieces, trim them and allow them to cool completely. Place in the refrigerator for about 1 hour. Prepare a brown chaud-froid sauce with some game stock, flavoured with truffle essence. Also prepare some Madeira-flavoured aspic jelly. Place the chilled pieces of pheasant on a rack and pour the chaud-froid sauce over them twice, refrigerating between the 2 applications.

Prepare various ingredients for a garnish; for example, thinly sliced pieces of truffle cut into fancy shapes, tarragon leaves, thinly sliced carrots and leeks, and pieces of hard-boiled (hard-cooked) egg white. Coat each item in aspic before arranging them on the joints of pheasant. Finally, coat the pheasant with the remaining aspic and place in the refrigerator to set. To serve, arrange on a serving dish garnished with chopped aspic or slices of aspic. Alternatively, arrange in a glass bowl and coat the entire arrangement with clear seasoned aspic.

## Game soufflé with Périgueux sauce

Pound 250 g (9 oz) cooked pheasant or partridge meat in a mortar with 150 ml (¼ pint, ⅔ cup) thick béchamel sauce flavoured with game stock. Season with salt and pepper. Add 3 egg yolks one by one, rub through a sieve and incorporate 3 stiffly whisked egg whites. Butter a 20 cm (8 in) soufflé mould and coat with flour. Add the mixture and bake in a preheated oven at 200°C (400°F, gas 6) for about 25 minutes. Serve with Périgueux sauce.

## Grilled pheasant à l'américaine

This recipe is particularly suitable for young pheasants. Split the pheasant along the back and flatten it gently. Season with salt and pepper, then fry in butter on both sides until the flesh is firm. Coat both sides with freshly made breadcrumbs seasoned with a large pinch of cayenne. Grill (broil) the pheasant slowly. Place on a dish and cover with grilled bacon rashers (slices). Garnish with grilled tomatoes and mushrooms, bunches of watercress and potato crisps (chips) or game chips. Serve with maître d'hôtel butter.

## Pheasant à l'alsacienne

Truss the pheasant and cook in butter in a flameproof casserole, for 25 minutes until lightly brown. Braise some sauerkraut and bacon rashers (slices) in goose fat . Put the sauerkraut in the casserole, with the pheasant on top. Cover and cook in a preheated oven at 190°C (375°F, gas 5) for another 25 minutes, or until the pheasant is tender. Cut the pheasant into portions. Slice some hot saveloys and cut up the hot bacon. Make a bed of sauerkraut on a hot dish, and garnish with the pheasant, bacon and saveloy.

## Pheasant à la Douro

Stuff the bird with boiled and peeled chestnuts, foie gras and prepared truffles. Tie, truss and bard the pheasant and brown in butter in a flameproof casserole. Add a few rashers (slices) of streaky bacon and 325 ml (11 fl oz, 1⅓ cups) white port. Season with salt and pepper, cover and cook over a very low heat for about 50 minutes.

## Pheasant à la géorgienne

Clean, bard and truss a young or hen pheasant. Place it in a saucepan with about 30 shelled walnuts. Add the juice of 3 oranges and 675 g (1½ lb) grapes, crushed and strained. Add 175 ml (6 fl oz, ¾ cup) Madeira or Malmsey and an equal quantity of very strong strained green tea. Then add 40 g (1½ oz, 3 tablespoons) butter. Season with salt and pepper. Cover the saucepan, bring to the boil, then reduce the heat and simmer for 45 minutes. Drain, untruss and discard the barding. Cook the pheasant in a preheated oven at 230°C (450°F, gas 8) for 15–20 minutes until brown. Place it on a serving dish with the walnuts arranged around it and pour over the reduced, strained cooking liquid or brown veal gravy.

## Pheasant à la languedocienne

Cut a pheasant into 4–6 pieces; season with salt and pepper. Prepare 4 tablespoons mirepoix; cook slowly in butter with a little thyme, powdered bay leaf, salt and pepper. Add the pieces of pheasant and lightly fry, then sprinkle with 1 tablespoon flour; cook until the flour turns golden. Moisten with 300 ml (½ pint, 1¼ cups) red wine and mix well. Add a few tablespoons of stock and a bouquet garni, then cover and cook for 20 minutes.

Drain the pheasant and arrange it in a flameproof earthenware dish with 12 cep or button mushrooms and a truffle cut into fine strips; moisten with 3 tablespoons Cognac or marc. Strain the pan juice, add some butter, whisk and pour over the pheasant. Put the lid on the dish, seal it with flour-and-water paste and cook in a bain marie in a preheated oven at 190°C (375°F, gas 5) for 40 minutes. Serve in the cooking dish.

## Pheasant à la normande

Brown the pheasant in butter in a flameproof casserole. Peel and slice 4 firm apples and fry quickly in butter. Place them in the bottom of the casserole with the pheasant on top. Cover and cook in a preheated oven at 240°C (475°F, gas 9) for about 45 minutes. Five minutes before serving, pour 100 ml

(4 fl oz, ½ cup) double (heavy) cream and 1 tablespoon Calvados over the pheasant. Untruss, carve into joints and serve very hot with the apples.

## Pheasant à la Sainte-Alliance

(from Brillat-Savarin's recipe) Hang a pheasant until it is very high, then pluck it and lard it with fresh firm bacon. Bone and draw 2 woodcock, separating the flesh and the offal (variety meats). Make a stuffing with the flesh by chopping it with steamed beef bone marrow, a little shredded pork fat, some pepper, salt, herbs and truffles. Stuff the pheasant with this mixture.

Cut a slice of bread 5 cm (2 in) larger than the pheasant all round, and toast it. Pound the livers and entrails of the woodcock with 2 large truffles, 1 anchovy, a little finely chopped bacon and a moderately sized lump of fresh butter. Spread this paste evenly over the toast. Roast the pheasant in a preheated oven at 230°C (450°F, gas 8); when it is cooked, spoon all the roasting juices over the toast on a serving dish. Place the pheasant on top and surround it with slices of Seville (bitter) orange. This highly flavoured dish is best accompanied by wine from Upper Burgundy.

## Pheasant Périgueux

Pluck, singe and gut (clean) a pheasant. Season the carcass inside and out, then put some slices of truffle between the skin and the flesh. Fry the pheasant in butter in a heavy-based pan then arrange on a slice of bread fried in butter. Prepare some Périgueux sauce with the cooking juices and serve separately. The dish can be garnished with quenelles of truffled game forcemeat.

## Pheasant with port

Cut 2 young pheasants, preferably hens, into 4 or 6 pieces each. Season with salt and pepper and brown in 50 g (2 oz, ¼ cup) butter in a frying pan. Soften

4 peeled, chopped shallots in 20 g (¾ oz, 1½ tablespoons) butter in a flame-proof casserole. Add the pheasant pieces and 250 ml (8 fl oz, 1 cup) port. Cover and simmer for 20 minutes. Fry 300 g (11 oz, 3½ cups) chanterelle mushrooms in butter. Remove the pheasant pieces and keep warm and deglaze the casserole with 250 ml (8 fl oz, 1 cup) double (heavy) cream. Add a little juice from the pan in which the chanterelles were cooked and boil down to reduce. Finish the sauce by gradually whisking in 65 g (2½ oz, 5 tablespoons) butter, cut into small pieces. Adjust the seasoning. Replace the pheasant pieces and the chanterelles in the hot sauce and allow to bubble for a few seconds. Arrange on a dish and serve with spätzle, Italian potato gnocchi or buttered noodles.

## Pheasant with truffles

At least 24 hours before cooking, insert some large slices of prepared truffle under the skin of a pheasant. Make a forcemeat with 250 g (9 oz) diced truffles and 350 g (12 oz) fresh pork fat and use it to stuff the pheasant. Cook in a preheated oven at 220°C (425°F, gas 7) for 50–55 minutes or for 55–60 minutes on a spit. (The pheasant may also be fried rather than roasted.) Place it on a large croûton, arrange some balls of game forcemeat around it and serve with Périgueux sauce.

## Pheasant with walnuts

Pound together 60 peeled fresh walnut kernels, 3 Petit-Suisse cheeses or 75 g (3 oz, ½ cup) cream cheese, ½ wine glass grape juice, the juice of 1 lemon, a few drops of port, ½ cup very strong tea and season with salt and pepper. Stuff a pheasant with this mixture. Brown the pheasant in butter in a sauté pan, season with salt and pepper then cover the pan and cook until the pheasant is tender (about 40 minutes).

## Roast pheasant

Truss and bard a young pheasant, brush with melted butter and season with salt and pepper. Roast in a preheated oven at 240°C (475°F, gas 9) for 30–40 minutes, depending on the size of the bird, basting 2 or 3 times. Fry some croûtons until golden brown. Untruss the pheasant and remove the barding fat. Place it on top of the croûtons and keep warm. Deglaze the roasting tin (pan) with a little poultry stock and serve this gravy separately. (The pheasant can be stuffed with truffles before roasting and the croûtons can be spread with a small amount of forcemeat made with the minced liver of the pheasant.)

## Salmi of pheasant

Pluck, draw, prepare and truss a young pheasant. Roast in a preheated oven at 240°C (475°F, gas 9) for only 20 minutes so that it is still rare. Set the roasting tin (pan) aside. Cut the pheasant into 6 pieces as follows: remove the legs; remove the wings, leaving sufficient white meat on the breast bone; cut the breast into 2 pieces, widthways. Trim each piece carefully and remove the skin. Place the portions of pheasant in a buttered sauté pan and add a dash of good-quality Cognac. Season with pepper. Cover and keep warm.

Crush the bones of the carcass, the skin and trimmings, and brown briskly with 1 unpeeled garlic clove in the roasting tin in which the pheasant was roasted. Reduce the heat and add 3 finely chopped shallots; cover and sweat the shallots gently for 5 minutes, then spoon or pour off excess grease. Deglaze with a dash of Cognac and add 500 ml (17 fl oz, 2 cups) good red wine. Season the mixture and add a bouquet garni. Cook the wine, uncovered, for a few minutes and then add a generous ladle of game stock. Simmer for 30 minutes, uncovered. Skim thoroughly. Strain the sauce through a chinois, pressing the mixture to extract as much of the juice as possible. Pour the liquor into a clean pan and bring back to simmering point. Correct the seasoning. Flavour the sauce with a little truffle juice and thicken with 50 g (2 oz, ¼ cup) foie gras pressed through a sieve, and pour over the pheasant. Fry a few sliced button mushrooms in butter, add to the pheasant and heat through gently, but thoroughly. Garnish with a few slices of truffle. Serve with garlic croûtons.

## Sautéed pheasant

Cut a young tender pheasant (preferably a hen) into 4 or 6 pieces. Season with salt and pepper, brown in butter and cook gently in a sauté pan. Keep the pieces of pheasant on a covered serving dish. Deglaze the sauté pan with 4 tablespoons white wine and a little veal stock; reduce the sauce by half and add some butter. Pour the sauce over the pheasant and serve very hot.

## Slices of pheasant with orange juice

Remove the flesh from a pheasant. Make a sauce as follows. Crush and pound the carcass and place it in a saucepan with some veal stock and a bottle of flat champagne. Add salt and pepper, bring to the boil and leave over a low heat to reduce. Press through a fine sieve and return to the heat. Add the minced (ground) heart and liver; cook for another 10 minutes. Cut the pheasant flesh into long, thin slices and sauté these in butter for 10 minutes, adding a handful of chopped parsley, chervil and chives. Arrange the slices on a dish. Add the cooking juice from the pheasant to the sauce, together with the strained juice of 1 orange. Stir and pour the hot sauce over the pheasant.

## Terrine of pheasant

Bone a pheasant weighing about 1.25 kg (2¾ lb) without damaging the breast meat. Cut the latter into even strips, together with 300 g (11 oz) bacon fat. Put the meat into a bowl with salt, pepper, ½ teaspoon quatre épices, 4 tablespoons brandy, a chopped bay leaf and a small sprig of thyme with the leaves removed. Thoroughly soak the meat in this mixture and marinate for 24 hours in a cool place. Put the rest of the pheasant in the refrigerator. Soak an intact pig's caul (caul fat) in cold water, then squeeze and wipe it dry.

Prepare a duxelles with 250 g (9 oz, 3 cups) button mushrooms, 2 or 3 shallots, salt and pepper.

Finely chop 350 g (12 oz) fresh belly of pork, 1 onion, the remaining pheasant meat and the blanched zest of an orange. Mix the duxelles and the chopped meat in a bowl with 2 eggs, pepper and salt. Work the mixture well to make it homogeneous, adding the marinade in which the strips of bacon fat and pheasant were steeped.

Line the terrine with the caul. Arrange a third of the forcemeat in an even layer. Cover with alternating strips of the marinated pheasant and bacon fat. Cover with the half the remaining forcemeat. Top with a thin layer of foie gras and diced truffle, then cover with the remainder of the forcemeat. Press down the caul on the contents of the terrine and trim. Place a bay leaf and 2 small sprigs of fresh thyme on top and then put on the lid.

Place the terrine in a bain marie, bring to the boil on the hob (stove top), then cook in a preheated oven at 180°C (350°F, gas 4) for 1½ hours. Remove from the oven and allow to cool. When lukewarm, take off the lid and replace with a weighted board. Allow the terrine to cool completely.

An aspic flavoured with port can be poured into the terrine and allowed to set. To preserve the terrine, cover with a fine layer of melted goose fat.

# Pigeon

## Pigeon, dressing a roasting bird

To pluck a bird more easily, chill it for a few hours in the refrigerator: the flesh will tighten and there will be less danger of tearing. Pluck each bird beginning with the large wing feathers, then the tail and proceed upwards to finish at the head. Singe and draw. Place a thin rasher (slice) of bacon on the back and breast of the bird. Truss by folding the head down between the wings.

## Pigeon compote

Season 4 pigeons with salt and pepper, inside and out, then place 3–4 juniper berries and 1 tablespoon marc brandy in each bird. Turn the birds over so that the marc is evenly distributed. Put a thin strip of bacon over the breasts and truss. Brown the pigeons in a flameproof casserole in 50 g (2 oz, ¼ cup) butter, then remove, drain and keep warm. In the same butter, brown 20 small (pearl) onions and 100 g (4 oz, ⅔ cup) smoked streaky bacon, cut into small pieces. Then add 150 g (5 oz, 1⅔ cups) thinly sliced mushrooms. When these have turned golden, add a bouquet garni, 200 ml (7 fl oz, ¾ cup) white wine and the same quantity of chicken stock. Reduce by two-thirds, return the pigeons to the casserole, cover and bring to the boil. Cook in a preheated oven at 230°C (450°F, gas 8) for 30 minutes.Remove the bouquet garni, untie the pigeons, arrange on a heated serving dish and spoon over the cooking liquid.

## Pigeons à la niçoise

Peel 18 small pickling (pearl) onions. Put them in a flameproof casserole with 20 g (¾ oz, 1½ tablespoons) butter. Season with salt and pepper. Add 3 table-

361

spoons water, cover and cook for 20 minutes over a moderate heat. Melt 40 g (1½ oz, 3 tablespoons) butter in a braising pan, add 6 pigeons, turning them over so they brown on all sides. Add 1 crumbled bay leaf and 2 pinches of winter savory. Pour over 100 ml (4 fl oz, 7 tablespoons) dry white wine and incorporate the drained onions. Simmer for 15 minutes. Add 200 g (7 oz) small black olives and cook for another 5–10 minutes. Steam 1 kg (2¼ lb) sugarsnap (snow) peas. Put them in a serving dish and arrange the pigeons on top, garnished with the olives, onions, a few bay leaves and sprigs of savory.

## Roast pigeons with shallot vinegar

Bone 2 pigeons, each weighing about 575 g (1¼ lb). In a medium saucepan, prepare a stock with the carcasses, 1 carrot and 2 onions cut into slices, a bouquet garni, 150 ml (¼ pint, ⅔ cup) white wine, salt and pepper. Add just enough water to cover and cook for 30 minutes. Strain the stock and boil down to reduce by a third to a half; the exact volume of stock will depend on the size of the pan and volume of water added.

Fry the pieces of pigeon in 1 tablespoon of olive oil, turning occasionally, until just cooked; deglaze with 2 tablespoons shallot vinegar, then add the pigeon stock.

Boil 800 g (1¾ lb) potatoes in their skins. Peel them, then mash with a fork, adding 100 g (4 oz, ½ cup) butter and 2 teaspoons ground cumin. Use two spoons to scoop the potatoes into quenelle shapes. Arrange the pieces of pigeon on 4 plates, surround with the quenelles and pour over the sauce.

## Squab à la minute

Split the bird in half lengthways. Remove the small bones, gently flatten the 2 halves and fry quickly in butter. When the squab is almost cooked, add 1 tablespoon chopped onion lightly fried in butter. Finish cooking. Arrange the squab on a dish and keep warm. Dilute the pan juices with a dash of brandy, thicken with a little dissolved meat essence and add 1½ teaspoons chopped parsley. Pour the sauce over the bird.

## Squabs en papillotes

Take 4 squabs and split each in half lengthways. Remove as many bones as possible, especially the breastbone. Season each half with salt and pepper, and fry in a casserole containing 50 g (2 oz, ¼ cup) butter to seal them. Prepare a duxelles from 40 g (1½ oz, ½ cup) mushrooms and 200 g (7 oz, 1¼ cups) raw unsmoked ham. Cut out 8 heart-shaped pieces of greaseproof (wax) paper, oil each piece lightly on one side and spread with the duxelles. Place a pigeon half on each and fold over the edges of the papillotes to seal. Cook in a preheated oven at 230°C (450°F, gas 8) until the paper cases have swollen and browned (about 15 minutes).

## Squabs with peas

Season 4 squabs with salt and pepper inside and out. Truss, then brown on all sides in 50 g (2 oz, ¼ cup) butter in a flameproof casserole. Remove and drain. Dice 150 g (5 oz, ¾ cup) slightly salted streaky bacon, scald for 5 minutes in boiling water, then drain and cool. Peel 12 small (pearl) onions. Brown the bacon and onions in the butter in which the pigeons were cooked, then, without removing them, deglaze the casserole with 175 g (6 fl oz, ¾ cup) white wine and 175 ml (6 fl oz, ¾ cup) stock. Reduce by half.

Return the pigeons to the casserole and add 800 g (1¾ lb, 3½ cups) fresh peas, shelled, 1 lettuce heart and a bouquet garni. Season with salt and pepper, cover and cook in a preheated oven at 220°C (425°F, gas 7) gently for about 30 minutes. Adjust the seasoning, remove the bouquet garni and serve from the casserole. The peas may be flavoured with savory if wished.

## Stuffed pigeons with asparagus tips

Starting at the backbone, bone 4 pigeons, each weighing about 400 g (14 oz). Prepare a forcemeat with 250 g (9 oz) noix of veal, 250 g (9 oz) fat bacon, 250 g (9 oz) calves' sweetbreads and 250 g (9 oz) foie gras. Chop all these ingredients very finely and add 25 g (1 oz, ¼ cup) broken truffle pieces and 1 egg. Blend together. Stuff the pigeons and then wrap each in a caul (caul fat), which will prevent the skin from drying while they are cooked.

Place the pigeons in a flameproof casserole, cover and cook over a gentle heat for about 15 minutes. Remove the pigeons, deglaze the casserole with 4 tablespoons vermouth and reduce over a brisk heat before pouring the sauce over the pigeons.

Serve with a gratin of asparagus tips prepared as follows: boil 32 asparagus tips in plenty of salted water, spread on a buttered gratin dish, cover with 100 ml (4 fl oz, 7 tablespoons) crème fraîche blended with 1 beaten egg yolk and brown under the grill (broiler).

# Quail

## Grilled quails

Pluck, draw and singe the quails. Split them down the centre of the back from the base of the neck to the tail and flatten slightly. Season with salt and pepper, brush with flavoured oil or melted butter and grill (broil) lightly for about 20 minutes. (Before cooking, the quails may be coated with fresh breadcrumbs.)

## Grilled quails petit-duc

Coat the quails with melted butter and breadcrumbs and grill (broil). Arrange them on a bed of Anna potatoes and place a large grilled mushroom on each quail. Heat a few tablespoons of game fumet with a little Madeira and butter and sprinkle this over the quails.

## Jellied stuffed quails à la périgourdine

Prepare and stuff the quails as described for stuffed quails in cases, adding diced foie gras to the forcemeat. Reshape the quails and wrap each one in a piece of muslin (cheesecloth) tied at both ends. Poach for 20–25 minutes in liquid meat aspic stock, flavoured with Madeira. Leave the quails to cool in the stock, but drain them before it sets. Unwrap them and dry with a cloth. Arrange them in a round, fairly shallow terrine. Clarify the aspic jelly and pour over the quails. Chill in the refrigerator before serving.

## Minute quails

Pluck, draw and singe the quails. Split them down the centre of the back from the base of the neck to the tail, flatten slightly and season with salt and pepper.

Sauté them briskly in butter. After 15 minutes add a small chopped onion, some parsley and some melted butter. Cover the pan and continue cooking for a further 5 minutes. Cut some mushrooms into thin slices, allowing 150 g (5 oz, 1½ cups) for 4 quails. Drain the quails and arrange them on a serving dish while still hot. Brown the mushrooms in the sauté pan. Add a dash of brandy and, optionally, a few tablespoons of game stock. Boil for 3–4 minutes and add a dash of lemon juice. Pour this sauce over the quails.

## Quail casserole

Pluck, draw and singe the quails. Smear the inside of each carcass with a knob of butter kneaded with salt and pepper, then truss each bird. Melt some butter in a flameproof casserole and fry the quails until golden. Add salt and pepper, cover and place in a preheated oven at 240°C (475°F, gas 9) for 12–18 minutes. When the birds are cooked, deglaze the dish with a little brandy.

## Quail casserole à la bonne femme

Pluck, draw, singe and truss the quails. Fry them in butter in a flameproof casserole until golden. Dice some potatoes and scalded bacon, and cook in butter in a separate pan. Add the fried potato and bacon to the quails and complete the cooking in the oven, as for quail casserole.

## Quail casserole Cinq-Mars

Pluck, draw, truss and singe the quails. Cut some carrots, onions and celery sticks into thin strips and soften in butter over a low heat, then add salt and pepper. Fry the quails in butter until golden, season with salt and pepper and cover with half the vegetable strips. Add 2–3 tablespoons sherry, cover and leave to cook in a preheated oven at about 240°C (475°F, gas 9) for 10 minutes.

Untruss the quails and arrange them in an ovenproof dish that can be taken to the table. Top with thinly sliced mushrooms (wild mushrooms if possible) and either thinly sliced truffles or truffle peel. Cover with the rest of the vegetables and add the cooking juices, 2 tablespoons brandy and some knobs of butter. Cover the dish and seal the lid with a flour-and-water paste. Place the dish in a bain marie and bring to the boil. Then place the bain marie in the oven at 200°C (400°F, gas 6) and leave to cook for another 30 minutes. Remove the lid and serve very hot in the same dish.

## Quail casserole with grapes

Pluck, draw and singe 8 quails. Wrap each one in a vine leaf and a very thin rasher (slice) of bacon, truss and fry in butter until golden. Add salt and pepper, cover the pan and leave to cook for another 10 minutes. Peel and seed about 60 large white grapes. Untruss the quails, arrange in an ovenproof dish (which can be taken to the table) and add the grapes. Sprinkle with the quails' cooking juices. Place the dish, without a lid, in a preheated oven at 240°C (475°F, gas 9) for 5 minutes. Just before serving, 2–3 tablespoons brandy can be added to the dish.

## Quail croustades à la périgueux

Prepare and cook some stuffed quails. Cover the bottom of each bread croustade with Périgueux sauce. Place a quail on it and coat with more sauce. Garnish with a slice of truffle and serve very hot.

## Quail pâté

Bone the quails. Stuff each with a piece of *à gratin* forcemeat about the size of a hazelnut, and the same amount of foie gras, studded with a piece of truffle, the whole well seasoned with salt, pepper and nutmeg, and sprinkled with a dash of brandy. Wrap each quail in a very thin rasher (slice) of bacon.

Line a hinged oval or rectangular mould with fine pastry, then with thin rashers of bacon. Cover with a layer of finely pounded forcemeat made of veal and equal proportions of lean and fat pork, bound with an egg, well seasoned, sprinkled with a little brandy and mixed with diced truffles. Next add a layer of *à gratin* game forcemeat, then half the stuffed quails, pressing down well. Cover with another layer of forcemeat, put in the rest of the quails and follow with a layer of forcemeat. Cover this with a layer of truffled forcemeat, flatten it and top with a layer of thin rashers of lean bacon. Seal with a pastry lid. Garnish with pieces of pastry cut in fancy shapes. Make a hole in the middle of the lid for steam to escape and brush the pastry top with beaten egg. Bake in a preheated oven at 180°C (350°F, gas 4) for about 1½ hours.

When cooked, leave the pâté to get cold and pour liquid game aspic stock through the hole in the top.

## Quails à la romaine

Brown 12 chopped small new onions and 100 g (4 oz, ⅔ cup) diced cooked ham in 25 g (1 oz, 2 tablespoons) butter. Add 1 kg (2¼ lb, 7 cups) shelled petits pois, a pinch each of salt and sugar, and a small bouquet garni. Cover and braise gently for 20 minutes. Dress, trim and truss 8 quails and brown quickly in butter in a flameproof casserole. Tip the vegetables on to the birds, cover and cook in a preheated oven at 230°C (450°F, gas 8) for 20 minutes.

## Quails en chemise

Stuff the quails with *à gratin* forcemeat, then truss, sprinkle with salt and pepper, and wrap each one separately in a small piece of pig's intestine. Tie up each end. Plunge the quails into boiling clear stock and poach for about 20 minutes. Drain, reduce the stock and coat the quails. A well-seasoned and well-reduced clarified chicken consommé may be used instead of stock.

## Quails in vine leaves

Wash and dry 4 large fresh vine leaves; if they are canned, rinse in plenty of water, sponge dry and remove the stalks. Draw 4 quails and season with salt and pepper. Generously butter the breast and legs. Place a vine leaf on the breast of each quail and fold the edges down under the bird. Wrap 2 thin rashers (slices) of bacon around each quail and fasten securely with string. Wrap each one tightly in foil. Cook en papillote in a preheated oven at 220°C (425°F, gas 7) for 20 minutes or in the ashes of a wood fire, or roast on a spit for 15 minutes. Remove the foil and string and serve the birds cut in two lengthways. Serve with potato chips (French fries) and watercress or small mushroom brochettes.

## Quails with cherries

Remove the stalks and stones (pits) from 1 kg (2¼ lb) morello cherries, then place them in a saucepan with 250 g (9 oz, generous 1 cup) sugar and 100 ml (4 fl oz, 7 tablespoons) water and leave them to cook for 8–10 minutes. Add 3 tablespoons redcurrant jelly and cook for a further 5 minutes. Roast some quails. When they are cooked, add the cherries and a little syrup to the roasting pan and reheat. Serve the quails surrounded by the cherries.

Alternatively, canned cherries in syrup may be used and the syrup thickened with a little arrowroot.

## Roast quails

Wrap the quails in vine leaves and then in thin rashers (slices) of larding bacon. Secure with string. Roast on a spit before a lively fire or in a preheated oven at 200°C (400°F, gas 6) for 15–20 minutes. Arrange each quail on a canapé. Garnish with watercress and lemon quarters. Serve the diluted pan juices separately.

## Stuffed quails à la financière

Prepare some stuffed quails in cases, coat them with a sauce made with their cooking juices mixed with Madeira, and glaze them in the oven. Arrange on fried croûtons or croustades of puff pastry. Garnish with finely sliced truffles and surround with a financière garnish.

## Stuffed quails à la gourmande

Pluck, draw and singe the quails. Season with salt and pepper, and stuff each bird with a mixture of butter, lean ham and chopped truffles (or truffle peel). Truss the birds and brown them in butter in a sauté pan. Cover the pan and finish cooking. Drain the quails, dilute the pan juices with champagne and reduce. Adjust the seasoning. Arrange the quails in a circle on a warm serving dish. Garnish the centre of the dish with boletus or chanterelle mushrooms sautéed in butter. Pour the pan juices over the quails.

## Stuffed quails à la Monselet

Pluck, draw and half-bone the quails. Stuff them with a salpicon of truffles and foie gras. Wrap each bird separately in a piece of muslin (cheesecloth) and poach them in a Madeira-flavoured game stock prepared from the bones and trimmings of the quails. Drain the birds, then unwrap them and place them in an ovenproof casserole together with a garnish of sliced artichoke hearts tossed in butter, some cultivated mushrooms and thick slices of truffles. Strain the stock, add an equal quantity of crème fraîche and boil to reduce. Pour this sauce over the birds. Cover the casserole and place in a preheated oven at 180°C (350°F, gas 4) for 10 minutes. Serve the quails in the casserole. Charles Pierre Monselet was a 19th century French writer and a friend of many restaurateurs; many recipes containing truffles, artichokes and Madiera are dedicated to him.

## Stuffed quails à la Souvarov

Pluck, draw and singe the quails. Stuff them with a salpicon of foie gras and truffles seasoned with salt and pepper and sprinkled with a dash of brandy. Truss the birds and fry briskly in very hot butter for 5 minutes. Season with salt and pepper. Cook some very small truffles in butter and place them in a casserole that is large enough to hold the quails. Arrange the quails in the casserole. Dilute the pan juices with Madeira (and possibly game stock), reduce, add a dash of brandy and pour the sauce over the birds. Cover the casserole and seal the lid with a flour-and-water paste. Cook in a preheated oven at 230°C (450°F, gas 8) for 15–18 minutes.

## Stuffed quails in cases

Pluck, draw and remove the bones from 8 quails. To 175 g (6 oz, ¾ cup) *à gratin* forcemeat, add 3 or 4 chicken livers and 1 tablespoon chopped truffle peel. Stuff the quails, reshape them and wrap each one in a piece of buttered greaseproof (wax) paper. Arrange them in a buttered dish so that they are tightly packed together and add a little melted butter. Season with salt and pepper. Cook (without a lid) in a preheated oven at 240°C (475°F, gas 9) for 18–20 minutes. Remove the quails from the dish and unwrap them. Place each bird in an oval paper case. Deglaze the cooking juices with some Madeira and pour over the quails. Put the cases in the oven for 5 minutes before arranging on a serving dish.

## Stuffed quails in cases à la Lamballe

Prepare the stuffed quails in cases, lining the base of each greaseproof (wax) paper case with a julienne of mushrooms and truffles blended with cream. Add some port to the pan juices in which the quails were cooked, blend in some crème fraîche and pour the resulting sauce over the quails.

## Stuffed quails in nests

Pluck, draw and bone the quails. Stuff them with game forcemeat mixed with chopped truffles. Wrap each bird in a small piece of muslin (cheesecloth) and make into a roll. Poach for 18 minutes in a stock prepared from the bones and trimmings, with added veal stock and Madeira. Drain the birds, unwrap and glaze lightly in the oven. Reduce the stock. Arrange each quail in a nest of straw potatoes and pour a little reduced stock over the top.

# Rabbit

## Rabbit coquibus

Joint a rabbit into small portions. Place in a large bowl with 250 ml (8 fl oz, 1 cup) white wine, a bouquet garni, including a sprig of savory and leave to marinate overnight.

The next day, drain and wipe the meat, reserving the marinade. Peel 24 small onions and blanch 24 strips of slightly salted belly pork or bacon. Heat 40 g (1½ oz, 3 tablespoons) butter in a large flameproof casserole and lightly brown the pieces of rabbit in it, together with the onions and bacon. Sprinkle with a little flour and cook until golden. Pour in the reserved marinade with the bouquet garni. Add enough stock to cover the pieces of rabbit and sprinkle with salt and pepper. Bring to the boil, then reduce the heat and cover the casserole. Allow to simmer for 15 minutes then add 500 g (18 oz) peeled new potatoes, cover and continue cooking for 45 minutes. Taste for seasoning before serving.

## Rabbit crépinettes

Use a 1.5 kg (3¼ lb) rabbit. Bone the saddle and legs and season with salt and pepper. Cut the saddle into 3 pieces. Soak a pig's caul. Clean and chop 1 or 2 shallots, 250 g (9 oz, 3 cups) mushrooms, a small sprig of parsley and 400 g (14 oz) smoked belly of pork (salt pork). Add some pepper, a pinch of thyme, some powdered bay leaf, and 1 tablespoon Cognac or marc (it is not necessary to add salt as the belly is salted). Mix the ingredients well and adjust the seasoning if necessary after browning a knob of the forcemeat in a frying pan and tasting it.

Fill the inside of each piece of rabbit with one-fifth of the forcemeat. Wipe the caul, stretch it gently and cut it into five. Roll each piece of stuffed rabbit in a piece of caul and place in a lightly buttered gratin dish. Brush these crépinettes with a little melted butter and cook in a preheated oven at 230°C (450°F, gas 8) until golden brown. Turn the crépinettes over to brown the other side and then reduce the temperature to 180°C (350°F, gas 4). Cook for a further 30 minutes. A little chicken stock flavoured with mustard may be poured into the cooking dish after the crépinettes have browned and they can be served coated with the resulting pan juices.

## Rabbit rillettes

Rillettes is a preparation of pork, rabbit, goose or poultry meat cooked in lard, then pounded to a smooth paste, potted and served as cold hors d'oeuvre.

Bone 4 wild rabbits, weigh the meat and cut it into large dice. Dice 1.4 kg (3 lb) fat streaky (slab) bacon. Melt 50–75 g (2–3 oz, 4–6 tablespoons) lard in a large frying pan and fry the bacon along with 8 peeled garlic cloves and a sprig of thyme; add the rabbit and cook until golden. Pour in 750 ml (1¼ pints, 3¼ cups) water and 1½ tablespoons salt for every 1 kg (2¼ lb) meat. Cover the pan and simmer gently for 3 hours. Adjust the seasoning.

When cooked, shred the meat using 2 forks and pour the mixture, still boiling hot, into small stoneware pots which have previously been scalded. Leave to cool. Fill the pots to the brim with melted lard, cover and chill.

## Rabbit rillettes en terrine with Parma ham

Cook 3 young rabbits in stock, seasoned with aromatic herbs. Remove the meat and shred it. Reduce the cooking juice by two-thirds, then strain it through a fine sieve and add it to the rabbit meat, together with 3 egg yolks and 2 tablespoons each of chopped fresh sage and marjoram. Season the mixture. Line a terrine with long, thin slices of Parma ham. Arrange a first layer of rillettes, then a row of preserved duck's gizzards, and cover with rillettes. Fold the ends of the Parma ham slices over the top and cook for 45 minutes in a bain marie in a preheated oven at 150°C (300°F, gas 2). Serve with thin slices of pear, marjoram leaves and some slender chives.

## Rabbit roasted in a caul

Soak a large pig's caul in fresh water. Joint a rabbit weighing 1.25 kg (2¾ lb); season the pieces with salt and pepper, sprinkle with a little dried thyme and plenty of mustard powder. Wipe the caul, stretch it on the worktop without tearing it, and cut it into 6 pieces. Wrap each piece of rabbit in a piece of caul and place the pieces in a roasting tin (pan) just large enough to hold them. Add 3 tablespoons water, put the tin in a preheated oven at 220°C (425°F, gas 7) and cook for 30 minutes, turning the pieces every 7–8 minutes. Add a little boiling water if necessary. Keep the pieces warm on a serving dish.

Skim the fat from the cooking juices remaining in the roasting tin and add 60 ml (2 fl oz) white wine and 200 ml (7 fl oz, ¾ cup) double (heavy) cream. Deglaze the tin and boil until reduced by half. Adjust the seasoning and pour the sauce over the rabbit. Serve with buttered noodles.

## Rabbit sautéed à la minute

Joint a rabbit weighing about 1.25 kg (2¾ lb). Sprinkle the pieces with salt and pepper and brown them in smoking hot butter, over a very brisk heat, stirring thoroughly so that all the pieces are evenly coloured. Arrange them in a pie dish and keep hot. Dilute the pan juices with 150 ml (¼ pint, ⅔ cup) white wine and add 1 chopped shallot. Boil down the sauce until it is very concentrated, then moisten with a few tablespoons of stock. Reduce again, then mix in 1 tablespoon butter and a squeeze of lemon juice. Pour the sauce over the rabbit and sprinkle with chopped parsley.

## Rabbit with mustard

Joint a rabbit weighing about 1.25 kg (2¾ lb). Spread the pieces with a mixture of 2 tablespoons strong mustard, 1 tablespoon oil, salt and ground pepper. Place the pieces in a flameproof dish and put in a preheated oven at 230°C (450°F, gas 8). After 5 minutes, sprinkle with 60 ml (2 fl oz, ¼ cup) water. Continue cooking, basting with the pan juices every 5 minutes. When the pieces of rabbit are cooked, arrange them on a heated serving dish and keep hot. Skim the fat from the cooking juices and add 2 tablespoons white wine to the pan; reduce slightly, stirring with a wooden spoon. Then add 60 ml (2 fl oz, ¼ cup) single (light) cream and some salt, stirring all the time; do not boil. Pour this sauce over the rabbit. Serve with pasta.

## Sautéed rabbit chasseur

Joint the rabbit and sauté the portions in a mixture of oil and butter. Sauté some strips of larding bacon with the rabbit. Add 150 g (5 oz, 1⅓ cups) thinly sliced raw mushrooms and cook for about 10 minutes more. Drain the rabbit and keep it hot. Brown 1 or 2 chopped shallots in the pan juices and add 100 ml (4 fl oz, 7 tablespoons) white wine and 1 tablespoon well-reduced tomato sauce. Reduce by a half and then add 1 tablespoon marc and 1 tablespoon chopped tarragon. Bring to the boil and coat the rabbit with the sauce. Sprinkle with parsley and serve very hot with steamed potatoes.

## Sautéed rabbit with prunes

Soak 350 g (12 oz, 2 cups) prunes in tea until swollen, then drain them. Sauté a rabbit of about 1.25 kg (2¾ lb) as in the recipe for rabbit sautéed *à la minute*. Pound the rabbit's liver with 1 tablespoon vinegar (or put through a blender). When the rabbit is cooked, keep hot in a serving dish. Dilute the pan juices with 150 ml (¼ pint, ⅔ cup) white wine, add the prunes, then reduce a little. Mix in the pounded liver to thicken the juices and adjust the seasoning. Pour the prunes and gravy over the rabbit.

## Wild rabbit with farm cider

Remove the bones from a baron (saddle and legs) of young rabbit weighing about 1.5 kg (3¼ lb) and reserve. Prepare a *brunoise* of carrots, celeriac, celery sticks and leeks (green parts). Blanch the vegetables separately, then allow to cool and bind together using 3 egg yolks. Sprinkle with salt and pepper. Prepare 200 ml (7 fl oz, ¾ cup) rabbit stock using the bones, 1 carrot, 1 onion, a bouquet garni, 250 ml (8 fl oz, 1 cup) farm cider, 250 ml (8 fl oz, 1 cup) water, salt, and pepper.

Spread the baron of rabbit out on its back, season with salt and pepper, and stuff it with the *brunoise*. Pull the sides of the legs and belly together over the *brunoise* and tie up with string. Place the rabbit in an ovenproof earthenware dish or casserole on a bed of diced vegetables (2 carrots, 2 red onions and 2 shallots) mixed with diced dessert (eating) apple. Roast it with butter in a preheated oven at 240°C (475°F, gas 9) for 15–20 minutes so that it remains pink. Keep it hot, covered with a sheet of foil.

Boil 1 litre (1¾ pints, 4⅓ cups) milk and let cool. Peel and slice 1 kg (2¼ lb) potatoes; shred half a green cabbage, blanch and cool. Arrange a layer of the potatoes, seasoned with salt and pepper, in a buttered ovenproof dish, then add a layer of the cabbage, a layer of Emmental cheese, and so on, ending with a layer of potatoes and Emmental. Add 4 well-beaten eggs and a few knobs of butter to the cooled milk and pour over the potatoes. Cook in a preheated oven at 200–220°C (400–425°F, gas 6–7) for 45 minutes. Keep hot.

For the sauce to accompany the rabbit, add 500 ml (17 fl oz, 2 cups) farm cider to the pan juices and reduce by two-thirds; add a small glass of demi-glace, the rabbit stock and 250 ml (8 fl oz, 1 cup) double (heavy) cream. Cook over a gentle heat for 5 minutes. Surround the rabbit with cress and serve it with the sauce, sprinkled with chopped chives, and the potato cake.

## Wild rabbit with Hermitage wine

Joint a rabbit weighing about 1.25 kg (2¾ lb) and season with salt and pepper. Cut 150 g (5 oz) fat bacon into dice. Peel 12 small white onions. Pound the rabbit's liver. Put the bacon in a saucepan and brown with the onions. Put the pieces of rabbit in the saucepan and sauté over a brisk heat; dust with flour and leave to brown slightly. Flame with 60 ml (2 fl oz, ¼ cup) Hermitage marc and moisten with (500 ml, 17 fl oz, 2 cups) of red Crozes-Hermitage. Add a little warm stock. Adjust the seasoning and add a bouquet garni made of thyme, bay leaf, parsley stalks and a garlic clove. Cook gently for about 1 hour. When the rabbit is cooked, take it out of the pan and keep hot. Remove the pan from the heat and add the liver and blood (to which a little vinegar has been added); blend with the pan juices off the heat. Return the pan to a gentle heat, so that the blood cooks without boiling. Strain the sauce and keep it hot. Arrange the rabbit in a deep earthenware dish and pour the sauce over it. Some fried croûtons may be placed around the dish.

# Snipe

## Hot snipe pâté Lucullus

Bone 8 snipe and lay them out flat on a working surface. Prepare some fine forcemeat *à la crème* and mix with a third of its volume of foie gras and chopped snipe's entrails. Spread the forcemeat over the birds and place a piece of foie gras and a piece of truffle in the middle. Reshape the birds and pour some Cognac over them.

Line an oval mould with pastry and spread over it a layer of forcemeat *à la crème* mixed with half its volume of *à gratin* forcemeat. Place the snipe in the mould, packing them close together and filling in the gaps with the forcemeat. Top with a layer of forcemeat and cover with some rashers (slices) of bacon. Cover the mould with a lid of pastry, seal and crimp the edges, then garnish with pastry motifs. Make an opening in the middle and brush with beaten egg.

Place the mould in a bain marie, bring to the boil over a moderate heat, then cook in a preheated oven at 180°C (350°F, gas 4) for about 1 hour. Cut away the pastry lid, take off the layer of bacon and unmould the pâté. Add to it a ragoût of truffles bound with a few spoonfuls of Madeira-flavoured game stock. Replace the pastry lid and heat the pâté in the oven. Serve immediately.

# Venison

## Burgundy sauce for venison

(from Carême's recipe) Pour into a saucepan a glass of old Burgundy wine, 2 tablespoons ordinary vinegar, 2 tablespoons sugar, the flesh of half a seeded lemon and half a pot of redcurrant jelly. Boil to reduce and add 2 tablespoons espagnole sauce. Reduce again, gradually mixing in the contents of a second glass of Burgundy. When the sauce has reached the correct consistency, rub it through a sieve.

## Consommé chasseur

Use game consommé. Cook 2 tablespoons finely shredded mushrooms in 3 tablespoons Madeira. Thicken the consommé slightly with tapioca. Add the mushrooms and sprinkle with chervil leaves. Small profiteroles filled with game purée may be served at the same time.

## Haunch of roebuck with capers

Trim the haunch and prepare a marinade with a bottle of red wine, 1½ table-spoons olive oil, pepper, 2 onions and 2 shallots (both thinly sliced), parsley, salt (in moderation) and pepper. Add the haunch and leave to marinate for at least 24 hours, basting it from time to time.

After draining, lard the meat with small strips of streaky (slab) bacon (250 g, 9 oz). Baste with melted butter, cook in a preheated oven at 200°C (400°F, gas 6) for at least 2 hours, basting occasionally with butter. Meanwhile, simmer the marinade, also for 2 hours. When the meat has finished cooking, mix 2 teaspoons cornflour (cornstarch) or arrowroot with a small cup of beef stock and add this mixture and the meat juices to the reduced marinade. To serve, add 1 tablespoon capers and about 40 g (1½ oz, 3 tablespoons) fresh butter to the sauce.

## Pan-fried venison with pears

First prepare a red wine sauce: bring 500 ml (17 fl oz, 2 cups) red Burgundy to the boil and flame it to evaporate the alcohol. Add 1 chopped shallot and reduce the sauce by three-quarters. Cook and purée 100 g (4 oz) carrots, then add them to the sauce with salt and pepper. Remove from the heat.

Peel and core 4 firm cooking pears and toss them in lemon juice. Quarter the pears lengthways and slice them into fine fans, leaving the slices just attached at the narrow ends. Melt 25 g (1 oz, 2 tablespoons) butter in a pan, add the pears, then cook gently until tender and browned around the edges.

Meanwhile, season 12 lean noisettes or medallions of venison steak, each weighing about 50 g (2 oz), with salt and pepper. Melt 25 g (1 oz, 2 tablespoons) clarified butter in a frying pan until foaming. Add the venison and cook over high heat for 2 minutes on each side, until well browned outside and still slightly pink in the middle.

Reheat the sauce and add 150 g (5 oz, ⅔ cup) butter, cut in small pieces, whisking hard continuously. Drain the venison on paper towels. Deglaze the pan with a little water and reduce for 1 minute, then whisk this into the sauce and add seasoning to taste. Drain the pears on paper towels. Coat warmed plates with the sauce, then arrange the venison and pears on top.

## Pomponnettes

A pomponnette is a small round rissole, filled with forcemeat or a finely minced salpicon, which is fried and served as a hot hors d'oeuvre.

Prepare 400–500 g (14–18 oz) lining pastry and leave in a cool place for about 2 hours. Prepare 250 g (9 oz, 1 cup) à gratin or game forcemeat, mushroom duxelles or a ham and mushroom salpicon bound with a very thick béchamel sauce. Roll out the pastry to a thickness of 3–4 mm (⅛ in) and cut into circles 7.5 cm (3 in) in diameter. Place a small amount of filling on the centre of each circle. Moisten the edges, draw them towards the middle like a small pouch and pinch firmly to seal. Deep-fry the pomponnettes in hot oil heated to 180°C (350°F) until golden. Drain on paper towels and serve hot.

## Roast haunch of roebuck

Skin and trim the haunch of young roebuck, pulling off the fine membrane which covers it. Lard with long strips of streaky (slab) bacon and place in an ovenproof dish; moisten with clarified butter, or brush with butter softened to room temperature, and sprinkle with salt and pepper. Roast the haunch in a preheated oven at 220°C (425°F, gas 7), basting several times, for 12–15 minutes per 1 kg (6–8 minutes per 1 lb); as soon as the meat is browned on all sides, add 250 ml (8 fl oz, 1 cup) boiling water to the dish. Serve it with a poivrade sauce and chestnut purée, together with baked apples filled with cranberry compote, or small mushroom croûtes.

## Roast saddle of roebuck with poivrade sauce

Remove the sinews from a saddle of roebuck and lard it with thin strips of bacon. Before roasting the saddle, it may be coated with olive oil to which pepper and herbs have been added and left to marinate for 3–4 hours. Roast the meat on a spit or in a preheated oven at 220°C (425°F, gas 7), allowing 12–15 minutes per 1 kg (6–8 minutes per 1 lb).

Serve with a poivrade sauce, braised chestnuts, and either dauphine potatoes, potatoes sautéed in butter, or potatoes scooped out and filled with a cranberry compote and baked in a buttered dish for about 15 minutes.

## Roebuck filets mignons

In principle, filets mignons are thin, tongue-shaped strips of meat situated beneath the saddle bone, but they may also be taken from the large fillets of the saddle. Trim these fillets, flatten them slightly and lard them with fat bacon. They may then be quickly sautéed in oil or butter, like cutlets, or oiled and grilled (broiled) under a high heat. Serve with poivrade sauce, chestnut purée, a fruit compote (especially of peaches) or a cherry or redcurrant sauce, according to choice. Generally speaking, all cutlet recipes are suitable.

## Roebuck noisettes with red wine and roast pear

Pour 500 ml (17 fl oz, 2 cups) red Burgundy into a saucepan and bring to the boil. Add 1 peeled, chopped shallot and reduce the liquid by three quarters. Stir in 100 g (4 oz, ¾ cup) puréed cooked carrots and stir well. Season with salt and pepper. Peel and core 4 firm pears. Cut in a fan shape. Melt 25 g (1 oz, 2 tablespoons) butter in a frying pan. Add the pears and cook gently. Heat 25 g (1 oz, 2 tablespoons) butter in a sauté pan until it starts foaming. Add 12 roebuck noisettes, weighing 50 g (2 oz) each. Season with salt and pepper. Cook over a high heat for 2 minutes on each side, keeping the inside pink. Reheat the red wine sauce. Incorporate 150 g (5 oz, ⅔ cup) butter, cut into pieces and whisk vigorously to obtain a smooth mixture. Season with salt and pepper. Remove the noisettes from the pan. Drain on paper towels. Deglaze the cooking juices in the pan with 1 small glass of water. Reduce for 1 minute and add to the red wine sauce. Drain the pears and pat dry. Pour the sauce on to 4 plates. Place the noisettes on top and surround with the roast pears.

## Roebuck sauce

Brown in butter 1 tablespoon thinly sliced onions and 40 g (1½ oz, ¼ cup) gammon or raw ham cut into small dice. Add 100 ml (4 fl oz, 7 tablespoons) vinegar and a bouquet garni, and reduce almost completely. Then add 200 ml (7 fl oz, ¾ cup) espagnole sauce and reduce for 25 minutes, skimming off the scum which forms. Remove the bouquet garni and add 3 tablespoons port and 2 teaspoons redcurrant jelly. Reheat, stirring well.

## Saddle of roebuck à la berrichonne

Trim a saddle of roebuck, removing the sinews and keeping the trimmings. Lard it with very thin strips of fat bacon and season with salt, pepper, thyme and a crushed bay leaf. Cover and set aside for 2–3 hours.

Meanwhile, clean and finely dice 100 g (4 oz, ⅔ cup) carrots and 100 g (4 oz, ⅔ cup) onions. Brown the game trimmings in oil, then add the diced vegetables, 40 g (1½ oz) shallots, 25 g (1 oz) celery, 2 garlic cloves, a bouquet garni, 8 peppercorns and 2 cloves. Add 1.5 litres (2¾ pints, 6½ cups) red wine, and cook gently for 1 hour.

Drain any juices off the saddle. Skim the cooking liquid and pass it through a conical strainer lined with coarse muslin (cheesecloth), then thicken with 50 g (2 oz) brown roux. Beat the sauce with 150 g (5 oz, ⅔ cup) butter, season with salt and pepper and finally work in 3 tablespoons pig's blood; keep the sauce hot in a bain marie.

Cook 4 peeled, cored and quartered pears in 500 ml (17 fl oz, 2 cups) red wine flavoured with a generous pinch of powdered cinnamon, then braise gently in butter some quarters of celeriac cut into half-moon shapes. Keep the poached pears and celeriac hot.

Roast the saddle in a preheated oven at 220°C (425°F, gas 7), allowing 12–15 minutes per 1 kg (6–8 minutes per 1 lb). Coat the bottom of a warm serving dish with some of the sauce and arrange the saddle on it, garnishing it with pears and celeriac quarters alternately. Serve the remaining sauce separately.

## Saddle of roebuck grand veneur

Trim the saddle, then lard it with strips of bacon that have been marinated in Cognac with chopped parsley, salt, pepper and a little oil. Roast it and arrange on a serving dish surrounded by braised chestnuts or chestnut purée and dauphine potatoes. Serve with a grand veneur sauce.

## Sautéed roebuck cutlets

Trim and flatten the cutlets slightly, sprinkle with salt and pepper, and sauté briskly in 2 tablespoons very hot oil and a knob of butter. Arrange them in a crown, alternating with croûtons of bread cut into the shape of hearts and fried in butter. The eye of the cutlets may be larded with a few thin strips of fat bacon arranged in a star.

## Sautéed roebuck cutlets à la crème

Season some roebuck cutlets with salt and pepper, dust with paprika and sauté them briskly in butter. Add a little lemon juice to a cream sauce and pour it over the cutlets. Serve with a chestnut purée or braised chestnuts.

## Sautéed roebuck cutlets à la minute

Prepare a marinade with 2 tablespoons olive oil, 1 very small crushed garlic clove, 2 teaspoons lemon juice, 2 teaspoons blanched and chopped lemon peel, 2 teaspoons chopped parsley, and salt and pepper. Marinate 8 roebuck cutlets in this mixture for 30 minutes, turning them over three or four times.

Clean 500 g (18 oz, 6 cups) small mushrooms (preferably wild) and sauté them briskly in butter, adding 1 chopped shallot and 1 small chopped onion. Drain the cutlets without wiping them and sauté them briskly in about 25 g (1 oz, 2 tablespoons) hot butter. Moisten them with a liqueur glass of Cognac and flame. Arrange the cutlets in a crown in a round serving dish, with the mushrooms in the centre. Serve with a lemon-flavoured apple compote and, if desired, a poivrade sauce.

## Sautéed roebuck cutlets à la mode d'Uzès

Prepare some croûtons fried in oil and some dauphine potatoes. Cut some blanched orange zest and pickled gherkins into fine strips. Sauté the cutlets briskly in oil and keep them hot. Make a sauce from the pan juice, vinegar, brown gravy and crème fraîche, then add the strips of orange zest and gherkins and a few shredded almonds. Coat the hot cutlets with this sauce and serve with the croûtons and the dauphine potatoes.

## Sautéed roebuck cutlets with cherries

Place 1 glass of port with the same amount of sweetened cherry juice and redcurrant jelly in a small saucepan. Add salt and pepper, ½ teaspoon lemon juice, a pinch of powdered ginger and, if desired, a dash of cayenne pepper. Heat gently for about 10 minutes, then add a large glass of cherries in syrup and reheat. Sauté the cutlets and coat with the cherry sauce; serve very hot.

## Sautéed roebuck cutlets with grapes

Fry some croûtons in oil and prepare a poivrade sauce. Macerate some large skinned and seeded grapes in Cognac. Sauté the cutlets briskly, then heat the grapes in the same frying pan. Serve the cutlets with the grapes, fried croûtons and poivrade sauce.

## Sautéed roebuck cutlets with juniper berries

Sauté the cutlets briskly and coat with a sauce made from the pan juice flavoured with crushed juniper berries. Serve with an unsweetened apple purée (apple sauce).

## Simple game consommé

For 5 litres (8½ pints, 5½ quarts) consommé, use the following: 2 kg (4¼ lb) shoulder or neck of venison, 1 kg (2¼ lb) forequarter of hare or the equivalent of rabbit, an old pheasant and an old partridge (these proportions may be modified according to availability), 300 g (11 oz) carrots, 300 g (11 oz) leeks, 300 g (11 oz) onions, 150 g (5 oz) celery, 50 g (2 oz, ¾ cup) parsley sprigs, 2 garlic cloves, 2 thyme sprigs, 1 bay leaf, 50 g (2 oz, ⅓ cup) juniper berries, 3 cloves and salt.

Clean the game, then brown it in a lightly greased pan in a preheated oven at about 240°C (475°F, gas 9). Put the game (including the meat juices) into the stockpot, add 6 litres (10 pints, 6½ quarts) cold water and bring to the boil. Meanwhile, prepare and chop the vegetables, and brown them in the pan. Tie the juniper berries and the cloves in a muslin (cheesecloth) bag. When the stock has come to the boil, add the vegetables and herbs and return to the boil. Simmer gently for 3½ hours. Remove surplus fat and strain the stock. It is now ready to serve as a soup or to be clarified in the same way as beef stock.

The game used in this consommé can be boned, made into a purée or salpicon, and used for various garnishes.

## Shoulder of roebuck with olives

Bone a shoulder of roebuck, leaving the knuckle bone, and marinate. Cut 200 g (7 oz) fat bacon into strips, roll them in salt and pepper, and lard the shoulder with them. Roll it up and tie fairly tightly. Heat 25 g (1 oz, 2 table-spoons) butter, 2 teaspoons oil and 2 tablespoons diced fatty bacon in a casserole. Brown the shoulder in the casserole, then cover and leave to cook gently for a good hour. Meanwhile stone (pit) some green and black (ripe) olives; blanch and drain the green ones. When the shoulder is cooked, remove it from the casserole. Skim the fat from the cooking liquid, add the olives and bring to the boil. Mix 2 teaspoons arrowroot with very little water, add it to the casserole and stir until it thickens. Pour the sauce over the shoulder and serve very hot, with a celery purée if desired.

## Three-hour leg of roebuck

Trim a leg of roebuck weighing 2.5–3 kg (5½–6½ lb). Cut 300 g (11 oz) fat bacon into thin strips and lard the leg with them. Brown on all sides in a braising pan containing 25 g (1 oz, 2 tablespoons) butter and 2 tablespoons oil. Heat a small glass of Cognac, pour it over the leg and flame. Cover and leave to cook for 1 hour over a gentle heat. Add 250 ml (8 fl oz, 1 cup) red wine, the juice of a lemon, 1 garlic clove, 1 or 2 small dried chilli peppers, salt and pepper, and leave to cook gently for another hour, keeping the lid on. Then mix 2 teaspoons flour and 2 teaspoons strong mustard with 250 ml (8 fl oz, 1 cup) red wine, pour over the leg and cook for a third hour. When time to serve, strain the sauce and thicken it with 4 teaspoons raspberry jelly. Blend 1½ tablespoons double (heavy) cream with 1 litre (1¾ pints, 4⅓ cups) thin chestnut purée and serve the leg, purée and sauce together.

# Wild boar

## Boar's-head brawn (head cheese)

Cook in court-bouillon 4 pigs' tongues, which have been blanched, peeled and soaked in brine for 4–5 days. Singe a boar's head weighing about 5 kg (11 lb), scrape it out carefully, and bone it completely, without tearing the skin. Cut off the ears and set aside; remove the tongue and the fleshy parts attached to the skin. Cut the lean meat into large, even-sized cubes and leave to marinate for 10 hours, with the tongue and the skin of the head, 5 carrots, 4 chopped onions, thyme, bay leaf, salt, pepper and 1 teaspoon mixed spice.

Cut into dice 2 cm (¾ in) square the boar's tongue, the cooked pigs' tongues, 500 g (18 oz) pickled tongue, 800 g (1¾ lb) ham, 1 kg (2¼ lb) boned and trimmed chicken meat and 500 g (18 oz) fat bacon. Add 400 g (14 oz) truffles (peeled and coarsely diced), 150 g (5 oz, 1 cup) shelled pistachio nuts and the pieces of lean meat from the head. Marinate for 2 hours in brandy, salt, pepper and ½ teaspoon mixed spice. Add 4.5 kg (10 lb) fine pork forcemeat and 4 eggs; mix all together well.

Spread out the skin of the head, with the outside underneath, on a cloth that has been soaked in cold water and wrung out. Lay the stuffing in the middle and fold the skin over the mixture. Wrap the head in the cloth, reshaping it into its original form, and tie it firmly.

Cook in aspic-jelly stock to which the bones and trimmings from the boar's head and the carcass and trimmings from the chicken have been added; simmer very gently for about 4½ hours. One hour before it is ready, put the ears into the stock to cook. Drain, leave to stand for 30 minutes, then unwrap the head, wash the cloth and wring it out well. Roll the head in the cloth again and bind with wide tape, taking care to keep the shape (start binding at the snout end). Leave to cool for at least 12 hours, then unwrap and wipe dry.

Using thin wooden cocktail sticks (toothpicks), fix the ears, coated with a layer of brown chaud-froid sauce or dissolved meat glaze, in their correct positions. Place the head on a rack and coat with the same sauce; put the tusks back in their sockets and make eyes with hard-boiled (hard-cooked) egg white and truffles. Lay the head on a large dish, garnish with truffles and shelled pistachio nuts and glaze with the aspic (which should have the consistency of unbeaten egg white). Chill in the refrigerator. In domestic cookery, where the truffles are omitted, the cooled head is simply covered with golden breadcrumbs. The ears are diced and added to the stuffing.

## Cutlets of marcassin with quinces

Peel and finely dice 100 g (4 oz) carrots, an equal quantity of onions, the white part of a leek and a stick of celery. Place in a saucepan with 450 g (1 lb) bones and trimmings of a *marcassin* (a wild boar under the age of six months), a garlic clove and a small bouquet garni and cook until well browned. Pour 1 bottle of a robust red wine into the saucepan and add 100 g (4 fl oz, 7 tablespoons) single (light) cream. Season with salt, stir and cook very gently for 1½ hours.

Skim off the fat, rub through a fine sieve and boil to reduce until about 300 ml (½ pint, 1¼ cups) liquid remains. Put this sauce on one side.

Prepare a stuffing: cook 400 g (14 oz) peeled, diced salsify in boiling water with a little lemon juice. Cook 200 g (7 oz, 1½ cups) thinly sliced onions and 200 g (7 oz, 2 cups) diced pears in a covered pan with a knob of butter for 30 minutes. Add the cooked salsify and adjust the seasoning. Prepare 6 crêpes. Spread the stuffing over the crêpes, roll them up, place in a greased gratin dish and bake in a preheated oven at 200°C (400°F, gas 6) for 15 minutes.

Peel 300 g (11 oz) quinces, cut into dice and boil in water with lemon juice until tender but slightly firm. Fry 12 *marcassin* cutlets until they are just slightly pink. Cover them with the quinces and a dash of rum. Bring the sauce to the boil and blend in 100 g (4 oz, ½ cup) butter, stirring over a low heat. When the sauce becomes glossy, pour it over the cutlets. Serve with the crêpes.

This recipe can be used for cutlets and noisettes of venison or wild boar.

## Saddle of wild boar with quince sauce

Cook 2 perfect quinces al dente in 1 litre (1¾ pints, 4⅓ cups) water, sweetened with 100 g (4 oz, ½ cup) caster (superfine) sugar. Peel and hollow them. Poach 100 g (4 oz, generous ½ cup) lentils in stock; 200 g (7 oz) cubed celeriac in vegetable stock; and 1 diced beetroot (red beet) in chicken stock.

Roast a saddle of wild boar in 50 g (2 oz, ¼ cup) goose fat, basting often. Take the meat out, degrease the roasting pan and deglaze with the quince cooking juices, 1 litre (1¾ pints, 4⅓ cups) brown wild boar stock and 1 teaspoon quince jelly. Reduce by four-fifths. Filter through a fine sieve and thicken with 25 g (1 oz, 2 tablespoons) butter.

Roast the quinces, cut into quarters, in 20 g (¾ oz, 1½ tablespoons) butter, adding a little caster (superfine) sugar to caramelize them. Heat the lentils, celeriac and beetroot separately. Garnish the edge of the plates with these vegetables, add 2 quarters of quince and the wild boar meat, carved off the saddle in aiguillettes or thin strips, and pour the sauce on top.

## Sweet-and-sour leg of marcassin (wild boar)

Soak the following ingredients separately in cold water: 12 prunes, 175 g (6 oz, 1 cup) currants and 175 g (6 oz, 1 cup) sultanas (golden raisins). Braise a leg of *marcassin* in the same way as a leg of pork. Drain and place in a long ovenproof dish. Strain the braising liquid and pour a few spoonfuls over the meat. Sprinkle 1 tablespoon sugar over the meat and brown in a preheated oven at 220°C (425°F, gas 7).

To make the sauce, first prepare a caramel using 4 sugar lumps, then add 4 tablespoons wine vinegar and 400 ml (14 fl oz, 1¾ cups) game stock. Boil for 10 minutes, then strain. Bake 4 tablespoons pine nuts, chop them coarsely and add to the sauce, together with the drained currants, sultanas and prunes, and 24 pickled cherries. Just before serving, melt 25 g (1 oz, 1 square) plain (semisweet) chocolate with the minimum of water and whisk it into the sauce, together with 15 g (½ oz, 1 tablespoon) beurre manié.

# Wild duck

## Puff-pastry piroshki

Make 400 g (14 oz) puff pastry. Prepare 5 tablespoons finely diced cooked game (wild duck, pheasant, young rabbit or partridge) or the same amount of white fish (fillets of whiting or pike) poached in a court-bouillon. Add to the diced meat 2 chopped hard-boiled (hard-cooked) eggs and 5 tablespoons long-grain rice cooked in stock. Mix thoroughly and adjust the seasoning.

Roll out the pastry very thinly and cut out 12 rounds, about 7.5 cm (3 in) in diameter. Pull slightly into oval shapes. Put a small amount of hash on to half of each piece, without going right to the edge. Brush the other half of each oval with beaten egg and fold over, pressing the edges together firmly. Score the top and brush with beaten egg. Cook in a preheated oven at 220°C (425°F, gas 7) for about 20 minutes until crisp, puffy and golden. Serve hot.

## Wild duck à la tyrolienne

Stew some cooking apples, adding a little cinnamon and mace, to form a hot apple purée. Stuff a wild duck with this purée, tie securely and place the duck on a spit for roasting. Boil 2 tablespoons red wine vinegar together with a small knob of butter (about the size of a walnut), ½ teaspoon caster (superfine) sugar and a few grains of coarsely ground pepper. Baste the duck constantly with this preparation while it is cooking on the spit, placing a small pan beneath to catch the juices. Cooking should take about 30–35 minutes. When finished, take the duck off the spit, untruss and arrange on a dish. Strain the collected juices into a saucepan and heat, adding 1½ teaspoons redcurrant jelly. Finally, pour this sauce over the duck.

## Wild duck à la Walter Scott

Draw, singe and truss a wild duck. Cook in a preheated oven at 220°C (425°F, gas 7). Meanwhile, fry the duck's liver in butter, mash and mix it with 20 g (¾ oz) foie gras. Fry 2 croûtons in clarified butter and spread them with the liver paste. Core 2 apples, stud each with 4 cloves and cook as for apples bonne femme. Dilute some Dundee marmalade with 2 tablespoons whisky and heat gently. When the duck is cooked, arrange it on a serving dish. Remove the cloves from the apples and place the latter on the croûtons, then pour the marmalade into the apples. Arrange the croûtons around the duck. Serve the juice in a sauceboat (gravy boat), without skimming off the fat.

## Wild duck au Chambertin

Roast the duck for 18–20 minutes in a preheated oven at 240°C (475°F, gas 9) or fry over a brisk heat, so that the flesh stays slightly pink. Arrange on a serving dish and cover with Chambertin sauce to which the pan juices have been added. Garnish with mushrooms and, if liked, with strips of truffle.

# Wild duck with pears

Pluck, draw and season a small wild duck. Roast it for about 30 minutes so that the flesh remains pink and leave it in its cooking dish. Make a caramel with 2 tablespoons caster (superfine) sugar and add 150 ml (¼ pint, ⅔ cup) red wine, a small stick of cinnamon, 6 coriander seeds, 6 black peppercorns and the zest of an orange and a lemon. Bring it to the boil and cook 2 peeled pears in it for no longer than 15 minutes.

Remove the breast fillets of the duck, bone the legs and put the carcass and bones to one side. Cut the pears in half, slice them and keep them warm. Dilute the duck cooking juices with 150 ml (¼ pint, ⅔ cup) red wine. Add the carcass and the pear cooking syrup. Bring to the boil, reduce and then strain. Cut the duck fillets and leg meat into thin slices. Cover with the sauce and surround with slices of pear (the finished dish may be warmed up for 30 seconds in a microwave cooker just before serving, if desired).

# Woodcock

## Woodcock, to prepare

Unlike poultry and other game birds, woodcock is not trussed with string as it trusses itself. The long pointed beak goes through the thighs and the legs are raised and held together. It is customary to remove the eyes of the woodcock, but not the intestines (except for the gizzard). After cooking, the intestines are spread on toast.

## Casserole of woodcock

Truss the woodcock and bard with thin bacon. Brown in some butter, season with salt and pepper, then place the woodcock in an ovenproof dish and roast in a preheated oven at 240°C (475°F, gas 9) for 15–18 minutes, basting frequently, until it is cooked. Drain the bird, remove the bacon and keep it warm. Pour a splash of brandy into the dish and, if possible, a few tablespoons of game stock. Remove the intestines and chop them with an equal quantity of fresh bacon. Add salt and pepper, a pinch of grated nutmeg and a splash of Cognac, Armagnac or Calvados. Fry a slice of bread (white or brown), spread it with the intestines and then put it in a very hot oven for a few minutes to cook the bacon. Serve the woodcock on the toast canapé and moisten with the cooking juices.

## Casserole of woodcock à la crême

Prepare and cook a woodcock as in the recipe for casserole of woodcock. Add to the casserole a dash of Cognac, Armagnac, or Calvados and a few tablespoons of crème fraîche. Return to the oven to warm through.

# Cold timbale of woodcock

Line a raised pie dish with lining pastry or hot water crust pastry and then with thin slices of bacon. Cover the bottom and sides of the lined dish with a game forcemeat flavoured with diced truffle. Bone 2 woodcocks, stuff with foie gras studded with truffle, roll up neatly to enclose the stuffing and form ballotines. Seal by frying in butter. Place the woodcock in the dish and fill the gaps between with the fine forcemeat mixed with foie gras and the chopped intestines, well seasoned and flavoured with a splash of Cognac. Spread a layer of game forcemeat over the whole, shaping it into a dome, then top with thin rashers (slices) of fat bacon. Cover with pastry and seal the edges to form a crimped ridge then garnish the top of the pie with pastry shapes. Make a small hole in the pastry lid for steam to escape. Bake in a preheated oven at 180°C (350°F, gas 4) for 1¼ hours. Allow to cool thoroughly before turning out of the mould. Serve on a dish covered with a napkin.

# Cold woodcock à la Diane

Roast the woodcock until rare and slice the meat. Pound the intestines with a knob of foie gras, a knob of butter, nutmeg and brandy. Sieve and season well. Reshape the sliced flesh around the intestine mixture, arranging it on large slices of raw truffle marinated in brandy to resemble a woodcock, and coat with a firm game aspic. Chill well in the refrigerator before serving.

# Hot woodcock pâté à la perigourdine

Bone 2 woodcocks, spread out the birds on a table, and fill with the stuffing in the recipe for woodcock casserole *à la perigourdine*. Roll up the woodcocks to enclose the stuffing and wrap each one separately in muslin (cheesecloth). Poach for 12 minutes in a Madeira braising stock prepared with the carcass and trimmings. Drain and allow to cool. Unwrap when cold.

Meanwhile, prepare a fine forcemeat composed of two-thirds game forcemeat and one-third veal forcemeat. Line the bottom and sides of an oval pâté mould with a thin layer of shortcrust pastry (basic pie dough) and spread the forcemeat over this. Place the ballotines side by side in the mould. Cover with 10 slices of foie gras fried in butter and 20 slices of truffle. Cover with the remaining forcemeat. Cover the pâté with a layer of pastry and seal and trim the edges. Make a hole in the pastry lid for the steam to escape. Garnish with shaped pastry trimmings and brush with egg. Place the pâté on a baking sheet and bake in a preheated oven at 180°C (350°F, gas 4) for 1¼ hours. Just before serving, pour a few tablespoons of Perigueux sauce into the pâté through the hole in the lid.

## Roast woodcock on toast

Truss the woodcock, bard, tie up with string and roast on a spit or in a preheated oven about 240°C (475°F, gas 9) for 18–20 minutes. Prepare a toast canapé as for casserole of woodcock and serve the woodcock on top of the canapé. The dish may be garnished with large peeled grapes.

## Sautéed woodcock in Armagnac

Cut the woodcock into pieces. Use the carcass and the trimmings to prepare a fumet and add rich demi-glace. Put the pieces of woodcock in a sauté pan just big enough to hold them and brown briskly in butter. Cover the pan and simmer for 8 minutes. Drain the pieces, arrange in a timbale or in a shallow dish and keep hot. Dilute the pan juices with 2 tablespoons Armagnac, add the strained concentrated woodcock fumet and boil for a few moments. Thicken this sauce with the chopped intestines, season with a small pinch of cayenne and add 1 teaspoon butter and a dash of lemon juice. Strain the sauce and pour it over the woodcock while it is piping hot.

## Truffled roast woodcock

Mix chicken forcemeat and finely diced truffles tossed in butter and use to stuff the woodcock. Insert a few slices of truffle between the skin and the flesh of the bird. Truss the bird, cover and leave in a cool place for 48 hours. Wrap the woodcock in buttered greaseproof (wax) paper and tie up with string. Cook in a preheated oven at about 240°C (475°F, gas 9) for 18–20 minutes.

Meanwhile, prepare the toast canapé as for casserole of woodcock. Serve the truffled woodcock on the toast. Deglaze the cooking pan with a splash of Cognac or Armagnac and pour over the bird.

## Woodcock à la Riche

Prepare à gratin forcemeat. Truss a woodcock and roast it in a preheated oven at 240°C (475°F, gas 9) for 10–12 minutes. Cut a slice of white bread large enough to hold the woodcock, fry until golden, then spread it thickly with the forcemeat. Warm a liqueur glass of Cognac, set it alight and pour immediately into the pan in which the woodcock was roasted to deglaze it. Add a purée consisting of 25 g (1 oz, 2 tablespoons) foie gras pounded with the same amount of butter, and mix with the pan juices until the sauce is quite smooth. Place the woodcock on the fried bread and pour over the sauce.

## Woodcock casserole à la perigourdine

Fill the woodcock with a stuffing made from the chopped intestines, diced foie gras, truffle, allspice and a dash of Armagnac. Truss the bird, brown in butter in a flameproof casserole, season, add 2 tablespoons Armagnac, cover and cook in a preheated oven at 240°C (475°F, gas 9) for 15–18 minutes. Remove the woodcock from the casserole and deglaze the dish with a little game or chicken stock. Reheat and serve the woodcock in the casserole. Very small peeled truffles may be cooked with this dish.

## Woodcock pâté (cold)

Prepare about 575 g (1¼ lb) game forcemeat *à gratin*. Remove the wings from 2 large woodcocks, season with salt and pepper and roast for about 10 minutes in a preheated oven at 230°C (450°F, gas 8) – they should still be very pink. Remove the flesh from the thighs and carcass and mince (grind) in a food processor with the liver and intestines. Add this minced (ground) meat to the forcemeat and adjust the seasoning.

Line an oval pâté mould with butter pastry. Coat the bottom and sides of the mould with a layer of forcemeat, then add the 4 wings. Cover with thick slices of truffle lightly fried in butter, spread the remaining forcemeat on top and cover with pastry. Pinch all round to seal.

Glaze the top with egg and garnish with shapes cut out from leftover pastry (rolled out thinly). Make a hole in the centre and insert a small smooth metal piping nozzle. Glaze the top again. and bake in a preheated oven at 190°C (375°F, gas 5) for about 1½ hours. Leave to cool completely, then pour in some chicken aspic through the 'chimney'. Keep the pâté cool.

## Woodcock salmi

A salmi is a stew made of woodcock, wild pheasant or partridge but domestic duck, pigeon or guinea fowl are also used. Pluck and singe 2 woodcock; truss and roast in a preheated oven at 220°C (425°F, gas 7) until two-thirds cooked.

Melt 50 g (2 oz, ¼ cup) butter in a sauté pan and add a carrot and an onion (both diced), a pinch of dried thyme and a pinch of powdered bay leaf. Cover and cook gently for 15 minutes. Then add a generous pinch of pepper and remove from the heat. Divide each woodcock into 4 joints, then skin them and arrange in a shallow heatproof serving dish; cover and keep warm.

Chop the skin and crush the bones of the carcasses; add to the diced vegetables, together with the roasting juices. Mix well with a wooden spoon for 4–5 minutes over a gentle heat. Then moisten with 200 ml (7 fl oz, ¾ cup) dry white wine and 400 ml (14 fl oz, 1¾ cups) thickened brown veal stock. Bring to the boil and cook gently for 15 minutes.

Meanwhile, clean 150 g (5 oz, 1⅔ cups) small button mushrooms and cook, covered, in the juice of ½ lemon, 2 tablespoons water and a pinch of salt, for 10 minutes. Drain and spoon the mushrooms over the woodcock, then flame with 2 tablespoons warmed brandy. Continue to keep warm.

Strain the sauce through a fine sieve, pressing the bones hard against the sides. Thicken with 1 tablespoon beurre manié, boil, then pour over the meat. Garnish with triangles of bread fried in butter.

## Woodcock soufflé with chestnuts

Pluck, singe and draw 2 woodcock. Remove the drumsticks and seal quickly in butter; bone them and cut the flesh into small dice. Thinly slice the white meat of the wings and breast, seize (brown) in butter and leave to cool.

To make the sauce, prepare and cut into small dice 1 small carrot, 1 small onion and 1 thinly sliced celery stick. Put these vegetables into a saucepan with 25 g (1 oz, 2 tablespoons) butter and the small bones and intestines of the woodcock. Fry together, flame with 1½ tablespoons brandy, then add some brown stock and a bouquet garni and boil gently, skimming several times. After cooking for 2 hours, strain the sauce through some muslin (cheesecloth), return to the boil, skim and strain once again. Keep warm.

Peel and steam 675 g (1½ lb) chestnuts, then purée in a food processor. Blend in 6 egg yolks, 50 g (2 oz, ¼ cup) butter, salt, pepper, a pinch of cayenne and the diced woodcock. Stiffly whisk 6 egg whites and fold them in. Butter a 20 cm (8 in) soufflé mould and pour this mixture into it, layering it with the slices of white meat. Finish with a layer of soufflé mixture. Bake in a preheated oven at 200°C (400°F, gas 6) for about 30 minutes. Serve with the sauce.

# Frogs
# &
# snails

# Frogs

## Frogs, to prepare

Skin the frogs by slitting the skin at the neck and pulling it back. Cut the backbone so that the legs are still joined to it and can be cooked in pairs. Cut off the feet. Skewer the legs and soak in very cold water. Change the water 3 or 4 times over 12 hours, so the flesh whitens and swells. Dry the legs and cook them according to the recipe; usually 3 pairs per serving are allowed.

## Brochettes of frogs' legs

Marinate the frogs' legs for at least 2 hours in a mixture of olive oil, lemon juice, grated garlic, finely chopped parsley and a pinch each of cayenne pepper, powdered bay leaf, salt and pepper. Drain, dry and thread the legs on to skewers. Fry for 7–10 minutes in the marinade oil, or grill (broil) gently for 15–20 minutes. Test with a fork to see if they are cooked. Sprinkle with chopped parsley and serve very hot, garnished with lemon slices.

## Fried frogs' legs

Season the prepared frogs' legs with salt and pepper and dip them in flour (or in egg and breadcrumbs). Sauté them in butter or olive oil in a shallow frying pan for 7–10 minutes over a brisk heat. Drain and arrange in a warm serving dish. Sprinkle with chopped parsley and lemon juice. If the frogs' legs were cooked in butter, pour it over them; otherwise use maître d'hôtel butter.

## Frogs' legs à la lyonnaise

Prepare the frogs' legs and sauté them in butter as for fried frogs' legs. Add 2 tablespoons finely chopped onion to the frying pan and brown the ingredients. (A finely chopped shallot may be added to the onions.) Arrange on a heated serving dish and sprinkle with chopped parsley and vinegar.

## Frogs' legs à la meunière

Prepare the frogs' legs, season with salt and pepper and dip them in flour. Sauté them in butter for 7–10 minutes over a brisk heat. Place in a timbale dish and sprinkle with chopped parsley. Keep hot. Heat some butter in the sauté pan until it turns brown; add the juice of ½ lemon and, if necessary, a little fresh butter. Pour this over the frogs' legs and serve immediately.

## Frogs'-leg fritots

Trim the frogs' legs and marinate them for 30 minutes in a mixture of oil, chopped garlic, chopped parsley, lemon juice, salt and pepper. Then dip them in a light batter and deep-fry until they are golden brown. Drain on paper towels and serve with fried parsley, quarters of lemon and either curry sauce or gribiche sauce. The frogs' legs can also be threaded on to small skewers before being dipped in the batter and fried.

## Frogs' legs with garlic purée and parsley juice

Remove the stalks from 100 g (4 oz, 2 cups) parsley and wash. Cook for 3 minutes in boiling water, allow to cool, then purée in a food processor or blender. Separate 4 heads of garlic into cloves and poach them for 2 minutes in salted boiling water. Remove the garlic cloves from the water, peel and return to the boiling water to cook for another 7–8 minutes or until the garlic is soft. Purée the garlic in a food processor or blender and put it into a saucepan with 500 ml (17 fl oz, 2 cups) milk. Season with salt and pepper. Season the frogs' legs with salt and pepper. Heat some olive oil and a knob of butter and fry the frogs' legs for 2–3 minutes until golden. Heat the parsley purée with 100 ml (4 fl oz, 7 tablespoons) water. Drain the frogs' legs on paper towels. Pour the parsley sauce into a warm serving dish. Arrange the garlic purée in the middle and surround with the frogs' legs.

## Gratin savoyard of frogs' legs

Allow 12 pairs of frogs' legs per person. Trim them, season with salt and pepper, dip in milk and then lightly flour. Fry in butter with shallots and a little chopped garlic, then drain and arrange them in a fairly large baking dish. Dilute the pan juices with Mandement wine (from the Côte de Mandement on the right bank of the Rhône, in the canton of Geneva) or with a fruity white wine; reduce and pour over the frogs' legs. Sprinkle with chopped chives and parsley, then squeeze the juice of 1 lemon over them. Mix together 250 ml (8 fl oz, 1 cup) double (heavy) cream, 75 g (3 oz, ¾ cup) grated Gruyère cheese and 2 egg yolks. Season with salt and pepper and pour over the frogs' legs. Brown under the grill (broiler) and serve garnished with a few fluted slices of lemon.

# Snails

## Snails, to prepare

Snails collected from the wild need to be starved for about 10 days to ensure they are rid of any poisonous leaves they may have eaten. (In Provence, instead of fasting, they are put on a diet of thyme, which helps the snails to eliminate poisonous material and also flavours their flesh.) Some authorities recommend that snails should not be purged with salt, because that risks spoiling their gastronomic quality. If they are purged, a small handful of coarse salt is required for 48 large snails, together with 5 tablespoons vinegar and a pinch of flour. Cover the vessel containing the snails and place a weight on top: leave to soak for 3 hours, stirring from time to time. Next, wash the snails in several changes of water to remove all the mucus, then blanch them for 5 minutes in boiling water. Drain the snails and rinse thoroughly in fresh water. Shell them and take out the black part (cloaca) at the end of the 'tail', but do not remove the mantle, comprising the liver and other organs, which represents a quarter of the total weight of the animal and is the most delicious and nutritious part.

Cultivated snails do not require the purification period but should be used on the day of purchase.

## Butter for snails

Finely chop 40 g (1½ oz) shallots and enough parsley to fill 1 tablespoon. Crush 2 garlic cloves. Add all these ingredients to 350 g (12 oz, 1½ cups) softened butter, 1 tablespoon salt and a good pinch of pepper. Mix well. (This quantity is sufficient to fill about 50 snail shells.)

## Escargots à l'arlésienne

Take some medium-sized snails, stand them in tepid water to remove the impurities and then blanch with a handful of salt. Remove them from their shells and drain. Put a little diced bacon into a saucepan, sprinkle with flour, moisten with dry white wine and add the snails, together with some garlic and plenty of herbs. Bring to the boil and cook gently for about 10 minutes. When the snails are cooked, drain and replace in their shells. Make a sauce with a glass of Madeira, a pinch of cayenne pepper and the juice of a lemon. Pour the sauce over the snails and sprinkle with chopped parsley.

## Snail broth

(from an ancient recipe) Prepare 36 snails. Shell them and put them in a saucepan containing 3 litres (5 pints, 13 cups) water. Add 400 g (14 oz) calf's head, 1 lettuce (cleaned and quartered), a handful of purslane leaves and a little salt. Heat, then skim. Bring to the boil, then reduce the heat and simmer for about 2 hours. Adjust the seasoning and strain.

## Snails à la bourguignonne

Put the shelled snails in a saucepan and cover them with a mixture of equal parts of white wine and stock. Add 1 tablespoon chopped shallot, 15 g (½ oz) onion and 75 g (3 oz) carrot per 1 litre (1¾ pints, 4⅓ cups) liquid and 1 large bouquet garni. Add salt, allowing 1 teaspoon per 1 litre (1¾ pints, 4⅓ cups).

Simmer for about 2 hours, then leave to cool in the cooking liquid. Meanwhile, boil the empty shells in water containing 1 tablespoon soda crystals per 1 litre (1¾ pints, 4⅓ cups). Drain them, wash in plenty of water and dry in the oven, without letting them colour. Prepare some butter for snails; at least 50 g (2 oz, ¼ cup) is required for 12 snails. Remove the snails from the cooking liquid. Place a little butter in the bottom of each shell, insert a snail and fill up the shell with more butter. Arrange in snail dishes and heat without letting the butter brown. Serve piping hot.

## Snails à la poulette

Cook 48 shelled snails as for snails *à la bourguignonne*, then drain. Prepare a white roux using 25 g (1 oz, 2 tablespoons) butter and 25 g (1 oz, ¼ cup) plain (all-purpose) flour. Add 250 ml (8 fl oz, 1 cup) chicken stock, 250 ml (8 fl oz, 1 cup) white wine and 1 bouquet garni. Cook briskly for about 15 minutes, or until the sauce is reduced by a third. Soften 1 large chopped onion in 20 g (¾ oz, 1½ tablespoons) butter in a saucepan. Add the snails and the sauce and cook for 5 minutes.

Meanwhile, mix 2 egg yolks and the juice of 1 lemon; chop a small bunch of parsley. Remove the bouquet garni from the saucepan. Blend a little of the hot sauce with the egg yolks and lemon juice, then add to the pan. Stir briskly and remove from the heat. Sprinkle with chopped parsley and serve hot.

## Snail feuilletés

Prepare about 500 g (1 lb 2 oz) puff pastry made with butter and roll it out to a thickness of about 3 mm (⅛ in). Cut out 8 rectangles measuring 14 × 9 cm (5½ × 3½ in). Arrange them on a baking sheet, cover loosely and leave them to stand for 30 minutes.

Prepare the garnish as follows. Finely chop 125 g (4½ oz, 1 cup) shelled pistachios. Cook 96 snails *à la bourguignonne*, but use champagne instead of white wine. Drain the snails, roll in flour and sauté in 4 tablespoons oil and 40 g (1½ oz, 3 tablespoons) butter. Add a dash of cayenne pepper, then a small glass of whisky, and flame, tilting the sauté pan in all directions. Then add 500 ml (17 fl oz, 2 cups) double (heavy) cream and heat to reduce, making sure the cream is oily but not curdled.

Brush the top of the rectangles of pastry with egg and make criss-cross patterns on them with the tip of a knife. Bake them in a preheated oven at 230°C (450°F, gas 8) for about 20 minutes (the feuilletés rise while baking). Add the chopped pistachios to the sauce and heat for 2–3 minutes. When the feuilletés are cooked, split them in two. Arrange the snails and some sauce on the bottom half of each feuilleté, replace the top halves and serve very hot. If any sauce remains, serve it separately.

## Snails grilled à la mode du Languedoc

Arrange some shelled snails on a grid (grill). Prepare a fire of vine shoots; as soon as the embers form a light ash, place the grid on top, sprinkle the snails with salt, pepper, thyme and crushed fennel and grill. Meanwhile, cook some diced fatty bacon in a frying pan until soft. Tip the cooked snails into a dish and baste with the sizzling bacon fat. Serve immediately with farmhouse bread and red wine.

# Basic recipes & classic additions

# Batters

## Coating batter

This batter is suitable for coating food before deep-frying. Sift 200 g (7 oz, 1¾ cups) plain (all-purpose) flour into a bowl. Add 2 teaspoons baking powder, 2 tablespoons groundnut (peanut) oil, a pinch of salt and 250 ml (8 fl oz, 1 cup) warm water. Mix the ingredients thoroughly and beat until smooth, then leave the batter to rest in a cool place for at least 1 hour. Just before using, fold in 2 stiffly whisked egg whites.

## Fritter batter (1)

Sift 250 g (9 oz, 2¼ cups) plain (all-purpose) flour into a bowl. Heat 200 ml (7 fl oz, ¾ cup) water until just lukewarm. Make a well in the middle and add 150 ml (¼ pint, ⅔ cup) beer, the warm water and a generous pinch of salt. Mix, drawing the flour from the sides to the centre of the well. Add 2 tablespoons groundnut (peanut) oil and mix. Leave to rest for 1 hour if possible. When required for use, stiffly whisk 2 or 3 egg whites and fold into the batter. Do not stir or beat. For sweet fritters, flavour the batter with Calvados, Cognac or rum. The batter may also be sweetened with 1½ teaspoons sugar and the oil replaced with the same amount of melted butter.

## Fritter batter (2)

Put 250 g (9 oz, 2¼ cups) sifted plain (all-purpose) flour in a mixing bowl. Make a well in the centre and add 1 teaspoon salt, 2 eggs and 300 ml (½ pint, 1¼ cups) groundnut (peanut) oil. Whisk the eggs and oil together, incorporating a little of the flour. Add 250 ml (8 fl oz, 1 cup) beer and, stirring well, gradually incorporate the rest of the flour. Allow to stand for about 1 hour. A few minutes before using the batter, whisk 3 egg whites stiffly and fold into the batter using a wooden spoon or rubber spatula.

## Savoury crêpe batter

Mix 500 g (18 oz, 4½ cups) plain (all-purpose) flour with 5–6 beaten eggs and a large pinch of salt. Then gradually add 1 litre (1¾ pints, 4⅓ cups) milk or, for lighter pancakes, 500 ml (17 fl oz, 2 cups) milk and 500 ml (17 fl oz, 2 cups) water. The batter may also be made with equal quantities of beer and milk, or the milk may be replaced by white consommé. Finally, add 3 tablespoons oil, either one with little taste, such as groundnut (peanut) oil or sunflower oil or, if the recipe requires it, use olive oil; 25 g (1 oz, 2 tablespoons) melted butter may also be added. Leave the batter to stand for 2 hours. Just before making the crêpes, dilute the batter with a little water (100–200 ml, 4–7 fl oz, ½–¾ cup).

# Butters

## Butters, to prepare

Whatever the ingredients, the butter must first be creamed, using a spoon or (for large quantities) an electric mixer. The following recipes give ingredients to flavour 225 g (8 oz, 1 cup) butter.

## Anchovy butter

Soak 100 g (4 oz) canned or bottled salted anchovies to remove the salt. Purée the fillets in a blender, season and, if liked, add a dash of lemon juice. Work into the softened butter. This butter is used for vol-au-vents, canapés and hors d'oeuvres and to accompany grilled (broiled) meat or cold white meat.

## Bercy butter or shallot butter for meat

Poach 500 g (18 oz) diced beef marrow in salted water and drain. Cook 1 tablespoon chopped shallots in 1 tablespoon butter in a saucepan without browning. Add 200 ml (7 fl oz, ¾ cup) dry white wine and heat gently. Soften 200 g (7 oz, ¾ cup) butter and add to the pan with the marrow, 1 tablespoon chopped parsley, the juice of ½ lemon, salt and pepper. This butter is poured on top of grilled (broiled) meat or may be served separately in a sauceboat.

## Chivry butter

Blanch 150 g (5 oz, 2 cups) mixed parsley, tarragon, chervil, chives and, if possible, salad burnet, and 2 tablespoons chopped shallot for 3 minutes in boiling water. Drain, cool in cold water and wipe dry. Chop very finely, add 200 g (7 oz, ¾ cup) butter, salt and pepper and press through a fine sieve.

## Green butter

Wring 1 kg (2¼ lb) raw crushed spinach in muslin (cheesecloth) until all the juice is extracted. Pour this juice into a dish and cook in a bain marie until separated, then filter through another cloth. Scrape off the green deposit left on this cloth and work it into the softened butter. This butter is used to garnish hors d'oeuvres and cold dishes.

## Lemon butter

Blanch the zest of a lemon, chop as finely as possible and work it into the softened butter in a blender with a dash of lemon juice, salt and pepper. This butter is used to garnish cold hors d'oeuvres.

## Maître d'hotel butter

Work 2 tablespoons finely chopped parsley, 1–2 dashes lemon juice and a pinch of salt into the softened butter. This butter is served with grilled (broiled) fish, fish fried in an egg-and-breadcrumb coating, poultry or meat and various steamed or boiled vegetables.

## Marchand de vin butter

Add 25 g (1 oz, ¼ cup) finely chopped shallots to 300 ml (½ pint, 1¼ cups) red wine and reduce by half. Add 300 ml (½ pint, 1¼ cups) beef consommé and reduce further until almost dry. Cream 150 g (5 oz, ⅔ cup) butter and mix it with the reduced wine mixture. Add 1 tablespoon finely chopped parsley and a little lemon juice and season with salt and pepper. Chill well.

## Noisette butter

Butter heated until it becomes nut brown; it is used to add a finishing touch to a variety of dishes, particularly fish.

## Sardine butter

Sardine butter is prepared in the same way as anchovy butter, using the filleted and skinned canned fish.

# Condiments & seasonings

## Apple compote

Prepare a syrup using 350 g (12 oz, 1½ cups) granulated sugar to 600 ml (1 pint, 2½ cups) water. Peel the apples, cut them into quarters, remove the pips (seeds) and cover them with lemon juice to prevent them from browning. Boil the syrup, add the apples and remove as soon as they are tender. Serve either warm or cold.

## Cherry syrup

Reduce some stoned (pitted) cherries to a purée in a food processor or blender. Strain the purée through a very fine sieve and leave the juice to ferment, covered, at room temperature for at least 24 hours. Decant and filter the juice. Add 1.5 kg (3¼ lb, 6½ cups) granulated sugar per 1 litre (1¾ pints, 4⅓ cups) of cherry juice and leave to dissolve. Transfer the sweetened juice to a saucepan, bring to the boil and strain. Store in bottles with airtight seals and keep in a cool place away from the light.

## Cranberry compote

Combine 500 g (18 oz, 2¼ cups) caster (superfine) sugar, the grated zest of ½ lemon and 200 ml (7 fl oz, ¾ cup) water in a saucepan; slowly bring to the boil, then boil for 5 minutes. Add 1 kg (2¼ lb) washed and stalked cranberries and cook over a high heat for 10 minutes. Remove the fruit from the liquid with a perforated spoon and place in a fruit dish. Reduce the syrup by one-third if the compote is to be eaten straight away, or by half if it is to be kept for a few days in the refrigerator. Pour the syrup over the fruit and allow to cool for 1 hour. Serve with vanilla-flavoured meringues.

## Curry powder

This is a useful general spice mixture and enough for seasoning 600–900 ml (1–1½ pints, 2½–3¾ cups) sauce or a dish to yield 4–6 portions, depending on the ingredients. Place 1 cinnamon stick, 4 cloves, 4 green cardamoms, 2 tablespoons cumin seeds and 4 tablespoons coriander seeds in a small saucepan. Roast the spices gently, shaking the pan frequently, until they are just aromatic. Remove the spices from the pan and allow to cool, then grind them to a powder in a spice grinder or in a mortar with a pestle. Stir in 2 teaspoons ground fenugreek, ½ teaspoon ground turmeric and ½ teaspoon chilli powder.

## Peach compote

Prepare a vanilla-flavoured syrup using the same proportions of sugar and water as for apple compote. Plunge the peaches in boiling water for about 30 seconds and cool them under cold running water. It should then be easy to peel them. Either leave them whole or cut them in half and remove the stones (pits). Poach the peaches in boiling syrup for 18 minutes if they are whole or for 13 minutes if they are halved.

# Preserved lemons

Wash 1 kg (2¼ lb) untreated lemons, wipe and cut into thick round slices. (Small lemons can simply be quartered lengthways.) Dust with 3 tablespoons fine salt and leave them to discharge their juices for about 12 hours. Drain them, place in a large jar and cover completely with olive oil. Leave in a cool place for 1 month before use. Close the jar firmly after opening and keep in a cool place away from light.

# Quatre épices or four spices

A mixture of spices, usually consisting of ground white pepper, grated nutmeg, powdered cloves and ground ginger or cinnamon. It is used in stews, *civets*, charcuterie, terrines and game dishes and is also found in Middle Eastern and Arab cookery.

# Raspberry jelly

This is made with equal quantities of redcurrants and raspberries. Pour the redcurrants into a pan and add 120 ml (4½ fl oz, ½ cup) water per 1 kg (2¼ lb) fruit. Boil until the berries soften and the juice comes out. Leave to cool, then place the redcurrants and raspberries in a cloth over a bowl and twist the cloth to extract the juice (for a very clear jelly, pour the fruit into a jelly bag and leave to drip overnight). Pour the juice into a pan, add 1 kg (2¼ lb, 4½ cups, firmly packed) sugar per 1 litre (1¾ pints, 4⅓ cups) fruit juice, and boil quickly until setting point is reached. Remove from the heat and pour immediately into clean, sterilized jars. Cover, seal and label.

# Redcurrant jelly (1)

Use either all redcurrants or two-thirds redcurrants and one-third white currants. Weigh 100 g (4⅔ oz) raspberries for each 1 kg (2¼ lb) currants.

Crush the currants and raspberries together and strain them through a cloth which is wrung at both ends. Measure the juice. Allow 1 kg (2¼ lb, 4½ cups) granulated sugar for each 1 litre (1¾ pints, 4⅓ cups) fruit juice. Heat the sugar in a pan with a little water – just enough in which to dissolve the sugar. Add the fruit juice and cook until setting point is reached, then pot and cover as usual.

## Redcurrant jelly (2)

Put the prepared and weighed currants in a pan, add a small glass of water for each 1 kg (2¼ lb) currants, then heat them gently until the skins burst and the juices come out. Add raspberries (the same proportion as in the previous recipe) and boil for a few seconds only. Strain the fruit and filter the juice. Continue as described above.

## Spiced salt

A mixture of dry table salt, ground white pepper and mixed spices in the proportions 10 : 1:1. It is used to season forcemeats, pies and terrines.

# Forcemeats, panadas, sausagemeats & stuffings

## Forcemeats, to prepare

Forcemeats are usually more refined and complex than stuffings. The ingredients for some forcemeats need to be very finely minced or even ground in a mortar or food processor and then forced through a sieve. Fine forcemeats need to be minced (ground) twice. Sometimes only some of the ingredients need to be minced. Season to taste and add 6 tablespoons brandy per 1 kg (2¼ lb) forcemeat. Allow 1 large egg to bind 450 g (1 lb) forcemeat.

## Sausagemeat, to prepare

Sausagemeat is a mixture of equal parts of lean pork and pork fat finely chopped and salted. All sinews and gristle must be removed. A range of other meats and seasonings may be used to make sausages.

## À gratin forcemeat

Fry 150 g (5 oz, 1 cup) finely chopped unsmoked bacon until cooked but not browned. Add 300 g (11 oz) chicken livers, 2 thinly sliced shallots, 50 g (2 oz, ⅔ cup) finely chopped mushrooms, ½ bay leaf and a thyme sprig. Season with salt, pepper and a little mixed spice and sauté quickly over a high heat. Allow to cool completely, then pound in a mortar (or purée in a blender) and press through a fine sieve. Cover with oiled greaseproof (wax) paper and chill until needed. This forcemeat is spread on the croûtons of fried bread that are used as a base for small roast game birds or served with salmis or *civets*.

## American stuffing

Cut some smoked belly of pork into very small dice and fry. Add some finely chopped onion and allow to sweat without colouring. Remove from the heat and add fresh breadcrumbs until the fat is completely absorbed. Season with salt and pepper, a little ground sage and the finest thyme. This forcemeat is used for stuffing young cockerels, young pigeons, guinea fowls and poussins.

## Chicken forcemeat

Dice 575 g (1¼ lb) chicken or other poultry meat, 200 g (7 oz) lean veal and 900 g (2 lb) bacon; work together in a blender until smooth. Add 3 eggs, 1 tablespoon salt and 200 ml (7 fl oz, ¾ cup) brandy. Mix well, press through a sieve and chill until required. This forcemeat is used for pâtés and terrines.

## Fine sausagemeat or fine pork forcemeat

Using the same mixture as for the sausagemeat recipe, finely mince (grind) the ingredients twice, or chop once and then press through a fine sieve. The seasonings are the same.

## Foie gras forcemeat

Finely pound in a mortar (or purée in a blender) 375 g (13 oz) lean pork, 450 g (1 lb) unsmoked streaky (slab) bacon and 250 g (9 oz) thinly sliced foie gras. Add 1½ teaspoons spiced salt and 100 ml (4 fl oz, 7 tablespoons) brandy, and press through a sieve. This forcemeat is used for making pâtés and terrines.

## Forcemeat for poultry

This consists of fine sausagemeat mixed with one-fifth of its weight each of fresh breadcrumbs and finely chopped onion cooked in a little butter until soft, together with chopped parsley. Chill until required.

## Game forcemeat

Prepare with the appropriate game meat in the same way as poultry force-meat. To make it richer, add thin slices of fresh foie gras or game liver forcemeat. This forcemeat is used for making pâtés and terrines.

## Godiveau lyonnais

The delicate forcemeat, consisting of veal and fat, is used to make quenelles, which are served as a hot entrée, used to fill vol-au-vent or to accompany meat dishes. The mixture, which must be very smooth, springy and yet firm, requires quite a long preparation time, because the raw meat and fat are pounded with cream or panada, eggs and seasoning.

Pound together in a mortar 500 g (18 oz) trimmed diced beef suet, 500 g (18 oz) frangipane panada and 4 egg whites (these ingredients may first be put through a blender). Add 500 g (18 oz) pike flesh and season with salt and pepper. Work vigorously with a spatula, then with a pestle. Rub through a fine sieve, place in an earthenware dish and work with a spatula until smooth.

## Godiveau with cream

Chop up 1 kg (2¼ lb) fillet of veal and pound it. Also chop up and pound 1 kg (2¼ lb) beef suet. Mix these ingredients together and add 1 tablespoon salt, ¼ teaspoon pepper, a pinch of grated nutmeg, 4 eggs and 3 egg yolks, grinding vigorously with a pestle the whole time. Rub the forcemeat through a fine sieve and spread it on a board. Leave on ice or in the refrigerator until the next day. Put the forcemeat back in the mortar and pound it again, gradually adding 750 ml (1¼ pints, 3¼ cups) single (light) cream.

To test the consistency of the godiveau, poach a small ball and rectify if necessary, adding a little iced water if it is too firm or a little egg white if it is too light. Shape into quenelles and poach.

## Liver forcemeat

Brown 250 g (9 oz, 12 slices) diced unsmoked streaky (slab) bacon in 25 g (1 oz, 2 tablespoons) butter in a sauté pan. Remove and drain. In the same fat, sauté 300 g (11 oz) pig's (pork), calf's, game or chicken liver cut into cubes. Mix 40 g (1½ oz, ¼ cup) finely chopped shallots and 75 g (3 oz, 1 cup) finely chopped cultivated mushrooms together. Replace the bacon in the sauté pan, add the mushrooms and shallots and season with salt, ground white pepper and allspice; then add a sprig of thyme and half a bay leaf. Mix together and sauté for 2 minutes.

Remove the cubes of liver. Deglaze the pan with 150 ml (¼ pint, ⅔ cup) dry white wine, pour the sauce over the cubes of liver and purée all the ingredients in a food processor or blender, together with 65 g (2½ oz, 5 tablespoons) butter and 3 egg yolks, until very smooth. Press the forcemeat through a sieve and store, covered, in the refrigerator. This forcemeat is used for making pâtés, terrines or meat loaves. Minced, cleaned truffle peelings can be added to it if wished. If game liver is used, add an equal amount of rabbit meat and replace the white wine with 100 ml (4 fl oz, 7 tablespoons) Madeira.

## Mousseline forcemeat

Pound 1 kg (2¼ lb) boned veal, poultry or game in a mortar (or purée in a blender) then press through a fine sieve. Whisk 4 egg whites lightly with a fork and add them to the meat purée a little at a time. Season with 4 teaspoons salt and a generous pinch of ground white pepper. Press through the sieve a second time, place in a terrine, then chill for 2 hours. Put the terrine in a bowl of crushed ice and work in 1.5 litres (2¾ pints, 6½ cups) double (heavy) cream using a wooden spoon. (It is essential to keep the cream and the pâté as cold as possible to prevent the mixture from curdling.) This forcemeat is used for fine quenelles, mousses and mousselines.

## Mushroom forcemeat

Sauté 2 peeled and finely chopped shallots and 175 g (6 oz, 2 cups) button mushrooms, also finely chopped, over a high heat in a frying pan, with 40 g (1½ oz, 3 tablespoons) butter and a generous pinch of grated nutmeg. When cooked, allow to cool. Make 100 g (4 oz) bread panada and purée it in a blender, adding the mushrooms and shallots. Finally, add 3 egg yolks and mix thoroughly (it is not necessary to sieve this forcemeat). It is used to stuff vegetables, poultry, game and fish.

## Panada, to prepare

A paste of variable composition used to bind and thicken forcemeats. A flour panada is used to thicken quenelle forcemeats; the flour is added all at once to boiling salted and buttered water, and the mixture is beaten well over the heat until it thickens (as for a choux paste). A frangipane panada (made with flour and egg yolks) is used for poultry and fish forcemeats; bread panada for fish forcemeats; potato panada for quenelles of white meat; and rice panada for various forcemeats.

## Panada, bread

Soak 250 g (9 oz, 4½ cups) fresh white breadcrumbs in 300 ml (½ pint, 1¼ cups) boiled milk until the liquid is completely absorbed. Pour this mixture into a saucepan and let it thicken over the heat, stirring it with a wooden spoon. Pour into a buttered dish and leave to cool.

## Panada, flour

Place 300 ml (½ pint, 1¼ cups) water, 50 g (2 oz, ¼ cup) butter and ½ teaspoon salt in a saucepan and bring to the boil. Add 150 g (5 oz, 1¼ cups) plain (all-purpose) flour, beat well over the heat with a wooden spoon, then cook until the mixture comes away from the edges of the saucepan. Pour the panada into a buttered dish, smooth the surface, cover with buttered paper and leave to cool.

## Panada forcemeat with butter

Purée 1 kg (2¼ lb) minced (ground) veal or poultry in a blender with salt, ground white pepper and grated nutmeg. Also blend 450 g (1 lb) potato or flour panada with an equal quantity of butter. Add the puréed meat and beat the mixture vigorously. Then add 8 egg yolks, one at a time. Press the forcemeat through a fine sieve, place in a terrine and work with a spatula until smooth. Chill, covered, until required. This forcemeat is used for quenelles, borders and meat loaves, and to stuff poultry and joints of meat.

## Panada forcemeat with cream

Pound 1 kg (2¼ lb) minced (ground) veal or poultry in a mortar (or reduce to a purée in a blender). Season with 2 teaspoons salt, a generous pinch of white pepper and some grated nutmeg. Add 4 lightly whisked egg whites one at a time, followed by 400 g (14 oz) bread panada. Beat vigorously until the mixture is very smooth. Press through a fine sieve over a terrine and chill for 1 hour, together with 1.5 litres (2¾ pints, 6½ cups) double (heavy) cream and 2 tablespoons milk. Then place the terrine in a basin of crushed ice or ice cubes. Add one-third of the cream to the forcemeat, working it in vigorously with a spatula. Lightly beat the remaining cream with the milk and then fold it into the forcemeat. Chill until needed. This forcemeat is used for quenelles.

## Panada, frangipane

Put 125 g (4½ oz, 1¼ cups) plain (all-purpose) flour and 4 egg yolks in a saucepan. Mix well, then add 90 g (3½ oz, ⅓ cup) melted butter, ½ teaspoon salt, some pepper and a pinch of nutmeg. Thin the mixture by blending it with 250 ml (8 fl oz, 1 cup) boiled milk, poured in gradually. Cook for 5–6 minutes, beating vigorously with a whisk. Pour the panada into a buttered dish, smooth the surface, cover with buttered paper and leave to cool.

## Panada, potato

Boil 300 ml (½ pint, 1¼ cups) milk seasoned with ½ teaspoon salt, a pinch of pepper and a pinch of grated nutmeg until it has reduced by one-sixth. Add 20 g (¾ oz, 1½ tablespoons) butter and 250 g (9 oz, 1¼ cups) thinly sliced boiled potatoes. Cook gently for 15 minutes, then mix well to obtain a smooth paste. Use this panada while still warm.

## Panada, rice

Add 200 g (7 oz, 1 cup) short-grain rice to 600 ml (1 pint, 2½ cups) white unclarified consommé to which 20 g (¾ oz, 1½ tablespoons) butter has been added and cook in a preheated oven at 160°C (325°F, gas 3) for about 50 minutes. Mix the cooked rice well with a wooden spoon to obtain a smooth paste. Leave to cool in a buttered dish.

## Poultry forcemeat

Dice 575 g (1¼ lb) chicken or other poultry meat, 200 g (7 oz) lean veal and 900 g (2 lb) bacon; work together in a blender until smooth. Add 3 eggs, 1 tablespoon salt and 200 ml (7 fl oz, ¾ cup) brandy. Mix well, press through a sieve and chill until required. This forcemeat is used for pâtés and terrines.

## Sausagemeat

Weigh out equal quantities of lean pork and fat bacon. Mince (grind) finely and add 3 tablespoons salt per 1 kg (2¼ lb) mince. Chopped truffle or truffle peelings may be added, or the mince may be seasoned with finely chopped onions, garlic, salt, pepper and herbs. Chopped mushrooms, wild or cultivated, may also be added.

## Truffled forcemeat

Truffle can be used to flavour any of the forcemeats, especially veal or game. The peelings can be cooked in the liquid to be used for a panada, and finely diced truffle or fine julienne can be added to the forcemeat after it has been sieved and mixed.

## Veal forcemeat (fine)

Pound 1 kg (2¼ lb) lean minced (ground) veal in a mortar (or reduce to a purée in a blender). Season with 1 tablespoon salt, some white pepper and grated nutmeg. Purée 300 g (11 oz) flour panada; when really soft, add the veal, together with 65 g (2½ oz, 4½ tablespoons) butter, and beat the mixture well. Finally, beating continuously, add 5 eggs and 8 yolks, one by one. Then add 1.25 litres (2¼ pints, 5½ cups) thick béchamel sauce. Press through a fine sieve and work with a spatula to make the forcemeat smooth. Chill until required. This forcemeat is used for borders and large quenelles.

# Garnishes & accompaniments

## Aubergine fritters

Peel some aubergines (eggplants), slice them and marinate for 1 hour in oil, lemon juice, chopped parsley, salt and pepper. Drain, dip in batter, deep fry in hot oil and serve with fried parsley. The same method may be used for broccoli, cardoons, celery, celeriac (celery root), courgettes (zucchini), cauliflower, marrow (squash) flowers, salsify, tomatoes and Jerusalem artichokes.

## Baked apples

Make a light circular incision round the middle of some firm cooking apples. Core them then put them in a large buttered ovenproof dish. Fill the hollows with butter mixed with caster (superfine) sugar. Pour a few tablespoons of water into the dish and cook in a preheated oven at 220°C (425°F, gas 7) until the apples are just tender, about 30 minutes.

## Boiled chestnuts

Place some peeled chestnuts in a saucepan and cover with cold water. Season with salt and pepper and add some chopped celery. Bring to the boil and simmer gently for 35–45 minutes. Drain well and serve with butter.

## Braised chestnuts

Peel some chestnuts and spread them evenly over the bottom of a large greased casserole. Place a bouquet garni and a celery stick in the centre, season with salt and pepper and add enough stock to just cover them. Cover the casserole and cook in a preheated oven at 220°C (425°F, gas 7) for about 45 minutes (do not stir the chestnuts during cooking in case they break). Serve with braised or roast meat.

## Château potatoes

Scrub some fairly small new potatoes, wash and wipe. Heat some butter in a shallow frying pan, add the potatoes and cook gently with the lid on. Add salt and pepper and serve with roast meat or with braised meat or fish.

## Conti, à la

Conti is the name given, in classic French cookery, to dressings made from lentils. For meat which is roasted, fried or braised, the garnish consists of a lentil purée cooked with streaky (slab) bacon cut into strips. Another Conti garnish consists of croquettes of lentil purée accompanied by potato rissoles. For eggs *sur le plat à la Conti*, the lentil purée should be piped along the edge of the dish. For Conti soup, the purée is diluted with stock and fresh butter and croûtons are added.

## Corn fritters

Make a smooth batter using 100 g (4 oz, 1 cup) plain (all-purpose) flour, 2 eggs and 100 ml (4 fl oz, 7 tablespoons) water. Add 225 g (8 oz, 1 cup) thawed frozen or drained canned sweetcorn. Stir well, adding seasoning to taste and a little grated nutmeg. Shallow fry spoonfuls of the sweetcorn in batter in a mixture of sunflower oil and butter until the fritters are golden underneath and set. Turn and cook the second sides until golden. Serve with deep-fried breadcrumb-coated chicken and fried bananas as American Maryland chicken.

## Dauphine potatoes

Peel 1 kg (2¼ lb) floury potatoes, cut into quarters and cook in salted water until very soft. Drain thoroughly and mash to a purée. Prepare some choux paste using 500 ml (17 fl oz, 2 cups) water, 125 g (4½ oz, ½ cup) butter, 250 g (9 oz, 2¼ cups) plain (all-purpose) flour, 7 eggs, a pinch of grated nutmeg, salt and pepper. Mix the dough with an equal volume of the potato purée. Heat some cooking oil to about 175°C (347°F) and drop the mixture into it a spoonful at a time. When the potato balls are puffed up and golden, drain on paper towels, dust with fine salt and serve very hot.

## Diablotin

A very thin, small round slice of bread (sometimes first coated with reduced béchamel sauce) sprinkled with grated cheese and browned in the oven. *Diablotins* are usually served with soup, particularly consommé.

## Financière, à la

This is a very rich classic garnish used for joints of meat, calves' sweetbreads and braised poultry. It may also be used as a filling for croûtes, timbales, bouchées or vol-au-vent. It consists of a ragoût of cockscombs, chicken quenelles, finely sliced mushrooms and shredded truffles flavoured with Madeira, all bound with a sauce containing Madeira and truffle essence. The same ingredients are used to make *attereaux à la financière*, the quenelles being optional. There is also a financière sauce which is flavoured with Madeira and truffles.

To make financière garnish, prepare some poached chicken quenelles and some cockscombs. Slowly cook some finely sliced mushrooms and shredded truffles in butter. Add a little Madeira. Bind all these ingredients with financière sauce (2).

## Française, à la

This describes a preparation of joints of meat served with asparagus tips, braised lettuce, cauliflower florets coated with hollandaise sauce and small duchess-potato nests filled with diced mixed vegetables. The sauce served with dishes *à la française* is a thin demi-glace – or a clear veal gravy.

Peas *à la française* are prepared with lettuce and onions.

## French beans in tomato sauce

Boil the French (green) beans in salted water until they are three-quarters cooked, and drain thoroughly. Cook them gently in butter for about 5 minutes, add a few tablespoons of concentrated tomato sauce and simmer. Turn into a dish and sprinkle with chopped parsley or basil.

## French beans with cream

Boil the French (green) beans in salted water until they are three-quarters cooked, Drain. Cover with single (light) cream and simmer until the cream is reduced by half. Add salt and pepper and transfer to a serving dish. A sprinkling of chopped parsley can also be added.

This dish can be prepared *à la normande*: for every 450 g (1 lb) beans, add 1 egg yolk and 40 g (1½ oz, 3 tablespoons) butter after removing the pan from the heat.

## Game chips or crisps (potato chips)

Crisps are served in France and Britain with apéritifs or with grills and roasts. This method of preparing fried potatoes is a very old one: it used to be called *pommes en liards* (the *liard* once being a small coin of some European countries). In the United States they are known as potato chips.

Wash and peel some large firm potatoes. Cut them into very thin round slices (preferably with a mandolin cutter or in a food processor) and immediately place them in cold water. Leave to soak for 10 minutes and then dry them thoroughly. Plunge the slices once only into frying oil at 185°C (365°F). Drain on paper towels and sprinkle with salt.

## Gratin dauphinois or potatoes dauphinois

Peel and thinly slice 1 kg (2¼ lb) potatoes and arrange them evenly in a generously buttered dish. Mix 2 whole eggs with a little milk, add 1 teaspoon salt, then whisk together with 600 ml (1 pint, 2½ cups) warmed milk or cream. Pour this mixture over the potatoes and dot with knobs of butter. Cook in a preheated oven at 220°C (425°F, gas 7) for about 50 minutes, if necessary protecting the top of the dish with foil towards the end of the cooking period.

The bottom of the dish can be rubbed with garlic, and a little grated nutmeg may be added at the same time as the salt. Some grated Gruyère may also be added: one layer is placed on the bottom of the dish and more grated Gruyère is sprinkled on the top.

## Milanaise, à la

Food prepared in the style of Milan is generally dipped in egg and breadcrumbs mixed with grated Parmesan cheese, then fried in clarified butter.

The name also describes a method of preparing macaroni (served in butter with grated cheese and tomato sauce), and a garnish for cuts of meat, made from macaroni with cheese, coarsely shredded ham, pickled tongue, mushrooms and truffles, all blended in tomato sauce.

Dishes cooked au gratin with Parmesan cheese are also described as *à la milanaise*.

## Mushrooms cooked in cream

Sauté the mushrooms in butter, cover them with boiling double (heavy) cream and simmer for 8–10 minutes, until reduced.

This preparation may be used as a filling for flans or vol-au-vent.

## Pasta dough

Sift 500 g (18 oz, 4½ cups) strong plain (bread) flour into a bowl and make a well in the middle. Dissolve 2 teaspoons salt (or less to taste) in 2 tablespoons water, put it in the well, then add 3 beaten eggs and 6 egg yolks. Gradually work the liquids into the flour to make a firm dough. Knead the dough thoroughly, working it with the heel of the hand until the dough is smooth and firm. Wrap the dough in a cloth or cling film (plastic wrap) and leave it in a cool place, but not the refrigerator, for 1 hour so it loses its elasticity.

To make noodles, divide the dough into pieces about the size of an egg and roll these into balls. Roll out each piece into a very thin pancake shape and lightly dust with flour then roll up loosely. Cut the dough into strips 1 cm (½ in) wide, then unroll the strips on a flat surface.

To cook the noodles, plunge them into boiling salted water, using 2.5 litres (4¼ pints, 11 cups) water for every 250 g (9 oz) fresh noodles. Boil fast for about 3 minutes, drain and serve tossed with butter.

## Peas à la française

Place 800 g (1¾ lb, 5¼ cups) fresh shelled peas in a saucepan with a shredded lettuce, 12 new small (pearl) onions, a bouquet garni composed of parsley and chervil, 75 g (3 oz, 6 tablespoons) butter cut into small pieces, 1 teaspoon salt, 2 teaspoons sugar and 4½ tablespoons cold water. Cover the pan, bring gently to the boil and simmer for 30–40 minutes. Remove the bouquet garni and mix in 1 tablespoon fresh butter just before serving.

## Piémontaise, à la

This describes various dishes that incorporate a risotto, sometimes accompanied by white Piedmont truffles. Arranged in a variety of ways – in darioles, in timbale moulds or as *coquettes* – the risotto is used to garnish poultry, meat and fish.

## Pilaf rice

Sweat some very finely chopped onions in butter without browning. Add the unwashed rice and stir until it becomes transparent. Add 1½ times its volume in boiling water. Season with salt and add a bouquet garni. Put some greaseproof (wax) paper over the rice and cover with a lid. Cook for 16–18 minutes in a preheated oven at 200°C (400°F, gas 6). Remove from the oven and allow to stand for 15 minutes. Add butter and fork the grains.

## Polenta

A cornmeal porridge that is the traditional basic dish of northern Italy (both Venice and Lombardy claim to have invented it). Polenta is traditionally made with water in a large copper pot, stirred with a big wooden spoon. The porridge is cooled in a round wooden tray and then cut into squares or diamond shapes. It can also be made with milk (for desserts), stock or with a mixture of white wine and water. Like rice and pasta, polenta is very versatile and is used for a large number of dishes: fritters, croquettes, gratins, croûtes and timbales. Served plain, with butter and cheese, in a sauce, or even flavoured with vegetables, ham or white truffle, polenta may accompany fish stews, meat ragoûts or brochettes of small birds.

Boil 1 litre (1¾ pints, 4⅓ cups) water with 1–2 teaspoons salt (or to taste), then add 250 g (9 oz, 2 cups) cornmeal and mix together thoroughly. Cook for 25–30 minutes, stirring continuously with a wooden spoon. Then add

50–65 g (2–2½ oz, 4–5 tablespoons) butter. Pour the porridge on to a damp plate, spreading it out in an even layer, and leave to cool completely. Cut into squares or diamond shapes and fry in butter until golden. Arrange on a serving dish and sprinkle with grated Parmesan cheese and noisette butter.

## Pommes Anna

Peel 1 kg (2¼ lb) potatoes and cut into thin even round slices. Wash, wipe and season with salt and pepper. Slightly brown 75 g (3 oz, 6 tablespoons) butter in a special casserole (or in a sauté pan) and arrange the potatoes in circular layers, making sure that they are evenly coated with butter, then compress them into a cake with a wooden spatula. Cover and cook in a hot oven for 25 minutes. Quickly turn the whole cake over on to a flat dish and slide it back into the casserole to brown the other side.

## Portugaise, à la

This describes various dishes (eggs, fish, kidneys, small pieces of meat and poultry) in which tomatoes predominate or are used as the garnish, often filled with a simple stuffing.

## Potato galette

Bake 6 large floury (baking) potatoes in the oven for 45–60 minutes until soft. Cut them open and remove the flesh, then mix 400 g (14 oz, 3¾ cups) of this with 4 egg yolks, added one by one, and 1 teaspoon salt. Soften 150 g (5 oz, ⅔ cup) butter with a spatula and mix it in. Roll the potato dough into a ball and flatten it with the palm of the hand. Shape it into a ball again and repeat the operation twice more. Butter a baking sheet and flatten the dough to form a galette 4 cm (1½ in) thick. Trace a pattern on the top with the point of a knife, brush it with beaten egg, and bake in a preheated oven at 220°C (425°F, gas 7) until golden brown. If the galette is to be served as a dessert, add to the dough 125 g (4½ oz, ½ cup) sugar, orange-flower water and chopped blanched orange and lemon rind (zest).

## Potato gnocchi

Cook 3 medium potatoes in boiling salted water for about 20 minutes. Meanwhile, grate 6–7 medium peeled potatoes and squeeze them in a cloth to extract as much water as possible. Peel and mash the cooked potatoes, then mix them with the grated raw potatoes. Add 100–125 g (4–4½ oz, 1 cup) plain (all-purpose) flour, a little grated nutmeg, salt and pepper, then 2 eggs, one after the other. Mix thoroughly. Boil some salted water and use 2 spoons to shape the paste into small, round portions. Drop them into the water and simmer for 6–8 minutes. Drain the gnocchi and place them on a cloth. Butter a gratin dish and arrange the gnocchi in it, coated with 200 ml (7 fl oz, ¾ cup) crème fraîche and sprinkled with grated cheese. Brown in a very hot oven.

## Potatoes à la boulangère

Slice 800 g (1¾ lb) peeled potatoes and brown them in 40 g (1½ oz, 3 tablespoons) butter. Slice 400 g (14 oz) onions and brown in 20 g (¾ oz, 1½ tablespoons) butter. Arrange alternate layers of potatoes and onions in a buttered ovenproof dish. Season with salt and pepper, then cover completely with stock. Cook in a preheated oven at 200°C (400°F, gas 6) for about 25 minutes, then reduce the heat to 180°C (350°F, gas 4) and leave to cook for 20 minutes more. If required, add a little stock while the potatoes are cooking.

## Ratatouille niçoise

Trim the ends of 6 courgettes (zucchini) and cut them into rounds (do not peel them). Peel and slice 2 onions. Cut the stalks from 3 green (bell) peppers, remove the seeds and cut them into strips. Peel 6 tomatoes, cut each one into 6 pieces and seed them. Peel and crush 3 garlic cloves. Peel 6 aubergines (eggplants) and cut them into rounds. Heat 6 tablespoons olive oil in a cast-iron pan. Brown the aubergines in this, then add the peppers, tomatoes and onions, and finally the courgettes and the garlic. Add a large bouquet garni containing plenty of thyme, salt and pepper. Cook over a low heat for about 30 minutes. Add 2 tablespoons fresh olive oil and continue to cook until the desired consistency is reached. Remove the bouquet garni and serve very hot.

## Rice à la créole

Thoroughly wash 500 g (18 oz, 2½ cups) long-grain rice and pour it into a sauté pan. Add salt and enough water to come 2 cm (¾ in) above the level of the rice. Bring to the boil and continue to boil rapidly with the pan uncovered. When the water has boiled down to the same level as the rice, cover the pan and cook very gently until the rice is completely dry (about 45 minutes). If preferred, the second part of the cooking process may be carried out in a cool oven.

## Rice à la grecque

Heat 3 tablespoons olive oil in a large saucepan until very hot, add 250 g (9 oz, 1¼ cups) unwashed long-grain rice and stir with a wooden spoon until the grains become transparent. Then add 2½ times its volume of boiling water, a handful of raisins, a small bouquet garni, a chopped onion, a small chopped garlic clove and season with salt and pepper. Lower the heat, cover the saucepan and leave to simmer for 16 minutes. Remove the bouquet garni. If wished, 2 tablespoons finely diced red (bell) pepper (which has been cooked in butter or oil) and 150 g (5 oz, 1 cup) peas (cooked and drained) may be added to the rice.

## Risotto à la milanaise

Heat 40 g (1½ oz, 3 tablespoons) butter or 4 tablespoons olive oil in a saucepan and cook 100 g (4 oz, ¾ cup) chopped onions very gently, without allowing them to brown. Add 250 g (9 oz, 1¼ cups) rice and stir until the grains are transparent. Add twice the volume of stock, a ladleful at a time, stirring with a wooden spoon and waiting until all the liquid has been absorbed before adding more. Taste and adjust the seasoning, add a small bouquet garni, then add 200 ml (7 fl oz, ¾ cup) thick tomato fondue, 500 g (18 oz) pickled ox (beef) tongue, ham and mushrooms (in equal proportions, all chopped) and a little white truffle and cook until heated through. Serve the risotto immediately.

## Risotto à la piémontaise

Prepare the rice as for risotto *à la milanaise*, but omit the tomato fondue, tongue, ham and mushrooms. Add 75 g (3 oz, ¾ cup) grated Parmesan cheese and 25 g (1 oz, 2 tablespoons) butter. Saffron may also be added.

## Romaine, à la

The name given to various French dishes inspired by the cuisine of the Italian region of Latium; these dishes include eggs with spinach, anchovies and Parmesan cheese; small birds casseroled with peas and ham; spinach loaf or soufflé. Sauce *à la romaine* is the classic sauce to serve with roast venison; it is a sweet-and-sour sauce made with dried vine fruits, game stock and pine kernels. Gnocchi *à la romaine* are made from semolina and grated cheese and are usually served as a first course. When used to garnish large joints of meat, they are put into tartlet cases (shells) and browned in the oven; they may be accompanied by small spinach loaves with a light tomato sauce or veal stock thickened with tomato.

## Royale, plain

A royale is a moulded custard which is cut into small dice, diamonds or stars, and used as a garnish for clear soup. Made from consommé and eggs, or a vegetable or poultry purée thickened with eggs, it is cooked in dariole moulds in a bain marie. When cooked, it is unmoulded and cut into the desired shapes.

Put some chervil into 150 ml (¼ pint, ⅔ cup) boiling consommé and leave to infuse for 10 minutes. Beat 1 egg with 2 yolks and add the consommé gradually, stirring constantly. Strain through a sieve lined with muslin (cheesecloth), skim and cook in a bain marie as for royale of asparagus.

## Royale of asparagus

Cook 75 g (3 oz) asparagus tips and 5 or 6 fresh spinach leaves in boiling water for a few minutes, then drain them. Add 1½ tablespoons béchamel sauce and 2 tablespoons consommé. Press through a sieve. Bind the mixture with 4 egg yolks, pour into dariole moulds and cook in a bain marie in a preheated oven at 200°C (400°F, gas 6) for 30 minutes.

## Royale of tomatoes

Mix 100 ml (4 fl oz, 7 tablespoons) concentrated tomato purée (paste) with 4 tablespoons consommé. Add salt and pepper, bind with 4 egg yolks and cook in a bain marie as for royale of asparagus.

## Russian salad

Boil and finely dice some potatoes, carrots and turnips; boil some French (green) beans and cut into short pieces. Mix together equal quantities of these ingredients and add some well-drained cooked petits pois. Bind with mayonnaise and pile up in a salad bowl. Garnish with a julienne of pickled tongue and truffles and add some finely diced lobster or langouste meat.

For a more elaborate dish, the ordinary mayonnaise can be replaced by thickened mayonnaise and the salad is poured into mould lined with aspic and garnished with slivers of truffle and pickled tongue. Chill in the refrigerator for 4 hours and remove from the mould just before serving.

# Salpicon

Ingredients that are diced, often very finely, then bound with sauce. Cooked meat or egg salpicons can be hot or cold. Savoury salpicons are used for filling or garnishing barquettes, vol-au-vent, canapés, croustades, croûtes, small meat pies, rissoles and tartlets. They are also used for making shaped cutlets, kromeskies and croquettes and for stuffing and garnishing poultry, game and some cuts of meat.

## Salpicons of meat, poultry, game, offal or egg

- *with brains* Diced poached brains, bound with allemande, béchamel or velouté sauce (hot).
- *à l'écossaise* Pickled tongue cut into small cubes and diced truffles, bound with reduced demi-glace (hot).
- *with foie gras* Finely diced foie gras, bound with Madeira, port or sherry sauce or game fumet (hot), or with aspic (cold); sautéed chicken livers can be added.
- *with game* Finely diced game meat bound either with white or brown sauce made with game fumet (from the same game as the salpicon) or with aspic.
- *with ham* Diced York, Prague or Paris ham, bound with demi-glace (hot), or with vinaigrette or mustard-flavoured mayonnaise (cold).
- *with hard-boiled (hard-cooked) eggs* Diced whites and yolks, bound with allemande, béchamel, cream or velouté sauce (hot), or with vinaigrette or mayonnaise with herbs (cold).

- *with lamb's or calf's sweetbreads* Sliced sweetbreads cooked in butter, bound with allemande, béchamel, demi-glace, Madeira or suprême sauce (hot).
- *with meat* Finely diced leftover beef, veal, mutton or pork, bound with white or brown sauce (used particularly for croquettes and kromeskies and for filling pies).
- *with poultry* Diced white poultry meat, bound with allemande, béchamel, cream, velouté, brown or demi-glace sauce or with veal stock (hot, for filling vol-au-vent, barquettes, croustades and poached eggs and croquettes), or with vinaigrette with herbs for filling cold barquettes or hard-boiled eggs.
- *à la reine* Diced white chicken meat, mushrooms and truffles, bound with allemande sauce (hot).
- *à la Saint-Hubert* Diced game meat, bound with reduced demi-glace made with game fumet (hot).
- *with veal* Diced cooked veal, bound with allemande, béchamel or demi-glace sauce or with veal stock (hot).

## Salpicon of truffles with cream sauce (hot)

Cut fresh truffles (raw or cooked in Madeira) or canned truffles into large or small dice, according to the requirements of the recipe. Sprinkle with salt and pepper. Cook gently in butter and bind with a few tablespoons of velouté or cream sauce.

## Straw potatoes

Peel some large firm potatoes, cut them into very thin strips and leave them to soak in plenty of cold water for 15 minutes. Drain and wipe thoroughly, then cook them in deep-frying oil at 180–190°C (350–375°F) until they are golden (about 5 minutes). Drain them on paper towels, dust them with fine salt and serve them piping hot.

## Sauerkraut à l'alsacienne

Thoroughly wash 2 kg (4½ lb) raw sauerkraut in cold water, then squeeze and disentangle it with your fingers. Peel 2 or 3 carrots and cut into small cubes. Peel 2 large onions and stick a clove in each.

Coat the bottom and sides of a flameproof casserole with goose fat or lard. Pile in half the sauerkraut and add the carrots, onions, 2 peeled garlic cloves, 1 teaspoon ground pepper, 1 tablespoon juniper berries and a bouquet garni. Add the rest of the sauerkraut, a raw knuckle of ham and 1 glass of dry white Alsace wine and top up with water. Season lightly with salt, cover and bring to the boil. Then transfer to a preheated oven at 190°C (375°F, gas 5) and cook for 1 hour. Add a medium-sized smoked shoulder of pork and 575–800 g (1¼–1¾ lb) smoked belly (salt pork). Cover, bring to the boil on the hob (stove top), then cook in the oven for a further 1½ hours.

Meanwhile, peel 1.25 kg (2¾ lb) potatoes. After 1½ hours, remove the pork belly from the casserole and add the potatoes. Leave to cook for a further 30 minutes. During this time, poach 6–8 Strasbourg sausages in barely simmering water. When the sauerkraut is cooked, remove and discard the bouquet garni and the cloves and return the pork belly for 10 minutes to reheat it. Arrange the sauerkraut in a large dish and garnish with the potatoes, sausages and meat cut into slices.

## Spätzle

Blend together 500 g (18 oz, 4½ cups) sifted plain (all-purpose) flour, 4 whole eggs, 2 tablespoons double (heavy) cream and 1 tablespoon fine salt. Season with pepper and grated nutmeg. Boil plenty of salted water in a large pan. Drop small spoonfuls of the dough into the boiling water, using a second spoon to shape them into little dumplings. Leave the spätzle to poach until they rise to the surface.

## Spinach in butter

Wash, trim and parboil some spinach, then drain and dry in a cloth. Melt a little butter in a frying pan and add the spinach. Season with salt, pepper and a little grated nutmeg. When all the moisture has evaporated, add more butter, allowing 50 g (2 oz, ¼ cup) butter to 500 g (18 oz, 3½ cups) cooked spinach. Arrange in a vegetable dish and garnish with fried croûtons. The spinach may also be sprinkled with noisette butter, if desired.

## Toulousaine, à la

This term describes a garnish for poached or pot-roasted poultry or a filling for croustades, tarts or vol-au-vent. It consists of a ragoût of small quenelles of poultry, lamb's sweetbreads or cockscombs and kidneys, mushrooms and truffles, bound with allemande sauce (or toulousaine sauce, a suprême sauce thickened and enriched with egg yolks and cream). Nowadays, the expression is more frequently applied to various dishes from south-western France.

## Vegetable macédoine with butter or cream

Peel and dice 250 g (9 oz) each of new carrots, turnips, French (green) beans and potatoes. Prepare 500 g (18 oz, 3½ cups) shelled peas. Add the carrots and turnips to a pan of boiling salted water. Bring back to the boil and add the beans, then the peas and finally the potatoes. Keep on the boil but do not cover. When the vegetables are cooked, drain them then tip into a serving dish and add butter or cream. Sprinkle with chopped herbs.

## Vegetable salpicons with cream sauce (hot)

Cut vegetables into large or small dice, according to requirements and partially cook as below. Finish cooking the salpicon in a little butter and bind with a few tablespoons of thick cream sauce or reduced velouté sauce.

- *artichoke hearts* Half-cooked in white stock.
- *aubergines (eggplants)* Half-cooked in butter or olive oil.
- *carrots* Three-quarters cooked in water and butter.
- *ceps or button mushrooms* Half-stewed in butter or oil.
- *green asparagus or French (green) beans* Half-cooked in salted boiling water.
- *onions* Half-cooked in butter.
- *tomatoes* Blanched for 1 minute and peeled.

## Vegetable salpicons with mayonnaise (cold)

Cook the chosen vegetable completely and leave to cool. Cut into small dice and bind with mayonnaise, which may be flavoured, coloured or thickened. Use any of these vegetables: artichoke hearts cooked in white stock; asparagus tips or French (green) beans cut into short pieces, boiled in salted water; peeled, diced celeriac, boiled in salted water; mushrooms cooked in butter; or potatoes, boiled in their skins then peeled.

## Vegetable salpicons with vinaigrette (cold)

Cook the chosen vegetable completely. Cool, dice and dress with seasoned vinaigrette flavoured with finely chopped herbs. Use any of the following: diced cooked beetroot with chervil and parsley; raw cucumber, sprinkled with salt, left to stand, rinsed, patted dry and diced, with mint or tarragon; tomatoes, blanched, peeled, seeded and diced, with basil or tarragon.

## Vichy carrots

Cut 800 g (1¾ lb) young carrots into thin rounds. Place in a sauté pan and just cover with water, adding 1 teaspoon salt and a generous pinch of sugar per 500 ml (17 fl oz, 2 cups) water. Cook gently until all the liquid is absorbed. Serve the carrots sprinkled with small pieces of butter and chopped parsley.

# Pastry & doughs

## Barquette cases

A barquette case is a a small boat-shaped tart made of shortcrust pastry (basic pie dough) or puff pastry, baked blind and then filled with various sweet or savoury ingredients. Sometimes the pastry boats are filled before they are baked. Savoury barquettes are served hot or cold as hors d'oeuvre or entrées.

## Bouchée cases

Dust the working surface with flour and roll out some puff pastry to a thickness of about 5 mm (¼ in). Using a round, crinkle-edged pastry (cookie) cutter, 7.5–10 cm (3–4 in) in diameter, cut out circles of pastry and place them on a damp baking sheet, turning them over as you do so. Use a 7.5–10 cm (3–4 in) ring cutter to stamp out rings of pastry. Brush the edge of the pastry bases with beaten egg and place the rings on top. Chill the cases in the refrigerator for about 30 minutes. Bake in a preheated oven at 220°C (425°F, gas 7) for 12–15 minutes. Using the point of a knife, cut out a circle of pastry from inside each bouchée, lift it out and set aside to use as a lid. If necessary remove any soft pastry inside the case. The bouchées are now ready to be filled.

## Bread croustades

Cut some thick stale bread into slices 5–6 cm (2–2½ in) thick, remove the crusts and trim to the desired shape. On the top, make a circular incision with the tip of a knife to a depth of 4–5 cm (1½–2 in) to mark the lid. Deep-fry the croustades in oil heated to 175–180°C (347–356°F) until they are golden.

Drain. Take off the lid and remove all the crumb from the inside. Line the croustades with a thin layer of forcemeat (according to the filling). Leave for 5–6 minutes at the front of a hot oven with the door open. Fill with the chosen mixture. All the fillings recommended for timbales and vol-au-vent are suitable for bread croustades. These croustades may also be made using round bread rolls.

## Brioche dough

Soften 225 g (8 oz, 1 cup) butter at room temperature. Crumble 7 g (¼ oz, ½ cake) fresh (compressed) yeast and stir in 1 tablespoon warm water. In a separate container stir 1 tablespoon sugar and a pinch of salt into 2 table-spoons cold milk. Sift 250 g (9 oz, 2¼ cups) strong plain (bread) flour, make a well in the centre, and add the yeast mixture and 1 lightly beaten egg. After working in a little flour, add the sugar and salt mixture, and another lightly beaten egg. Continue to work the dough until it becomes smooth and elastic. It should stretch easily. Mix a third of the dough with the softened butter, then add the second and finally the remaining third of the dough to the mixture.

Put the dough in a 2 litre (3½ pint, 9 cup) container, cover with a cloth, and leave to rise in a warm place until it has doubled in volume. Then separate the dough into 3 pieces, knead lightly and leave to rise again. Leave to rest for a few hours in a cool place: the dough is now ready to be shaped and baked.

- *Standard brioche dough* This is prepared in exactly the same way, but the quantity of butter is reduced to 175 g (6 oz, ¾ cup).
- *Pâte levée pour tartes* This yeasted brioche dough is used for tarts and flans. Prepare as for brioche dough, but use 250 g (9 oz, 2¼ cups) plain (all-purpose) flour, 7 g (¼ oz, ½ cake) fresh (compressed) yeast, ½ teaspoon salt, 2 teaspoons caster (superfine) sugar, 2 eggs, 100 g (4 oz, ½ cup) butter and 6 tablespoons milk.

## Butter pastry for pâté en croûte

This pastry can be used for hot or cold pâtés. Put 500 g (18 oz, 4½ cups) sifted plain (all-purpose) flour in a heap on the worktop and make a well in the centre. Add 2 teaspoons salt, 125 g (4½ oz, ½ cup) butter, 2 whole eggs and about 3 tablespoons water. Mix together, then knead lightly. Roll into a ball, cover and keep cool for 2 hours before use.

## Choux paste

To make about 40 small buns, 20 larger buns or éclairs, measure 250 ml (8 fl oz, 1 cup) water or milk and water (in equal proportions) into a saucepan. Add a large pinch of salt and 65 g (2½ oz, 5 tablespoons) butter cut into small pieces. Heat gently until the butter melts, then bring to the boil. As soon as the mixture begins to boil, take the pan off the heat, add 125 g (4½ oz, 1 cup) plain (all-purpose) flour all at once and mix quickly. Return the saucepan to the heat and cook the paste until it thickens, stirring: it takes about 1 minute for the paste to leave the sides of the saucepan. Do not overcook the mixture or beat it vigorously as this will make it greasy or oily. Remove from the heat and cool slightly. Beat in 2 eggs, then 2 more eggs, one after the other, continuing to beat hard until a smooth glossy paste is obtained. Use as required.

## Flaky pastry

Mix 75 g (3 oz, ⅓ cup) butter with 75 g (3 oz, ⅓ cup) lard or white vegetable fat (shortening) by chopping both types of fat together. Divide into quarters and chill. Rub a quarter of the fat into 225 g (8 oz, 2 cups) plain (all-purpose) flour, then mix in 7–8 tablespoons cold water to make a soft dough.

Knead the dough lightly on a floured surface, then roll it out into a long rectangle measuring about 15 × 35 cm (6 × 14 in). Mark the pastry across into thirds. Dot another quarter of the prepared fat in lumps over the top two thirds of the pastry. Fold the bottom third over the fat on the middle third, then fold the top third down. Press the edges together and give the pastry a quarter turn in a clockwise direction. Chill the pastry for 15 minutes, then roll it out as before and dot with another portion of fat. Fold and chill the pastry for 30 minutes. Repeat the rolling and folding twice more – once with the remaining portion of fat and once without any additional fat. Chill the pastry for 15–30 minutes between each rolling and at the end, before rolling it out and using as required.

## Gougères (basic recipe)

Make 500 g (18 oz) unsweetened choux paste. After adding the eggs, blend in 100 g (4 oz, 1 cup) grated Gruyère cheese and a pinch of white pepper. Butter a baking sheet and shape the dough into small balls using a spoon or into a ring using a piping (pastry) bag. Brush with beaten egg, sprinkle with flakes of Gruyère and cook in the oven at 200°C (400°F, gas 6) for about 20 minutes until golden brown. Leave to cool in the oven with the heat switched off and the door half-open.

## Hot water crust pastry

This close-textured firm pastry is used as a crust for raised or moulded pies, such as pork or game pies, or as a casing for pâtés. It is cooked at a lower temperature than puff or shortcrust pastries. Mix 350 g (12 oz, 1½ cups) plain (all-purpose) flour with ½ teaspoon salt in a bowl. Heat 4 tablespoons milk and 4 tablespoons water with 100 g (4 oz, ½ cup) lard or 50 g (2 oz, ¼ cup) each of lard and butter over gentle heat until the fat has melted completely. Then bring the mixture to the boil and immediately pour it into the flour. Working quickly, stir the liquid into the flour to make a dough, then knead it lightly together by hand in the bowl. (Take care as the mixture is very hot.) Do not over-knead the dough or it will become greasy.

Press or roll out the dough as required. If the dough is rolled out into too large a sheet or too thinly, it breaks up easily, so for lining large moulds, begin by rolling out the dough, then press it into the mould, thinning it out evenly with the fingertips. For small pies, allow the dough to cool and set slightly (1–2 minutes is usually enough), when small portions can be rolled thinly and evenly to give a smooth result without breaking.

## Lining pastry

This is a basic shortcrust pastry made by the French method and used for lining flans and tarts. Sift 250 g (9 oz, 2¼ cups) plain (all-purpose) flour on to a board. Make a well in the centre and add ½ teaspoon salt and 125 g (4½ oz, ½ cup) butter (softened at room temperature and cut into pieces). Start to mix the ingredients and then add 2 tablespoons water (the quantity of water required may vary depending on the type of flour used). Knead the dough gently, using the heel of the hand, shape it into a ball, wrap it in foil and set aside in a cool place for at least 2 hours if possible.

A richer pastry can be made by increasing the butter to 150 g (5 oz, ⅔ cup) and by adding 1 small egg and 2 tablespoons caster (superfine) sugar.

## Profiteroles

Prepare some choux paste with 250 ml (8 fl oz, 1 cup) water, a pinch of salt, 2 tablespoons sugar, 125 g (4½ oz, 1 cup) plain (all-purpose) flour and 4 eggs. Using a piping (pastry) bag with a plain nozzle, pipe out balls of dough the size of walnuts on to a greased baking sheet and brush them with beaten egg. Cook in a preheated oven at 200°C (400°F, gas 6) for about 20 minutes until crisp and golden; allow to cool in the oven.

# Puff pastry

Put 500 g (18 oz, 4½ cups) plain (all-purpose) flour on a board in a circle, making a well in the middle. Since flours differ, the exact proportion of water to flour is variable. Into the centre of this circle put 1½ teaspoons salt and about 300 ml (½ pint, 1¼ cups) water. Mix and knead until the dough is smooth and elastic. Form into a ball and leave to stand for 25 minutes.

Roll out the dough into square, mark a cross in the top and roll out the wedges to form an evenly thick cross shape. Put 500 g (18 oz, 2¼ cups) softened butter in the middle of this dough. (The butter should be softened with a wooden spatula until it can be spread easily.) Fold the ends of the dough over the butter in such a way as to enclose it completely. Leave to stand for 10 minutes in a cold place, until rested and firmed slightly.

The turning operation (called *tournage* in French) can now begin. Roll the dough with a rolling pin on a lightly floured board in such a way as to obtain a rectangle 60 cm (24 in) long, 20 cm (8 in) wide and 1.5 cm (⅝ in) thick. Fold the rectangle into three, give it a quarter-turn and, with the rolling pin at right angles to the folds, roll the dough out again into a rectangle of the same size as the previous one. Again fold the dough into three and leave to stand for about 15 minutes and chill if too sticky. Repeat the sequence (turn, roll, fold) a further 4 times, leaving the dough to stand for about 15 minutes after each folding. After the sixth turn, roll out the dough in both directions and use according to the recipe.

# Puff pastry croustades

Sprinkle the worktop with flour and roll out puff pastry to a thickness of about 1–2 cm (½–¾ in). Using a pastry (cookie) cutter, cut rounds 7.5–10 cm (3–4 in) in diameter. With a smaller cutter, make a circle centred on the first, with a diameter 2 cm (¾ in) smaller, taking care not to cut right through the pastry: this smaller circle will form the lid of the croustades. Glaze with egg yolk and place in a preheated oven at 230°C, (450°F, gas 8). As soon as the crust has risen well and turned golden, take the croustades out of the oven. Leave until lukewarm, then take off the lid and, with a spoon, remove the soft white paste which is inside. Leave to cool completely.

Alternatively, roll the pastry to a thickness of only 5 mm (¼ in) and cut half of it into circles 7.5–10 cm (3–4 in) in diameter, and the rest into rings of the same external diameter and 1 cm (½ in) wide. Brush the base of the rings with beaten egg and place them on the circles; glaze with beaten egg and cook.

## Shortcrust pastry

Sift 225 g (8 oz, 2 cups) plain (all-purpose) flour into a bowl and stir in a pinch of salt, if required. Add 50 g (2 oz, ¼ cup) chilled butter and 50 g (2 oz, ¼ cup) chilled lard or white vegetable fat (shortening). Cut the fat into small pieces, then lightly rub them into the flour until the mixture resembles breadcrumbs. Sprinkle 3 tablespoons cold water over the mixture, then use a roundbladed knife to mix it in. The mixture should form clumps: press these together into a smooth ball. Chill the pastry for 30 minutes before baking. Roll out and use as required.

## Vol-au-vent case

Prepare 500 g (18 oz) fine puff pastry. Divide it in half and roll out each half to a thickness of 5 mm (¼ in). Cut out 2 circles, 15 cm (6 in) in diameter. Place 1 pastry circle on a slightly dampened baking sheet. Using a 12–13 cm (4¾–5 in) round cutter, remove the centre of the second circle. Dampen the top of the pastry circle and place the outer ring from the second one on top. Turn the ring over as you place it on the circle so that the slightly floury underside is uppermost.

Roll the central circle of pastry from the ring to the same size as the vol-au-vent. Dampen the border of the vol-au-vent and place this third layer on top. Glaze the top with beaten egg top then use a small knife to score around the inside of the border. This marks the lid covering the well in the vol-au-vent; scoring it without cutting through completely makes it easier to remove when cooked. Mark a pattern on top of the lid by lightly scoring it in a criss-cross pattern.

Bake in a preheated oven at 220°C (425°F, gas 7) for about 15 minutes until well-risen and golden-brown. After taking it out of the oven, place the vol-au-vent on a wire rack; carefully cut out the lid without breaking it, place it on the wire rack, and remove the soft pastry from the inside of the vol-au-vent. Keep hot. Reheat the filling, fill the case with it, place the lid on top and serve very hot.

## White bread

Blend 15 g (½ oz, 1 cake) fresh (compressed) yeast with a little warm water taken from 400 ml (14 fl oz, 1¼ cups). Add more of the water to thin the paste to a milky consistency, then cover and leave in a warm place until frothy. Alternatively, dissolve 1 teaspoon sugar in the warm water, then sprinkle on 2 teaspoons standard (regular) dried yeast. Leave in a warm place for 10 minutes until dissolved and frothy.

Mix 675 g (1½ lb, 6 cups) strong white (bread) flour and 2 teaspoons salt and rub in 15 g (½ oz, 1 tablespoon) butter. Add the yeast liquid to the dry ingredients and mix to form a firm dough, adding a little extra flour if it is too sticky. Turn the dough on to a lightly floured surface and knead until smooth and elastic. Shape the dough into a ball, place inside a large oiled plastic bag, and leave to rise in a warm place until doubled in size.

Remove from the plastic bag, then knock back (punch down). Shape into loaves or rolls. Cover with a cloth and leave to rise until doubled in size.

Bake in a preheated oven at 200°C (400°F, gas 6) for about 40 minutes for a large loaf, 30–35 minutes for small loaves, or 15–20 minutes for rolls.

- *Using dried yeast* Always follow the packet instructions, as products vary. As a guide, standard (regular) dried yeast should be sprinkled over lukewarm water to which a little sugar has been added. Cover and leave, without stirring, until the yeast granules have absorbed the water, dissolved and become frothy. Then stir well.

Easy-blend dried (active dry) yeast should be added to the flour and other dry ingredients before any liquid is added. The liquid should be slightly hotter than normal – hand-hot, rather than lukewarm – and the dough should then be mixed and kneaded as usual.

Fast-action easy-blend dried (quick-rising dry) yeast should be mixed with the dry ingredients and the water and dough prepared as for easy-blend dried yeast. After kneading, the dough should be shaped and proved – this yeast requires one rising, not two.

# Sauces, dressings & marinades

## Aïoli

Peel 4 large garlic cloves (split them in two and remove the germ if necessary). Pound the garlic with 1 egg yolk in a mortar or blender. Add salt and pepper and, while pounding or blending, very gradually add 250 ml (8 fl oz, 1 cup) olive oil, as for a mayonnaise. The sauce is ready when it is thick and creamy. The bulk of the sauce is sometimes increased by adding 2 teaspoons mashed boiled potato.

## Albufera sauce

Prepare a suprême sauce using 500 ml (17 fl oz, 2 cups) thick rich chicken velouté sauce, 400 ml (14 fl oz, 1¾ cups) white chicken stock, 400 ml (14 fl oz, 1¾ cups) crème fraîche and 50 g (2 oz, ¼ cup) butter. While the sauce is cooking, sweat 150 g (5 oz) sliced sweet (bell) peppers in 50 g (2 oz, ¼ cup) butter. Allow to cool, then purée the peppers in a blender. Work in 150 g (5 oz, ⅔ cup) butter and press through a sieve. Reduce the suprême sauce to 500 ml (17 fl oz, 2 cups), then add 3 tablespoons veal stock and 2 teaspoons of the pepper butter. Rub through a fine sieve. Serve the sauce hot.

## Allemande sauce

(from Carême's recipe) Prepare some velouté; pour half of it into a saucepan with an equal quantity of good chicken consommé containing some mushroom skins and stalks but no salt. Place the pan on a high heat and stir with a wooden spoon until it boils. Then cover the pan and simmer gently for about an hour to reduce the sauce; skim off the fat and return it to a high heat, stirring with the wooden spoon so that it does not stick to the pan. When the sauce is thoroughly reduced and well thickened, it should leave a fairly thick covering on the surface of the spoon. When poured, it should make a coating similar to that of redcurrant jelly at its final stage of cooking.

Remove the saucepan from the heat and make a liaison of 4 egg yolks mixed with 2 tablespoons cream. Put this through a sieve and add a knob of unsalted butter, the size of a small egg, cut up into small pieces. Pour this a little at a time into the velouté, taking care to stir with the wooden spoon to thicken as the liaison blends in. When completely thickened, place the allemande on a moderate heat, stirring all the time, and as soon as it has begun to bubble slightly, remove from the heat and add a dash of grated nutmeg. When well blended, press through a sieve.

## Allemande sauce based on meat stock

Using a wooden spatula, mix together 2 or 3 egg yolks (according to size) and 400 ml (14 fl oz, 1¾ cups) white meat stock in a heavy-based saucepan over a low heat. Then stir in 500 ml (17 fl oz, 2 cups) velouté. Bring to the boil, whisking constantly to prevent the sauce from sticking, and reduce until it coats the spatula. Check seasoning. Cut 50 g (2 oz, ¼ cup) butter into small pieces and mix into the sauce. Place in a bain marie. This sauce may be flavoured with a fumet of truffle or mushrooms.

## Apple sauce

Cook pieces of peeled apples with a small quantity of sugar until they are soft; flavour with a little ground cinnamon or cumin. In northern Europe, this sauce is served with roast pork as well as roast goose and duck.

## Aurore sauce or pink sauce

The traditional sauce is made by adding 500 ml (17 fl oz, 2 cups) very thick puréed tomato sauce to 200 ml (7 fl oz, ¾ cup) velouté sauce. Finish with 50 g (2 oz, ¼ cup) butter and put the sauce through a sieve.

Today, however, sauce aurore is a light béchamel sauce flavoured with tomato purée (paste) and butter.

## Béarnaise sauce

Put 1 tablespoon chopped shallots, 2 tablespoons chopped chervil and tarragon, a sprig of thyme, a piece of bay leaf, 2½ tablespoons vinegar, and a little salt and pepper in a pan. Reduce by two-thirds, then allow to cool slightly. Mix 2 egg yolks with 1 tablespoon water, add to the pan and whisk over a very low heat. As soon as the egg yolks have thickened, add 125 g (4½ oz, ½ cup) butter in small pieces, a little at a time, whisking continuously. Adjust the seasoning, adding a dash of cayenne pepper if desired, and a little lemon juice. Add 1 tablespoon each of chopped chervil and tarragon and mix. The sauce can be kept in a warm bain marie until required, but it must not be reheated once it has cooled.

## Béchamel sauce

Gently heat 500 ml (17 fl oz, 2 cups) milk with 1 bay leaf, a thick slice of onion and 1 blade of mace. Remove from the heat just as the milk boils, cover the pan and set aside for at least 30 minutes. Strain the milk and discard the flavouring ingredients. Melt 40 g (1½ oz, 3 tablespoons) butter over a low heat in a heavy-based saucepan. Add 40 g (1½ oz, 6 tablespoons) flour and stir briskly until the mixture is smoothly blended, without allowing it to change colour. Gradually stir in the milk and bring to the boil, beating well to prevent any lumps from forming. Season with salt and pepper and (according to the use for which the sauce is destined) a little grated nutmeg. Simmer the sauce gently for 3–5 minutes, stirring from time to time.

## Beurre manié

Beurre manié is a classic thickening mixture for sauces, casseroles and other cooking liquors.

To thicken 500 ml (17 fl oz, 2 cups) stock or sauce, work together 25 g (1 oz, 2 tablespoons) butter and 25 g (1 oz, 4 tablespoons) plain (all-purpose) flour. Add this paste to the boiling liquid and whisk over the heat for 2 minutes.

## Bitter orange sauce

Peel the rind (zest) of 1 Seville orange in strips running from top to bottom, ensuring that it is very thin: any pith left on it would make it bitter. Cut each strip into small pieces and place in a little boiling water. Allow to boil for a few minutes, then drain and put in a pan with some espagnole sauce, a little game extract, a pinch of coarsely ground pepper and the juice of ½ Seville orange. Boil for a few moments, then add a little good-quality butter.

## Bordelaise sauce

(from a recipe by Carême) Place in a saucepan 2 garlic cloves, a pinch of tarragon, the seeded flesh of a lemon, a small bay leaf, 2 cloves, a glass of Sauternes and 2 teaspoons Provençal olive oil. Simmer gently. Skim off all the fat from the mixture and mix in enough espagnole sauce to provide sauce for an entrée and 3–4 tablespoons light veal stock. Reduce the mixture by boiling down and add half a glass of Sauternes while still simmering. Strain the sauce when it is the right consistency. Just before serving add a little butter and the juice of ½ lemon.

## Breton sauce

Cut the white part of 1 leek, ¼ celery heart and 1 onion into thin strips. Soften gently in a covered pan with 1 tablespoon butter and a pinch of salt for about 15 minutes. Add 2 tablespoons thinly sliced mushrooms and 175 ml (6 fl oz, ¾ cup) dry white wine. Reduce until dry. Add 150 ml (¼ pint, ⅔ cup) thin velouté sauce and boil vigorously for 1 minute. Adjust the seasoning and stir in 1 tablespoon double (heavy) cream and 50 g (2 oz, ¼ cup) butter. Serve immediately.

## Brown bitter orange sauce for roast duck

Cut the rind of 1 Seville orange (or 1 sweet orange) and ½ lemon into thin strips; blanch, cool and drain. Heat 20 g (¾ oz, 1½ tablespoons) granulated sugar and 1 tablespoon good wine vinegar in a saucepan until it forms a pale caramel. Add 200 ml (7 fl oz, ¾ cup) brown veal stock (or well-reduced bouillon) and boil vigorously for 5 minutes. Add the juice of the orange and a dash of lemon juice. Strain and add the blanched rind. The sauce can be flavoured with a small amount of Curaçao added just before serving.

## Brown roux

Make a white roux, but cook it very gently for 15–20 minutes, stirring constantly, until it becomes a light brown colour.

## Butter sauce (1)

Mix together 25 g (1 oz, 2 tablespoons) melted butter and 25 g (1 oz, ¼ cup) plain (all-purpose) flour in a heavy-based saucepan. Whisk in 250 ml (8 fl oz, 1 cup) salted boiling water. Over a very low heat, gradually incorporate 100 g (4 oz, ½ cup) butter cut into small pieces, stirring constantly. Season with salt and pepper and strain, if necessary.

## Butter sauce (2)

(from Carême's recipe) Put 1 scant tablespoon flour and a little butter into a saucepan over a gentle heat. Blend them together with a wooden spoon, remove from the heat and add 4¼ tablespoons water or consommé, a little salt, some grated nutmeg and the juice of ½ lemon. Stir constantly over a brisk heat, and as soon as it comes to the boil, remove the sauce. Stir in a large piece of butter. The sauce should be velvety and very smooth, with a rich but delicate flavour.

## Caper sauce

To accompany English-style boiled mutton, prepare melted butter sauce, adding the mutton cooking juices to the roux, followed by well-drained capers and a little anchovy essence (extract) or a purée of desalted anchovies.

## Chambertin sauce

Peel and dice 2 carrots and 2 onions. Soften them with 20 g (¾ oz, 1½ table-spoons) butter in a shallow frying pan. Add a bouquet garni, 100 g (4 oz, 1¼ cups) chopped mushrooms (including stalks and peelings), half a chopped garlic clove, meat or poultry trimmings and season with salt and pepper. Moisten with 500 ml (17 fl oz, 2 cups) Chambertin (or another fine red burgundy) and cook for at least 20 minutes in a covered pan. Remove the lid and reduce by a third. Pass through a conical strainer and bind with 1 tablespoon beurre manié.

## Charcutière sauce

Soften 3 tablespoons peeled chopped onions by frying gently in a covered pan, in 1 tablespoon lard (shortening). Sprinkle with 1 tablespoon white dried breadcrumbs until lightly coloured. Add 3 tablespoons white wine and

3 tablespoons stock and boil for 3–4 minutes. Stir in 2 tablespoons finely diced gherkins (sweet dill pickles) and then 1 tablespoon mustard. Adjust the seasoning before serving.

## Chasseur sauce

Sauté 150 g (5 oz, 1⅓ cups) finely chopped mushrooms (mousserons if possible) and 2 chopped shallots in butter. Add 100 ml (4 fl oz, 7 tablespoons) white wine and reduce by half. Then add 150 ml (5 fl oz, ⅔ cup) stock and 2 tablespoons reduced tomato sauce and reduce by a further third. Add 1 teaspoon beurre manié (or arrowroot) and boil for 2 minutes. Finally add 25 g (1 oz, 2 tablespoons) butter and 1 tablespoon chopped herbs (tarragon, chervil and parsley).

## Chaud-froid sauce, brown for game

Mix 500 ml (17 fl oz, 2 cups) demi-glace and 500 ml (17 fl oz, 2 cups) greatly reduced and clarified game fumet (it must have the consistency of wobbly jelly). Gradually pour the hot mixture over 16 egg yolks and add 200 g (7 oz, ¾ cup) butter, whisking all the time.

## Chaud-froid sauce, brown for meat

To make 500 ml (17 fl oz, 2 cups) sauce, put 350 ml (12 fl oz, 1½ cups) demi-glace glaze and 200 ml (7 fl oz, ¾ cup) light brown gelatinous stock into a heavy-based sauté pan. Reduce by a good third over a high heat, stirring with a spatula and gradually adding 400 ml (14 fl oz, 1¾ cups) aspic. Test the consistency by pouring a little sauce on to a chilled surface: if it is not thick enough, add several tablespoons of aspic and reduce again. Remove from the heat, add 2 tablespoons Madeira or any other dessert wine; strain through muslin (cheesecloth). Stir the sauce until completely cooled.

The following variations may be used for this brown chaud-froid sauce:

- *Game chaud-froid* Prepare a game fumet with the carcasses and trimmings of the game used; replace the light brown stock with 100 ml (4 fl oz, 7 tablespoons) game fumet and flavour the sauce with Madeira or any other dessert wine.

- *Niçoise, à la* Add 3–4 anchovy fillets, completely desalted, reduced to a purée and pressed through a sieve, then strain the sauce and add 1 tablespoon coarsely shredded tarragon leaves.

- *Orange, à l'* For ducks and ducklings. Prepare a duck fumet with the carcasses and giblets of the poultry and use it in place of the light brown stock; reduce the chaud-froid sauce more than usual so that adding orange juice does not make it too weak; blend the juice of 1 orange with the sauce, strain through muslin (cheesecloth), add 2 tablespoons orange zest cut into fine strips, blanched, cooled and drained.

## Chaud-froid sauce for chicken

Soften 5 leaves of gelatine in 120 ml (4½ fl oz, ½ cup) cold water. Then dissolve the gelatine in the water. Make a very pale roux with 125 g (4½ oz, ½ cup) butter and 100 g (4 oz, 1 cup) plain (all-purpose) flour, leave it to cool, then gradually add 1 litre (1¾ pints, 4⅓ cups) reduced boiling stock, stir briskly over the heat. Leave to simmer gently for 10 minutes, then add a small glass of brandy and the same of port, and 400 ml (14 fl oz, 1¾ cups) double (heavy) cream, spoonful by spoonful. Finally stir in the dissolved gelatine. Leave this chaud-froid sauce to cool, stirring to prevent a skin from forming.

## Chaud-froid sauce, white for poultry

Soak a knuckle of veal in cold water, drain and place it in a braising pan with 1.5 kg (3¼ lb) chicken and turkey carcasses, 3 litres (5 pints, 13 cups) cold water, 3–4 onions cut into quarters, 1 onion stuck with 4 cloves, 3–4 white parts of leek, 3–4 celery sticks sliced and cut into sections, a large bouquet garni and some ground pepper. Do not add salt: the broth must reduce a great deal. Cover, bring to the boil, then half uncover and skim; leave to simmer gently for about 3 hours, occasionally skimming off the surface fat. Strain and leave to cool: the broth will change into jelly.

Bring the jellied broth back to the boil. For every 1 litre (1¾ pints, 4⅓ cups) broth, add 100 ml (4 fl oz, 7 tablespoons) double (heavy) cream, one after the other, 16 egg yolks blended one at a time into the cream-jelly mixture and, as it cools, 300 g (11 oz, 1⅓ cups) fresh butter. Leave the sauce to cool, but for coating meat and poultry do not allow it to set.

## Chivry sauce for eggs and poultry

Put 100 ml (4 fl oz, 7 tablespoons) dry white wine, 1 teaspoon finely chopped shallot and 1 tablespoon chopped chervil and tarragon in a small saucepan. Reduce by half. Add 300 ml (½ pint, 1¼ cups) chicken velouté and reduce by a third. Finally add 2 tablespoons chivry butter and press through a fine sieve.

## Choron sauce

Dilute 200 ml (7 fl oz, ¾ cup) béarnaise sauce with 2 tablespoons well reduced and sieved tomato purée. The purée must be very concentrated.

## Cream sauce

Add 100 ml (4 fl oz, 7 tablespoons) double (heavy) cream to 200 ml (7 fl oz, ¾ cup) béchamel sauce and boil to reduce by one-third. Remove from the heat and add 25–50 g (1–2 oz, 2–4 tablespoons) butter and 60–100 ml (2–4 fl oz, ¼–scant ½ cup) double (heavy) cream. Stir well and strain. This sauce is served with vegetables, fish, eggs and poultry.

## Demi-glace

Boil down to reduce by two-thirds a mixture of 500 ml (17 fl oz, 2 cups) espagnole sauce and 750 ml (1¼ pints, 3¼ cups) clear brown stock. Remove from the heat, add 3 tablespoons Madeira and strain. A handful of sliced mushroom stalks may be added during cooking.

## Devilled sauce, English

Add 1 tablespoon chopped shallots to 150 ml (¼ pint, ⅔ cup) red wine vinegar and reduce by half. Then add 250 ml (8 fl oz, 1 cup) espagnole sauce and 2 tablespoons tomato purée (paste). Cook for 5 minutes. Just before serving, add 1 tablespoon Worcestershire sauce, 1 tablespoon Harvey sauce or spiced vinegar, and a dash of cayenne pepper. Strain the sauce. This sauce is generally served with grilled (broiled) meat.

## Devilled sauce

Mix together 150 ml (¼ pint, ⅔ cup) dry white wine with 1 tablespoon vinegar, then add 1 tablespoon finely chopped shallots, a sprig of thyme, a small piece of bay leaf and a generous twist of the peppermill. Reduce the sauce by two-thirds, then add 200 ml (7 fl oz, ¾ cup) demi-glace and boil for 2–3 minutes. Strain the sauce through a sieve. Just before serving, add 1 teaspoon chopped parsley and check the seasoning, adding a little cayenne pepper if liked. Alternatively, omit straining the sauce and add 1 tablespoon butter or beurre manié.

## Dried cherry sauce

(from Carême's recipe) Wash 225 g (8 oz, 1 cup) dried cherries. Pound them in a mortar and place them in a saucepan with 1½ tablespoons icing (confectioner's) sugar, 350 ml (12 fl oz, 1½ cups) good-quality Burgundy wine, 2 tablespoons vinegar, a pinch of ground coriander and a little grated lemon zest. Bring to the boil and simmer for 20–25 minutes. Then stir in 4 tablespoons espagnole sauce and the juice of 1 lemon and mix well. Reduce the sauce, stirring continuously over a brisk heat, and then rub through a sieve. This sauce is served with venison.

## Duxelles sauce

Prepare 4 tablespoons mushroom duxelles. Add 100 ml (4 fl oz, 7 tablespoons) white wine and reduce until almost completely dry. Add 150 ml (¼ pint, ⅔ cup) demi-glace sauce and 100 ml (4 fl oz, 7 tablespoons) sieved tomato sauce. Boil for 2–3 minutes, pour into a sauceboat (gravy boat), and sprinkle with chopped parsley.

Alternatively, the duxelles may be moistened with 150 ml (¼ pint, ⅔ cup) consommé and 100 ml (4 fl oz, 7 tablespoons) sieved tomato sauce and thickened with 1 tablespoon beurre manié.

## Espagnole sauce (1)

(from Carême's recipe) Put 2 slices of Bayonne ham into a deep saucepan. Place a noix of veal and 2 partridges on top. Add enough stock to cover the veal only. Reduce the liquid rapidly, then lower the heat until the stock is reduced to a coating on the bottom of the pan. Remove it from the heat. Prick the noix of veal with the point of a knife so that its juice mingles with the stock. Put the saucepan back over a low heat for about 20 minutes. Watch the liquid as it gradually turns darker.

To simplify this operation, scrape off a little of the essence with the point of a knife. Roll it between the fingers. If it rolls into a ball, the essence is perfectly reduced. If it is not ready, it will make the fingers stick together.

Remove the saucepan from the heat and set it aside for 15 minutes for the essence to cool. (It will then dissolve more readily.) Fill the saucepan with clear soup or stock and heat very slowly.

Meanwhile prepare a roux: melt 100 g (4 oz, ½ cup) butter and add to it enough flour to give a rather liquid consistency. Put it over a low heat, stirring from time to time so that gradually the whole mixture turns a golden colour. As soon as the stock comes to the boil, skim it, and pour 2 ladles into a roux. When adding the first ladleful of stock, remove the roux from the heat, then replace it and stir in the second ladleful until the mixture is perfectly smooth. Now pour the thickened sauce into the saucepan with the veal noix. Add parsley and spring onions (scallions), ½ bay leaf, a little thyme, 2 chives, and some mushroom trimmings. Leave to simmer, stirring frequently. After 1 hour skim off the fat, then 30 minutes later, skim off the fat again.

Strain through a cloth into a bowl, stirring from time to time with a wooden spoon so that no skin forms on the surface, as easily happens when the sauce is exposed to the air.

## Espagnole sauce (2)

Make a brown roux with 25 g (1 oz, 2 tablespoons) butter and 25 g (1 oz, ¼ cup) plain (all-purpose) flour. Add 1 tablespoon mirepoix, 50 g (2 oz, ⅔ cup) chopped mushrooms and 1 kg (2¼ lb) crushed tomatoes. Stir in 2.25 litres (4 pints, 10 cups) brown stock and simmer gently for 3–4 hours, skimming the sauce occasionally. Pass through a very fine sieve, or preferably strain through muslin (cheesecloth), when cold.

## Financière sauce (1)

(from Carême's recipe) Put some shredded lean ham, a pinch of mignonette (coarsely ground white pepper), a little thyme and bay leaf, some shredded mushrooms and truffles, and 2 glasses of dry Madeira into a saucepan and simmer over a gentle heat until reduced. Add 2 tablespoons chicken consommé and 2 tablespoons well-beaten espagnole sauce. Reduce by half then press through a fine sieve. Strain the sauce, then heat it again, stirring in 3 tablespoons Madeira. Reduce to the desired consistency and serve in a sauceboat (gravy boat).

When this sauce is intended for a game entrée, the chicken consommé is replaced by game fumet. Add a little butter just before serving.

## Financière sauce (2)

Make 200 ml (7 fl oz, ¾ cup) Madeira sauce, adding 100 ml (4 fl oz, 7 tablespoons) truffle essence while it is reducing. This sauce is usually used to bind the financière garnish.

## Grand veneur sauce

Prepare a poivrade sauce using the trimmings from a piece of cooked venison, and boil it down to obtain at least 200 ml (7 fl oz, ¾ cup). Strain the liquid, then blend it with 1 tablespoon redcurrant jelly and 2 tablespoons cream. Whisk. If the sauce is to accompany hare, mix 1 tablespoon hare's blood with 2 tablespoons strained marinade and add this mixture to the reduced and strained sauce.

## Green sauce

For 400 ml (14 fl oz, 1¾ cups) sauce, prepare 300 ml (½ pint, 1½ cups) mayonnaise and 100 ml (4 fl oz, 7 tablespoons) purée of green herbs (spinach, watercress, parsley, chervil and tarragon), blanched for 1 minute in boiling water, then cooled under cold running water. Dry thoroughly then pound in a mortar. Mix the 2 preparations together and rub through a sieve. Use like classic mayonnaise.

## Hollandaise sauce

Pour 4 tablespoons water into a pan with a pinch of salt and a pinch of ground pepper. Place the base of the saucepan in a bain marie of hot water: do not allow the water to approach boiling point, but keep it hot. In another saucepan, melt 500 g (18 oz, 2¼ cups) butter without letting it get too hot. Beat 5 egg yolks with 1 tablespoon water and pour into the pan containing the warmed water. With the pan still in the bain marie, whisk the sauce until the yolks thicken to the consistency of thick cream; add the melted butter slowly, whisking all the time, and then add 2 tablespoons water, drop by drop. Adjust the seasoning and add 1 tablespoon lemon juice. The sauce can be strained.

## Hungarian sauce

Peel and chop some onions and fry them in butter, without browning them. Season with salt and pepper and sprinkle with paprika. For 6 tablespoons cooked onion add 250 ml (8 fl oz, 1 cup) white wine and a small bouquet garni. Reduce the liquid by two-thirds. Pour in 500 ml (17 fl oz, 2 cups) velouté sauce (with or without butter enrichment). Boil rapidly for 5 minutes, strain through a strainer lined with muslin (cheesecloth) and finish with 50 g (2 oz, ¼ cup) butter.

## Italian sauce

Clean and chop 250 g (9 oz, 2 generous cups) button mushrooms, 1 onion and 1 shallot. Heat 5 tablespoons olive oil in a saucepan, add the chopped vegetables and cook over a high heat until the juices from the mushrooms are completely evaporated. Add 150 ml (¼ pint, ⅔ cup) stock, 6 tablespoons tomato purée (paste), salt, pepper and a bouquet garni and cook gently for 30 minutes. Just before serving, add 1 tablespoon diced lean ham and 1 tablespoon chopped parsley.

## Lyonnaise sauce

Cook 3 tablespoons finely chopped onions in 15 g (½ oz, 1 tablespoon) butter. When the onions are well softened, add 500 ml (17 fl oz, 2 cups) vinegar and 500 ml (17 fl oz, 2 cups) white wine. Reduce until almost evaporated, then add 200 ml (7 fl oz, ¾ cup) demi-glace. Boil for 3–4 minutes, then strain the sauce or serve it unstrained. Add 1 tablespoon tomato purée (paste) to this sauce if liked.

Alternatively, sprinkle the cooked onions with 1 tablespoon flour and cook until golden, deglaze with 175 ml (6 fl oz, ¾ cup) vinegar and 175 ml (6 fl oz, ¾ cup) white wine, then add some meat stock or pan juices. Boil for a few minutes and serve as above.

## Madeira sauce (modern recipe)

Put 1 kg (2¼ lb) crushed veal bones into an ovenproof dish and place in a preheated oven at 240°C (475°F, gas 9). Turn the bones over from time to time so that they colour evenly. Meanwhile, dice 2 carrots and 1 large onion. When the bones are golden, add the vegetables and cook until golden, then drain the bones and vegetables and place in a large pan. Remove the fat from any juices in the cooking dish and add 1 litre (1¾ pints, 4⅓ cups) stock or water. Scrape the sides of the dish well and stir the residue into the liquid.

Quickly bring to the boil, skim, and add 2 finely chopped celery sticks, 200 g (7 oz) peeled and seeded tomatoes, 1 peeled crushed garlic clove, a bouquet garni and 1 tablespoon tomato purée (paste). Bring to the boil, cover and simmer gently for 2 hours. Strain and then add some tarragon and 100 g (4 oz, 1¼ cups) finely chopped mushrooms. Bring to the boil. Dissolve 1 tablespoon cornflour (cornstarch) in 200 ml (7 fl oz, ¾ cup) Madeira and pour in a stream into the boiling sauce, whisking it in. Strain and reheat before serving.

## Madeira sauce (old recipe)

Add 3 tablespoons Madeira to 200 ml (7 fl oz, ¾ cup) reduced meat juices and heat through.

## Marinade for ingredients of pâtés and terrines

Season the ingredients with salt, pepper and mixed spice. Add a little crushed thyme and a finely chopped bay leaf. Moisten with brandy – for example, about 150 ml (¼ pint, ⅔ cup) brandy for the ingredients of a duck terrine – and marinate for 24 hours in a cool place.

## Marinade for large cuts of meat and game

Season the meat with salt, pepper and mixed spice. Place in a dish just large enough to hold it. Add 1 large chopped onion, 2 chopped shallots, 1 chopped carrot, 2 crushed garlic cloves, 2–3 sprigs of parsley, a sprig of thyme, ½ bay leaf (coarsely chopped) and a clove. (For a daube add a piece of dried orange peel.) Cover completely with red or white wine (according to the recipe) and 1 liqueur glass of brandy. Cover and marinate for 6 hours to 2 days in a cool place, turning the meat 2 or 3 times so it is thoroughly infused with the marinade. The marinade can be used in cooking if the meat is to be braised.

## Marinade for meats en chevreuil

*En chevreuil* is the term used for meat prepared and served like venison. Roughly chop 75 g (3 oz) onions, 75 g (3 oz) carrots, 2 fine shallots, 3–4 celery sticks and 1 garlic clove and brown lightly in oil, adding a little chopped parsley and crumbled thyme, 1 clove, a piece of bay leaf and some ground pepper. Moisten with 750 ml (1¼ pints, 3¼ cups) white wine and 175 ml (6 fl oz, ¾ cup) white wine vinegar, and cook gently for 30 minutes. Leave to cool completely then pour over the meat, already seasoned with salt and pepper.

## Marinade for small cuts of meat, fish and poultry

Season the meat or fish with salt and pepper and sprinkle with the following: 1 large chopped onion, 2 chopped shallots, 1 finely chopped carrot, a sprig of thyme, a finely chopped bay leaf, 1 tablespoon chopped parsley, a small crushed garlic clove, a clove and 12 black peppercorns. Moisten with the juice of a lemon and 300 ml (½ pint, 1¼ cups) oil (preferably olive oil) and marinate in a cool place for 2–12 hours.

## Mayonnaise

Half an hour before making the mayonnaise, ensure that all the ingredients are at room temperature. Put 2 egg yolks, a little salt and white pepper, and a little vinegar (tarragon, if available) or lemon juice in a medium bowl. 1 teaspoon white mustard can also be added. Stir quickly with a wooden spoon or whisk and as soon as the mixture is smooth use a tablespoon to blend in about 300 ml (½ pint, 1¼ cups) olive oil. Add the oil drop by drop, with a few drops of vinegar, taking care to beat the sauce against the sides of the bowl. The whiteness of the sauce depends on this continued beating. As it increases in volume, larger quantities of oil can be added in a thin trickle and also more vinegar or lemon juice. It is essential to add the ingredients slowly and sparingly to avoid curdling.

## Mornay sauce

Heat 500 ml (17 fl oz, 2 cups) béchamel sauce. Add 75 g (3 oz, ¾ cup) grated Gruyère cheese and stir until all the cheese has melted. Take the sauce from the heat and add 2 egg yolks beaten with 1 tablespoon milk. Bring slowly to the boil, whisking all the time. Remove from the heat and add 2 tablespoons double (heavy) cream (the sauce must be thick and creamy). For browning at a high temperature or for a lighter sauce, the egg yolks are omitted.

## Mushroom duxelles sauce

Prepare 4 tablespoons mushroom duxelles. Chop 250 g (9 oz, 3 cups) button mushrooms very finely with 1 onion and 1 shallot. Melt a large knob of butter, add the vegetables, season and cook over a brisk heat until the vegetables are browned and the liquid from the mushrooms has evaporated. Add 100 ml (4 fl oz, 7 tablespoons) white wine and reduce until almost completely dry. Add 150 ml (¼ pint, ⅔ cup) demi-glace sauce and 100 ml (4 fl oz, 7 tablespoons) sieved tomato sauce. Boil for 2–3 minutes, pour into a sauceboat (gravy boat), and sprinkle with chopped parsley.

Alternatively, the duxelles may be moistened with 150 ml (¼ pint, ⅔ cup) consommé and 100 ml (4 fl oz, 7 tablespoons) sieved tomato sauce and thickened with 1 tablespoon beurre manié.

## Mustard sauce with cream

Mix 1 part Dijon mustard with 2 parts double (heavy) cream. Season with salt, pepper and a little lemon juice. Whisk thoroughly until the sauce becomes slightly mousse-like. This sauce is served with white meat and poultry.

## Noisette sauce

Noisette sauce is a hollandaise sauce to which a few spoonfuls of noisette butter are added.

Noisette butter is butter heated until it becomes nut brown; it is used to add a finishing touch to a variety of dishes.

## Parsley sauce

Prepare 250 ml (8 fl oz, 1 cup) butter sauce then add 1 tablespoon chopped blanched parsley and sharpen with a little lemon juice. This sauce is served with calf's head, poached chicken, boiled rabbit, boiled ham and braised veal.

## Périgueux sauce

Clean, peel and dice some truffles and gently braise them in butter for 10 minutes. Then add them to some Madeira sauce just before mixing in the cornflour (cornstarch) and Madeira.

## Piquante sauce

Prepare 250 ml (8 fl oz, 1 cup) devilled sauce with wine vinegar. Just before serving, add 3 tablespoons coarsely chopped gherkins and 1 generous tablespoon chopped parsley. This sauce is served with pork chops, boiled tongue or slices of beef.

## Poivrade sauce

Finely dice 150 g (5 oz) scraped or peeled carrots with the cores removed, 100 g (4 oz, ⅔ cup) onions and 100 g (4 oz) green (unsmoked) streaky (slab) bacon. Cut 50 g (2 oz, ½ cup) celery into thin strips. Sweat very gently for about 20 minutes with 25 g (1 oz, 2 tablespoons) butter, a sprig of thyme and half a bay leaf. Add 500 ml (17 fl oz, 2 cups) vinegar and 100 ml (4 fl oz, 7 tablespoons) white wine, then reduce by half.

Make a brown roux with 40 g (1½ oz, 3 tablespoons) butter and 40 g (1½ oz, ⅓ cup) plain (all-purpose) flour. Add 750 ml (1¼ pints, 3¼ cups) beef or chicken stock and cook gently for 30 minutes. Skim the fat from the mirepoix and add to the roux. Deglaze the mirepoix pan with 100 ml (4 fl oz, 7 tablespoons) white wine and add to the sauce, together with 2 tablespoons finely chopped mushrooms.

Cook gently for a further hour, adding a little stock if the sauce reduces too much. Crush about 10 black peppercorns, add to the sauce and leave to simmer for 5 minutes. Then strain the sauce through coarse muslin (cheesecloth) or a very fine strainer.

If this sauce goes with marinated meat, use the strained marinade to deglaze the cooking pan and dilute the roux. If it is to be served with game, cut the trimmings from the game into small pieces and add to the mirepoix.

## Portuguese sauce

Finely chop 2 large onions and cook in 1 tablespoon olive oil until soft. Peel, seed and crush 4 tomatoes and add to the onions, together with 2 crushed garlic cloves. Bring to the boil, cover and cook slowly for 30–35 minutes, stirring from time to time, until the tomatoes are reduced to a pulp. Moisten with 150 ml (¼ pint, ⅔ cup) stock and season with ground pepper. Leave to cook for a further 10 minutes. Bind with 2 teaspoons beurre manié and sprinkle with chopped parsley.

## Poulette sauce

Whisk 2 or 3 egg yolks with 400 ml (14 fl oz, 1¾ cups) white veal or poultry stock. Heat for about 10 minutes, whisking all the time, adding the juice of ½ or 1 lemon and 50 g (2 oz, ¼ cup) butter. Remove from the heat when the sauce coats the spoon. Keep the sauce warm in a bain marie until needed, stirring from time to time to stop a skin from forming.

## Provençal sauce

Heat 2 tablespoons olive oil in a heavy-based saucepan. Soften in it without browning 3 tablespoons peeled and chopped onions, then add 800 g (1½ lb, 3 cups) peeled, seeded and crushed tomatoes and cook gently for about 15 minutes. Add a crushed garlic clove, a bouquet garni, 200 ml (7 fl oz, ¾ cup) dry white wine and 200 ml (7 fl oz, ¾ cup) meat stock. Leave to cook, covered, for 15 minutes, then adjust the seasoning, remove the lid and reduce the sauce by half. Add some fresh chopped parsley or basil just before serving.

## Ravigote sauce (cold)

Prepare 120 ml (4½ fl oz, ½ cup) plain vinaigrette with mustard. Add ½ teaspoon chopped tarragon, 1 teaspoon chopped parsley, 1 teaspoon fines herbes, 2 teaspoons chervil, 1 finely chopped small onion and 1 tablespoon dried and chopped capers.

## Red wine sauce

Cook the meat, game or poultry in 150 ml (¼ pint, ⅔ cup) mirepoix cooked in butter, 500 ml (17 fl oz, 2 cups) red wine, 1 garlic clove and some mushroom skins. Remove the main ingredients, then reduce the liquid by one-third. Thicken with beurre manié, add a few drops of anchovy essence, if liked, season with a pinch of cayenne pepper and strain.

## Red wine sauce (bourguignonne style)

Cut 75 g (3 oz) bacon into small strips, blanch, drain and cook in butter until golden brown. Finely chop some onions and mushrooms, mix together and cook 4–5 tablespoons of the mixture in butter, together with 2 generous tablespoons mirepoix. Stir in the diced bacon and transfer the mixture to the pan in which the chicken or meat has been cooked. Stir well and cook until golden brown. Add 2 tablespoons flour and stir well. Then add 500 ml (17 fl oz, 2 cups) red wine, 200 ml (7 fl oz, ¾ cup) stock, a bouquet garni, salt and pepper. Reduce by two-thirds. When ready to use, sieve the sauce and thicken with 50 g (2 oz, ¼ cup) beurre manié.

## Robert sauce

Cook 2 finely chopped onions until golden brown in 25 g (1 oz, 2 table-spoons) butter or lard. Sprinkle with 1 tablespoon flour and continue to cook until the mixture browns. Add 200 ml (7 fl oz, ¾ cup) white wine and 300 ml

(½ pint, 1¼ cups) stock, or 100 ml (4 fl oz, 7 tablespoons) white wine, 200 ml (7 fl oz, ¾ cup) vinegar and 100 ml (4 fl oz, 7 tablespoons) water, then boil until reduced by one-third. Adjust the seasoning. Mix together 1 tablespoon mustard and a little of the sauce, then add it to the rest of the sauce, mixing thoroughly away from the heat.

## Rouennaise sauce

Pound 150 g (5 oz) duck livers in a mortar. Peel and chop 75 g (3 oz, ½ cup) shallots and cook until golden in 20 g (¾ oz, 1½ tablespoons) butter. Pour 325 ml (11 fl oz, 1⅓ cups) red wine into the pan and boil until the liquid is reduced by half. Add 25 g (1 oz, ¾ cup) chopped parsley and 2 litres (3½ pints, 9 cups) demi-glace sauce. Adjust the seasoning and put aside. Just before serving, reheat if necessary, add the pounded duck livers and mix well to obtain a smooth sauce.

## Royale sauce

Mix together 200 ml (7 fl oz, ¾ cup) chicken velouté sauce and 100 ml (4 fl oz, 7 tablespoons) white chicken stock. Reduce by half, adding 100 ml (4 fl oz, 7 tablespoons) double (heavy) cream during the reduction. Just before serving, add 2 tablespoons finely chopped raw truffle, then whisk in 50 g (2 oz, 4 tablespoons) butter, and finally add 1 tablespoon sherry.

## Sainte-Menehould sauce

Melt 15 g (½ oz, 1 tablespoon) butter in a saucepan. Add 15 g (½ oz, 2 tablespoons) finely chopped onion, cover and cook very gently for 10 minutes until soft. Season with salt, pepper, a pinch of thyme and a pinch of powdered bay leaf and add 100 ml (4 fl oz, 7 tablespoons) white wine and 1 tablespoon vinegar. Reduce until all the liquid has evaporated, then moisten with 200 ml (7 fl oz, ¾ cup) demi-glace sauce. Boil over full heat for 1 minute, then add a pinch of cayenne pepper. Remove from the heat and blend in 1 tablespoon each of mustard, very finely diced gherkins, chopped parsley and chervil.

## Sauce with fines herbes

Make 250 ml (8 fl oz, 1 cup) demi-glace sauce or brown stock and add 2 tablespoons chopped parsley, chervil and tarragon. Reduce, press through a very fine sieve, add a few drops of lemon juice and adjust the seasoning. This sauce is served with poached poultry.

## Supreme sauce

Prepare a velouté with a white roux, comprising 40 g (1½ oz, 3 tablespoons) butter and 40 g (1 ½ oz, 6 tablespoons) plain (all-purpose) flour and 750 ml (1¼ pints, 3¼ cups) well-seasoned and well-reduced chicken consommé. Add 500 ml (17 fl oz, 2 cups) white chicken stock and reduce it by at least half. Add 300 ml (½ pint, 1¼ cups) crème fraîche and reduce the sauce to about 600 ml (1 pint, 2½ cups), at which point it should be thick enough to coat the back of the spoon. Remove the pan from the heat and stir in 50 g (2 oz, ¼ cup) butter. Strain through a very fine sieve and keep warm in a bain marie until ready to use.

## Tartare sauce

Prepare some mayonnaise, replacing the raw egg yolk with hard-boiled (hard-cooked) egg yolk. Add some finely chopped chives and chopped spring onion (scallion).

Alternatively, a mixture of raw egg yolk and hard-boiled egg yolk can be used, and chopped herbs can replace the chives and onion.

## Tortue sauce

Infuse a bouquet garni and a few sprigs of basil in 500 ml (17 fl oz, 2 cups) dry white wine. Lightly cook in butter 150 g (5 oz) smoked ham, 3 onions and 3 carrots (both cut into dice). Sprinkle with 3 tablespoons flour and brown. Add the strained white wine and 300 ml (½ pint, 1¼ cups) beef stock. Add 2–3 tablespoons concentrated tomato purée (paste), cover and cook very gently for at least 30 minutes.

## Truffle sauce

Cook a very fresh black truffle in a mixture of half Madeira, half meat stock, with a little tomato purée (paste), for 10 minutes. Drain and cut into julienne strips. Cover the pan tightly and reduce the liquid to a few teaspoonfuls, then add 2 egg yolks and the julienne. Thicken with 200 g (7 oz, ¾ cup) clarified butter, as for a béarnaise sauce. Season with salt and pepper.

This sauce is served with white meats, Lauris asparagus and poached fish.

## Velouté sauce

Stir 2.75 litres (4¾ pints, 12 cups) white veal or chicken stock into a pale blond roux made with 150 g (5 oz, ⅔ cup) butter and 150 g (5 oz, 1¼ cups) plain (all-purpose) flour. Blend well together. Bring to the boil, stirring until the first bubbles appear. Cook the velouté very slowly for 30 minutes, skimming frequently. Strain the sauce through a cloth and stir until it is completely cold.

Velouté may be prepared either in advance or just before it is required. As the white stock used for making it is seasoned and flavoured, it is not necessary to add other flavourings. An exception is made for skins and trimmings of mushrooms, which may be added when available, this addition making the sauce yet more delicate.

## Villeroi sauce

Prepare 200 ml (7 fl oz, ¾ cup) allemande sauce, dilute with 4 tablespoons white stock flavoured with a little mushroom essence, then reduce until it coats the back of a spoon. Put through a strainer and stir until the sauce is barely tepid.

## White bitter orange sauce for roast duck

Deglaze the dish in which the duck has been cooked with 175 ml (6 fl oz, ¾ cup) dry white wine. Cut the rind of 1 Seville orange (or 1 sweet orange if Seville oranges are not available) and ½ lemon into thin strips; blanch, cool and drain. When the sauce has almost completely reduced, add 150 ml (¼ pint, ⅔ cup) white consommé or stock and boil for 5 minutes. Thicken the sauce with 1 teaspoon cornflour (cornstarch) or arrowroot mixed with 2 tablespoons cold water. Add the juice of the orange and a splash of lemon juice. Strain, add the rind and season with salt and pepper.

## White roux

Melt the butter in a heavy-based saucepan, then clarify it. Add the same weight (or a little more) of sifted plain (all-purpose) flour – up to 125 g (4½ oz, 1 cup) flour for 100 g (4 oz, ½ cup) butter. To make 1 litre (1¾ pints, 4⅓ cups) béchamel sauce, the roux should contain 75 g (3 oz, ¾ cup) flour and the same weight of butter; to make 1 litre (1¾ pints, 4⅓ cups) velouté sauce, use 50–65 g (2–2½ oz, ½–⅔ cup) flour and the same weight of butter.

Mix the butter and flour, stirring constantly with a wooden spoon and covering the whole bottom of the saucepan, so that the roux does not colour unevenly and become lumpy. Continue to cook in this way for 5 minutes, until the mixture begins to froth a little. Take the pan off the heat and leave it to cool until time to add the liquid (milk, white stock, fish stock). To avoid lumps forming this must be poured boiling on to the cold roux. Use a whisk to mix the roux and heat gradually while whisking constantly. (Alternatively, the cold liquid may be whisked gradually into the warm roux.)

## White sauce

Make 100 g (4 oz, ½ cup) pale blond roux using 50 g (2 oz, ¼ cup) butter and 50 g (2 oz, ½ cup) plain (all-purpose) flour. Blend in 1 litre (1¾ pints, 4⅓ cups) white stock (chicken or veal). Bring to the boil and cook gently for 1½ hours, skimming from time to time.

# Stocks, consommés, aspics & glazes

## Aspic

- *Meat aspic* Brown 1 kg (2¼ lb) leg of beef and 500 g (18 oz) knuckle of veal, cut into pieces, 1 calf's foot, 500 g (18 oz) veal bones, and 250 g (9 oz) bacon rind, trimmed of fat, in a preheated oven at 200°C (400°F, gas 6). Peel and shred 2 onions, 4 carrots and 1 leek. Place all these ingredients in a stockpot together with a large bouquet garni, 1 tablespoon salt and pepper. Add 3 litres (5 pints, 13 cups) water and bring to the boil. Skim, then add a ladleful of very cold water and simmer for 5 hours. Carefully strain the liquid through a strainer lined with muslin (cheesecloth), let it cool completely and put it in the refrigerator so that the fat which solidifies on the surface can be removed easily. Clarify the stock with 200 g (7 oz) lean beef, 2 egg whites and a small bouquet of chervil and tarragon.

- *Enriched aspic* The meat aspic can be flavoured with Madeira, port, sherry or with any other liquor. If this is done, the flavouring is added just before straining the aspic.
- *White aspic* This is made as for meat aspic, but the meat and bones are not browned.
- *Game aspic* This is obtained by adding to meat aspic 1.25 kg (2¾ lb) game carcasses and trimmings, which have been previously browned in the oven, and several juniper berries.
- *Chicken aspic* This is obtained by adding to meat aspic either a whole chicken or 1.5 kg (3¼ lb) chicken carcasses and giblets, both browned in the oven.

## Beef consommé (clear)

For 3 litres (5 pints, 13 cups) stock, use 800 g (1¾ lb) lean beef, chopped and trimmed, 100 g (4 oz) carrots, 100 g (4 oz) leeks and 2 egg whites. Clean the carrots and leeks then cut them into small dice. Put them into a saucepan with the chopped beef and the egg whites. Add the stock cold, or at most, tepid. Heat gently, stirring constantly, until the stock is just boiling. Then reduce the heat, if necessary, to prevent the stock from boiling, and simmer very gently for 1½ hours. Remove surplus fat and strain the consommé through a damp cloth.

## Beef consommé (simple)

Cut up 2 kg (4½ lb) lean beef and 1.5 kg (3¼ lb) shin of beef (beef shank) (with bone) and put them into a big stockpot. (To extract the maximum amount of flavour from the bones, ask the butcher to break them into chunks.) Add 7 litres (12 pints, 7½ quarts) cold water. Bring to the boil and carefully remove the scum that forms on the surface. Season with coarse salt (it is better to adjust the seasoning at the end than to add too much at the beginning). Add 3 or 4 large carrots, 400 g (14 oz) turnips, 100 g (4 oz) parsnips, 350 g (12 oz) leeks tied in a bundle, 2 celery sticks, sliced, a medium-sized onion with 2 cloves stuck in it, a garlic clove, a sprig of thyme and half a bay leaf. Simmer very slowly so that boiling is hardly perceptible, for 4 hours. Remove the meat and very carefully strain the stock. Remove surplus fat carefully.

## Brown veal stock

Bone 1.25 kg (2¾ lb) shoulder of veal and the same amount of knuckle of veal. Tie them together with string and brush with melted dripping. Crush 500 g (18 oz) veal bones as finely as possible. Brown all these ingredients in a large flameproof casserole or saucepan. Peel and slice 150 g (5 oz) carrots and 100 g (4 oz) onions, then add them to the pan. Cover and leave to sweat for 15 minutes. Add 250 ml (8 fl oz, 1 cup) water and reduce to a jelly-like consistency. Repeat the process. Add 3 litres (5 pints, 13 cups) water or white stock and bring to the boil. Skim and season. Leave to simmer very gently for 6 hours. Skim off the fat and strain through a fine sieve or, better still, through muslin (cheesecloth).

## Chicken consommé (simple)

Proceed as for simple beef consommé, but replace the lean beef by a small chicken and 3 or 4 giblets browned in the oven, and the shin of beef (beef shank) by 800 g (1¾ lb) veal knuckle. For clarification, proceed as for clear beef consommé, using 4 or 5 chopped chicken giblets instead of the chopped beef. The chicken may then be used for croquettes or patties.

## Court-bouillon with wine

The wine should be chosen for its fruity flavour. The amount of wine can be increased if the amount of water is reduced by the same quantity. Red wine may also be used, especially if the court-bouillon is to be used to make an aspic jelly, which will then have a pale pink colour. The most common use of court-bouillon is for poaching fish or shellfish; however, it is also used for offal (variety meats), such as brains, and for some white meat and poultry.

For every 2.5 litres (4¼ pints, 11 cups) water, add 500 ml (17 fl oz, 2 cups) dry white wine, 50 g (2 oz, ⅓ cup) grated carrot, 50 g (2 oz, ⅓ cup) grated onion, a sprig of thyme, a piece of bay leaf, 25 g (1 oz, 2 tablespoons) coarse salt and possibly a small celery stick, chopped, and a sprig of parsley (although these have a strong flavour). Add 2 teaspoons peppercorns 10 minutes before the end of the cooking time.

## Giblet bouillon

Put the giblets from 2 chickens in a pan with 2 litres (3½ pints, 9 cups) cold water and bring to the boil. Chop 4 carrots, 2 turnips, 3 leeks (white part only), 2 celery sticks and a small piece of parsnip. Skim the liquid, then add the vegetables together with an onion stuck with cloves, a bouquet garni, salt and pepper. Simmer gently until completely cooked (about 1½ hours). Just before serving, bone the giblets and return the meat to the bouillon, adding the juice of ½ lemon and some chopped parsley. Adjust the seasoning.

If desired, this can be prepared in the Greek way by cooking 2 handfuls of rice in the stock and thickening it with a whole beaten egg.

## Light brown stock

Scald 150 g (5 oz) fresh pork rind and 125 g (4½ oz) knuckle of ham for 4–5 minutes. Bone 1.25 kg (2¾ lb) lean stewing beef (leg or blade) and cut into cubes, together with the same amount of knuckle of veal. Peel 150 g (5 oz) carrots and 150 g (5 oz) onions, cut into slices, then brown on the hob (stove top) in a large flameproof casserole with all the meat, 500 g (18 oz) crushed veal or beef bones and the pork rind. Add 1 bouquet garni, 1 garlic clove, 500 ml (17 fl oz, 2 cups) water and reduce to a jelly-like consistency. Add another 500 ml (17 fl oz, 2 cups) water and reduce to a jelly again. Add 2.5–3 litres (4¼–5 pints, 11–13 cups) water and 2 teaspoons coarse salt; bring to the boil and simmer very gently for 8 hours. Skim off the fat and strain through a fine sieve or, better still, through muslin (cheesecloth).

## Meat glaze

This is commonly known as *glace de viande*. Remove all the fat from a brown stock. When it is as clear as possible, boil it down by half. Strain through a muslin cloth (cheesecloth), then boil it down again and strain. Continue this process until it will coat the back of a spoon, each time reducing the temperature a little more as the glaze becomes more concentrated. Pour the meat glaze into small containers and keep them in the refrigerator.

• *Poultry or game glaze* A similar method is used with a poultry or game stock to obtain a poultry or game glaze.

## Stocks (quick)

Home cooks no longer have stockpots bubbling away permanently on a corner of the stove. However, stock is still the basis of many recipes, so here are a few simple and quick recipes. Depending on the purpose of these stocks, a little thyme or parsley and salt and pepper may be added. Stock can be kept for 2–3 days in the refrigerator or frozen for longer storage. Good-quality stock is also available from supermarkets, where it is usually sold chilled.

• *Beef* Roughly chop 100–150 g (4–5 oz) beef, 1 small carrot, 1 white leek,

1 small celery stick, 1 onion and a clove. Place all the ingredients in 1.5 litres (2¾ pints, 6½ cups) water and simmer gently for 20 minutes. Strain.

- *Veal* Use the same method as for quick beef stock but use lean veal.
- *Chicken* Use the same method as for quick beef stock but with 400–500 g (14–18 oz) chicken wings instead of the beef.

## Thick veal stock

Reduce 2 litres (3½ pints, 9 cups) brown veal stock by a quarter. Thicken with 2 tablespoons arrowroot blended with 3 tablespoons clear cold veal stock. Strain through muslin (cheesecloth) or a fine sieve.

## Tomato veal stock

Add 200 ml (7 fl oz, ¾ cup) fresh tomato purée to 2 litres (3½ pints, 9 cups) brown veal stock. Reduce by a quarter. Strain through a fine sieve or, better still, through muslin (cheesecloth).

## Vegetable bouillon

Use vegetables that are generally included in a stockpot – carrots, onions, leeks, celery, garlic cloves, tomatoes and turnips are typical. Potatoes and parsnips tend to make the stock cloudy; strongly flavoured vegetables give the stock a distinctive flavour – for example, broccoli, cauliflowers, swede (rutabaga) or fennel. Chop the vegetables, put them in a large saucepan and cook them gently in butter, then pour boiling water over them to cover. A bouquet garni, salt and pepper (optional) should be added and the broth is simmered until the vegetables are cooked.

Alternatively, simply add all the ingredients to boiling water and simmer until cooked, either conventionally or using a pressure cooker. In both cases, the broth must be strained before it can be served.

## White chicken stock

Prepare in the same way as for ordinary white stock, but with the addition of a small chicken (which can be used afterwards in another recipe) or double the quantity of giblets, that is from two chickens.

## White stock

This is made with white meat or poultry, veal bones, chicken carcasses and aromatic vegetables.

Bone an 800 g (1¾ lb) shoulder of veal and a 1 kg (2¼ lb) knuckle of veal, then tie them together with string. Crush the bones. Put the bones, meat and 1 kg (2¼ lb) chicken giblets or carcasses in a pan. Add 3.5 litres (6 pints, 3½ quarts) water, bring to the boil and skim. Add 125 g (4½ oz) sliced carrots, 100 g (4 oz) onions, 75 g (3 oz) leeks (white part only), 75 g (3 oz) celery and 1 bouquet garni and season. Simmer gently for 3½ hours. Skim off the fat then strain the stock through a very fine sieve or muslin (cheesecloth).

# Purées & vegetable flavouring mixtures

## Chestnut purée

Boil some peeled chestnuts, drain them, press them through a sieve and place the purée in a saucepan. Add 150 ml (¼ pint, ⅔ cup) double (heavy) cream per 1 kg (2¼ lb) chestnuts and reheat, stirring constantly. Then add 50 g (2 oz, ¼ cup) butter and adjust the seasoning. If the purée is too thick, add a little of the strained cooking liquid.

Chestnut purée can be used to make soup or a savoury soufflé.

## Garlic purée

Blanch some garlic cloves, then gently sweat them in butter. Add a few spoonfuls of thick béchamel sauce and either press the mixture through a sieve or liquidize in a food processor or blender. Garlic purée is used in sauces and stuffings.

## Matignon mixture

This is a vegetable mixture used as a complementary ingredient in various braised or fried dishes. For the *au maigre* (meatless) version, cook 125 g (4½ oz, 1¼ cups) sliced carrots, 50 g (2 oz, ½ cup) chopped celery, and 25 g (1 oz, ¼ cup) sliced onions gently in butter. Add salt, a sprig of thyme, ½ bay leaf and a pinch of sugar. When the vegetables are very soft, add 6 tablespoons Madeira and boil to reduce until the liquid has nearly evaporated.

For the *au gras* version (with meat), add 100 g (4 oz, ½ cup) lean diced bacon to the mixture with the onions.

## Mirepoix with meat

Peel and finely dice 150 g (5 oz) carrots and 100 g (4 oz) onions. Cut 50 g (2 oz) celery and 100 g (4 oz) raw ham (or blanched streaky (slab) bacon) into fine strips. Heat 25 g (1 oz, 2 tablespoons) butter in a saucepan and add the ham and vegetables, together with a sprig of thyme and half a bay leaf. Stir the ingredients into the butter, cover and cook gently for about 20 minutes until the vegetables are very tender.

## Mushroom duxelles

Clean and trim 250 g (9 oz, 3 cups) button mushrooms and chop them finely, together with 1 onion and 1 large shallot. Melt a large knob of butter in a frying pan, add the chopped vegetables, salt and pepper and a little grated nutmeg (unless the duxelles is to accompany fish). Cook over a brisk heat until the vegetables are brown and the water from the mushrooms has evaporated. If the duxelles is for use as a garnish, stir in 1 tablespoon cream at the last minute.

## Soubise purée

Peel and thinly slice 1 kg (2¼ lb) white onions and place in a saucepan with plenty of salted water. Bring to the boil, then drain the onions and place in a saucepan with 100 g (4 oz, ½ cup) butter, salt, pepper and a pinch of sugar. Cover and cook over a gentle heat for 30–40 minutes (the onions should not change colour). Then add to the onions a quantity of boiled rice or thick béchamel sauce equal to one quarter of the volume of the onion. Mix thoroughly and cook for a further 20 minutes. Adjust the seasoning, press through a very fine sieve and stir in 75 g (3 oz, 6 tablespoons) butter.

## Tomato fondue

A fondue is a preparation of vegetables cut into thin pieces and cooked slowly in butter over a very low heat until they are reduced to a pulp. Peel and chop 100 g (4 oz, ¾ cup) onions. Peel, seed and finely chop 800 g (1¾ lb) tomatoes. Peel and crush 1 garlic clove. Prepare a bouquet garni rich in thyme. Soften the onions in a heavy-based saucepan with 25 g (1 oz, 2 tablespoons) butter, or a mixture of 15 g (½ oz, 1 tablespoon) butter and 2 tablespoons olive oil, or 3 tablespoons olive oil. Then add the tomatoes, salt and pepper, the garlic and bouquet garni. Cover the pan and cook very gently until the tomatoes are reduced to a pulp. Remove the lid, stir with a wooden spatula and continue cooking, uncovered, until the fondue forms a light paste. Taste and adjust the seasoning, then press through a sieve and add 1 tablespoon chopped parsley or other herbs.

## Vegetable mirepoix

This mirepoix is cooked in the same way as mirepoix with meat, but the ham or bacon is omitted and the vegetables are shredded into a brunoise.

# Index

**A**

à gratin forcemeat 421
accompaniments
   429–45
Agnès Sorel tartlets 215
Agnès Sorel timbales
   215
aiguillettes of duckling
   with honey
   vinegar 282
aïoli 455
Albufera sauce 455
Algerian lamb with
   prunes, tea and
   almonds 121
allemande sauce 455–6
almonds, Algerian lamb
   with prunes, tea
   and 121
American stuffing 422
Amiens duck pâté 282–3
amourettes 165
   amourette fritters 165
   amourettes au
      gratin 165
anchovy butter 415

andouillettes
   andouillettes *à la*
      *lyonnaise* 207
   andouillettes *à la*
      *tourangelle* 207
   grilled andouillette 101
apples
   apple compote 417
   apple sauce 456
   baked apples 429
   boudin *à la*
      *normande* 209
   chicken with
      cider 247–8
   goose in the pot 312
   guinea fowl salad with
      fruit 330
   knuckle of veal
      braised in cider 72–3
   pheasant *à la*
      *normande* 355–6
   roast goose with fruit
      313–14
   roast turkey stuffed
      with dessert apples
      318–19

wild duck *à la*
   *tyrolienne* 392
wild duck *à la Walter*
   *Scott* 392
Armagnac, sautéed
   woodcock in 396
artichoke hearts
   chicken medallions
      Beauharnais 241
   chicken with
      artichokes 246
   escalopes casimir 68–9
   medallions of veal
      Alexandre 73
   noisettes Beauharnais
      143
   sauté of lamb with
      artichokes 151
   tournedos marigny 60
   tournedos masséna 60
artichokes, Jerusalem,
   roast loin of pork
   with 115–16
asparagus
   calves' sweetbreads
      princesse 189

493

# Picture acknowledgements

Cabanne P. et Ryman C. *Coll. Larousse* colour plates 4, 5, 13, 14; **CZAP** *Coll. Larousse* colour plate 16; **Magis J.-J.** *Coll. Larousse* colour plates 1, 3, 8, 9, 12; **Magis J.-J.** *La Photothèque culinaire* colour plate 11; **Miller G.** *Coll. Larousse* colour plates 7, 10; **Overseas** *La Photothèque culinaire* colour plate 2; **Studiaphot** *Coll. Larousse* colour plate 6; **Sudres J.-D.** *Coll. Larousse* colour plate 15.

Editorial Director **Jane Birch**
Executive Editor **Nicky Hill**
Design Manager **Tokiko Morishima**
Editorial team **Anne Crane, Lydia Darbyshire, Bridget Jones, Cathy Lowne**
Index **Hilary Bird**
Cover design **Tokiko Morishima**
Senior Production Controller **Ian Paton**
Picture Research **Jennifer Veall**
Typesetting **Dorchester Typesetters**